Multicentury Fire and Forest Histories at 19 Sites in Utah and Eastern Nevada

Emily K. Heyerdahl, Peter M. Brown,
Stanley G. Kitchen, and Marc H. Weber

United States Department of Agriculture / Forest Service

Rocky Mountain Research Station

General Technical Report RMRS-GTR-261WWW

December 2011

Abstract

Our objective is to provide site-specific fire and forest histories from Utah and eastern Nevada that can be used for land management or additional research. We systematically sampled fire scars and tree-recruitment dates across broad gradients in elevation and forest type at 13 sites in Utah and 1 in eastern Nevada to characterize spatial and temporal variation in historical fire regimes as well as forest structure and composition. We collected similar data non-systematically at five additional sites in Utah. These 19 sites include a broad range of forest types (from pinyon-juniper woodlands to spruce-fir forests) and fire regime types. In this report, we summarize local-scale spatial and temporal variation with site-specific details of historical fire regimes and forests that will be useful for local natural resource and fire management of the individual sites. For each site, we report topography, chronologies of fire and tree recruitment, and properties derived from those chronologies such as time-averaged fire regime parameters (mean fire interval and fire severity) and changes in forest composition and structure that have occurred since the late 1800s.

Keywords: fire scars, dendrochronology, crossdate, fire history, fire regimes, forest structure

Authors

Emily K. Heyerdahl is a Research Forester with the U.S. Department of Agriculture (USDA) Forest Service, Rocky Mountain Research Station, Fire Sciences Laboratory in Missoula, Montana.

Peter M. Brown is the founder and Director of Rocky Mountain Tree-Ring Research, Fort Collins, Colorado—a nonprofit research organization involved in tree-ring studies around the world.

Stanley G. Kitchen is a Research Botanist with the USDA Forest Service, Rocky Mountain Research Station, Shrub Sciences Laboratory in Provo, Utah.

Marc H. Weber was a Biologist with the USDA Forest Service, Rocky Mountain Research Station, Fire Sciences Laboratory in Missoula, Montana. He is a Geographer with the U.S. Environmental Protection Agency, Western Ecology Division in Corvallis, Oregon.

Acknowledgments

For help with field collection and sample processing, we thank Dan Bentley, Jim Bentley, Stephanie Carlson, Brandon Collins, Katie L. Collins, Gerad Dean, Chris Gentry, David Hanley, Joslin Heyn, Myron Holland, Andy Kitchen, Kevin Lee Hayes, Covy D. Jones, Gary Jorgensen, Brian Latta, Rachel Laurie, Kristy Miller, Heidi Neeley, Brad Newton, Eric O'Neil, Matt Proett, Becca Pyne, Matt Pyne, James P. Riser II, Gretchen Baker, Tyson Swetnam, Jeff Taylor, Tonya Thygerson, Heather Vice, Clay Waley, Brad Weaver, Nancy Williams, and Rosalind Wu. For help with logistics, we thank Evan Boshell, Robert Campbell, Linda Chappell, Rob Cruz, Kevin Greenhalgh, Gary Hall, Susie Hatch, Donna Owens, Jolie Pollet, Clark Tucker, and L.J. Western. We thank Aaron Wilson and Ann Wolf for help with data and GIS analysis and/or for assistance with figures, and Denny Simmerman for help with photographs and figures. For reviews of the manuscript, we thank Matthew Bekker, Robert Campbell, Linda Chappell, Beth Corbin, Peter Fulé, Sherel Goodrich, George Gruell, Bob Keane, Don Long, Doug Page, James P. Riser II, William Romme, and Elaine Kennedy Sutherland. We acknowledge primary funding from the Joint Fire Science Program under Project JFSP 01C-3-3-22 with additional funding from the USDA Forest Service (Fishlake National Forest and Rocky Mountain Research Station); USDI Bureau of Land Management, Utah State Office; and Rocky Mountain Tree-Ring Research, Inc. (partly through Research Joint Venture Agreement 03-JV-11222048-043 between the UDSA Forest Service, Rocky Mountain Research Station, and Rocky Mountain Tree-Ring Research, Inc.).

Contents

Introduction

Diverse forest and woodland ecosystems occur across landscape, elevational, and climatic gradients in Utah and eastern Nevada (Mauk and Henderson 1984; Youngblood and Mauk 1985). However, quantitative data on historical fire regimes are generally lacking for most of these ecosystems (but see Kitchen 2010; Madany and West 1983; Stein 1988; Wadleigh and Jenkins 1996). Furthermore, we have little information on the effect that variation in historical fire regimes had on the composition and structure of forests and woodlands or on the effect that recent fire exclusion may have had on current composition and structure. Such information is critical for forest management, especially regarding when and where fuel treatments, fire, or ecological restoration are needed or appropriate (for example, Allen and others 2002; Covington and others 1997; Falk 2006; Schoennagel and others 2004). This information is also crucial for inferring the drivers of regional variation in fire regimes through time and across space. Such drivers include climate, forest type, topography, and land use (for example, Brown and others 2008a).

We reconstructed crossdated (annually accurate) fire and forest histories from systematically sampled grids of plots at 13 sites in Utah and 1 site in eastern Nevada. In addition, we reconstructed fire histories and some forest histories at another five sites in Utah, some sampled systematically and others targeted only for a history of low-severity fires. The 19 sites include a broad range of forest types (pinyon-juniper woodlands to spruce-fir forests) and fire regime types. We have already used these histories to infer the drivers of variation in fire through time and space across the region (Brown and others 2008a; Kitchen 2010). While these studies are useful for managing fire and forests at regional scales, the site specific details of fire and forest history that we have not previously published will help other researchers and land managers understand and manage forests and fire at local scales. For example, understanding the departure of current forests from historical conditions can support management plans for specific areas to land management agencies and the public. Also, the local-scale properties of historical fire regimes, such as mean fire interval, can be compared to modern regimes to understand how they may have changed over the past century.

Our objective is to provide site-specific fire and forest histories that can be used for land management or additional research. We describe the study area and methods in a single section that applies to all sites, but we provide detailed results for each site in separate appendices. For each site, we include site and fire maps, interpret chronologies of fire and tree recruitment, estimate time-averaged properties of past fire regimes (frequency and severity), and show how these characteristics varied across the site by forest type and topography.

Methods

Study Area

We sampled sites in forests and woodlands across the Colorado Plateau of southern and central Utah, the Wasatch Plateau in central Utah, the Wah Wah Mountains and Snake Range in the eastern Great Basin, and the Uinta and northern Wasatch Range (fig. 1; table 1). The region is a complex of valleys, canyons, mountains, plateaus, and mesas that range in elevation from 2950 to 13,528 ft.

Sampling Design for Gridded Sites

We distributed 14 gridded sites across Utah, generally outside wilderness areas, on public lands managed by the USDA Forest Service, Bureau of Land Management, or National Park Service. We selected sites that covered a range of topography and forest type in an area that had road access but minimal forest management and no recent fires. We identified potential sampling sites based on local knowledge and selected final sampling sites during field reconnaissance.

Prior to sampling, we mapped plot locations for each site on a 0.31-mile grid oriented in the cardinal directions, using Universal Transverse Mercator coordinates (UTMs). In the field, we navigated to each plot using handheld global positioning system receivers. However, some plots were in areas we could not sample because they occurred in streams; on dramatic changes in slope such as ridges; roads; skid-trails; mudslides; or in areas that could not be safely sampled such as cliffs. In these cases, moving 164 ft along a random azimuth generally relocated plot center to an area we

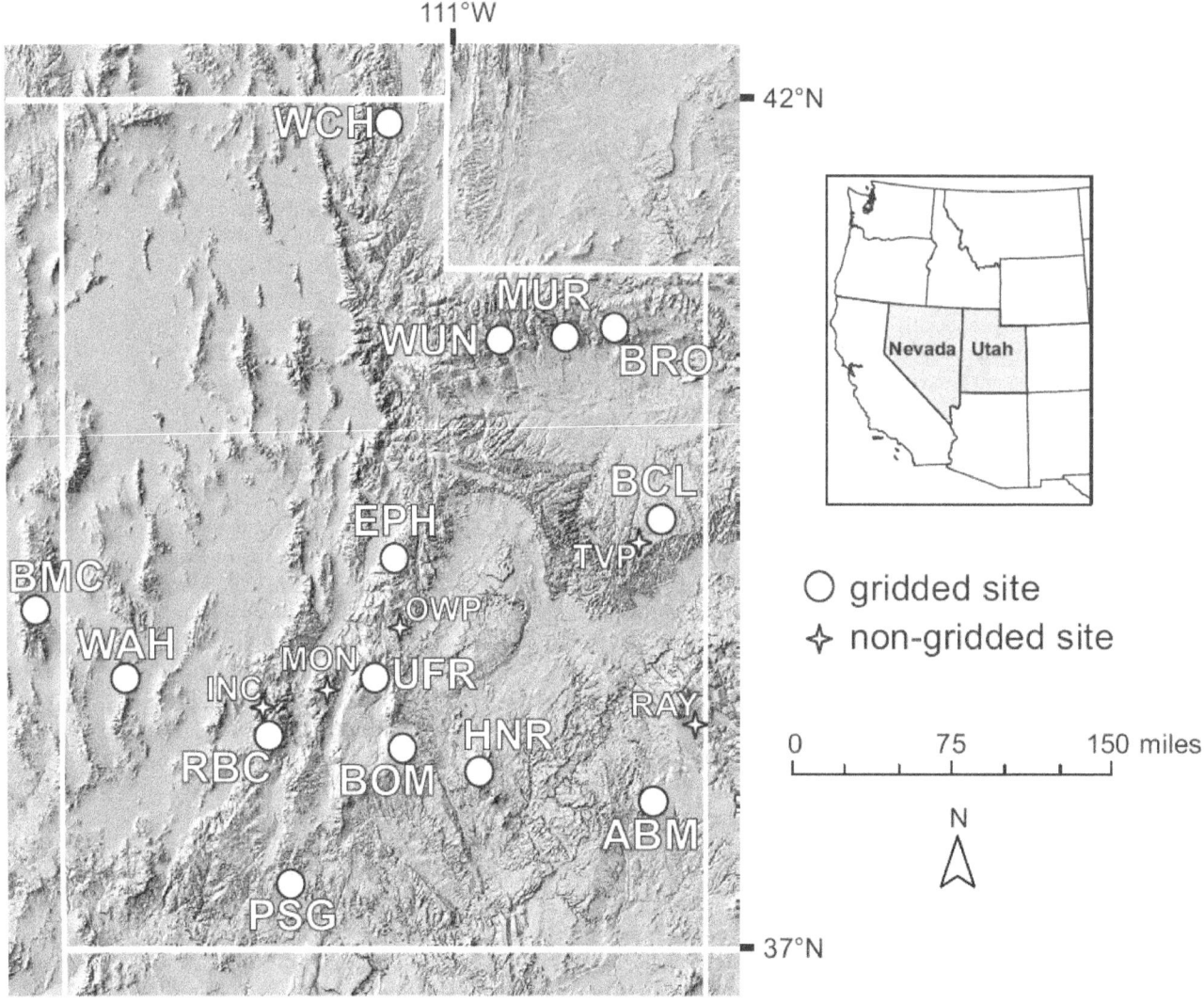

Figure 1—Locations of our fire and forest history sites in Utah and eastern Nevada against a background of elevation. Characteristics of each site are given in table 1.

could sample. We sampled 24 to 30 plots at most of the gridded sites (average 28 plots) but 44 plots at one site (Beaver River [RBC]; table 1) and 15 plots at another (Mytoge Mountains [UFR]). We sampled a total of 395 plots over 28,263 acres (table 1). The sites ranged from 1391 to 2837 acres and encompassed all of the plots plus a buffer of 0.16 mile, equal to one-half the average distance between plots. We were unable to sample 48 plots, either because we could not relocate plot center to a place we could sample or because the plot lacked trees ≥8 inches in diameter at breast height (DBH, 4.5 ft). Our final plots were 0.31 mile apart on average but ranged from 0.16 to 0.44 mile apart.

At each sampled plot, we recorded UTMs, elevation, slope, and aspect. At most plots, we took four photographs (one in each cardinal direction). We visually estimated ground cover for each plot as the percentage of rock, litter, bare ground, forbs, grasses, and shrubs, and we recorded the dominant understory plants for most plots. To compute an index of soil moisture at each plot (Topographic Relative Moisture Index; Parker 1982), we recorded topographic position (valley bottom, lower slope, middle slope, upper slope, or ridge top) and slope shape (concave, convex, or straight). In the office, we evaluated whether the topography of the sampled plots was representative of the topography of the site by comparing the distribution of plots among three topographic parameters (elevation, slope, and aspect) to that of the land area at the site. We derived the topographic characteristics of the land area from a digital elevation model (98 ft resolution; Utah AGRC 2004).

Table 1—Amount of evidence used to reconstruct fire and forest histories. The number of crossdated, fire-scarred sections does not include trees with fire dates that did not occur on at least two trees at the site. Of the 889 crossdated fire-scarred trees sampled at gridded sites, 301 were trees that we also sampled for recruitment date. Trees at MON were sampled for a previous study (Chappell 1997) but were crossdated for this study. All Universal Transverse Mercator (UTM) coordinates are relative to the 1927 North American Datum (NAD27) and lie in UTM zone 12, except for the Snake Range site (BMC), which is in zone 11.

Site code	Site name	National Forest or other land ownership	Area (acres)	Area (ha)	Number of plots sampled	Trees in plots		Fire-scarred trees		Location of Center of Site	
						Number sampled	Number cross-dated	Number sampled	Number cross-dated	UTM E	UTM N
Gridded											
ABM	Abajo Mountain	Manti-La Sal	2223	897	26	737	697	76	55	636081	4192853
BCL	Book Cliffs	Bureau Land Mgmt.	1788	722	29	883	707	30	11	636624	4379720
BMC	Snake Range	Great Basin Natl. Park	1569	633	24	674	507	128	103	735944	4323652
BOM	Boulder Mountain	Dixie	1963	792	30	892	788	114	95	463505	4227120
BRO	Brownie Creek	Ashley	1842	744	30	841	731	74	69	604433	4500480
EPH	Ephraim Canyon	Manti-La Sal	1876	757	29	856	724	38	26	457943	4353018
HNR	Henry Mountains	Bureau Land Mgmt.	2280	920	30	868	626	25	18	514716	4213697
MUR	Central Uinta Mountains	Ashley	2218	895	30	810	610	97	83	576529	4498031
PSG	Paunsaugunt Plateau	Dixie	2262	913	29	844	661	73	46	385172	4142590
RBC	Beaver Creek	Fishlake	2837	1145	44	1332	913	194	164	373558	4231772
UFR	Mytoge Mountains	Fishlake	1391	562	15	447	402	22	13	442816	4269737
WAH	Wah Wah Mountains	Bureau Land Mgmt.	1593	643	24	730	610	130	125	276630	4276601
WCH	Bear River Range	Uinta-Wasatch-Cache	2166	874	30	909	564	18	16	458199	4637430
WUN	Western Uinta Mountains	Ashley	2255	910	25	745	524	74	65	531727	4489112
TOTAL			28,263	11,410	395	11,568	9064	1093	889		
Non-gridded											
INC	Indian Creek	Fishlake	624	252	6	182	146	36	34	368989	4254123
MON	Monroe Mountain	Fishlake	---	---	0	0	0	11	11	414263	4260309
OWP	Old Woman Plateau	Fishlake	49	20	0	0	0	17	16	463477	4305011
RAY	Ray Mesa	Bureau Land Mgmt.	15	6	4	118	97	19	16	664652	4241779
TVP	East Tavaputs Plateau	Bureau Land Mgmt.	10	4	0	0	0	19	16	621022	4363832
TOTAL			698	282	10	300	243	102	94		

Tree Demography at Gridded Sites

At each plot, we used *n*-tree density-adapted sampling to reconstruct tree demography (recruitment and death dates) and historical and current forest structure (Jonsson and others 1992; Lessard and others 2002). This method allowed us to sample the same number of trees in every plot (roughly 30) regardless of tree density, which varied greatly across the study area. This method has been successfully used elsewhere (Brown and others 2008b; Brown and Wu 2005; Heyerdahl and others 2006). At each plot, we sampled live or dead trees that were ≥8 inches DBH and closest to plot center, up to a maximum of 35 trees (minimum 6 trees, average 29 trees; fig. 2). We estimated plot size using the distance between plot center and the farthest tree sampled (area of plot = π × [distance to farthest tree]^2). The farthest tree was 20 to 207 ft from plot center (average 73 ft). Consequently, plot size ranged from 0.03 to 3.09 acres with an average of 0.38 acres.

For each tree in the plot, we noted species, measured diameter with calipers at breast height (DBH) and sampling height (4 to 6 inches, and recorded the azimuth and distance from plot center. From live trees, we removed increment cores 4 to 6 inches above ground level. All heights were measured along the slope contour. We attempted to obtain increment cores that were no more than a field-estimated 10 rings from pith but removed a maximum of four cores from any given tree and retained the one that was closest to pith. From dead trees (logs, snags, and stumps) that were sound enough to sample, we used a chain saw to remove a full or partial cross section that included pith from what would have been approximately 4 to 6 inches above ground level. From dead trees that were not sound enough to sample, we did not remove a section but instead tallied them and noted whether or not they were charred.

All cores and sections were sanded until the cell structure was visible with a binocular microscope. We assigned calendar years to tree rings using a combination of mainly visual crossdating of ring widths and occasional cross-correlation of measured ring-width series (Grissino-Mayer 2001; Holmes 1983). For crossdating, we used ring-width chronologies that we developed for our sites and the species we sampled as well as chronologies that we downloaded from the International Tree-Ring Data Bank (http://www.ncdc.noaa.gov/paleo/treering.html). Crossdating is the process of matching climatically driven patterns of wide and narrow rings or other ring features, such as latewood width, from trees within and among sites to identify and account for false or partially absent rings (Stokes and Smiley 1968). Crossdating is possible because year-to-year variation in ring width or density is determined in part by year-to-year variation in climate, which was generally homogeneous across large parts of the region (Meko and others 1993).

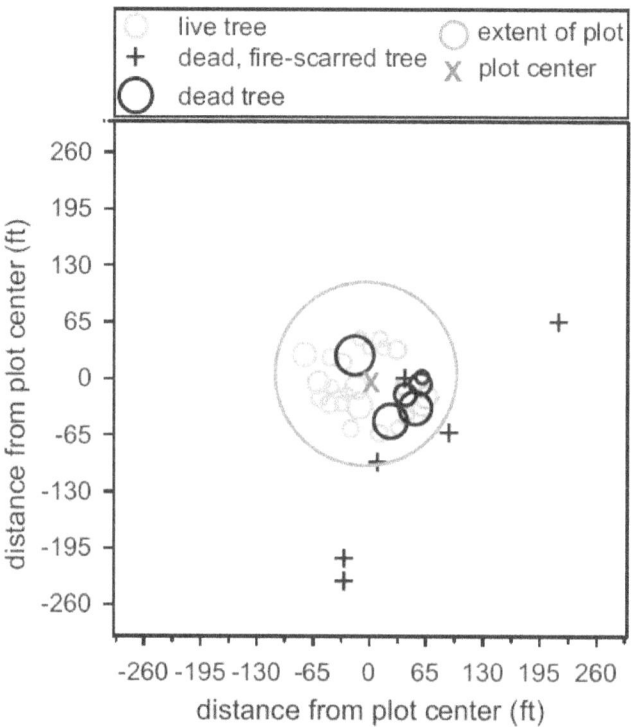

Figure 2—Schematic map of trees sampled at plot BOM17L. The diameter of the green and black symbols is proportional to DBH. We sampled the 30 trees that were ≥8 inches DBH and closest to plot center (whether living [green symbol] or dead [black symbol]). The size of this plot (the area within the blue circle) is 0.5 acres. In addition, we searched within 260 ft of plot center and found four fire-scarred trees (black symbols outside the blue circle).

USDA Forest Service RMRS-GTR-261WWW. 2011.

Slowly varying trends in ring width, such as those generated by stand dynamics, occurred in our samples in addition to the year-to-year variation that was driven by climate, but these trends did not affect our ability to crossdate individual live or dead trees. If we were unable to visually match the ring-width patterns from a sample to a ring-width chronology, we measured the width of the rings on the sample and statistically compared them to the chronology. This statistical comparison suggested possible dates for the rings on our samples, which we then verified on the wood to obtain final, exact calendar years for every tree ring. A total of 11,568 trees occurred in our plots and we removed wood samples from 10,284 of them (table 1). Of those, we were able to crossdate samples from 9064 trees. We excluded samples that we could not crossdate from analyses that relied on dates, such as fire frequency, but included them in analyses that did not, such as modern tree density and composition.

We estimated tree-recruitment dates from pith dates at sampling height (4 to 6 inches above ground level. Samples from most trees (70 percent) did not intersect the pith, so we estimated the number of years to pith based on the curvature of the innermost rings sampled (Applequist 1958; Duncan 1989) and subtracted this number from the innermost crossdated ring date. The average correction was eight years with a standard deviation of eight years. We did not correct for the number of years to reach sampling height because accurately measuring sampling height is challenging, especially where ground level may have changed at the base of trees that are several hundred years old and because the rate of vertical tree growth can vary through time. Therefore, we report recruitment dates—in other words, the date at which the tree reached a height of 4 to 6 inches.

Historical and Current Forest Structure and Composition

We assigned each plot to a category of historical (1860) and modern (2000) vegetation roughly following classifications developed for the LANDFIRE zones that cover our study area (zones 16, 17, and 23; table 2; fig. 3; Comer and others 2003; LANDFIRE 2006; Rollins and Frame 2006). We classified historical vegetation into rough approximations of LANDFIRE Biophysical Settings (BpS). BpS categories represent the vegetation communities that would exist under given environmental conditions (climate, soils, and landscape physiography) and historical disturbance regimes.

Table 2—Forest types that we assigned to plots and the names and codes of the LANDFIRE Biophysical Setting (BpS) and Existing Vegetation Type (EVT) categories from which our forest types are roughly derived (Comer and others 2003; LANDFIRE 2006).

Forest type used in this study	Category used in LANDFIRE BpS and EVT	BpS code	EVT code
spruce-fir	Rocky Mountain Subalpine Dry-Mesic Spruce-Fir Forest and Woodland	10550	2055
spruce-fir	Rocky Mountain Subalpine Mesic-Wet Spruce-Fir Forest and Woodland	10560	2056
limber-bristlecone	Inter-Mountain Basins Subalpine Limber-Bristlecone Pine Woodland	10200	2020
lodgepole	Rocky Mountain Lodgepole Pine Forest	10500	2050
aspen	Rocky Mountain Aspen Forest and Woodland	10110	2011
aspen-mixed conifer	Inter-Mountain Basins Aspen-Mixed Conifer Forest and Woodland	10610	2061
mixed conifer	Southern Rocky Mountain Dry-Mesic Montane Mixed Conifer Forest and Woodland	10510	2051
mixed conifer	Southern Rocky Mountain Mesic Montane Mixed Conifer Forest and Woodland	10520	2052
ponderosa pine	Southern Rocky Mountain Ponderosa Pine Woodland	10540	2054
ponderosa pine	Southern Rocky Mountain Ponderosa Pine Savanna	11170	2117
mountain mahogany	Inter-Mountain Basins Curl-Leaf Mountain Mahogany Woodland and Shrubland	10620	2062
pinyon-juniper	Colorado Plateau Pinyon-Juniper Shrubland	11020	2102
pinyon-juniper	Colorado Plateau Pinyon-Juniper Woodland	10160	2016
pinyon-juniper	Great Basin Pinyon-Juniper Woodland	10190	2019
oak	Rocky Mountain Gambel Oak-Mixed Montane Shrubland	11070	2107
sagebrush	Inter-Mountain Basins Montane Sagebrush Steppe	11260	2126
shrubland	Rocky Mountain Lower Montane-Foothill Shrubland	10860	2086

Figure 3—Photographs of the range of forest types sampled for this study (table 2). Site and plot identifiers and cardinal direction in which the photograph was taken (north [N], south [S], east [E], or west [W]) are provided to the right of each photo. All photographs were taken between 2002 and 2005.

Figure 3—*Continued.*

BpS is similar in concept to potential natural vegetation (Schmidt and others 2002). We assigned BpS categories to each plot based on the species and numbers of trees that we estimated were alive in that plot in 1860. Based on our crossdated samples, some plots (66 plots or 16 percent) lacked live trees in 1860. For these plots, we assigned BpS based on the dominant understory vegetation recorded at the plot. For example, in several plots, there was evidence that woody vegetation had expanded into what we inferred were historically sagebrush or grassland ecosystems. Similarly, we classified modern vegetation into rough approximations of LANDFIRE Existing Vegetation Types (EVT). We assigned EVT categories to each plot based on the species and number of trees present in that plot in 2000. Our plots fell into 17 different BpS and EVT categories but we combined some to form 12 forest-type categories that were consistent across the region (table 2). For example, we combined "Southern Rocky Mountain Ponderosa Pine Woodland" with "Southern Rocky Mountain Ponderosa Pine Savanna" to form a single "ponderosa pine" category and "Colorado Plateau Pinyon-Juniper Woodland" with "Great Basin Pinyon-Juniper Woodland" to form a single "pinyon-juniper" category. The classes we assigned to plots in this study (table 2) follow general BpS and EVT categories but are not directly comparable to them (see also Swetnam and Brown 2010). We report tree density by modern forest type but otherwise analyze only historical forest type.

For each site, we estimated changes in forest structure and composition over time by estimating the historical (1900) and modern (2000) density of trees ≥8 inches DBH at each plot and pooling them by forest type. To compute density at a plot in 1900, we divided the number of all dated trees that were alive in that plot in 1900 by the area of the plot. Note that the density of trees in 1900 does not include trees we were unable to crossdate or from which we were unable to remove a wood sample. Therefore, we have likely underestimated density in 1900 in some plots. To compute density in 2000, we divided the number of all trees that were alive when we sampled a plot (regardless of whether or not we removed a wood sample and crossdated it) by the area of that plot.

Fire Scars at Gridded Sites

We reconstructed a history of surface fires by using a chain saw to remove one to several partial cross sections from 1093 fire-scarred trees (table 1; Arno and Sneck 1977). Most of these trees (668 trees) were in our plots. This includes 364 of the trees that we sampled for recruitment date plus 304 trees that we searched for in a larger plot—in other words, we searched within approximately 260 ft of plot center, corresponding to an area of 5 acres (fig. 2). We sampled the remaining 461 fire-scarred trees as we encountered them between plots. We sanded and crossdated these samples, as previously described, for recruitment date samples and, again, we excluded any samples that we could not crossdate from further analyses.

We identified the calendar year of the tree ring in which each scar formed to determine the year of fire occurrence. We identified the position of each scar within a ring (ring boundary, early-earlywood, middle-earlywood, late-earlywood, latewood, or unknown; fig. 4) because this information could be used to infer the season of fire occurrence (Dieterich and Swetnam 1984). In addition to fire scars, we obtained a small amount of supporting evidence of surface fires (8 percent of fire records), mostly from eroded fire scars (ones for which much or all of the overlapping, curled rings were destroyed by subsequent fires or rot) but also from abrupt changes in the width of annual rings. However, because factors other than surface fires can cause abrupt changes in cambial growth, we used ring-width changes as evidence of surface fire only when they were synchronous with a fire scar on other samples at the same site. In the northern hemisphere, the season of cambial dormancy (the period corresponding to the ring boundary) spans two calendar years—from the time the cambium stops growing in the fall of one year until it resumes in the spring of the following year. For the southern sites (Abajo Mountain [ABM], Snake Range [BMC], Boulder Mountain [BOM], Ephraim Canyon [EPH], Henry Mountains [HNR], Indian Creek [INC], Monroe Mountain [MON], Old Woman Plateau [OWP], Paunsaugunt Plateau [PSG], RBC, UFR, and Wah Wah Mountains [WAH]), we assigned ring-boundary scars to the *following* calendar year because most modern fires in southern Utah burn early in the cambial growing season (Barrows 1978; Kitchen and McArthur 2003; Swetnam 1990). In contrast, the remaining sites are to the north (Wasatch Range [WCH], Western Uinta Mountains [WUN], Central Uinta Mountains [MUR], Brownie Creek [BRO], Book Cliffs [BCL], and East Tavaputs Plateau [TVP]), and so we assigned ring-boundary scars to the *preceding* calendar year because most modern fires in northern Utah burn late in the cambial growing season (Brown and others 2008a). Occasionally however, some late-season fires occur in southern

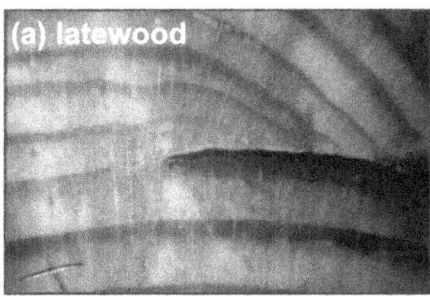

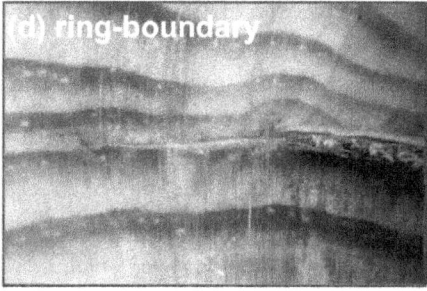

Figure 4—Examples of fire scars on ponderosa pine trees that differ in their intra-ring positions, which can be combined with information on cambial phenology to indicate the season in which a fire burned.

Utah and some early season fires occur in northern Utah. In addition, scars from a given fire can have a range of intra-annual positions because the timing of radial growth varies across the landscape (Fritts 1976) and because fires may burn for several months (Parsons and van Wagtendonk 1996). Therefore, when a site had many ring-boundary scars but some late-season scars at southern sites (or early-season scars at northern sites), we assigned all of the scars to the preceding year (or the following year at northern sites; 134, or 4 percent, of scar dates changed). We were unable to determine the intra-ring position of some scars (26 percent) because they were obscured by rot or insect galleries or because the rings were very narrow. For each site, we report the distribution of fire scars by intra-ring position of species for which at least 20 fire scars occurred during the period from 1650 to 1900.

Cohorts at Gridded Sites

For each plot, we inferred a history of severe fires (fires that killed some or all of the overstory trees) based on the occurrence of cohorts of trees and occasionally on tree death dates (Brown and others 2008b; Heyerdahl and others 2001). We assumed all of the cohorts we identified were recruited in response to high-severity fires, although it is likely that some of these cohorts were recruited after trees were killed by other disturbances such as insect outbreaks, wind, drought, or interactions among these disturbances (Brown 2006; DeRose and Long 2007; Kulakowski and Veblen 2002). Furthermore, while tree death dates can accurately indicate fire dates, estimated recruitment dates of trees in cohorts are not accurate fire dates because tree-ring determination of recruitment dates is not exact and trees may establish in fire-created openings over a period of years (Oliver and Larsen 1990).

We identified a cohort of trees at a plot when five or more trees were recruited within 20 years. More than one cohort could be identified at a plot but we required that every cohort date be preceded by at least 30 years with no recruitment to avoid identifying cohorts from continuous recruitment. We also identified severe fires at a plot when five or more trees died in the same year. We were not always able to obtain both pith and death dates for the dead trees we sampled because the sapwood of many tree species decays more rapidly than the heartwood. In identifying cohorts, we only included dates from trees whose outer rings were not decayed. We excluded the death dates of stumps even though trees killed by fire may have subsequently been harvested because we did not have harvesting dates. We estimated the year of the fire that created the opening in which a cohort established as the earliest recruitment date within that cohort. Although cohorts and scars occurred in the same or neighboring plots and may have been created by the same fire, we did not assign cohorts to fire-scar dates because low-severity fires were generally too frequent for us to unequivocally associate each cohort with a single fire-scar date. We present chronologies of fire scars and cohorts in fire charts (Grissino-Mayer 1995).

Plot-Composite Fire Regimes at Gridded Sites

Fire Intervals (Low-Severity Fires Only)

During the analysis period (1650 to 1900) for each plot, we estimated plot-composite fire intervals as the interval between years in which fire scarred two or more trees at the site (Dieterich 1980). We assumed that scar dates recorded on two or more trees were unlikely to have been created by factors other than fire, for example lightning or falling trees or branches. We report plot-composite intervals, pooled by forest type, for those forest types with 10 or more intervals at a site.

Fire Severity

To infer fire severity at plots before 1900, we assumed that fire-scar dates are evidence of low-severity fire, cohorts are evidence of high-severity fire, and a combination of the two is evidence of mixed-severity fire (table 3). We assigned *low severity* to plots that had three or more fire-scar dates but no cohorts and *high severity* to plots that had no fire-scar dates, a single cohort, and no trees recruited prior to the cohort (with the exception of trees killed by the fire that resulted in the cohort). More than one cohort can be present in a plot if a fire does not kill all the overstory trees but leaves some residual trees (Turner 2010). For example, if a cohort established in 1619 in response to a fire that killed all the trees in a plot, a second cohort could have established in 1899 in response to a fire that killed some, but not all of the trees in the 1619 cohort. Therefore, we assigned *mixed severity* to plots that had (1) one or more fire-scar dates and one or more cohorts or (2) a cohort plus trees that were recruited prior to the cohort. We were able to infer historical fire severity at most plots (55 percent) using these criteria.

Table 3—Criteria used to assign historical fire severity to plots at gridded sites. Note that plots could be assigned to mixed severity if they contained either of two kinds of evidence. Twelve of the 395 plots were classified as not historically forested because they lacked both trees recruited before 1900 and undated remnant trees. Another 26 were unclassified because they did not meet the criteria for any of our categories of fire severity.

Fire severity	Number of fire-scar dates[a]	Number of cohorts[b]	Additional evidence
Assumed no fire over the period of record	0	0	No charred remnants; pre-1900 trees dominated[c] by species with non-winged seeds (pinyons, junipers), lack serotinous cones, or do not sprout
High	0	1	No recruitment pre-dates the cohort
Assumed high	0	0	Pre-1900 trees dominated by Engelmann spruce, white fir, subalpine fir, quaking aspen, or lodgepole pine
Mixed	0	≥1	Recruitment pre-dates at least one of the cohorts
Mixed	≥1	≥1	
Assumed mixed	<3	0	Pre-1900 trees dominated by ponderosa pine, Douglas-fir, Great Basin bristlecone pine, or limber pine
Low	≥3	0	

[a] Recorded on ≥2 trees at a site.
[b] Five or more trees with recruitment and/or death dates within 20 years, preceded by 30 years with no recruitment. Death dates can be from snags or logs but not from stumps. Cohorts that initiated after 1900 are not included.
[c] Defined here as ≥50 percent of the trees at a plot were recruited before 1900.

Table 4—Common and scientific names of the species mentioned in the text. Nomenclature follows Welsh and others (1993) and USDA NRCS (2002).

Common name	Scientific name
Colorado pinyon	*Pinus edulis* Engelmann
common juniper	*Juniperus communis* Linnaeus
curl-leaf mountain mahogany	*Cercocarpus ledifolius* Nuttall in Torrey & Gray
Douglas-fir	*Pseudotsuga menziesii* (Mirbel) Franco
Engelmann spruce	*Picea engelmannii* Parry ex Engelmann
Gambel oak	*Quercus gambelii* Nuttall
Great Basin bristlecone pine	*Pinus longaeva* D.K. Bailey
limber pine	*Pinus flexilis* James
lodgepole pine	*Pinus contorta* Douglas ex Loudon
ponderosa pine	*Pinus ponderosa* Douglas ex Lawson & Lawson
quaking aspen	*Populus tremuloides* Michaux
Rocky Mountain juniper	*Juniperus scopulorum* Sargent
Rocky Mountain maple	*Acer glabrum* Torrey
singleleaf pinyon	*Pinus monophylla* Torrey & Frémont
subalpine fir	*Abies lasiocarpa* (Hooker) Nuttall
Utah juniper	*Juniperus osteosperma* (Torrey) Little
white fir	*Abies concolor* (Gordon & Glendinning) Lindley ex Hildebrand

The remaining plots did not have sufficient fire scars and/or cohorts to meet our criteria for low, high, or mixed severity, so instead, we inferred severity from the life-history strategies of the trees occurring in those plots. We assigned *assumed mixed severity* to plots with fewer than three fire-scar dates and no cohorts whose pre-1900 trees were dominated (in other words, at least half of the trees were recruited by 1900) by ponderosa pine (scientific names and authorities for overstory species are provided in table 4), Douglas-fir, Great Basin bristlecone pine, or limber pine (Agee 1993; Brown and Smith 2000; Wright and Bailey 1982). These species have relatively thick bark and generally high crowns and, therefore, tend to be adapted to low-severity fire regimes. We assigned *assumed high severity* to plots that lacked both fire scars and cohorts, and whose pre-1900 trees were dominated by Engelmann spruce, white fir, subalpine fir, quaking aspen, or lodgepole pine. These species have winged seeds (in the case of spruce and fir), predominately serotinous cones (lodgepole pine), or can sprout (aspen), all of which are characteristics that allow them to recolonize an area relatively fast after high-severity fire. We assigned *assumed no fire* to plots with (1) no fire-scar dates or cohorts, (2) no charred dead trees, and (3) pre-1900 trees dominated by species that have non-winged seeds (pinyon or juniper), lack serotinous cones, and do not sprout. A few plots did not fit the requirements for any of our categories and were not assigned an historical fire severity (6 percent), and a few were assumed to be not historically forested (3 percent) because they lacked both trees before 1900 and undated dead trees. While plots in the last three categories (assumed no fire, unclassified, and not historically forested) may have sustained fire in the past, we found no evidence of fire over the period of record.

Relative Fire Extent (Low-Severity Fires Only)

For every fire year that was recorded by a scar or fire-caused injury on two or more trees at a site, we used the location of fire-scarred trees sampled in and between plots to estimate the relative extent of low-severity fires. It is likely that we underestimated the extent of most of the fires that we reconstructed because they intersected the boundaries of our study sites. Therefore, we term our estimates "relative fire extent" to indicate that we are not able to reconstruct a complete fire-size distribution. To estimate relative fire extent, we divided each site into cells containing a single plot, where the boundaries of each cell lay halfway between a plot and its nearest neighbors (Mark 1987). The cells containing sampled plots averaged 63 acres in area and ranged from 37 to 101 acres. We estimated relative fire extent as the sum of the area of all cells with evidence of fire in that year. Because many fires intersected the boundaries of the sites and because not all trees were recording during every fire year (in other words, the trees at some plots were too young to show evidence of fire or the trees were not susceptible to scarring), we also computed relative fire extent as a percentage of recording area (area of cells with evidence of fire divided by area of cells with recording trees). We sampled a few trees outside of the cells (one tree each at EPH, HNR, and MUR) and mapped fire-scar dates from these trees but did not include them in our estimates of relative fire extent. While it is likely that many of the fires we reconstructed included small patches to extensive areas of high-severity fire, we unfortunately could not map the extent of these higher-severity fires because we generally could not reconstruct them with annual accuracy.

Spatial Variation in Fire Regimes within Gridded Sites

At each site, we graphically compared fire frequency at each plot to elevation, forest type, and an index of soil moisture at that plot—the topographic relative moisture index (TRMI; Parker 1982). This index of soil moisture is the sum of indices of four slope parameters that we measured in the field: aspect, slope, topographic position, and slope configuration. Our measure of fire frequency was the number of fire dates we reconstructed from fire scars and cohorts of trees from 1650 to 1900.

Non-Gridded Sites

In addition to the 14 gridded sites, we report fire history from five sites in Utah. We sampled two of these sites on grids in a manner similar to that used for the gridded sites but including only a few plots (Ray Mesa [RAY] and INC). At the remaining three sites, we only sampled fire-scarred trees (TVP, OWP, and MON). All tree-ring samples collected at these sites were sanded and crossdated, as previously described for the gridded sites.

The East Tavaputs Plateau (TVP) is approximately 24 miles southwest of BCL in woodland dominated by ponderosa pine and pinyon-juniper with scattered Douglas-fir. We sampled this site because it was one of the few locations on the Tavaputs Plateau with the concentration of fire-scarred trees that we needed for our regional study of the climate drivers of fire (Brown and others 2008a). We sampled 19 fire-scarred trees (15 ponderosa pine and 4 Douglas-fir) over an area of approximately 10 acres.

Ray Mesa (RAY) is located on the south side of the La Sal Mountains. The site is dominated by sagebrush meadows and pinyon-juniper woodlands and forests. We intended to sample a grid of plots in this area but did not find a suitable location. Instead, we sampled four plots in a manner similar to that used for the gridded sites to provide information for a project that was being conducted by the Bureau of Land Management. The ponderosa pine we sampled occurred mainly in drainages or rocky areas on the mesa. In four plots spread over 15 acres, we sampled 118 trees for recruitment dates and 11 trees for fire scars. We also removed partial cross sections from eight targeted fire-scarred ponderosa pine trees over an area of 4 acres, approximately 2.5 miles east of the plots.

Indian Creek (INC) is dominated by ponderosa pine, mixed conifer, aspen, and curlleaf mountain mahogany and is approximately 14 miles north of RBC. Similar to RAY, we intended to sample a grid of plots in this area but were not able to find a suitable environmental gradient over which to sample. Instead, we sampled six plots over 624 acres in a manner similar to that used for the gridded sites. We sampled 82 trees for recruitment dates and 15 trees for fire scars. We also sampled 21 fire-scarred trees that we encountered between plots.

Old Woman Plateau (OWP) is a relatively flat mesa bounded by steep canyons and cliffs to the east, north, and south and is dominated by ponderosa pine. We searched a portion of the mesa for trees with multiple fire scars and removed partial cross sections from 17 ponderosa pine trees over an area of 49 acres. Similar to TVP, we collected fire-scarred trees from this site for use in our analysis of the regional climate drivers of fire (Brown and others 2008a).

Monroe Mountain (MON) was sampled in a previous study conducted by the Fishlake National Forest (Chappell 1997). Fire-scarred and recruitment-date sections were removed from approximately 40 trees at approximately 16 locations. We were able to crossdate fire-scarred sections from 10 of these trees (6 ponderosa pine, 2 Douglas-fir, 1 quaking aspen, and 1 Colorado pinyon). The trees are spread along an approximately 35-mile north-south transect (in areas 2, 3, 5, 11, 15, 22, and 23, sampled by Chappell [1997]) but we lack exact locations for the individual trees.

Results and Discussion

Our fire and forest history tree-ring collection from Utah and eastern Nevada is the largest of its type from a single region for a single study. We sampled over 11,000 trees and were able to crossdate samples from more than 9000 of them. In this section, we briefly describe several overall aspects of these data and briefly review studies from which we inferred some of the causes of regional variation. In Appendices A through S, we provide details of the fire and forest histories we reconstructed for each site.

Many of our plots had evidence of a range of fire severities through time, but it is also likely that individual fires were of mixed severity across space, as has been documented elsewhere for modern fires (Lentile and others 2005). For example, at BRO we found evidence of a widespread fire in 1871 in the form of fire scars in 15 of the 16 cells that were recording that year (fig. H-7). We also identified nine cohorts with initial recruitment dates between 1871 and 1879, two of which occurred in plots that lacked fire scars in 1871. It is likely that these cohorts established in response to the same fire that created the scars. However, this site is unusual among our sites in that it had relatively few low-severity fires. At other sites, low-severity fires were generally more frequent, so a given cohort may have established in response to one of several low-severity fires.

It is challenging to reconstruct fire severity from tree rings. Our ability to identify cohorts of trees is limited by the accuracy with which we can reconstruct recruitment dates. Even though our fire-scar dates are annually accurate and we can date each tree ring on our recruitment samples to the correct calendar year, we cannot obtain annually accurate fire years from recruitment dates alone because there may have been climate driven delays in post-fire establishment. These inaccuracies interact with our rules for identifying cohorts and, thus, it is likely that we failed to identify some cohorts. Furthermore, we assumed that all of the cohorts we identified established in response to fire, but it is likely that some of these cohorts established after trees were killed by other disturbances such as insect outbreaks, wind, drought, or interactions among these factors (Brown 2006; DeRose and Long 2007; Kulakowski and Veblen 2002).

We were unable to assign fire severity to some of our plots (6 percent), but this does not imply that they necessarily lacked fire during the period of record. In fact, we found a few fire scars in some of these plots and others were surrounded by plots that sustained fire in the past. For example, the tree-ring evidence from plot BRO 14E (fig. R-1) did not meet our criteria for any category of fire severity. However, in most of the surrounding plots we reconstructed between one and four fire dates from both fire scars and cohorts. Given that the earliest recruitment date in plot BRO 14E post dates fire dates from most of the surrounding plots (fig. R-7), it is likely that this plot sustained a high-severity fire in the recent past.

We obtained death dates for 1121 trees, many of which occurred on or before 1900 (87 percent), but we were surprised that we were able to associate only a few of these death dates with high-severity fires based on our criterion of five or more trees dying in the same year. We suggest that trees died as a result of factors other than fire.

It was also challenging to estimate tree density and fire extent. Our estimates of tree density are conservative. We probably underestimated tree density in 1900 because some trees may have established before 1900 but had died and been consumed by fire or rot since then and because we were able to obtain pith dates for only 71 percent of the trees that occurred in our plots. In addition, our estimates of modern tree density did not include very small trees because the estimates were made only from trees that were at least 8 inches DBH when sampled. Another challenge to determining modern tree density was that the number of years it took for trees that were ≥8 inches DBH to reach sampling height (4 to 6 inches) likely varied both within and among our sites. For example, trees at the relatively mesic WCH site that were 8 to 9 inches DBH when sampled were recruited between 1782 and 1959, whereas trees of the same size at the relatively dry WAH site were recruited between 1243 and 1893, indicating that growth was generally slower at the dry WAH site. We estimated the extent of low-severity fires within our sites but did not capture the full distribution of relative fire extents that burned the landscape in the past. Many of the low-severity fires we reconstructed intersected the site boundary so the full extent of these fires was not reconstructed. For example, from 1650 to 1900 at BMC, most fire years (74 percent) burned in at least one cell on the boundary of the site (fig. F-12).

The season during which a fire burns can have ecological consequences for forest structure or understory composition (Harrington 1993; Kerns and others 2006; Knapp and others 2009). We report the intra-ring position of fire scars that could be used to infer the seasonal timing of past fires, but such inferences require data on the phenology of cambial growth, in other words, the seasonal timing of radial growth. Unfortunately, very little is known about cambial phenology in this region. In the future, we may be able to estimate the seasonal timing of past fires using the results of phenology studies that are now underway.

We present details of the spatial and temporal variation we found at our sites in appendices to this report, but we have inferred the causes of that variation in three other studies so far. First, we used fire-scar dates from 18 of the sites reported here (all except BCL) in an analysis of the climate drivers of regional-fire years between 1630 and 1900 (Brown and others 2008a). We found that years when fires were widespread across the region (31 years with fire at ≥20 percent of sites) had drier than average summers, whereas years with no fires at any site (100 years) were wetter than average. In addition, prior wet summers were associated with regional fire years in mixed-conifer and ponderosa pine forest types, possibly by increasing fine fuel amount and continuity, but prior wet summers were not associated with regional-fire years in spruce-fir or pinyon-juniper forests. We also found associations between fire and El Niño-Southern Oscillation (ENSO). Regional-fire years tended to occur during La Niña years when dry conditions prevailed across most of the study area, whereas non-fire years tended to occur during El Niño years when wet conditions prevailed across most of the study area. However, while dry conditions were associated with ponderosa pine and mixed-conifer forests throughout the study area, ENSO forcing was seen only in southeastern sites, which supports a hypothesis that a geographic pivot line in Pacific Basin teleconnections occurs at approximately latitude 40° N.

Second, Kitchen (2010) used fire chronologies from six new sites in combination with fire histories from four of our gridded sites (BMC, INC, RBC, and WAH) to explore in greater detail three aspects of historical fire patterns in the eastern Great Basin. First, using fire-scar data from four sites, he evaluated the competing risks for over- and under-estimation of point mean fire interval using individual-tree and composite fire chronologies. He recommended estimating mean fire interval from multiple-tree chronologies derived from sample areas of approximately 1.2 acres for heterogeneous landscapes. He also suggested that a correction factor be applied to mean fire intervals calculated from single-tree chronologies. Second, he found that the climate drivers of fire at 10 sites scattered just south of latitude 40° N were similar to those found in our broader study (Brown and others 2008a). Years of widespread fire were drier than average, whereas years with no fires were wetter than average. Widespread fires were more likely to occur in La Niña years and just after wet-to-dry transitions in multi-year precipitation oscillations. Local fire years occurred under a broad range of conditions. Kitchen (2010) cited a bimodal seasonality pattern as evidence of the influence of Native American ignitions on the fire regime. Third, spatial and temporal variation in the frequency, severity, and size of fires and tree recruitment patterns were explored for two sites. Point mean fire interval varied 10-fold within sites demonstrating strong topographic control of the fire regime. Surface fire was predominant at upper-elevation sub-alpine stands; however, intervals were longer than at lower-elevation mixed-conifer stands. Most fires were small and together accounted for only a minor proportion of area burned. Recruitment pulses varied spatially from stand to landscape scales and were often synchronous with fire-quiescent periods, consistent with the notion of a dynamic mixed-severity fire regime especially at mid-elevations.

Third, Swetnam and Brown (2010) compared vegetation characteristics derived through simulation modeling for use in fire regime condition class (FRCC; Hann and Bunnell 2001; Hardy and others 2001; Schmidt and others 2002) and LANDFIRE with those we reconstructed from tree rings at 11 of our gridded sites (WCH, MUR, WUN, UFR, WAH, INC, BOM, RBC, HNR, ABM, and PSG). First, the BpS categories assigned to plots did not differ significantly from the composition of the plot in 1880 that was derived from tree rings for ponderosa pine, aspen, and mixed-conifer BpS, but they did differ significantly for spruce-fir, pinyon-juniper, and lodgepole pine BpS. Second, LANDFIRE map data were approximately 58 percent accurate for BpS and approximately 60 percent accurate for EVT. These results suggest that the reference condition definitions used in FRCC assessments could be improved by additional sampling to determine the relationship of tree age to size. Additionally, more empirical data are needed to better parameterize FRCC vegetation models, especially in low-frequency fire types.

Management Implications

The site specific data we report here are important for managing fire and forests, especially at the broad spatial and temporal scales we present. While the fire and forest histories we report provide a foundation for management, many other factors are critical to determining actual management actions and desired conditions (Allen and others 2002; Hood and Miller 2007; Keeley and others

2009). Restoring the regimes we reconstructed may not be feasible if it would conflict with other objectives such as reducing invasive species. Nonetheless, quantitative data on fire and forest history provides a baseline for identifying recent changes that are unusual and perhaps incompatible with protecting specific species or habitats (Keeley and others 2009). These data are still valuable in the face of changing climate (Fulé 2008). The Forest Service's recent directive "Ecological restoration and resilience" (Interim Directive No. 2020-2010-1; March 3, 2010; http://www fs.fed.us/ im/directives/fsm/2000/id_2020-2010-1.doc) recognizes that "Ecosystems are dynamic and change is inevitable," and that "Knowledge of past and current ecosystem dynamics, current and desired conditions, climate change projections, and human uses is fundamental to planning restoration activities." The data we present here can also be used as reference dynamics for process-centered restoration (Falk 2006).

For More Information

Our fire-scar and tree-recruitment dates and associated metadata are available from the International Multiproxy Paleofire Database (IMPD), a permanent, public archive maintained by the Paleoclimatology Program of the National Oceanic and Atmospheric Administration in Boulder, Colorado (http://www.ncdc noaa.gov/paleo/impd/paleofire html). The wood samples we collected are permanently archived and their current location(s) are provided in the metadata that are archived at the IMPD.

References

Agee, J.K. 1993. Fire ecology of Pacific Northwest forests. Washington, DC: Island Press. 493 p.

Allen, C.D., M. Savage, D.A. Falk, K.F. Suckling, T.W. Swetnam, T. Schulke, P.B. Stacey, P. Morgan, M. Hoffman, and J.T. Klingel. 2002. Ecological restoration of southwestern ponderosa pine ecosystems: A broad perspective. Ecological Applications. 12:1418-1433.

Applequist, M.B. 1958. A simple pith locator for use with off-center increment cores. Journal of Forestry. 56:141.

Arno, S.F. and K.M. Sneck. 1977. A method for determining fire history in coniferous forests of the Mountain West. General Technical Report INT-GTR-42. Ogden, Utah: U.S. Department of Agriculture, Forest Service, Intermountain Forest and Range Experiment Station. 28 p.

Barrows, J.S. 1978. Lightning fires in southwestern forests. Final report. Fort Collins, Colorado: U.S. Department of Agriculture, Forest Service, Rocky Mountain Forest and Range Experiment Station. 154 p.

Brown, J.K. and J.K. Smith, eds. 2000. Wildland fire in ecosystems: Effects of fire on flora. General Technical Report RMRS-GTR-42-vol. 2. Ogden, Utah: U.S. Department of Agriculture, Forest Service, Rocky Mountain Research Station. 257 p.

Brown, P.M. 2006. Climate effects on fire regimes and tree recruitment in Black Hills ponderosa pine forests. Ecology. 87:2500-2510.

Brown, P.M. and R. Wu. 2005. Climate and disturbance forcing of episodic tree recruitment in a southwestern ponderosa pine landscape. Ecology. 86:3030-3038.

Brown, P.M., E.K. Heyerdahl, S.G. Kitchen, and M.H. Weber. 2008a. Climate effects on historical fires (1630-1900) in Utah. International Journal of Wildland Fire. 17:28-39.

Brown, P.M., C.L. Wienk, and A.J. Symstad. 2008b. Fire and forest history at Mount Rushmore. Ecological Applications. 18:1984-1999.

Chappell, L. 1997. A fire history study conducted on the Monroe Mountain demonstration area. Final report. Richfield, Utah: U.S. Department of Agriculture, Forest Service, Fishlake National Forest. 25 p.

Comer, P., D. Faber-Langendoen, R. Evans, S. Gawler, C. Josse, G. Kittel, S. Menard, M. Pyne, M. Reid, K. Schulz, K. Snow, and J. Teague. 2003. Ecological systems of the United States: A working classification of U.S. terrestrial systems. NatureServe, Arlington, Virginia. 75 p.

Covington, W.W., P.Z. Fulé, M.M. Moore, S.C. Hart, T.E. Kolb, J.N. Mast, S.S. Sackett, and M.R. Wagner. 1997. Restoring ecosystem health in ponderosa pine forests of the Southwest. Journal of Forestry. 95:23-29.

DeRose, R.J. and J.N. Long. 2007. Disturbance, structure, and composition: Spruce beetle and Engelmann spruce forests on the Markagunt Plateau, Utah. Forest Ecology and Management. 244:16-23.

Dieterich, J.H. 1980. The composite fire interval: A tool for more accurate interpretation of fire history. Pages 8-14 in: M.A. Stokes and J.H. Dieterich, tech. coords. Proceedings of the fire history workshop; 20-24 October, 1980; Tucson, Arizona. General Technical Report RM-81. Fort Collins, Colorado: U.S. Department of Agriculture, Forest Service, Rocky Mountain Forest and Range Experiment Station.

Dieterich, J.H. and T.W. Swetnam. 1984. Dendrochronology of a fire-scarred ponderosa pine. Forest Science. 30:238-247.

Duncan, R.P. 1989. An evaluation of errors in tree age estimates based on increment cores in kahikatea (*Dacrycarpus dacrydiodes*). New Zealand Natural Sciences. 16:31-37.

Falk, D.A. 2006. Process-centred restoration in a fire-adapted ponderosa pine forest. Journal for Nature Conservation. 14:140-151.

Fritts, H.C. 1976. Tree rings and climate. New York, New York: Academic Press. 567 p.

Fulé, P.Z. 2008. Does it make sense to restore wildland fire in changing climate? Restoration Ecology. 16:526-531.

Grissino-Mayer, H.D. 1995. Tree-ring reconstructions of climate and fire history at El Malpais National Monument, New Mexico. Tucson, Arizona: University of Arizona. 407 p. Dissertation.

Grissino-Mayer, H.D. 2001. Evaluating crossdating accuracy: A manual and tutorial for the computer program COFECHA. Tree-Ring Research. 57:205-221.

Hann, W.J. and D.L. Bunnell. 2001. Fire and land management planning and implementation across multiple scales. International Journal of Wildland Fire. 10:389-403.

Hann, W., D. Havlina, A. Shlisky, [and others], eds. 2003. Interagency and The Nature Conservancy fire regime condition class [Homepage of Fire Regime Condition Class, USDA Forest Service, U.S. Department of the Interior, The Nature Conservancy, and Systems for Environmental Management], [Online]. Available: http://www.frcc.gov [2007, December 27].

Hardy, C.C., K.M. Schmidt, J.M. Menakis, and N.R. Samson. 2001. Spatial data for national fire planning and fuel management. International Journal of Wildland Fire. 10:353-372.

Harrington, M.G. 1993. Predicting *Pinus ponderosa* mortality from dormant season and growing season fire injury. International Journal of Wildland Fire. 3:65-72.

Heyerdahl, E.K., L.B. Brubaker, and J.K. Agee. 2001. Spatial controls of historical fire regimes: a multiscale example from the Interior West, USA. Ecology. 82:660-678.

Heyerdahl, E.K., R.F. Miller, and R.A. Parsons. 2006. History of fire and Douglas-fir establishment in a savanna and sagebrush-grassland mosaic, southwestern Montana, USA. Forest Ecology and Management. 230:107-118.

Holmes, R.L. 1983. Computer-assisted quality control in tree-ring dating and measurement. Tree-Ring Bulletin. 43:69-78.

Hood, S.M. and M. Miller, eds. 2007. Fire ecology and management of the major ecosystems of southern Utah. General Technical Report RMRS-GTR-202. Fort Collins, CO: U.S. Department of Agriculture, Forest Service, Rocky Mountain Research Station. 110 p.

Jonsson B., S. Holm, and H. Kallur. 1992. A forest inventory method based on density-adapted circular plot size. Scandinavian Journal of Forest Research. 7:405-421.

Keeley, J.E., G.H. Aplet, N.L. Christensen, S.C. Conard, E.A. Johnson, P.N. Omi, D.L. Peterson, and T.W. Swetnam. 2009. Ecological foundations for fire management in North American forest and shrubland ecosystems. General Technical Report PNW-GTR-779. Portland, OR: U.S. Department of Agriculture, Forest Service, Pacific Northwest Research Station. 92 p.

Kerns, B.K., W.G. Thies, and C.G. Niwa. 2006. Season and severity of prescribed burn in ponderosa pine forests: Implications for understory native and exotic plants. Écoscience. 13: 44-55.

Kitchen, S.G. 2010. Historic fire regimes of eastern Great Basin (USA) mountains reconstructed from tree rings. Provo, Utah: Brigham Young University. 166 p. Dissertation.

Kitchen, S.G. and E.D. McArthur. 2003. Ponderosa pine fire history in a southeastern Great Basin stand. Pages 152-156 in: K.E.M. Galley, R.C. Klinger, and N.G. Sugihara, eds. Proceedings of Fire Conference 2000: The first national congress on fire ecology, prevention, and management. Miscellaneous Publication No. 13, Tall Timbers Research Station, Tallahassee, Florida.

Knapp, E.E., B.L. Estes, S.N. Skinner. 2009. Ecological effects of prescribed fire season: A literature review and synthesis for managers. General Technical Report PSW-GTR-224. Albany, California: U.S. Department of Agriculture, Forest Service, Pacific Southwest Research Station. 80 p.

Kulakowski, D. and T.T. Veblen. 2002. Influences of fire history and topography on the pattern of a severe wind blowdown in a Colorado subalpine forest. Journal of Ecology. 90:806-819.

LANDFIRE. 2006. The national map. National existing vegetation type and biophysical settings layers. (2006, September—last update). U.S. Department of Interior, Geological Survey. [Online]. Available: http://gisdata.usgs net/website/landfire/ [2008, October 21].

Lentile, L.B., F.W. Smith, and W.D. Sheppard. 2005. Patch structure, fire-scar formation, and tree regeneration in a large mixed-severity fire in the South Dakota Black Hills, USA. Canadian Journal of Forest Research. 35:2875-2885.

Lessard, V.C., T.D. Drummer, and D.D. Reed. 2002. Precision of density estimates from fixed-radius plots compared to N-tree distance sampling. Forest Science. 48:1-5.

Madany, M.H. and N.E. West. 1983. Livestock grazing-fire regime interactions within montane forests of Zion National Park, Utah. Ecology. 64:661-667.

Mark, D.M. 1987. Recursive algorithm for determination of proximal (Thiessen) polygons in any metric space. Geographical Analysis. 19:264-272.

Mauk, R.L. and J.A. Henderson. 1984. Coniferous forest habitat types of northern Utah. General Technical Report INT-GTR-170. Ogden, Utah: U.S. Department of Agriculture, Forest Service, Intermountain Research Station. 89 p.

Meko, D., E.R. Cook, D.W. Stahle, C.W. Stockton, and M.K. Hughes. 1993. Spatial patterns of tree-growth anomalies in the United States and southern Canada. Journal of Climate. 6:1773-1786.

National Wildfire Coordinating Group (NWCG). Glossary of wildland fire terminology, [Online]. Available: http://www.nwcg.gov/pms/pubs/glossary/pms205.pdf [2008, November 28].

Oliver, C.D. and B.C. Larson. 1990. Forest stand dynamics. New York, New York: McGraw-Hill. 467 p.

Parker, A.J. 1982. The topographic relative moisture index: An approach to soil-moisture assessment in mountain terrain. Physical Geography. 3:160-168.

Parsons, D.J. and J.W. van Wagtendonk. 1996. Fire research and management in the Sierra Nevada National Parks. Pages 25-48 in: W.L. Halvorson and G.E. Davis, eds. Science and ecosystem management in the National Parks. Tucson, Arizona: University of Arizona Press.

Rollins, M.G. and C.K. Frame, tech. eds. 2006. The LANDFIRE prototype project: Nationally consistent and locally relevant geospatial data for wildland fire management. General Technical Report RMRS-GTR-175. Fort Collins, Colorado: U.S. Department of Agriculture, Forest Service, Rocky Mountain Research Station. 416 p.

Schmidt, K.M., J.P. Menakis, C.C. Hardy, W.J. Hann, and D.L. Bunnell. 2002. Development of coarse-scale spatial data for wildland fire and fuel management. General Technical Report RMRS-GTR-87. Fort Collins, Colorado: U.S. Department of Agriculture, Forest Service, Rocky Mountain Research Station. 41 p.

Schoennagel, T., T.T. Veblen, and W.H. Romme. 2004. The interaction of fire, fuels, and climate across Rocky Mountain forests. BioScience. 54:661-676.

Stein, S.J. 1988. Fire history of the Paunsaugunt Plateau in southern Utah. Great Basin Naturalist. 48:58-63.

Stokes, M.A. and T.L. Smiley. 1968. An introduction to tree-ring dating. Chicago, Illinois: University of Chicago Press. 73 p.

Swetnam, T.L. 2006. Fire regime condition class accuracy: A comparison to tree-ring fire histories. Tucson, Arizona: University of Arizona. 111 p. Thesis.

Swetnam, T.L. and P.M. Brown. 2010. Comparing selected fire regime condition class (FRCC) and LANDFIRE vegetation model results to tree-ring data. International Journal of Wildland Fire. 19:1-13.

Swetnam, T.W. 1990. Fire history and climate in the Southwestern United States. Pages 6-17 in: J.S. Krammes, tech. coord. Proceedings of symposium on Effects of fire in management of southwestern U.S. natural resources; November 15-17, 1988. General Technical Report RM-GTR-191. Fort Collins, Colorado: U.S. Department of Agriculture, Forest Service, Rocky Mountain Forest and Range Experiment Station.

U.S. Department of Agriculture and Natural Resources Conservation Service [USDA, NRCS]. 2002. The PLANTS database, version 3.5. National Plant Data Center, Baton Rouge, Louisiana [Online]. Available: http://plants.usda.gov [2008, October 8].

Utah Automated Geographic Reference Center [AGRC]. 2004. Homepage of Utah AGRC, State of Utah Online Services, [Online]. Available: http://agrc.utah.gov/agrc_sgid/dem.html [2004, September 1].

Wadleigh, L. and M.J. Jenkins. 1996. Fire frequency and the vegetative mosaic of a spruce-fir forest in northern Utah. Great Basin Naturalist. 56:28-37.

Welsh, S.L., N.D. Atwood, S. Goodrich, and L.C. Higgins, eds. 1993. A Utah flora. Second edition, revised. Provo, Utah: Brigham Young University. 986 p.

Wright, H.A. and A.W. Bailey. 1982. Fire ecology, United States and southern Canada. New York, New York: Wiley. 501 p.

Youngblood, A.P. and R.L. Mauk. 1985. Coniferous forest habitat types of central and southern Utah. General Technical Report INT-GTR-187. Ogden, Utah: U.S. Department of Agriculture, Forest Service, Intermountain Research Station. 89 p.

Appendix A. Henry Mountains, Bureau of Land Management (HNR)

Topography

We sampled 30 plots over 2280 acres near Willow and Dugout Creeks on the west side of Mount Ellen, Kanab Field Office, Bureau of Land Management, in Garfield County, Utah (figs. 1 and A-1). The plots were separated by 0.29 miles on average (range 0.22 to 0.33 miles) and averaged 0.95 acres in area (range 0.14 to 2.13 acres). Plots were sampled within cells that averaged 63 acres and ranged from 52 to 74 acres. Plots ranged in elevation from 7892 to 10,289 ft (fig. A-2). They ranged in slope from 5 to 64 percent, but all except one plot had slopes less than 50 percent. The plots were sampled on a range of aspects, but most were on south or west aspects (83 percent). The distribution of the plots by elevation or aspect did not differ from the distribution of the landscape by more than 10 percent in any category except for gentle and moderate slopes, which were under and over sampled, respectively (fig. A-2). We took four photographs each at 12 of the plots.

Tree Demography

Of the 868 trees that occurred in the plots, most (97 percent) were Utah juniper, Colorado pinyon, ponderosa pine, Douglas-fir, quaking aspen, or limber pine, but 10 subalpine fir and 13 Engelmann spruce trees also occurred (fig. A-3). Most of these trees were living (94 percent) and the rest were snags (3 percent) or logs (3 percent). We were able to remove and crossdate wood samples from most of these trees (626 trees or 72 percent) and obtained actual or estimated pith dates for 621 of them. These pith dates ranged from 1325 to 1972, but many post-dated 1900 (296 trees; fig. A-4). The death dates we obtained for one snag and one log were 1961 and 1900, respectively.

Historical and Current Forest Structure and Composition

The plots included a range of historical and modern forest types (sagebrush, pinyon-juniper, ponderosa pine, mixed conifer, aspen, and spruce-fir; table A-1). Some plots changed forest type between 1860 and 2000: three sagebrush and one ponderosa pine plot converted to mixed conifer. In 1900, tree density averaged 18 trees per acre and ranged from 0 to 79 trees per acre (fig. A-5). In 2000, tree density averaged 50 trees per acre and ranged from 13 to 218 trees per acre. However, we likely underestimated historical tree density because we could not obtain recruitment or earliest-ring dates for 242 of the 868 trees that occurred in the plots and only an earliest-ring date for another 5 trees.

Fire Scars

We were able to remove and crossdate fire-scarred samples from 18 trees. Only 3 of these trees were sampled in 2 of the 30 plots at this site. We sampled the 15 other fire-scarred trees as we encountered them between plots over 1057 acres throughout the site (fig. A-6). Most of the 18 fire-scarred trees were ponderosa pine (89 percent), and the rest were limber pine. Most were living (67 percent) and the rest were snags or stumps. These 18 trees yielded 97 fire scars and 7 eroded fire scars or abrupt changes in ring width (figs. A-4 and A-7), none of which was recorded on only a single tree. We were able to assign an intra-ring position to 94 percent of the 77 fire scars that occurred during the analysis period (1650 to 1900). Of the scars that occurred on ponderosa pine trees, most (62 percent) occurred on the boundary between two rings (fig. A-8).

Post-Fire Cohorts

We identified 12 cohorts of trees from estimated recruitment dates at 11 of the plots. Six of these cohorts were recruited before 1900 (1626 to 1853) and were identified from 39 trees (5 to 8 trees per cohort), about half of which were ponderosa pine (49 percent) and the rest were Colorado pinyon (18 percent), Engelmann spruce (15 percent), Douglas-fir (13 percent) or limber pine (5 percent; figs. A-4 and A-7). The cohorts recruited before 1900 occurred in plots with a range of forest types: ponderosa pine (50 percent of cohorts), spruce-fir (17 percent), and mixed conifer (17 percent), and pinyon-juniper (17 percent).

Spatial Variation in Fire Regimes

We reconstructed too few fire intervals in plots during the analysis period (1650 to 1900) to compute plot-composite fire intervals by forest type at this site. The tree-ring record before 1900 was less than 100 years long for 6 of the 30 plots at this site (fig. A-9).

We inferred that five pinyon-juniper plots did not sustain fire over the period of record (table A-2). Two plots were not historically forested, and we could not infer historical fire severity at two others because they did not meet our requirements for any of the severity categories. We assigned the remaining plots to the mixed or high fire severity categories.

From 1650 to 1900, the 22 low-severity fires we reconstructed within our 2280-acre sampling area averaged 109 acres and ranged from 59 to 195 acres (fig. A-10), equivalent to 24 to 100 percent of the recording area (in other words, the combined area of cells containing recording, fire-scarred trees during a given year). Recording area varied among fire years, ranging from 121 to 374 acres. We likely underestimated the extent of low-severity fires because most fires intersected the boundary of the site (fig. A-11).

Table A-1—Distribution of plots at HNR by historical (1860) and modern (2000) forest types (table 2).

Historical forest type (1860)	Modern forest type (2000)					Total plots in 1860
	Spruce-fir	Aspen	Mixed conifer	Ponderosa pine	Pinyon-juniper	
Spruce-fir	1					1
Aspen		2				2
Mixed conifer			5			5
Ponderosa pine			1	11		12
Pinyon-juniper					7	7
Sagebrush			3			3
Total plots in 2000	**1**	**2**	**9**	**11**	**7**	**30**

Table A-2—Distribution of plots at HNR by historical forest type (1860; table 2) and fire severity (table 3).

Forest type	High	Assumed high	Mixed	Assumed mixed	Assumed no fire	Not historically forested	Unclassified
Spruce-fir			1				
Aspen		2					
Mixed conifer			1	4			
Ponderosa pine			3	7		1	1
Pinyon-juniper	1				5		1
Sagebrush				2		1	
Total	**1**	**2**	**5**	**13**	**5**	**2**	**2**

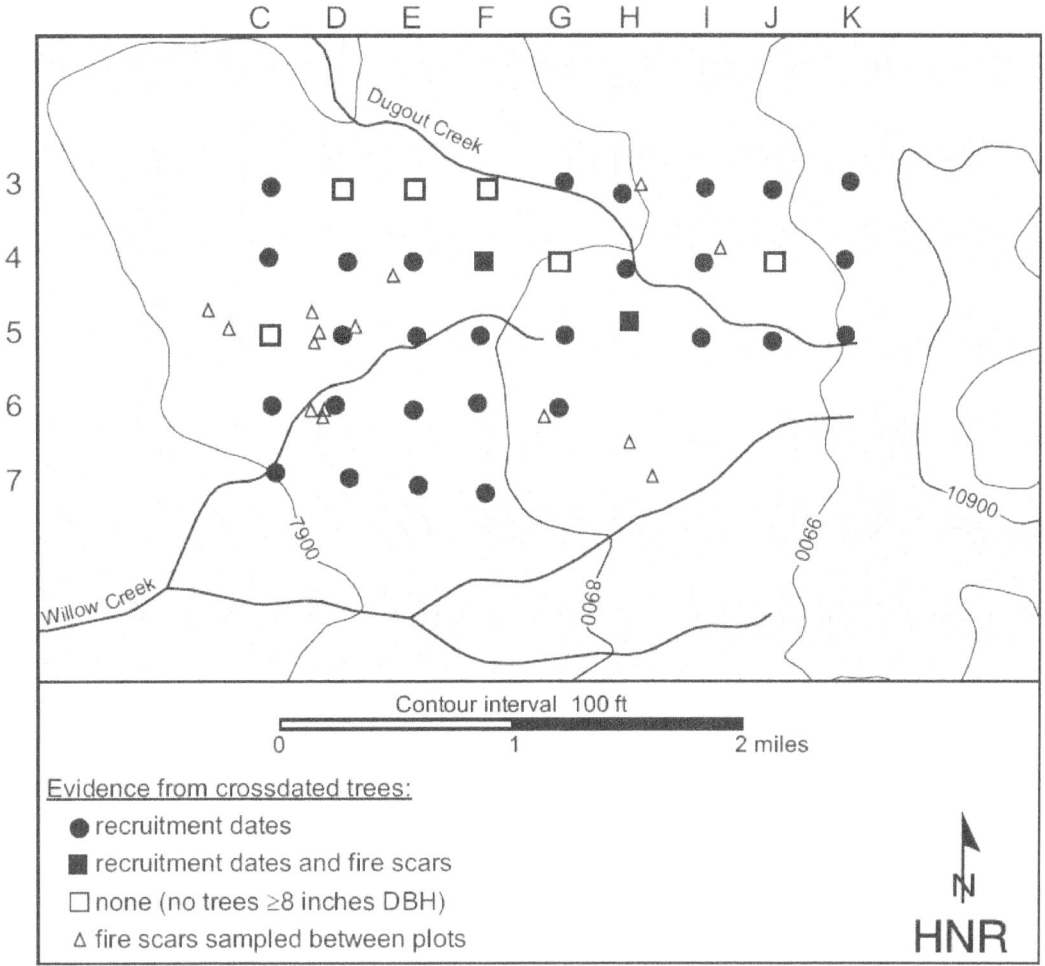

Figure A-1—Locations of plots and crossdated fire-scarred trees that were sampled outside plots. Two of the fire-scarred trees were sampled within plots and are not mapped individually. Plots are identified by column and row, in other words, the northwestern most plot is 3C, the next plot to the east is 3D, and so forth.

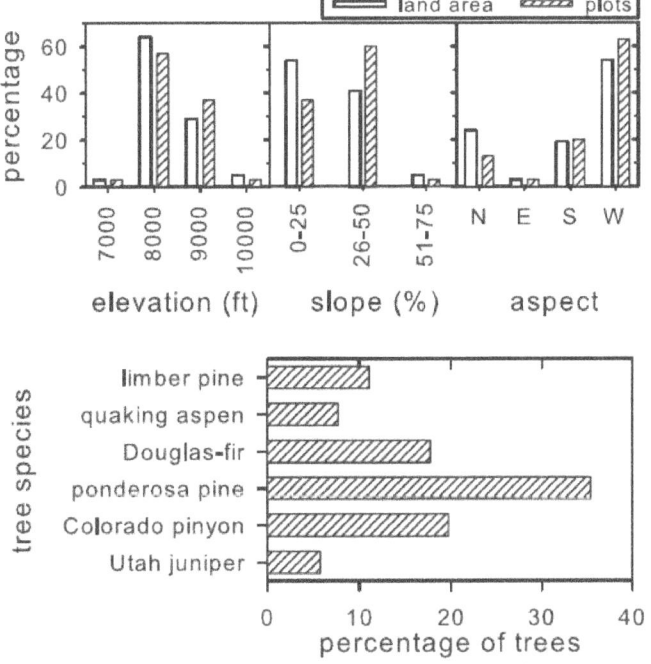

Figure A-2—Distribution of sampled plots and land area at HNR by topography. Aspect classes are 90° wide, beginning with 46° for east (E). Land area was derived from a digital elevation model (Utah AGRC 2004).

Figure A-3—Distribution by species of the 868 live and dead trees ≥8 inches DBH that occurred in plots at HNR, regardless of whether or not we removed wood samples and crossdated them. Not shown are 10 subalpine fir and 13 Engelmann spruce trees.

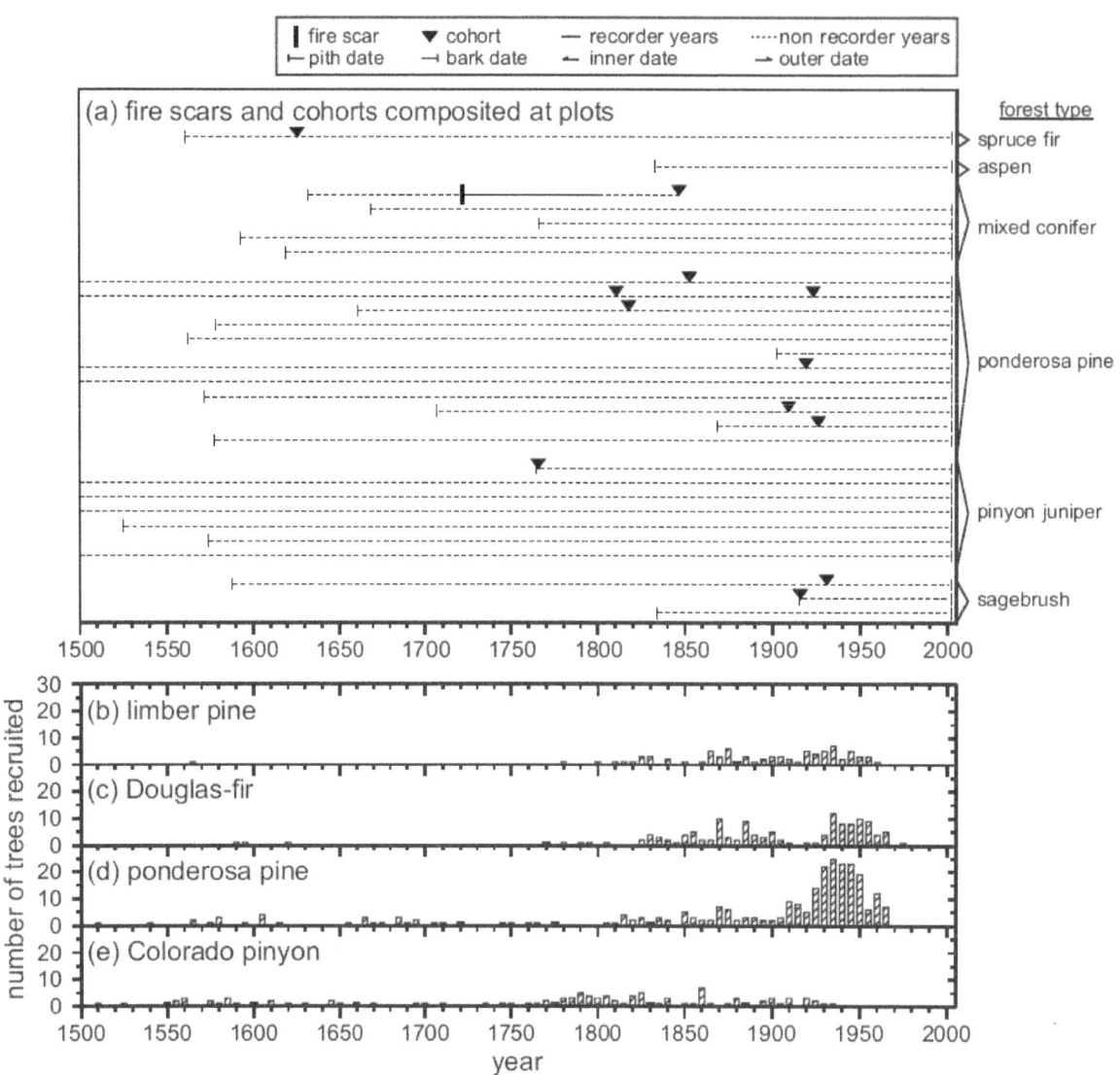

Figure A-4—Chronologies of fire and tree recruitment at HNR. In (a), horizontal lines are plot-composite fire-scar and cohort dates by forest type. Non-recorder years precede the first scar, whereas recorder years generally follow it, but non-recorder years can also occur when the catface margin is consumed by subsequent fires or rot. In (b) through (e), recruitment dates are given for species comprising ≥10 percent of trees with such dates. The latter part of the distribution is incomplete because we only cored trees that were ≥8 inches DBH.

                                              USDA Forest Service RMRS-GTR-261WWW. 2011.

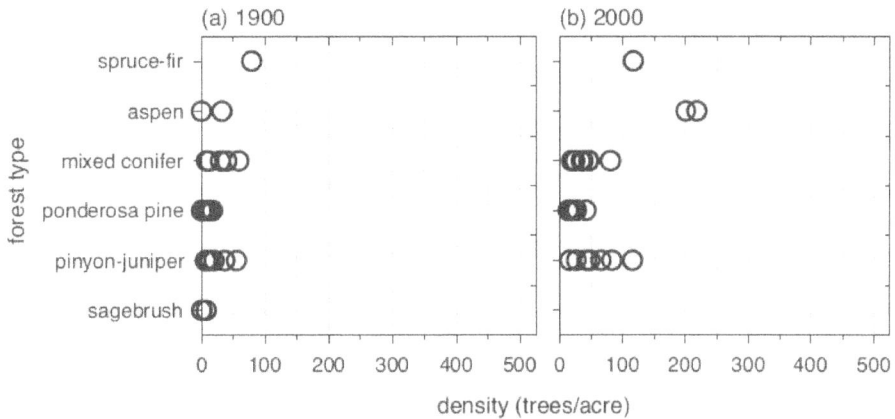

Figure A-5—Density of trees ≥8 inches DBH that were alive at each plot at HNR (a) in 1900 and (b) in 2000, by forest type (table 2).

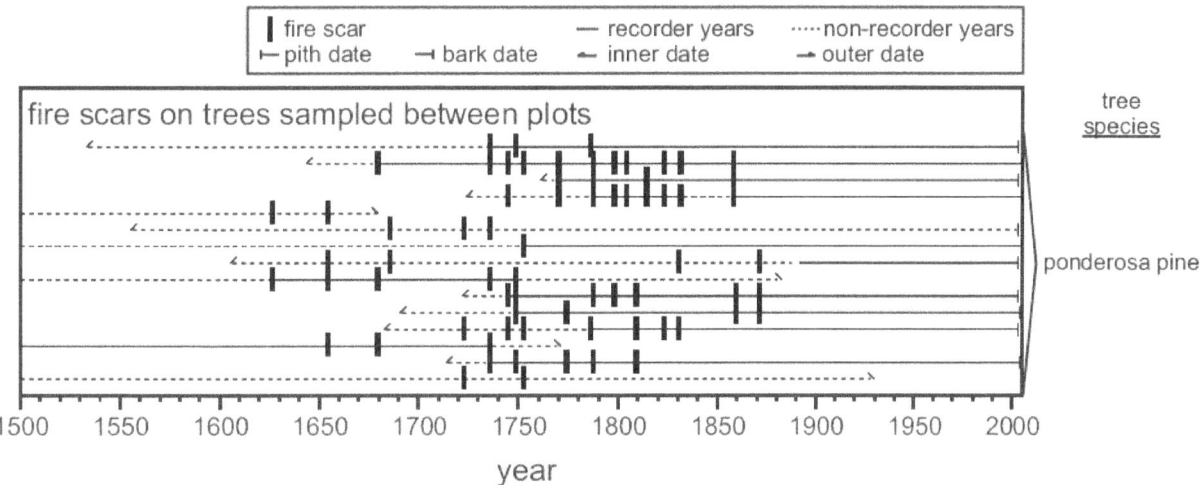

Figure A-6—Chronology of low-severity fires recorded on the 15 trees sampled between plots, over approximately 1057 acres at HNR.

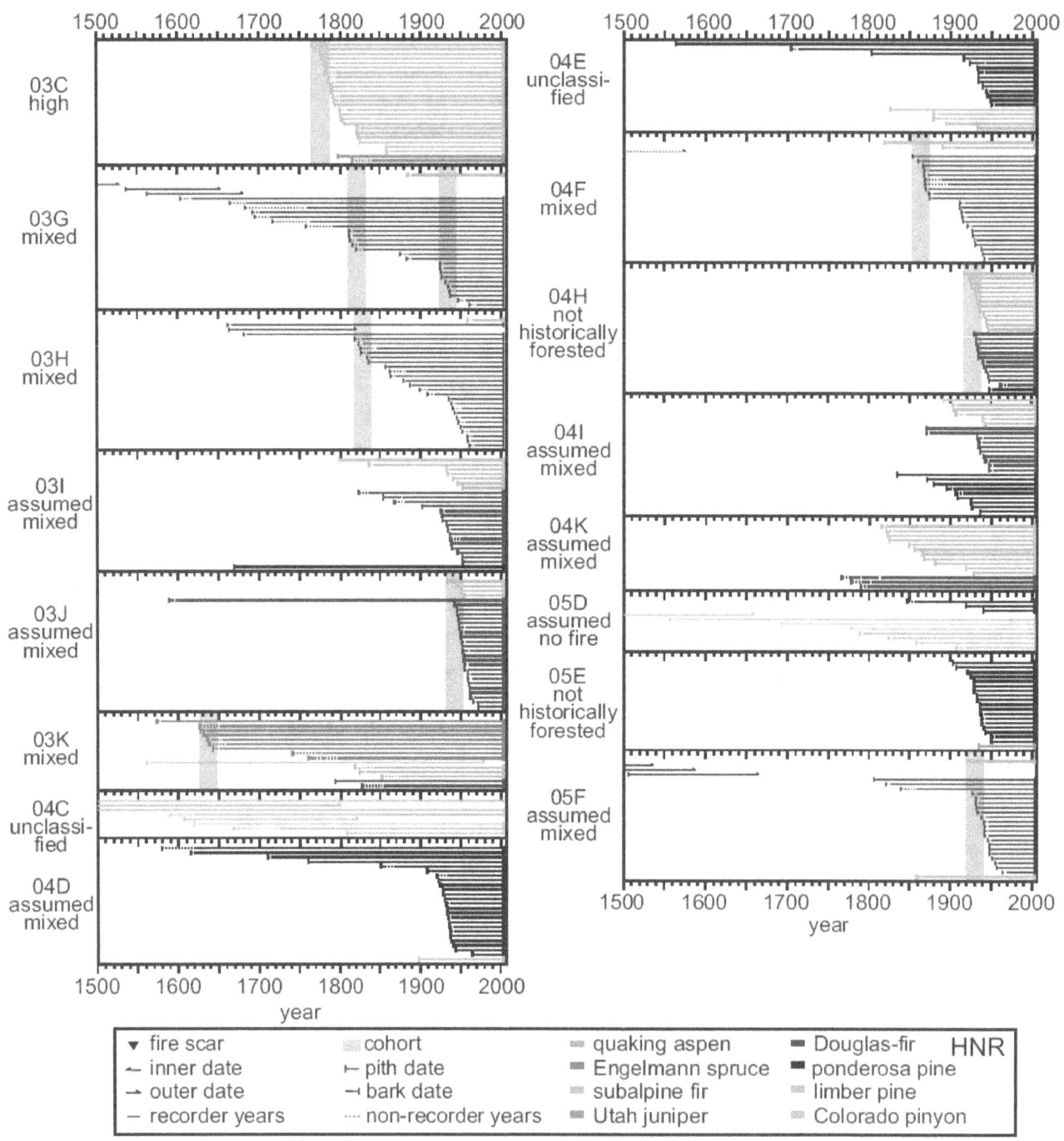

Figure A-7—Fire-demography diagrams (FDDs, Brown and others 2008b) showing chronologies of tree demography (recruitment and death), fire scars, and cohorts at each plot. Bark dates on four stumps are shown as outer dates. Inferred fire severity (table 3) is indicated to the left of each panel. Plot 6G is not shown because it contained only quaking aspen with center rot from which we could not obtain recruitment dates.

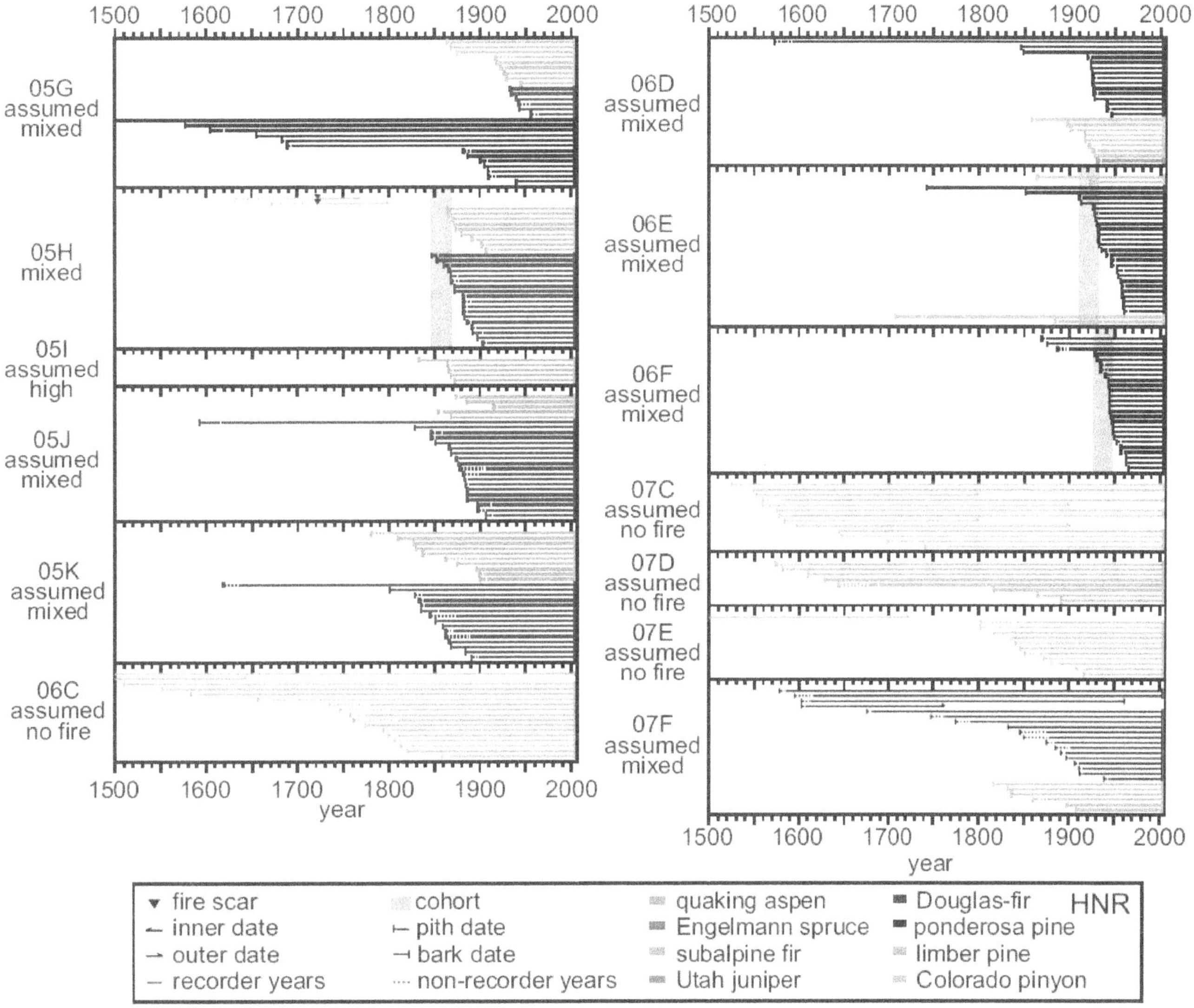

05G
assumed
mixed

05H
mixed

05I
assumed
high

05J
assumed
mixed

05K
assumed
mixed

06C
assumed
no fire

06D
assumed
mixed

06E
assumed
mixed

06F
assumed
mixed

07C
assumed
no fire

07D
assumed
no fire

07E
assumed
no fire

07F
assumed
mixed

1500 1600 1700 1800 1900 2000
year

1500 1600 1700 1800 1900 2000
year

▼ fire scar	cohort	quaking aspen	■ Douglas-fir	HNR
⊢ inner date	⊢ pith date	Engelmann spruce	■ ponderosa pine	
→ outer date	⊣ bark date	subalpine fir	limber pine	
— recorder years	···· non-recorder years	Utah juniper	Colorado pinyon	

Figure A-7—*Continued.*

Figure A-8—Intra-ring position of fire scars
sampled in and between plots at HNR
from 1650 to 1900, as a percentage
of the number of scars for which the
position could be determined (given in
parentheses). Not shown is the intra-
ring position for one fire scar on a
limber pine tree.

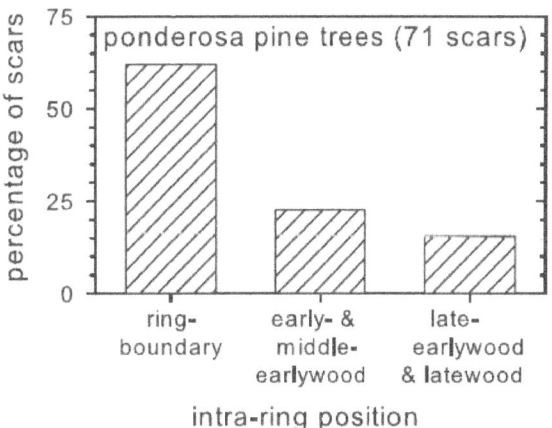

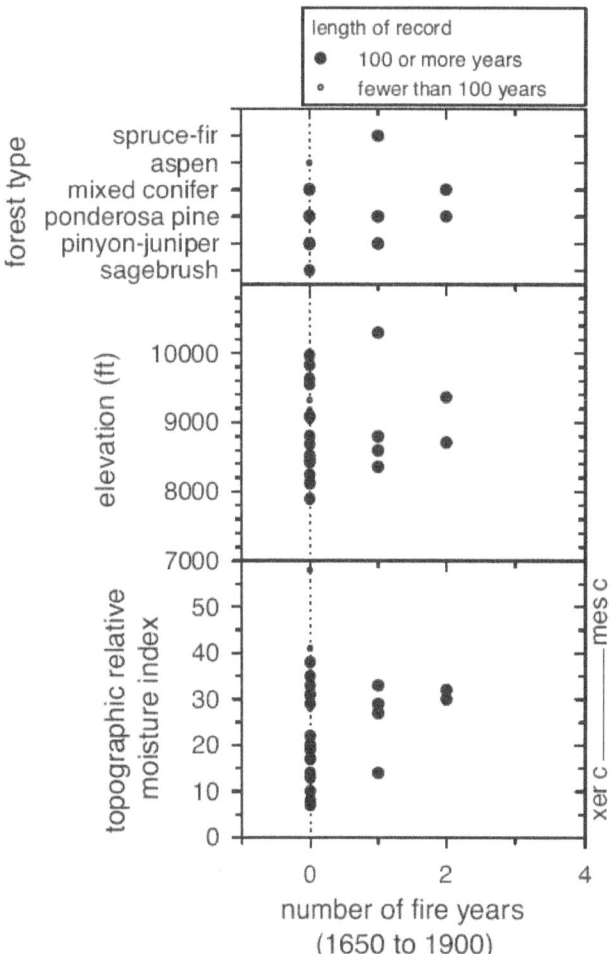

Figure A-9—Variation in fire among plots at HNR with topography, forest type, and relative soil moisture availability (Parker 1982). Number of fire years includes both fire-scar and cohort dates. Plots with no reconstructed fires during this period fall on the dotted line.

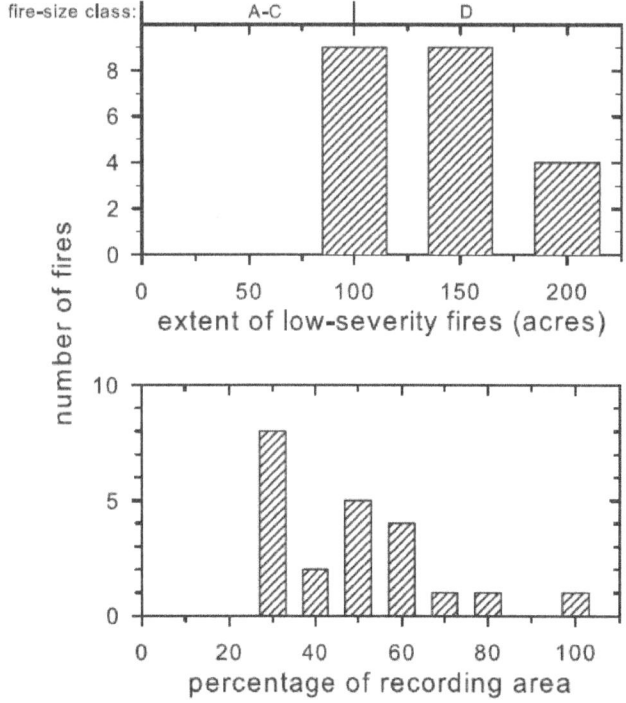

Figure A-10—Relative extent of low-severity fires within the 2280-acre HNR site from 1650 to 1900, as area (top) and as a percentage of the recording area (in other words, the combined area of cells containing recording, fire-scarred trees during each year; bottom). Commonly used fire-size classes are indicated at the top (NWCG 2007).

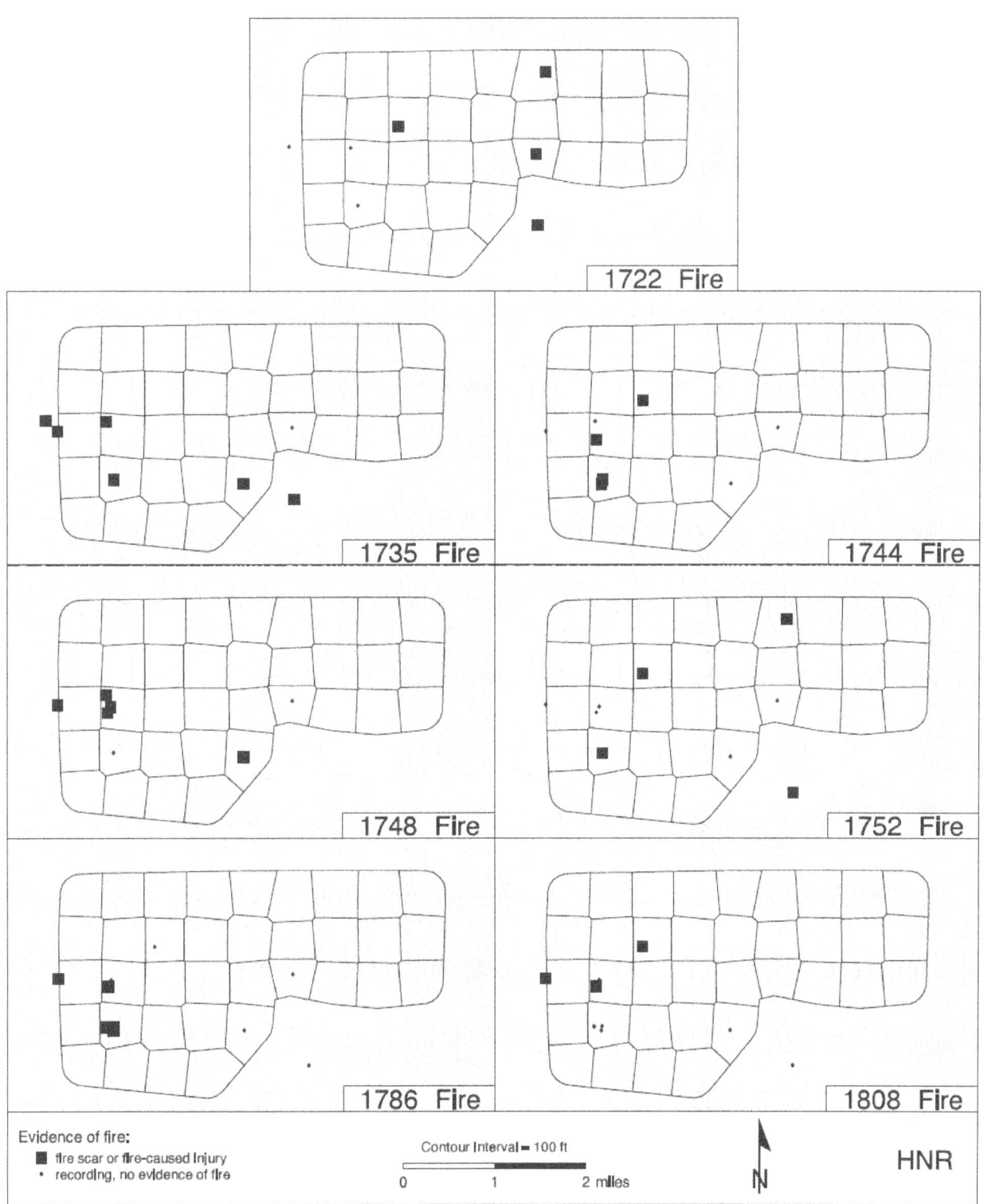

Figure A-11—Maps of years with evidence of low-severity fires in three or more cells at HNR. "Recording, no evidence of fire" indicates at least one tree was alive at that location during that year but did not have a fire scar or fire-caused injury. Empty cells indicate that no fire-scarred trees were recording in that cell during that year. Cohort dates are not mapped.

Appendix B. Wah Wah Mountains, Bureau of Land Management (WAH)

Topography

We sampled 24 plots over 1593 acres near Lawson Cove Canyon, Fillmore Field Office, Bureau of Land Management in Millard County, Utah (figs. 1 and B-1). The plots were separated by 0.29 miles on average (range 0.16 to 0.36 miles) and averaged 0.43 acres in area (range 0.21 to 1.11 acres). Plots were sampled within cells that averaged 61 acres and ranged from 32 to 70 acres. Plots ranged in elevation from 7197 to 8806 ft (fig. B-2) and ranged in slope from 12 to 58 percent. They were sampled on a range of aspects, but most were on north or east aspects (83 percent). The distribution of the plots by elevation, aspect, or slope did not differ from the distribution of the landscape by more than 10 percent in any category except north and east aspects, which were over and under sampled, respectively (fig. B-2). We took between one and four photographs each at 22 of the plots.

Tree Demography

Of the 730 trees that occurred in the plots, all were Utah juniper, singleleaf pinyon, Rocky Mountain juniper, ponderosa pine, white fir, Douglas-fir, or Great Basin bristlecone pine, except 3 trees we could not identify (fig. B-3). Most of these trees were living (74 percent) and the rest were snags (9 percent), logs (16 percent), or stumps (1 percent). We were able to remove and crossdate wood samples from most of these trees (610 trees or 84 percent) and obtained actual or estimated pith dates for 576 of them. These pith dates ranged from 558 to 1893 (fig. B-4). The death dates we obtained for 98 logs and snags ranged from 1419 to 2003.

Historical and Current Forest Structure and Composition

The plots included a range of historical and modern forest types (pinyon-juniper, mixed conifer, and limber-bristlecone; table B-1). One limber-bristlecone plot converted to mixed conifer between 1860 and 2000. In 1900, tree density averaged 61 trees per acre and ranged from 22 to 112 trees per acre (fig. B-5). In 2000, tree density averaged 61 trees per acre and ranged from 21 to 112 trees per acre. However, we likely underestimated historical tree density because we could not obtain recruitment or earliest-ring dates for 120 of the 730 trees that occurred in the plots and only an earliest-ring date for another 34 trees.

Fire Scars

We were able to remove and crossdate fire-scarred samples from 129 trees, 4 of which had only scars that were recorded on a single tree and so were excluded from further analyses. Of the remaining 125 trees, about half (65 trees) were sampled in 19 of the 24 plots at this site (1 to 14 trees per plot, average 3 trees). We sampled the 60 other fire-scarred trees as we encountered them between plots over 1163 acres throughout the site (fig. B-6). Most of the 125 fire-scarred trees were ponderosa pine (74 percent) and the rest were Great Basin bristlecone pine, white fir, singleleaf pinyon, Utah juniper, and Rocky Mountain juniper. Most were snags, logs, and stumps (66 percent) and the rest were live trees. These 125 trees yielded 369 fire scars and 79 eroded fire scars or abrupt changes in ring width (figs. B-4 and B-7). However, four of these scar dates were eliminated from further analyses because they were recorded on only a single tree at the site. We were able to assign an intra-ring position to 87 percent of the 271 fire scars that occurred during the analysis period (1650 to 1900). Of the scars that occurred on ponderosa pine trees, half (52 percent) occurred on the boundary between two rings (fig. B-8).

Post-Fire Cohorts

We identified eight cohorts of trees from estimated recruitment dates at eight of the plots. All 8 cohorts were recruited before 1900 (1527 to 1786) and were identified from 56 trees (5 to 11 trees per cohort), most of which were white fir (66 percent), ponderosa pine (16 percent), and Utah juniper (11 percent) with a few Douglas-fir and singleleaf pinyon trees (figs. B-4 and B-7). Most of the cohorts occurred in plots of the mixed conifer forest type (88 percent of cohorts) with the rest occurring in pinyon-juniper plots (12 percent).

Spatial Variation in Fire Regimes

During the analysis period (1650 to 1900), plot-composite low-severity fire intervals that were pooled among mixed conifer plots averaged 20 years (range 2 to 86 years; fig. B-9). The tree-ring record before 1900 was longer than 100 years for all 24 plots at this site (fig. B-10).

We inferred that one pinyon-juniper plot did not sustain fire over the period of record (table B-2). We could not infer historical fire severity at four plots because they did not meet our requirements for any of the severity categories. We assigned the remaining plots to the low, mixed, or high fire severity categories.

From 1650 to 1900, the 50 low-severity fires we reconstructed within our 1593-acre sampling area averaged 172 acres and ranged from 61 to 604 acres (fig. B-11), equivalent to 5 to 53 percent of the recording area (in other words, the combined area of cells containing recording, fire-scarred trees during a given year). Recording area varied among fire years, ranging from 845 to 1279 acres. We likely underestimated the extent of low-severity fires because most fires intersected the boundary of the site (fig. B-12).

Table B-1—Distribution of plots at WAH by historical (1860) and modern (2000) forest types (table 2).

Historical forest type (1860)	Modern forest type (2000)		Total plots in 1860
	Mixed conifer	Pinyon-juniper	
Limber-bristlecone	1		1
Mixed conifer	17		17
Pinyon-juniper		6	6
Total plots in 2000	**18**	**6**	**24**

Table B-2—Distribution of plots at WAH by historical forest type (1860; table 2) and fire severity (table 3).

Forest type	Assumed high	Mixed	Assumed mixed	Low	Assumed no fire	Unclassified
Limber-bristlecone				1		
Mixed conifer	5	7	1	3		1
Pinyon-juniper		1		1	1	3
Total	**5**	**8**	**1**	**5**	**1**	**4**

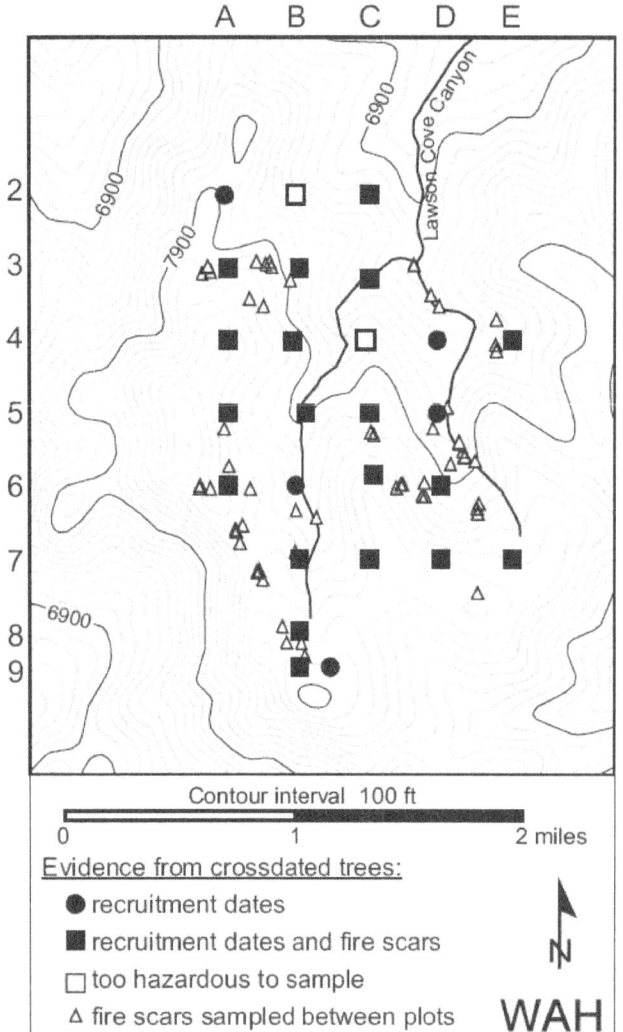

Figure B-1—Locations of plots and crossdated fire-scarred trees that were sampled outside of plots. About half of the fire-scarred trees were sampled within plots and are not mapped individually. Plots are identified by column and row, in other words, the northwestern most plot is 2A, the next plot to the east is 2B, and so forth.

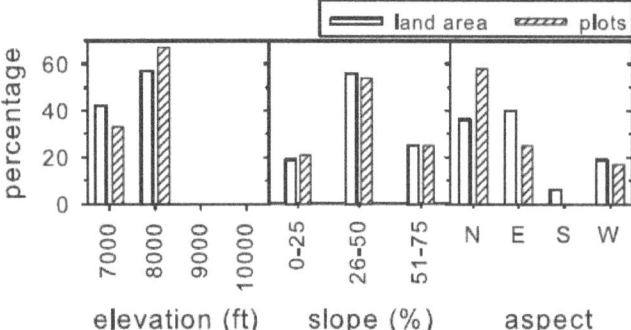

Figure B-2—Distribution of sampled plots and land area at WAH by topography. Aspect classes are 90° wide, beginning with 46° for east (E). Land area was derived from a digital elevation model (Utah AGRC 2004). One percent of the land area was below 7000 ft and is not shown here.

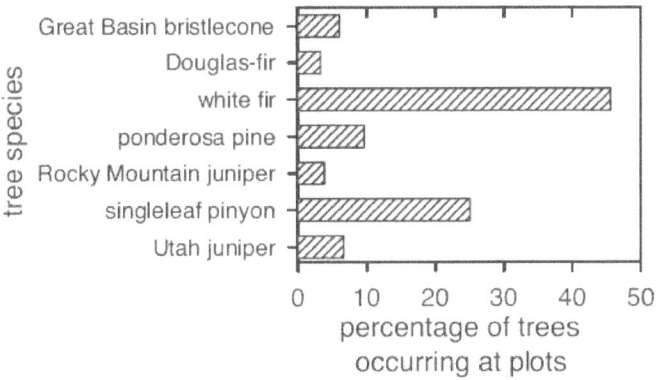

Figure B-3—Distribution by species of the 730 live and dead trees ≥8 inches DBH that occurred in plots at WAH, regardless of whether or not we removed wood samples and crossdated them. Not shown are three trees of unknown species.

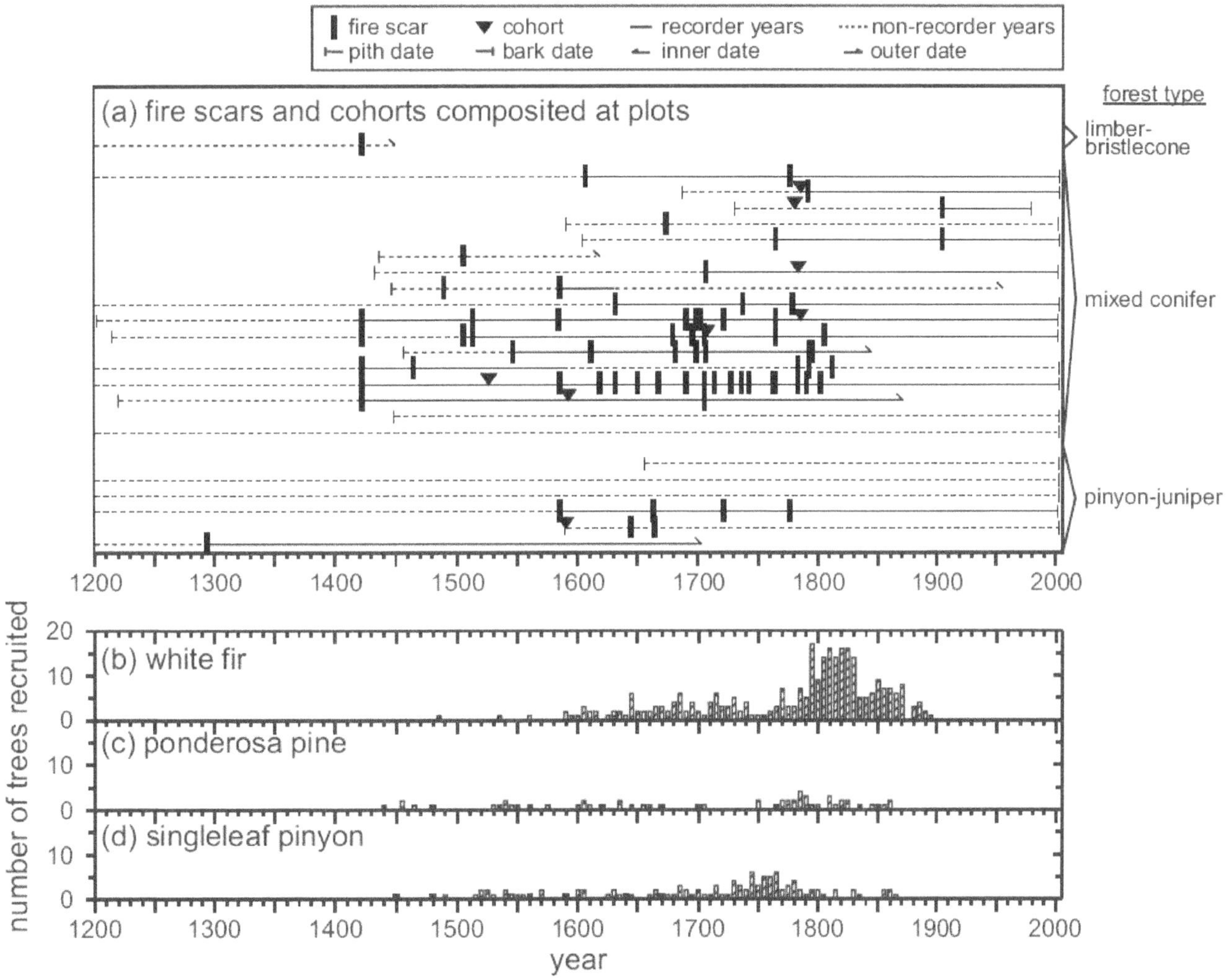

Figure B-4—Chronologies of fire and tree recruitment at WAH. In (a), horizontal lines are plot-composite fire-scar and cohort dates by forest type. Non-recorder years precede the first scar, whereas recorder years generally follow it, but non-recorder years can also occur when the catface margin is consumed by subsequent fires or rot. In (b) through (d), recruitment dates are given for species comprising ≥10 percent of trees with such dates. The latter part of the distribution is incomplete because we only cored trees that were ≥8 inches DBH.

(a) 1900
(b) 2000
forest type
limber-bristlecone
mixed conifer
pinyon-juniper
0
100
200
300
400
500
density (trees/acre)

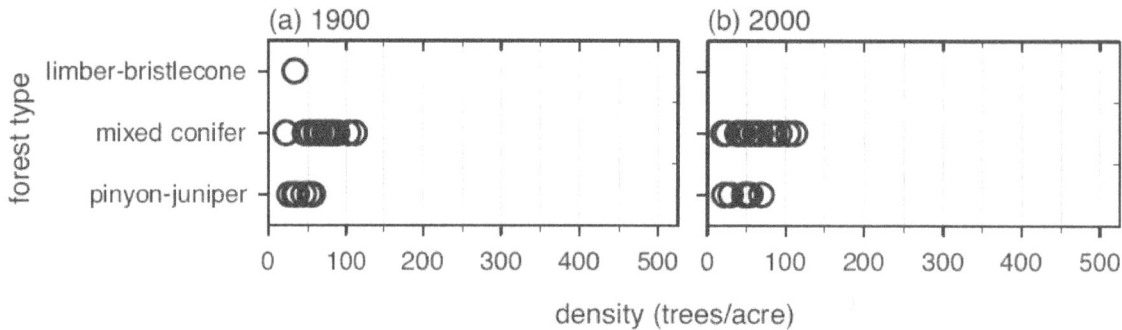

Figure B-5—Density of trees ≥8 inches DBH that were alive at each plot at WAH (a) in 1900 and (b) in 2000, by forest type (table 2).

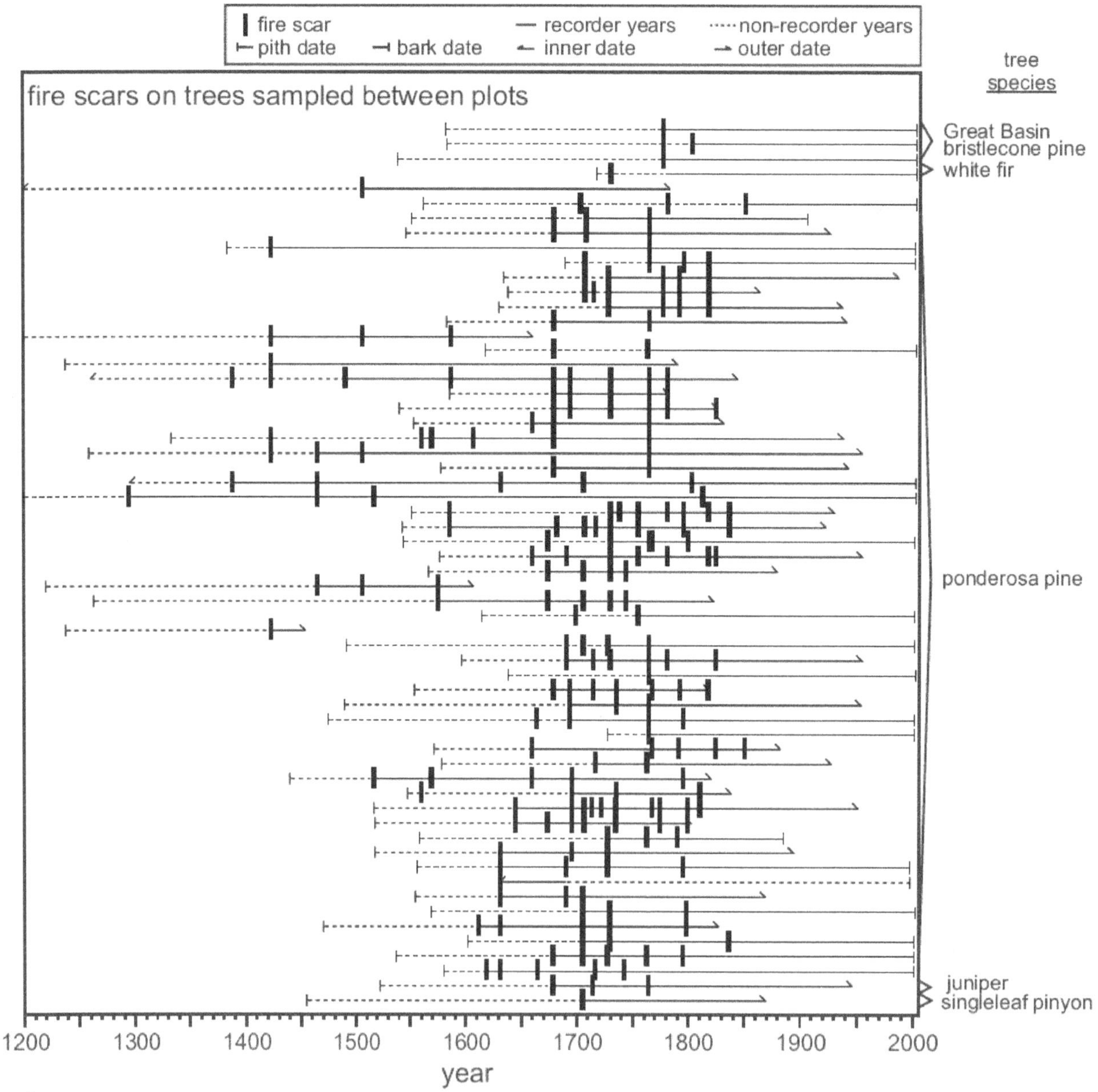

fire scar
pith date
bark date
recorder years
inner date
non-recorder years
outer date
fire scars on trees sampled between plots
tree species
Great Basin bristlecone pine
white fir
ponderosa pine
juniper
singleleaf pinyon
1200
1300
1400
1500
1600
1700
1800
1900
2000
year

Figure B-6—Chronology of low-severity fires recorded on the 60 trees sampled between plots over approximately 1163 acres at WAH.

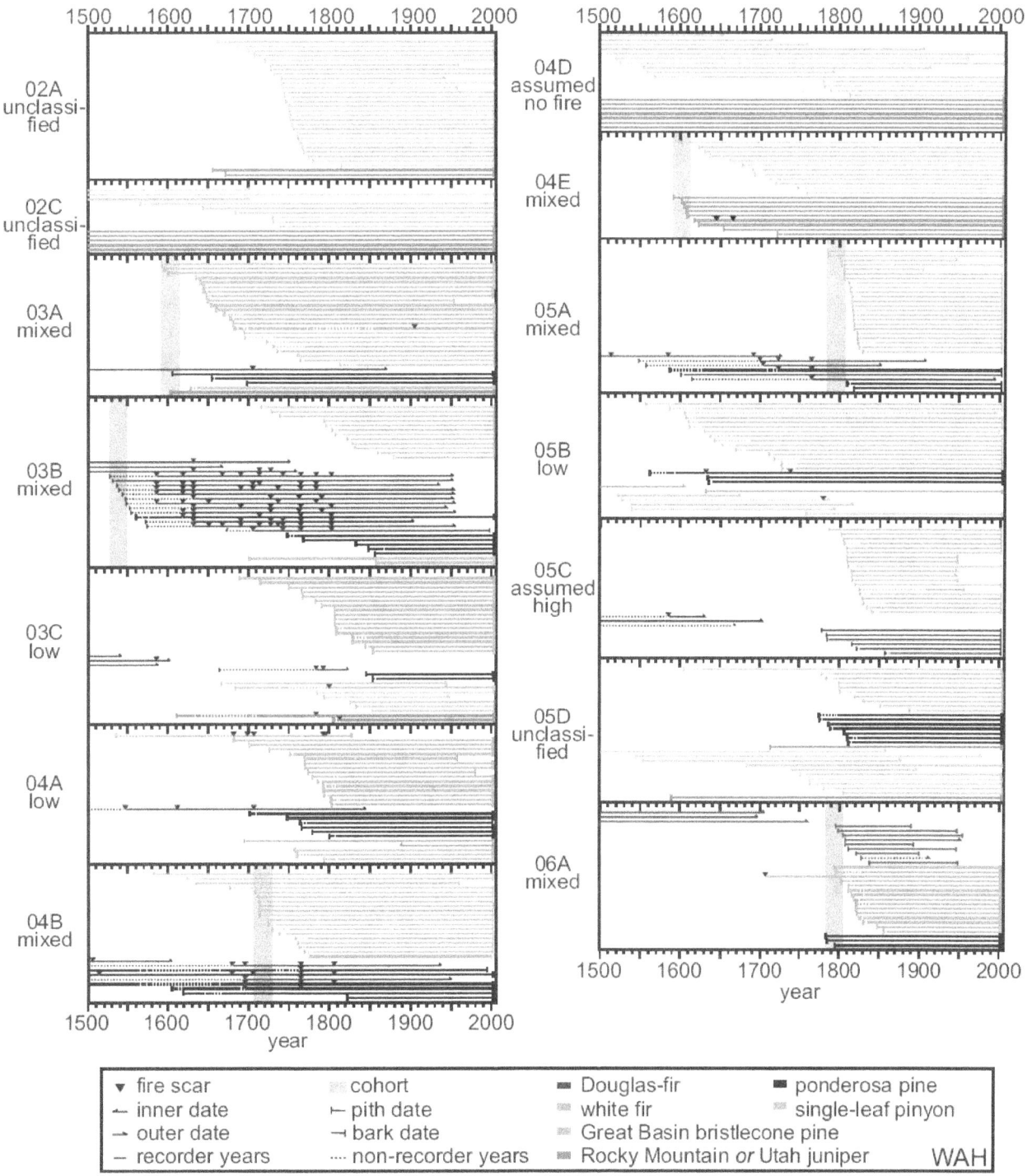

Figure B-7—Fire-demography diagrams (FDDs, Brown and others 2008b) showing chronologies of tree demography (recruitment and death), fire scars, and cohorts at each plot. Bark dates on 20 stumps are shown as outer dates. Not shown are 60 fire-scarred trees sampled between plots. Inferred fire severity (table 3) is indicated to the left of each panel. Most of the trees (60 percent) in the combined Rocky Mountain and Utah juniper category are Utah juniper.

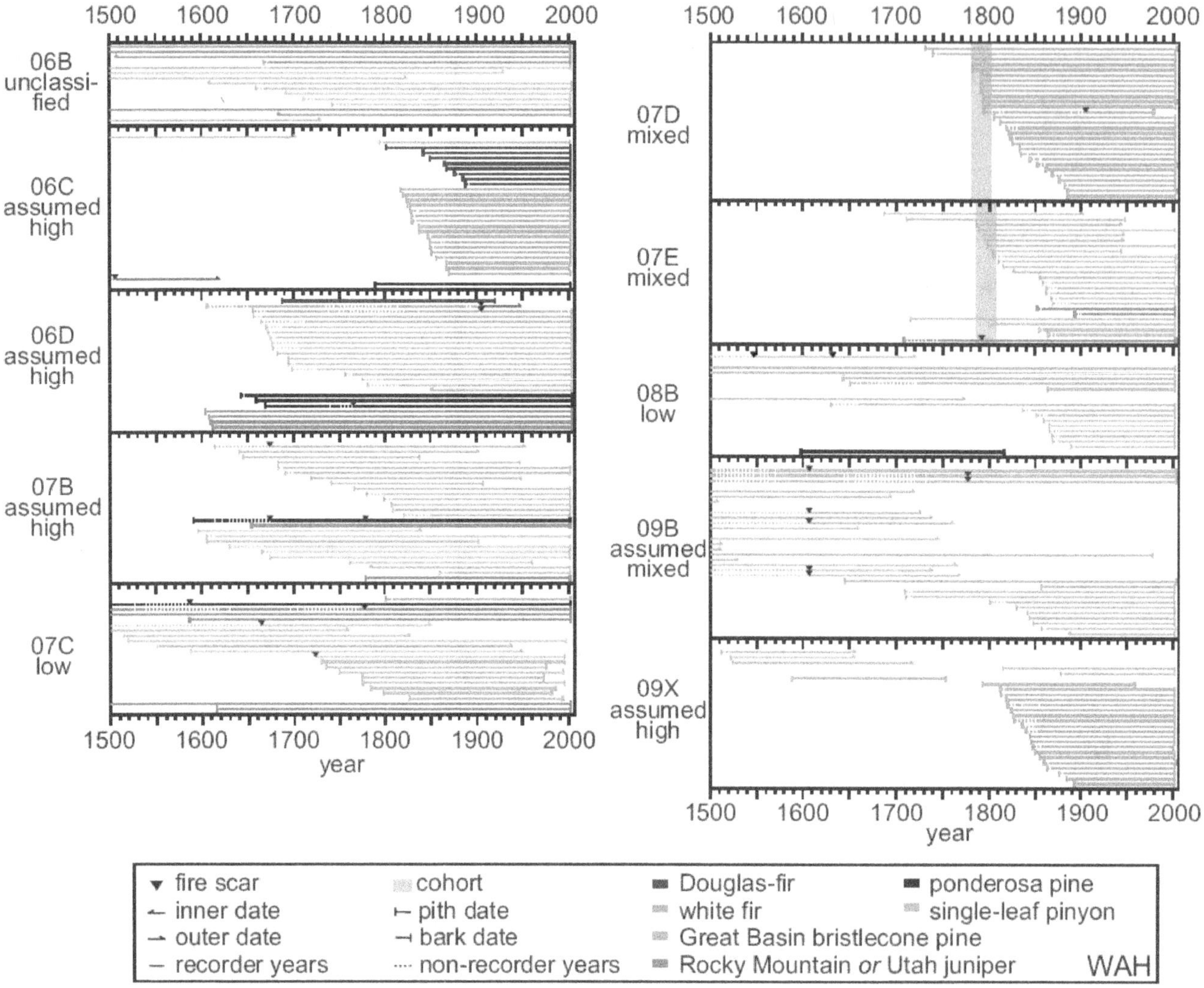

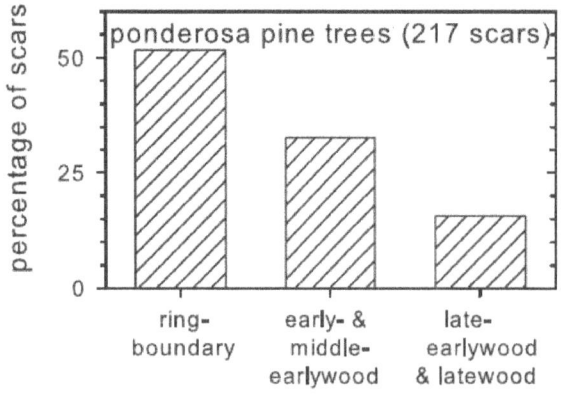

Figure B-7—*Continued.*

Legend:
- ▼ fire scar
- ⊢ inner date
- → outer date
- — recorder years
- ▒ cohort
- ⊢ pith date
- ⊣ bark date
- ···· non-recorder years
- ▬ Douglas-fir
- ▬ white fir
- ▬ Great Basin bristlecone pine
- ▬ Rocky Mountain *or* Utah juniper
- ▬ ponderosa pine
- ▒ single-leaf pinyon

WAH

ponderosa pine trees (217 scars)

Figure B-8—Intra-ring position of fire scars sampled in and between plots at WAH from 1650 to 1900, as a percentage of the number of scars for which the position could be determined (given in parentheses). Not shown are intra-ring positions for 18 fire scars on Utah juniper, singleleaf pinyon, Rocky Mountain juniper, white fir, and Great Basin bristlecone pine trees.

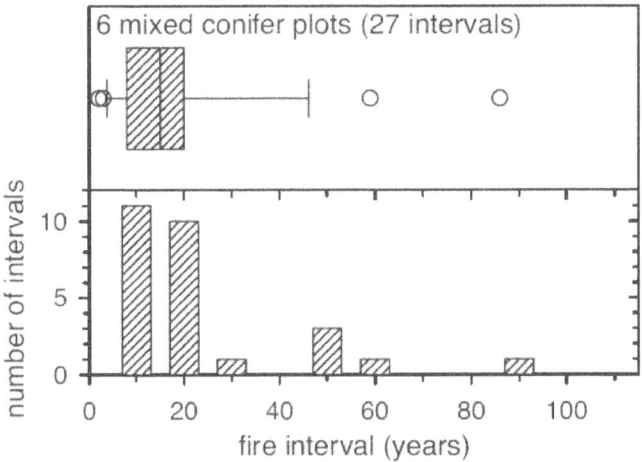

Figure B-9—Plot-composite intervals between low-severity fires in mixed conifer plots at WAH from 1650 to 1900. Plots averaged 0.43 acres. The box (top panel) encloses the 25th to 75th percentiles and the whiskers enclose the 10th to 90th percentiles of the distribution of intervals. The vertical line indicates the median fire interval, and all values falling outside the 10th to 90th percentiles are shown as circles. In the histogram (bottom panel), the same intervals are plotted in 10-year bins (1 to 10 years, 11 to 20 years, and so forth).

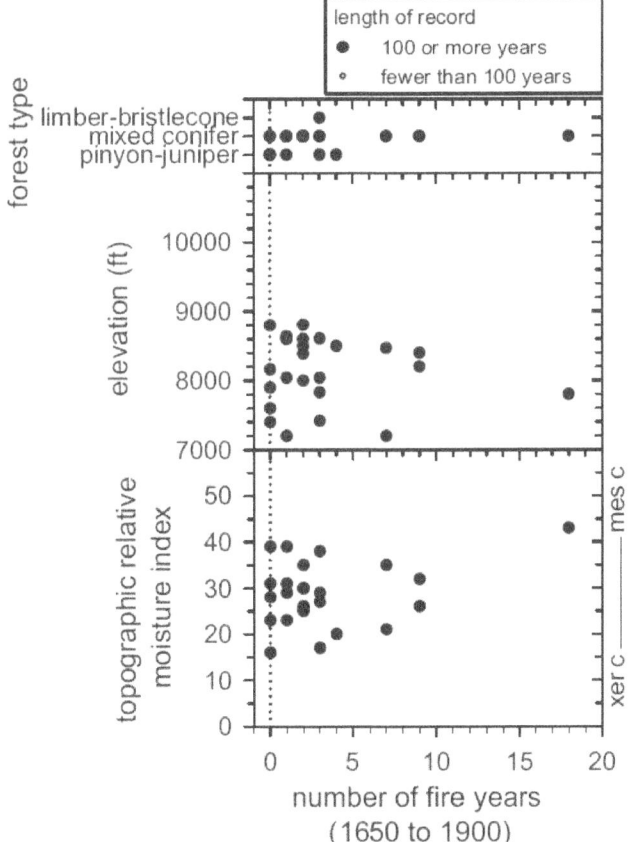

Figure B-10—Variation in fire among plots at WAH with topography, forest type, and relative soil moisture availability (Parker 1982). Number of fire years includes both fire-scar and cohort dates. Plots with no reconstructed fires during this period fall on the dotted line.

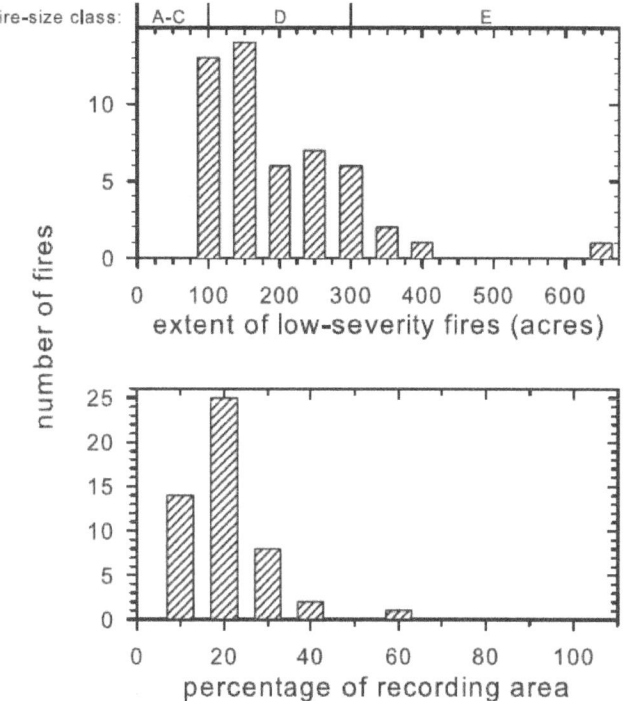

Figure B-11—Relative extent of low-severity fires within the 1593-acre WAH site, from 1650 to 1900, as area (top) and as a percentage of the recording area (in other words, the combined area of cells containing recording, fire-scarred trees during each year; bottom). Commonly used fire-size classes are indicated at the top (NWCG 2007).

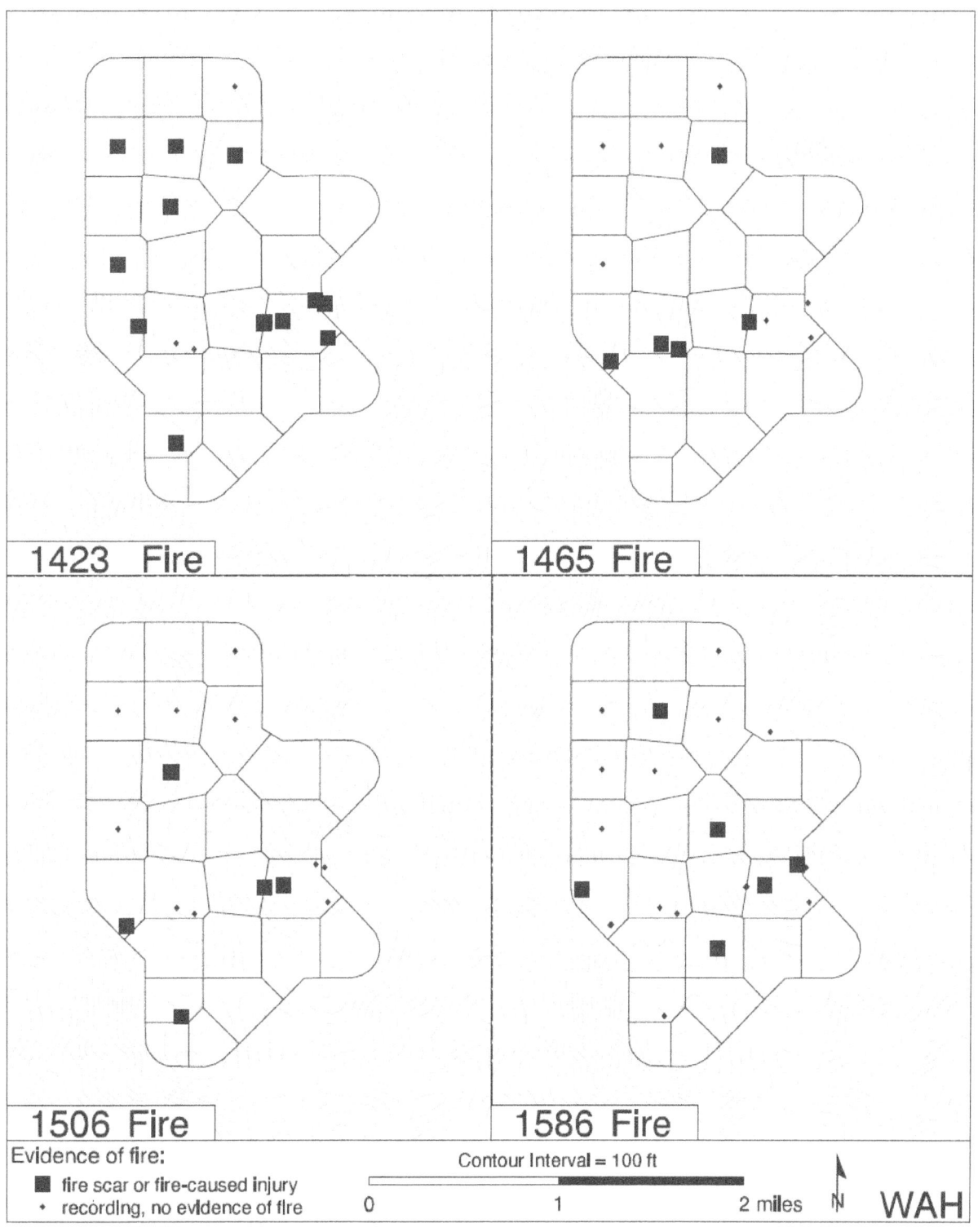

Figure B-12—Maps of years with evidence of low-severity fires in three or more cells at WAH. "Recording, no evidence of fire" indicates at least one tree was alive at that location during that year but did not have a fire scar or fire-caused injury. Empty cells indicate that no fire-scarred trees were recording in that cell during that year. Cohort dates are not mapped.

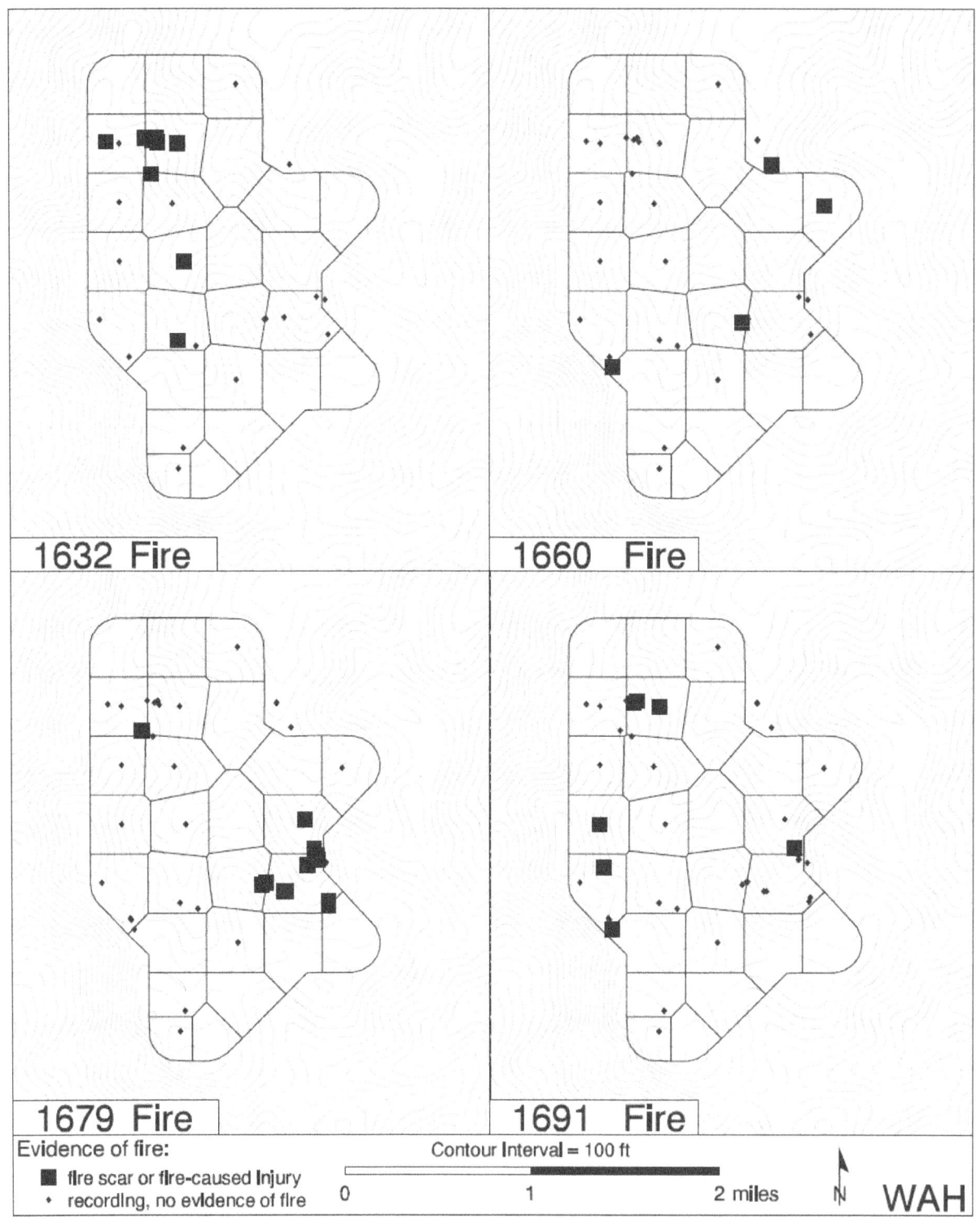

1632 Fire

1660 Fire

1679 Fire

1691 Fire

Evidence of fire:

■ fire scar or fire-caused Injury

♦ recordlng, no evldence of flre

Contour Interval = 100 ft

0   1   2 miles

N

WAH

Figure B-12—*Continued.*

 USDA Forest Service RMRS-GTR-261WWW. 2011.

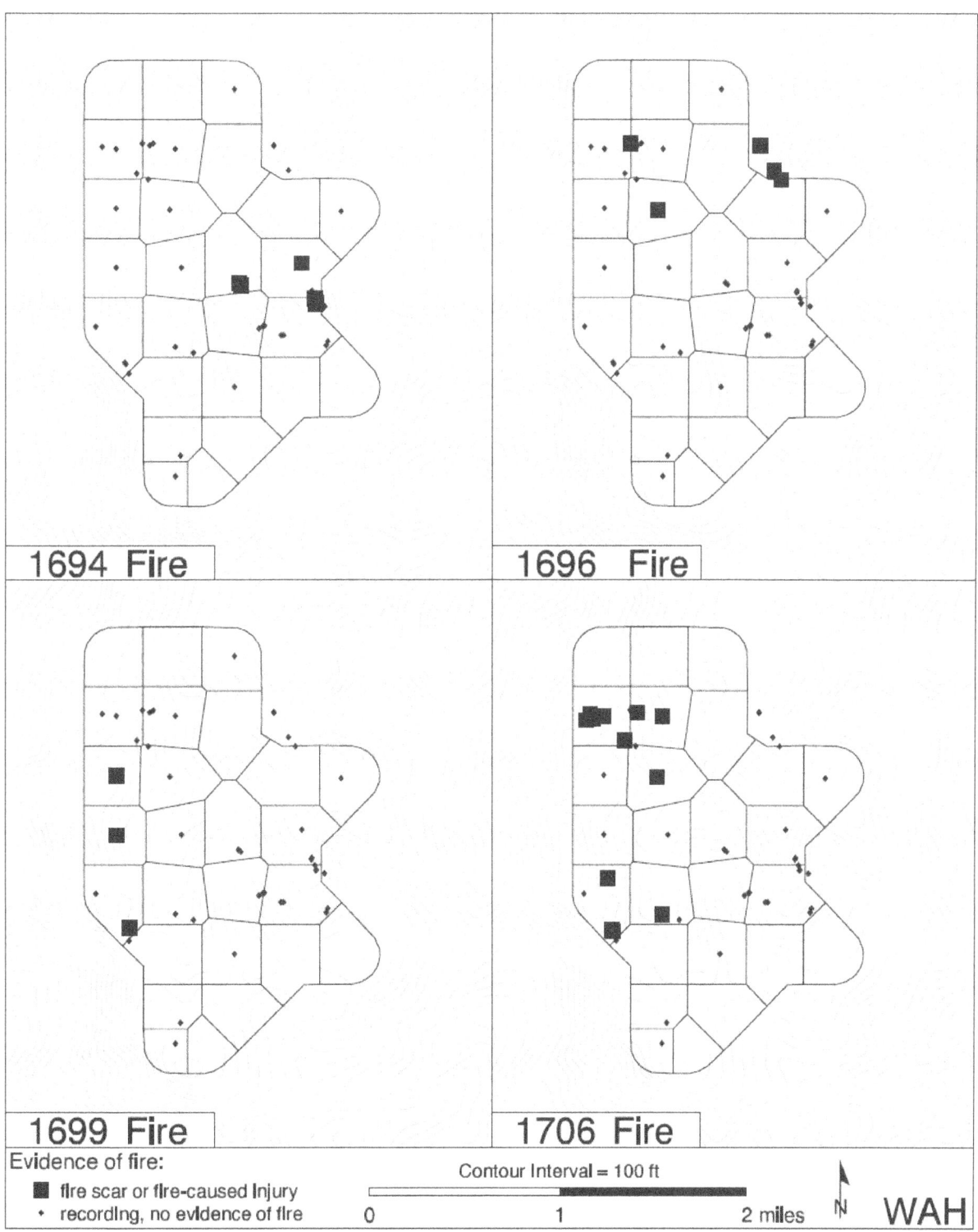

1694 Fire

1696 Fire

1699 Fire

1706 Fire

Evidence of fire:
■ fire scar or fire-caused Injury
• recording, no evidence of fire

Contour Interval = 100 ft

0   1   2 miles

N

WAH

Figure B-12—*Continued.*

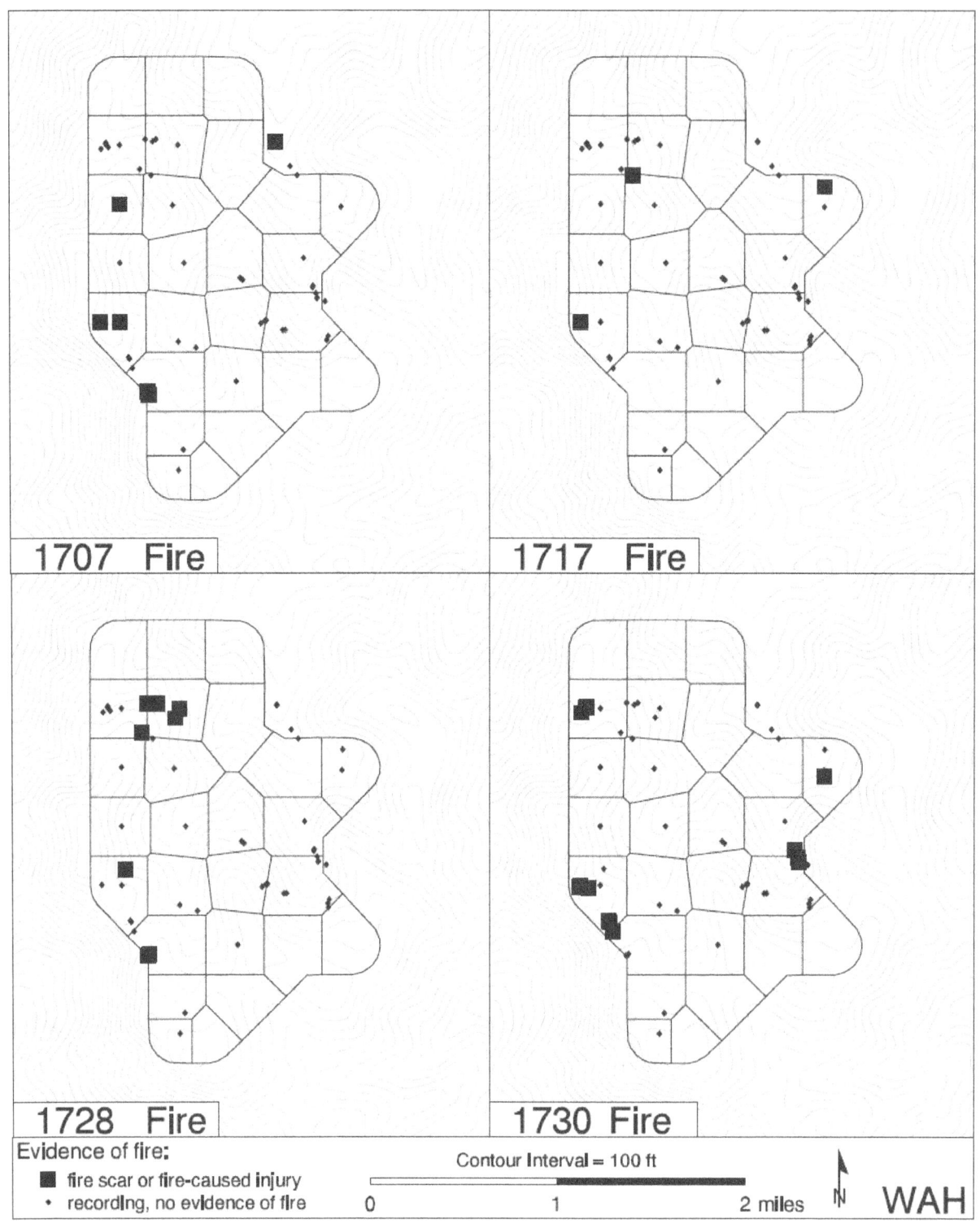

1707 Fire

1717 Fire

1728 Fire

1730 Fire

Evidence of fire:
■ fire scar or fire-caused injury
• recording, no evidence of fire

Contour Interval = 100 ft

0   1   2 miles

N

WAH

Figure B-12—*Continued.*

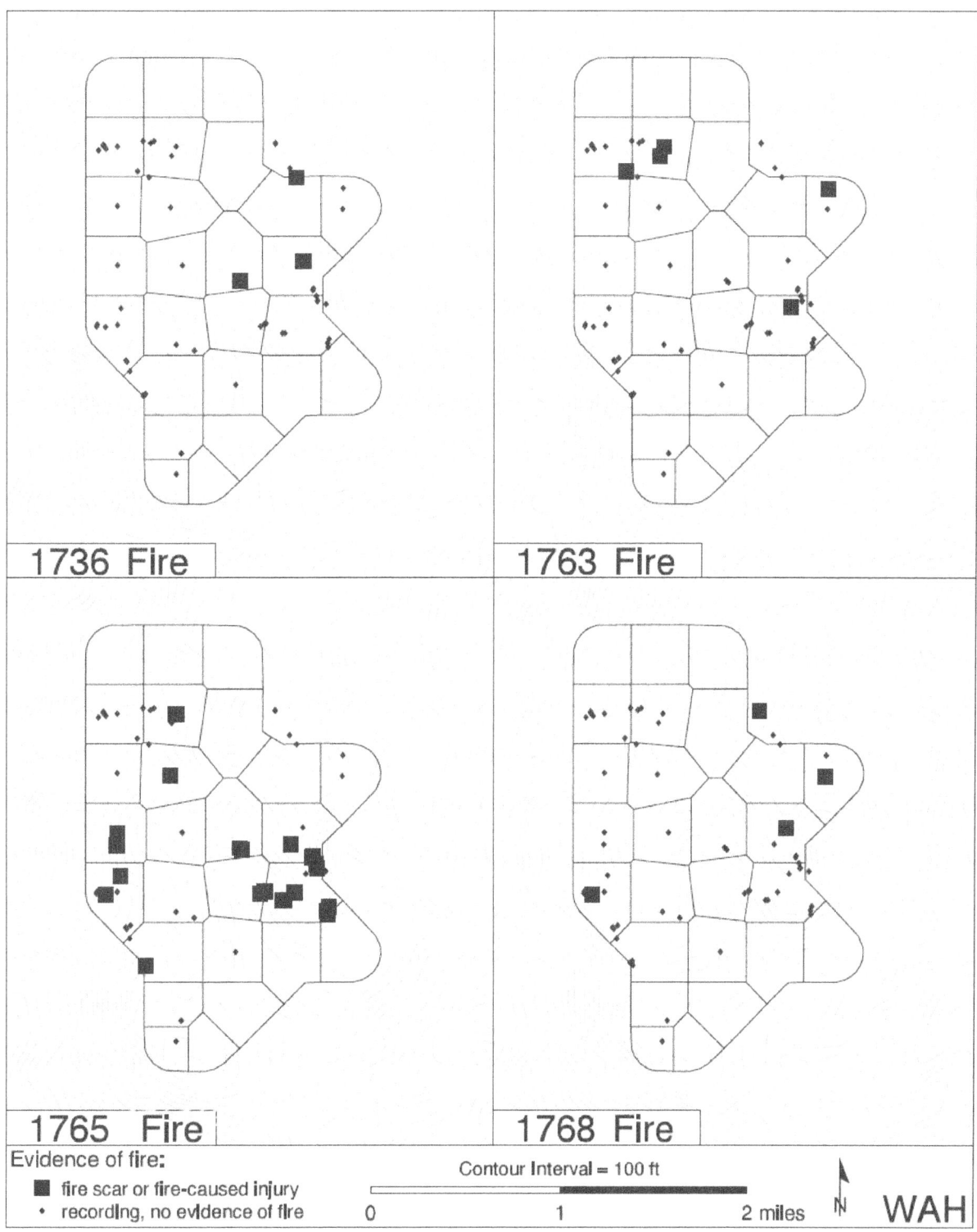

1736 Fire

1763 Fire

1765 Fire

1768 Fire

Evidence of fire:
■ fire scar or fire-caused injury
• recording, no evidence of fire

Contour Interval = 100 ft

0   1   2 miles

N

WAH

Figure B-12—*Continued*.

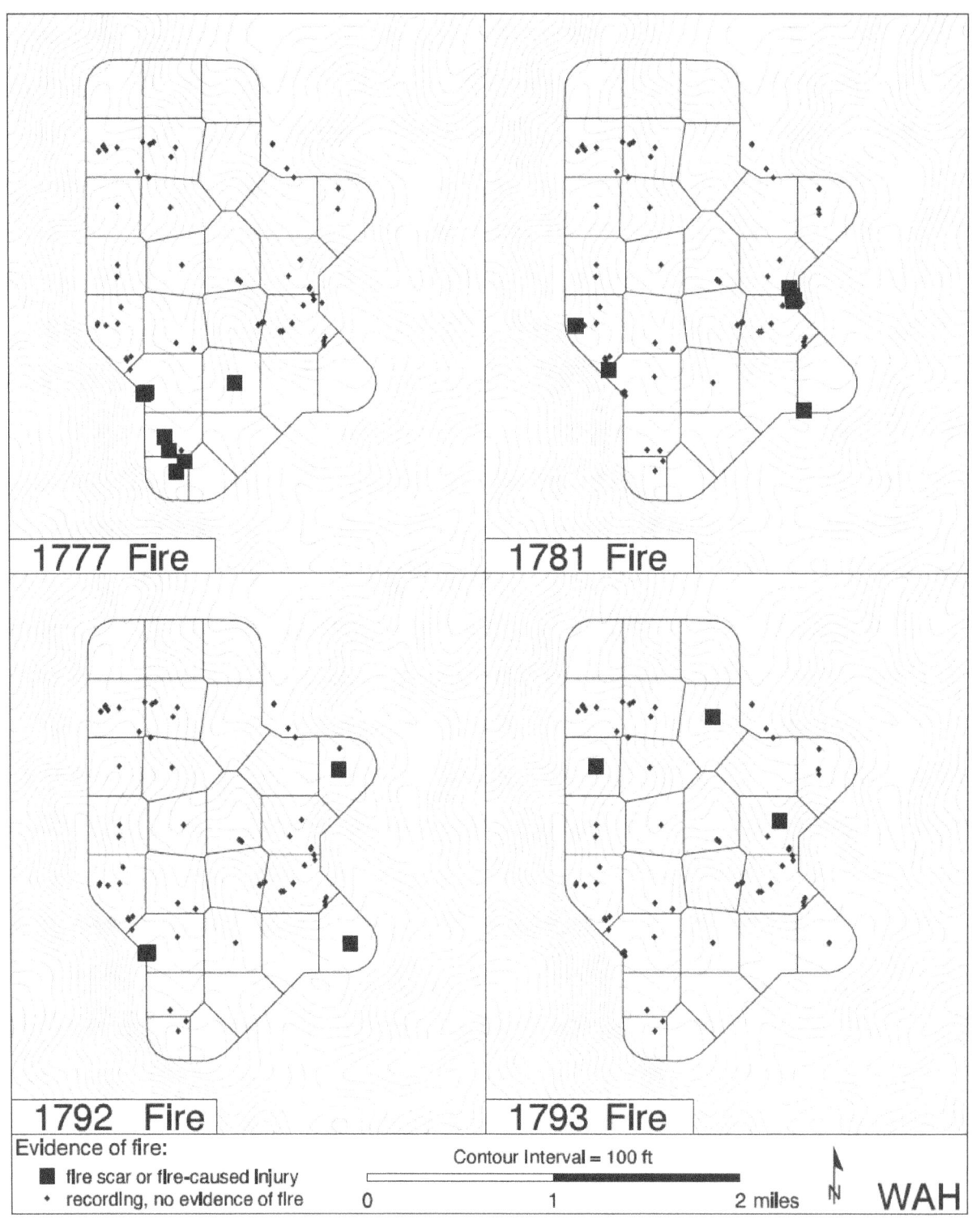

1777 Fire

1781 Fire

1792 Fire

1793 Fire

Evidence of fire:

■ fire scar or fire-caused injury

• recording, no evidence of fire

Contour Interval = 100 ft

0   1   2 miles

N

WAH

Figure B-12—*Continued.*

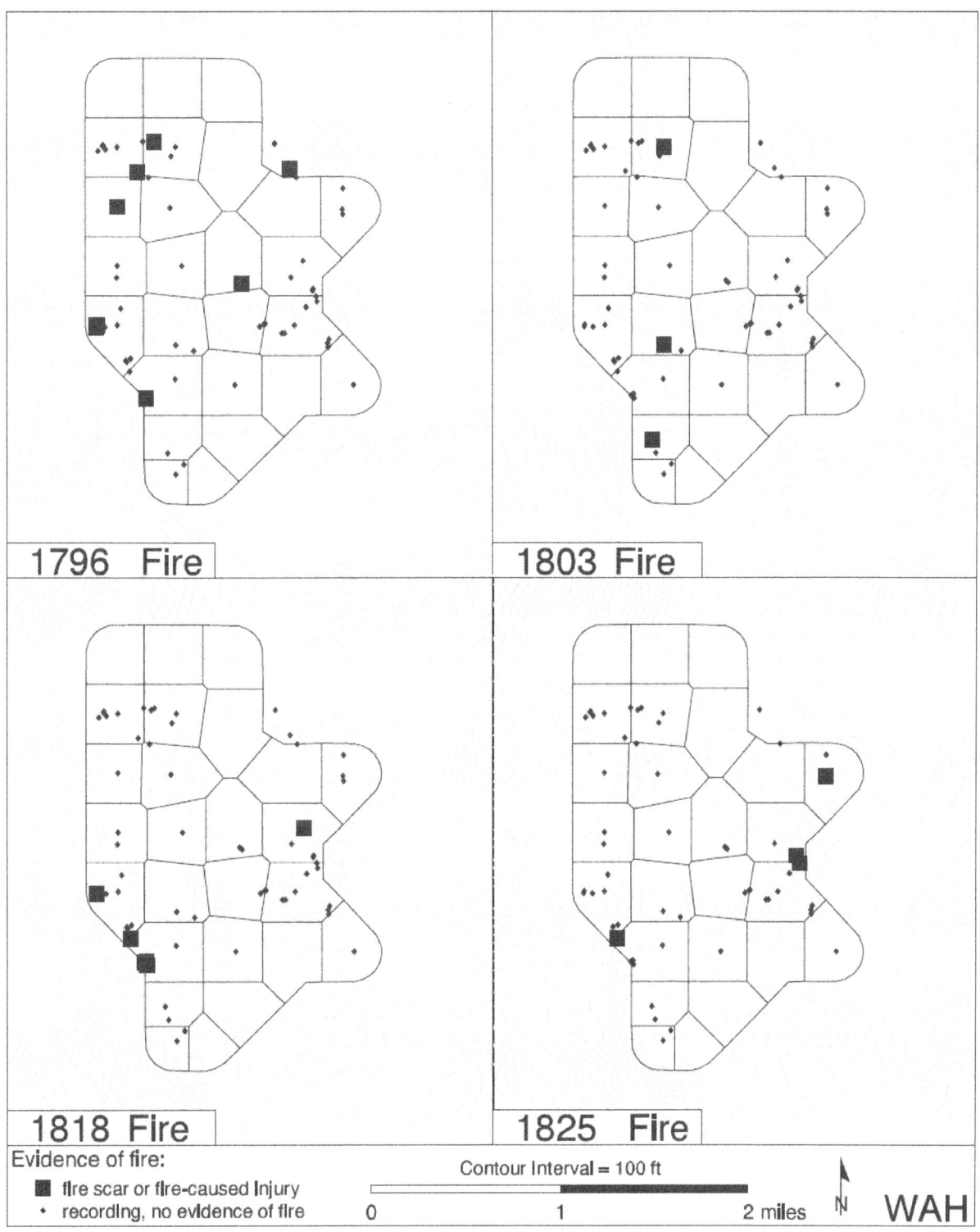

1796 Fire

1803 Fire

1818 Fire

1825 Fire

Evidence of fire:
■ fire scar or fire-caused injury
• recording, no evidence of fire

Contour Interval = 100 ft

0   1   2 miles

N

WAH

Figure B-12—*Continued.*

Appendix C. Book Cliffs, Bureau of Land Management (BCL)

Topography

We sampled 29 plots over 1788 acres near Pine Spring and Hideout Creeks, Vernal Field Office, Bureau of Land Management in Uintah County, Utah (figs. 1 and C-1). The plots were separated by 0.30 miles on average (range 0.25 to 0.31 miles) and averaged 0.36 acres in area (range 0.15 to 1.01 acres). Plots were sampled within cells that averaged 62 acres and ranged from 56 to 72 acres. Plots ranged in elevation from 6957 to 7357 ft (fig. C-2). They ranged in slope from 0 to 71 percent, but all except two plots had slopes less than 50 percent. The plots were sampled on a range of aspects. The distribution of the plots by elevation, aspect, or slope differed from the distribution of the landscape by more than 10 percent only for north and south aspects, which were over and under sampled, respectively (fig. C-2). We took between two and four photographs each at 10 of the plots.

Tree Demography

All of the 883 trees that occurred in the plots were Utah juniper, Colorado pinyon, Rocky Mountain juniper, ponderosa pine, or Douglas-fir, except 2 trees that we could not identify (fig. C-3). Most of these trees were living (73 percent) and the rest were snags (14 percent), logs (12 percent), or stumps (1 percent). We were able to remove and crossdate wood samples from most of these trees (707 trees or 80 percent) and we obtained actual or estimated pith dates for 616 of them. These pith dates ranged from 1220 to 1978, including 30 trees that post-dated 1900 (fig. C-4). The death dates we obtained for 100 logs and snags ranged from 1660 to 2004.

Historical and Current Forest Structure and Composition

The plots included a range of historical and modern forest types (pinyon-juniper, ponderosa pine, and mixed conifer; table C-1). Some plots changed forest type between 1860 and 2000: one pinyon-juniper and one ponderosa pine plot converted to mixed conifer plots. In 1900, tree density averaged 74 trees per acre and ranged from 15 to 147 trees per acre (fig. C-5). In 2000, tree density averaged 81 trees per acre and ranged from 24 to 166 trees per acre. However, we likely underestimated historical tree density because we could not obtain recruitment or earliest-ring dates for 176 of the 883 trees that occurred in the plots and only an earliest-ring date for another 91 trees. Three of these trees had earliest-ring dates between 1901 and 1920 and therefore may have been living before 1900.

Fire Scars

We were able to remove and crossdate fire-scarred samples from 20 trees, 9 of which had only scars that were recorded on a single tree and so were excluded from further analyses. Of the remaining 11 trees, 5 were sampled in 4 of the 29 plots at this site. We sampled the six other fire-scarred trees as we encountered them between plots, over 245 acres at the north end of the site (fig. C-6). Most of the 11 fire-scarred trees were ponderosa pine (82 percent) and the rest were Douglas-fir trees. Nearly half were logs or snags (45 percent) and the rest were live trees. These 11 trees yielded 23 fire scars (figs. C-4 and C-7). However, 11 of these scar dates were eliminated from further analyses because they were recorded on only a single tree at the site. Only two of these scars occurred during the analysis period (1650 to 1900) and we were not able to assign an intra-ring position to either of them.

Post-Fire Cohorts

We identified six cohorts of trees from estimated recruitment dates at six of the plots. All of the cohorts were recruited before 1900 (1532 to 1728) and were identified from 34 trees (5 to 8 trees per cohort), all of which were Utah juniper (47 percent), Colorado pinyon (38 percent), or Douglas-fir (15 percent; figs. C-4 and C-7). The cohorts recruited before 1900 occurred in plots with one of two forest types: pinyon-juniper (88 percent of cohorts) and mixed conifer (17 percent).

Spatial Variation in Fire Regimes

We reconstructed only a single low-severity fire during analysis period (1650 to 1900) and so did not compute plot-composite fire intervals by forest type at this site. This fire occurred in 1759 and was 122 acres in extent, equivalent to 48 percent of the recording area. All the plots at this site had a record longer than 100 years (fig. C-8).

We inferred that half of the plots at this site did not sustain fire over the period of record, including 14 pinyon-juniper plots and 1 mixed conifer plot (table C-2). We could not infer historical fire severity at two plots because they did not meet our requirements for any of the severity categories. We assigned the remaining plots to the mixed or high fire severity categories.

From 1650 to 1900, we reconstructed only a single low-severity fire within our 1788-acre site that was 122 acres in extent, equivalent to 48 percent of the 252-acre recording area (in other words, the combined area of cells containing recording, fire-scarred trees during a given year). We likely underestimated the extent of this low-severity fire because it intersected the boundary of the site (fig. C-9).

Table C-1—Distribution of plots at BCL by historical (1860) and modern (2000) forest types (table 2).

Historical forest type (1860)	Modern forest type (2000)		Total plots in 1860
	Mixed conifer	Pinyon-juniper	
Mixed conifer	9		9
Ponderosa pine	1		1
Pinyon-juniper	2	17	19
Total plots in 2000	**12**	**17**	**29**

Table C-2—Distribution of plots at BCL by historical forest type (1860; table 2) and fire severity (table 3).

Forest type	High	Mixed	Assumed mixed	Assumed no fire	Unclassified
Mixed conifer		1	5	1	2
Ponderosa pine			1		
Pinyon-juniper	2	3		14	
Total	**2**	**4**	**6**	**15**	**2**

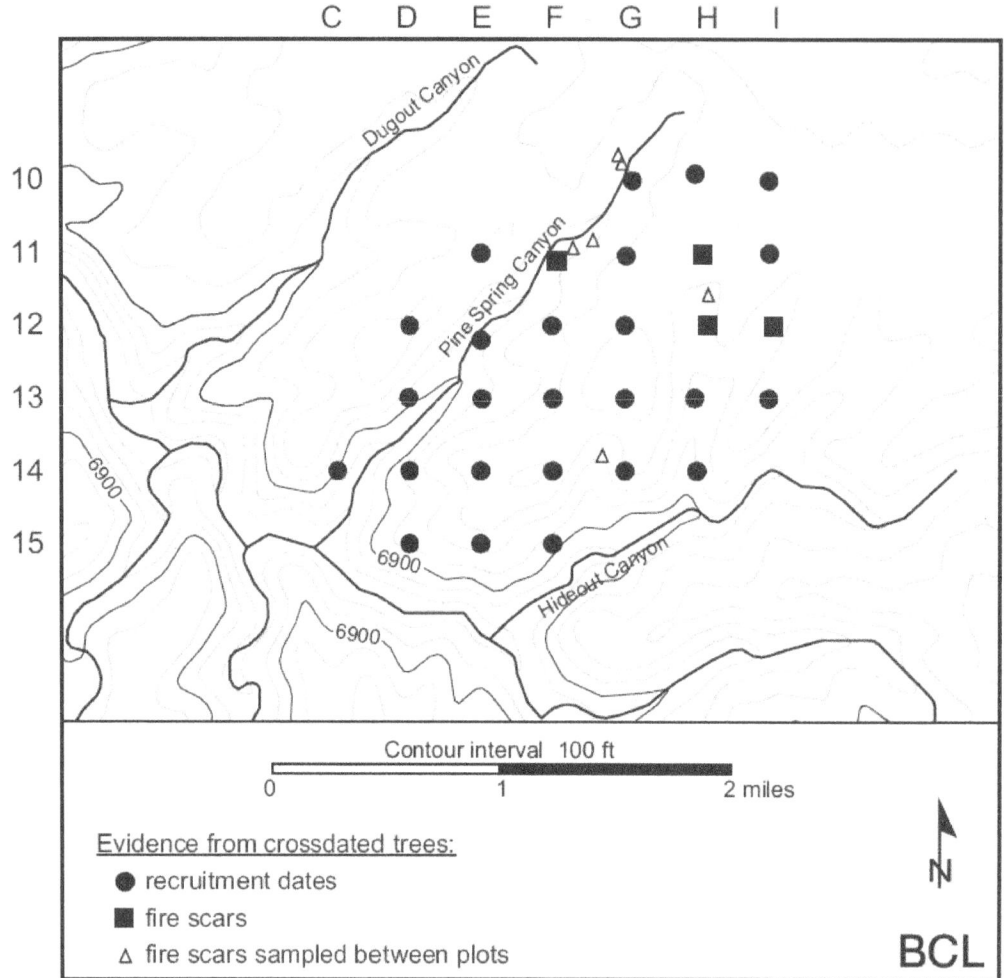

Figure C-1—Locations of plots and crossdated fire-scarred trees that were sampled outside plots. About half of the fire-scarred trees were sampled within plots and are not mapped individually. Plots are identified by column and row, in other words, the northeastern most plot is 10I, the next plot to the west is 10H, and so forth.

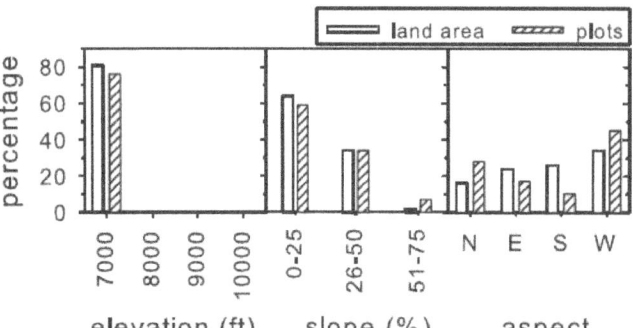

Figure C-2—Distribution of sampled plots and land area at BCL by topography. Aspect classes are 90° wide, beginning with 46° for east (E). Land area was derived from a digital elevation model (Utah AGRC 2004). Nineteen percent of the land area and 24 percent of the plots were sampled below 7000 ft and are not shown here.

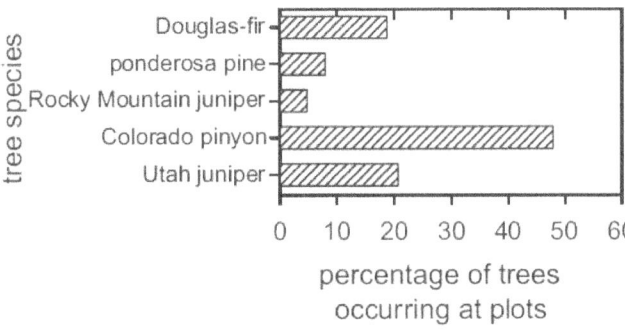

Figure C-3—Distribution by species of the 883 live and dead trees ≥8 inches DBH that occurred in plots at BCL, regardless of whether or not we removed wood samples and crossdated them. Not shown are two trees of unknown species.

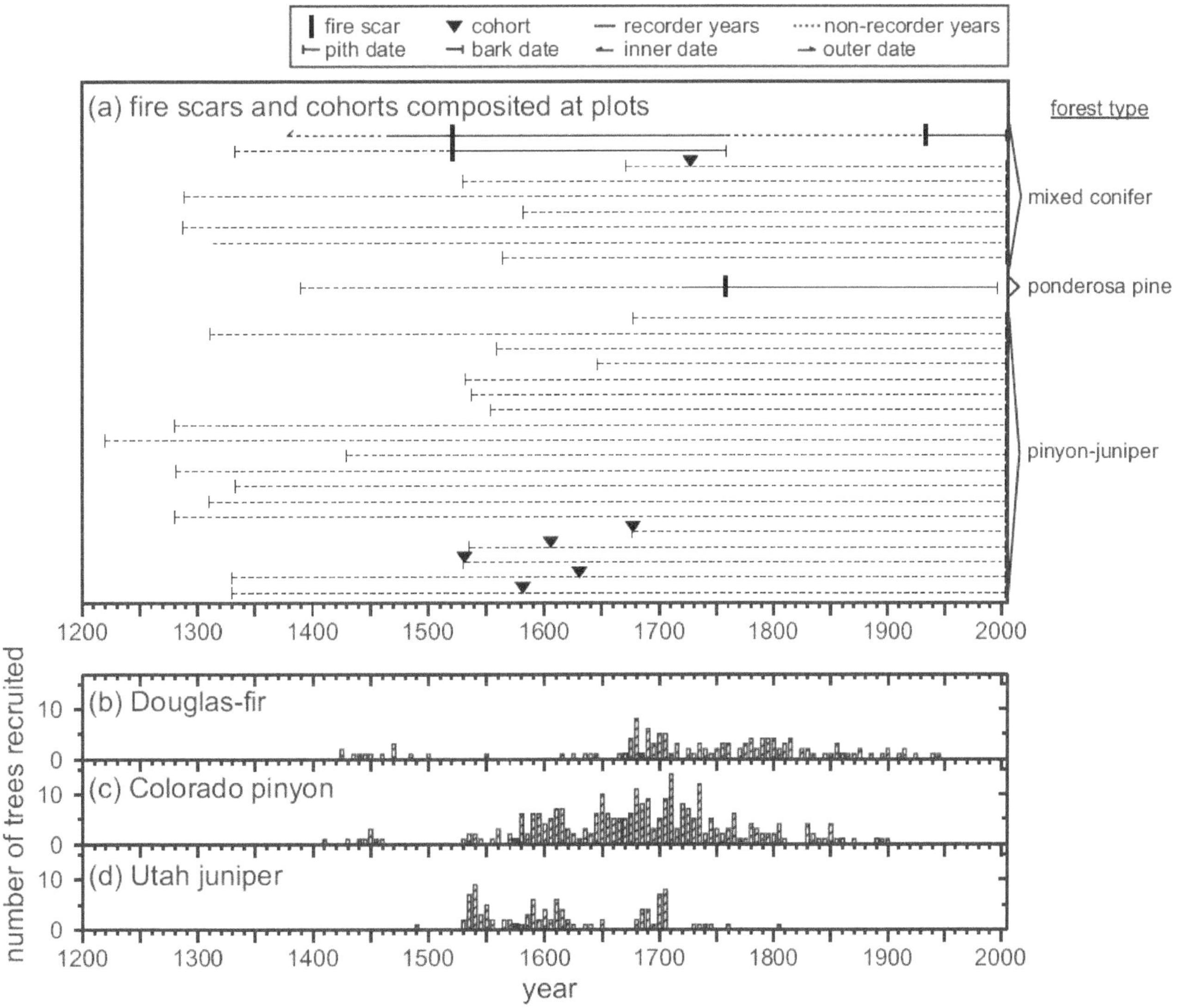

Legend:
| fire scar | ▼ cohort | — recorder years | ····· non-recorder years |
| ⊢ pith date | ⊣ bark date | — inner date | → outer date |

(a) fire scars and cohorts composited at plots

forest type

mixed conifer

ponderosa pine

pinyon-juniper

(x-axis: 1200 1300 1400 1500 1600 1700 1800 1900 2000)

number of trees recruited

(b) Douglas-fir 10 0

(c) Colorado pinyon 10 0

(d) Utah juniper 10 0

(x-axis: 1200 1300 1400 1500 1600 1700 1800 1900 2000)

year

Figure C-4—Chronologies of fire and tree recruitment at BCL. In (a), horizontal lines are plot-composite fire-scar and cohort dates by forest type. Non-recorder years precede the first scar, whereas recorder years generally follow it, but non-recorder years can also occur when the catface margin is consumed by subsequent fires or rot. In (b) through (d), recruitment dates are given for species comprising ≥10 percent of trees with such dates. The latter part of the distribution is incomplete because we only cored trees that were ≥8 inches DBH.

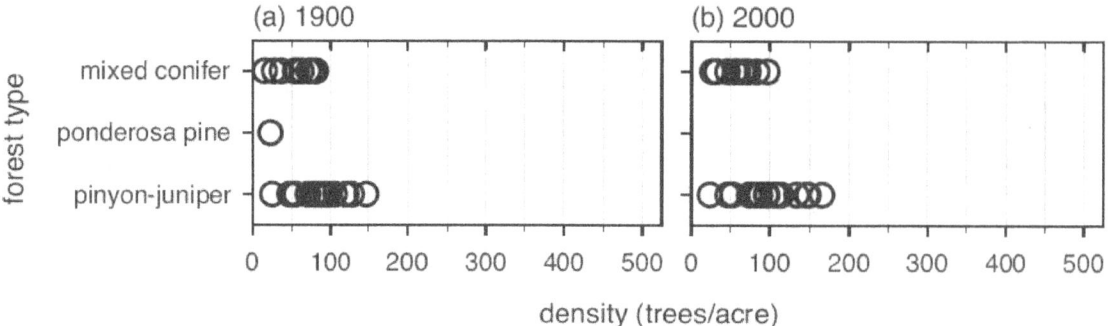

Figure C-5—Density of trees ≥8 inches DBH that were alive at each plot at BCL (a) in 1900 and (b) in 2000, by forest type (table 2).

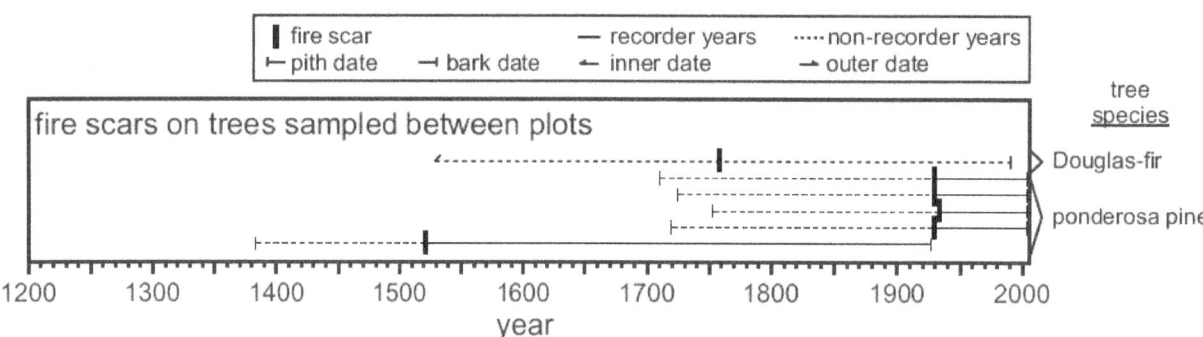

Figure C-6—Chronology of low-severity fires recorded on the six trees sampled between plots over approximately 245 acres in the eastern portion of the BCL site.

    USDA Forest Service RMRS-GTR-261WWW. 2011.

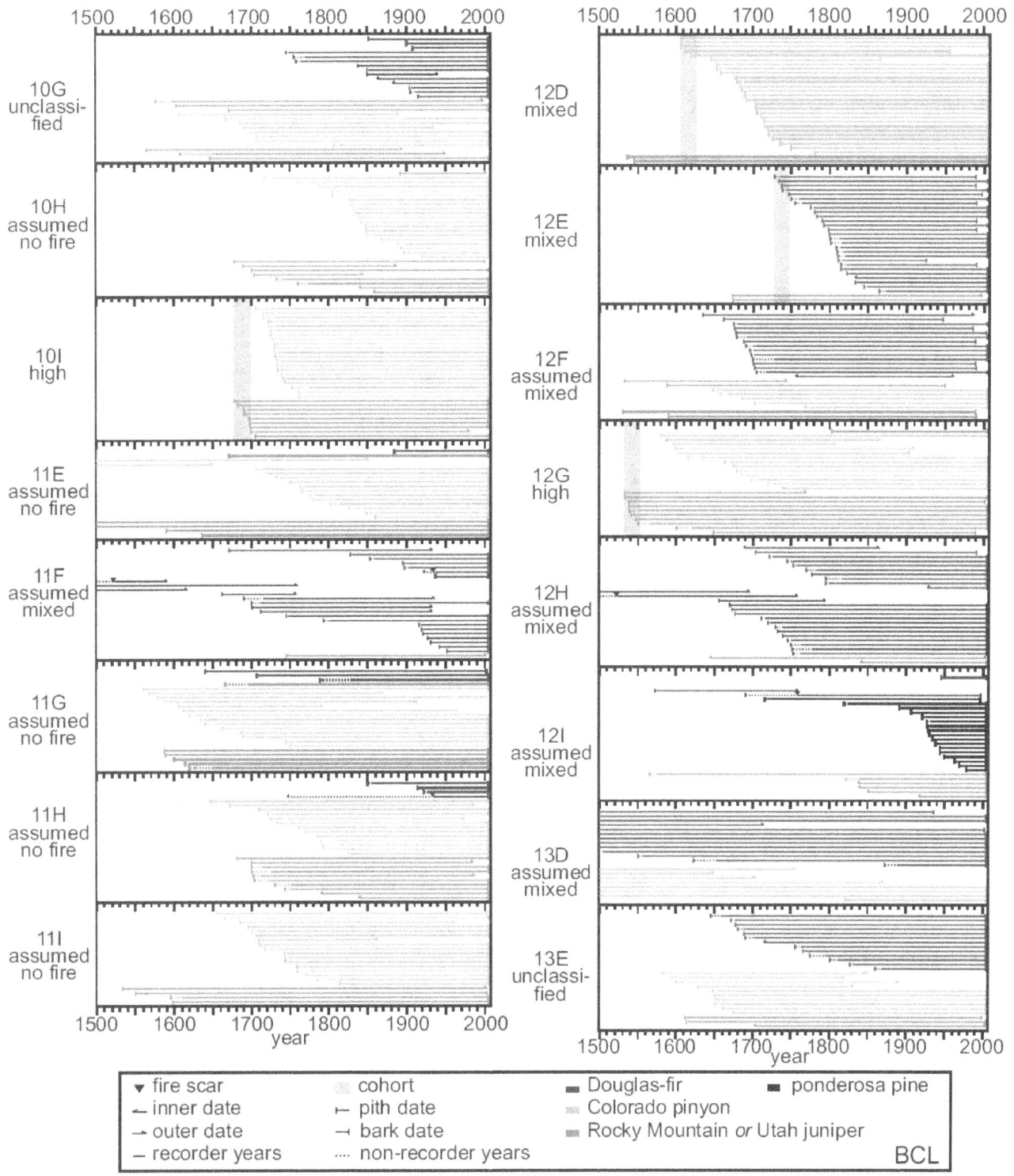

Figure C-7—Fire-demography diagrams (FDDs, Brown and others 2008b) showing chronologies of tree demography (recruitment and death), fire scars, and cohorts at each plot. Bark dates on 13 stumps are shown as outer dates. Not shown are six fire-scarred trees sampled between plots. Inferred fire severity (table 3) is indicated to the left of each panel. Most of the trees (84 percent) in the combined Rocky Mountain and Utah juniper category are Utah juniper.

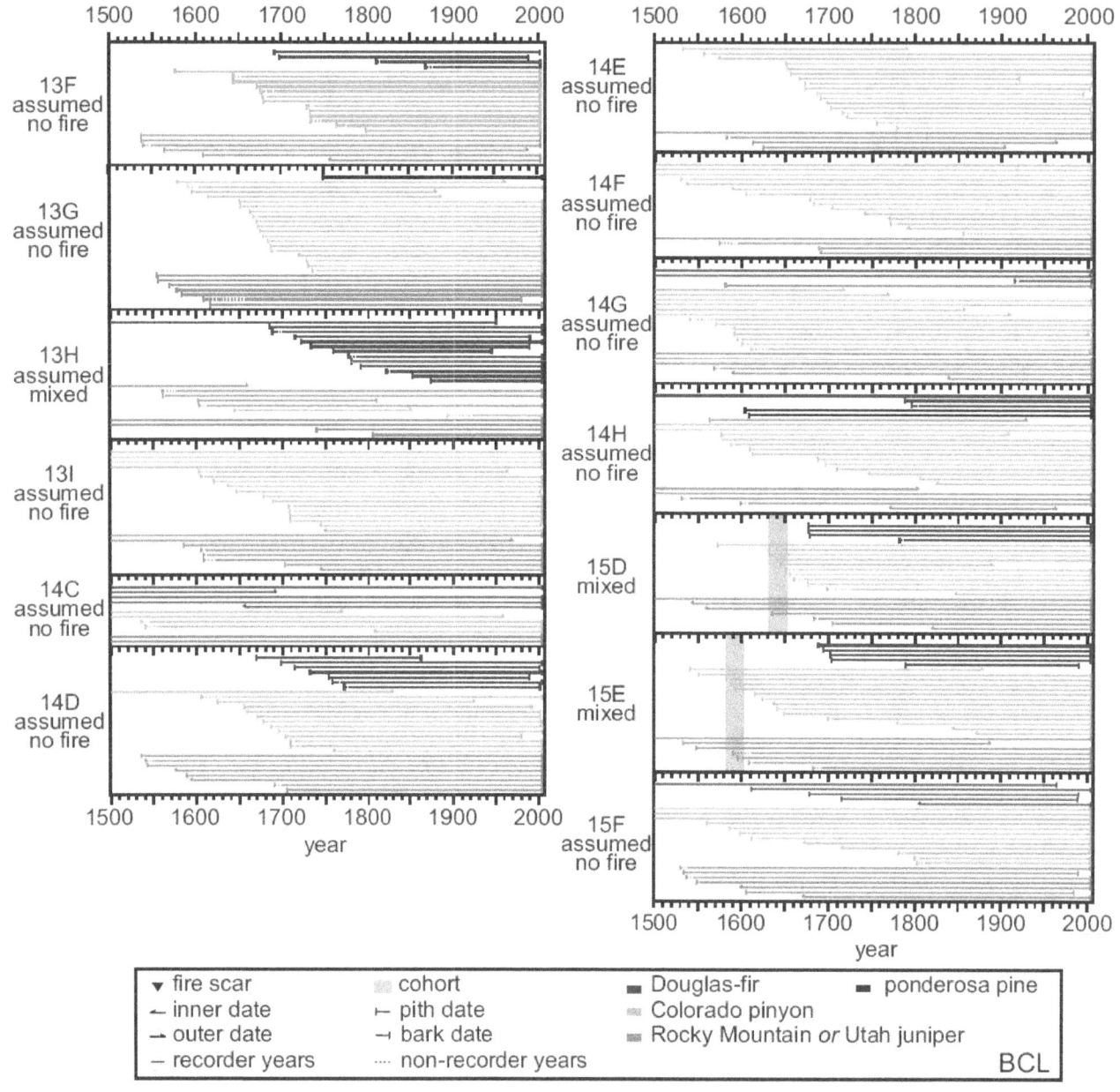

Figure C-7—*Continued*.

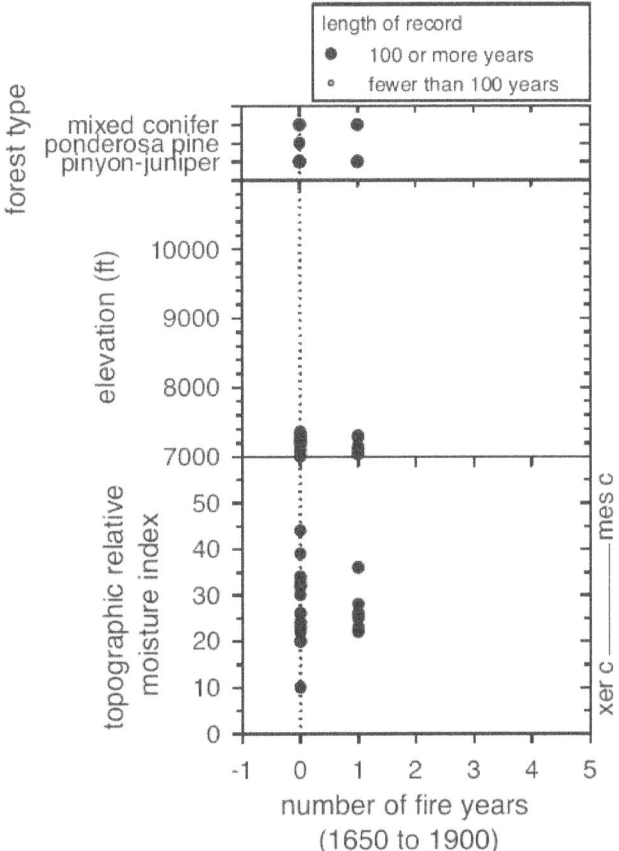

Figure C-8—Variation in fire among plots at BCL with topography, forest type, and relative soil moisture availability (Parker 1982). Number of fire years includes both fire-scar and cohort dates. Plots with no reconstructed fires during this period fall on the dotted line.

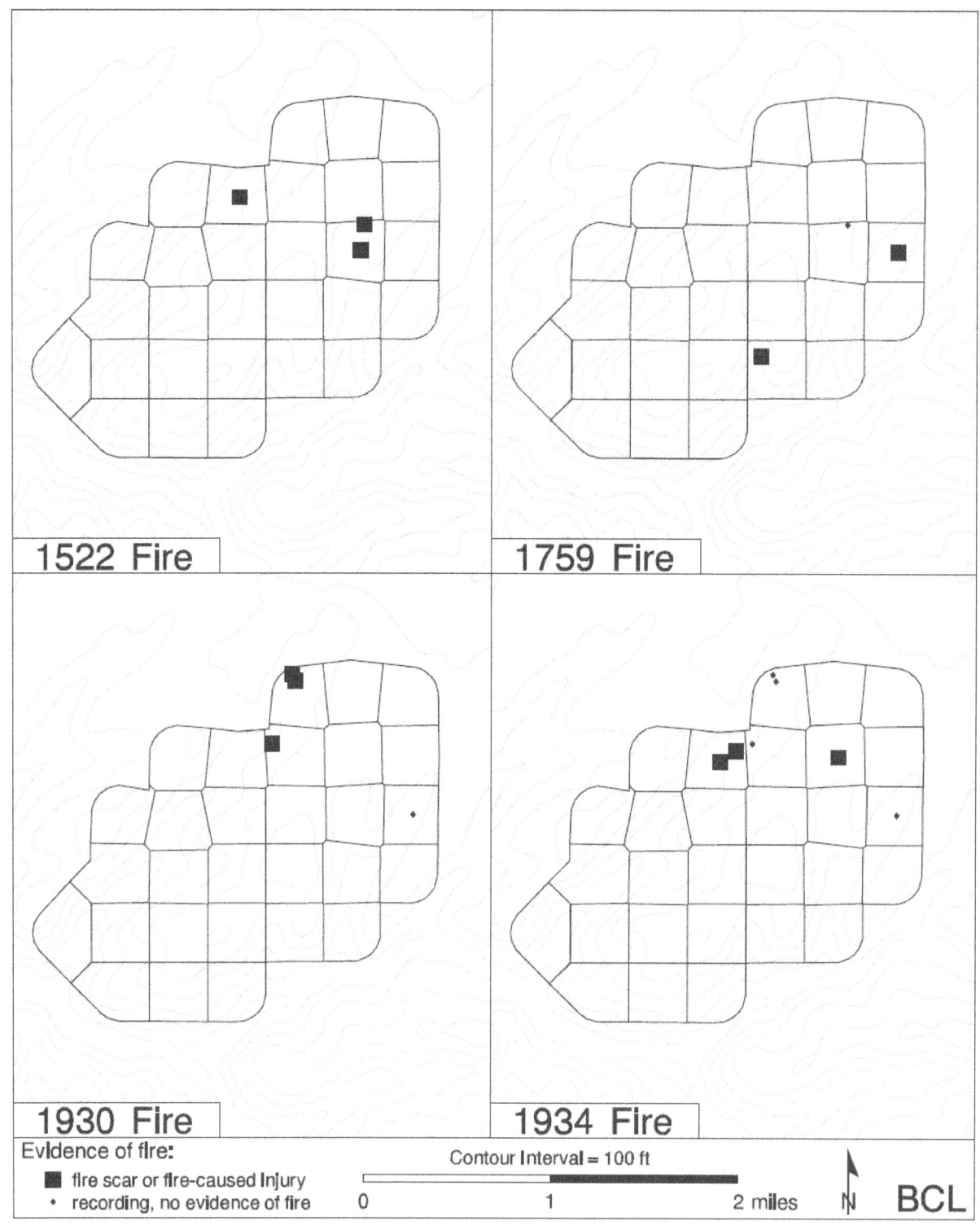

1522 Fire

1759 Fire

1930 Fire

1934 Fire

Evidence of fire:

■ fire scar or fire-caused injury

• recording, no evidence of fire

Contour Interval = 100 ft

0   1   2 miles   N   BCL

Figure C-9—Maps of years with evidence of low-severity fires in three or more cells at BLC. "Recording, no evidence of fire" indicates at least one tree was alive at that location during that year but did not have a fire scar or fire-caused injury. Empty cells indicate that no fire-scarred trees were recording in that cell during that year. Cohort dates are not mapped.

Appendix D. East Tavaputs Plateau, Bureau of Land Management (TVP)

In 2004, we removed fire-scarred partial cross sections from 19 trees (15 ponderosa pine and 4 Douglas-fir) over an area of approximately 10 acres on the Tavaputs Plateau, approximately 24 miles southwest of BCL, near Pine Springs Canyon, Vernal Field Office, Bureau of Land Management, in Uintah County, Utah (fig. 1). We sampled in woodland dominated by ponderosa pine and pinyon-juniper with scattered Douglas-fir. We sampled this site because it was one of the few locations on the Tavaputs Plateau where we found a concentration of fire-scarred trees for our regional study of the climate drivers of fire (Brown and others 2008a). All but one of these trees were dead when sampled. We were able to crossdate samples from 16 of them (12 ponderosa pine and 4 Douglas-fir). Three fire years were recorded by fire scars on two or more trees at this site (fig. D-1). We were able to assign an intra-ring position to more than half (54 percent) of the fire scars, but there were too few of these to report the distribution of scars by this feature (16 on ponderosa pine trees and 5 on Douglas-fir trees).

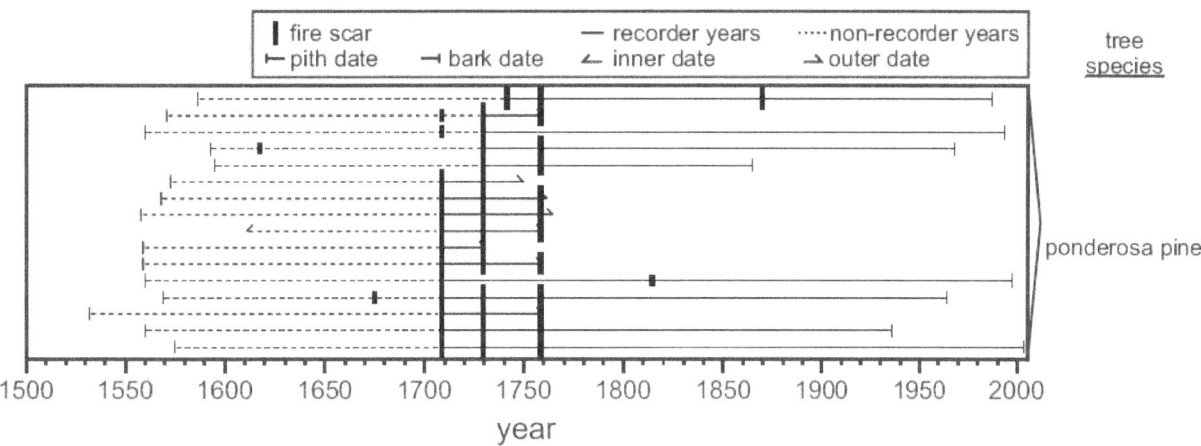

Figure D-1—Chronology of low-severity fires from trees sampled over 10 acres at TVP. Each horizontal line indicates the length of record for a single tree. Non-recorder years precede the first scar at a plot, whereas recorder years generally follow it. However, non-recorder years also occur when the margin of the catface is consumed by subsequent fires or rot.

Appendix E. Ray Mesa, Bureau of Land Management (RAY)

Topography

We sampled 4 plots over 15 acres on Ray Mesa, Monticello Field Office, Bureau of Land Management in San Juan County, Utah (figs. 1 and E-1). The plots were separated by 0.13 miles on average (range 0.08 to 0.27 miles) and averaged 0.40 acres in area (range 0.19 to 0.59 acres. Plots ranged in elevation from 7377 to 7475 ft. They ranged in slope from 0 to 10 percent. We did not take photographs at this site.

Tree Demography

All of the 118 trees that occurred in the plots were Utah juniper, Colorado pinyon, or ponderosa pine (fig. E-2). Most of these trees were living (78 percent) and the rest were snags (6 percent), logs (13 percent), or stumps (3 percent). We were able to remove and crossdate wood samples from most of these trees (97 trees or 82 percent), and we obtained actual or estimated pith dates for 85 of them. These pith dates ranged from 1566 to 1926 and only three of them post-dated 1900 (fig. E-3). The death dates we obtained for nine logs and snags ranged from 1795 to 2000.

Historical and Current Forest Structure and Composition

The plots included two historical and modern forest types (pinyon-juniper and ponderosa pine; table E-1). No plots changed forest type between 1860 and 2000 at this site. In 1900, tree density averaged 64 trees per acre and ranged from 41 to 101 trees per acre (fig. E-4). In 2000, tree density averaged 71 trees per acre and ranged from 38 to 133 trees per acre. However, we likely underestimated historical tree density because we could not obtain recruitment or earliest-ring dates for 21 of the 118 trees that occurred in the plots and only an earliest-ring date for another 12 trees. Five of these trees had earliest-ring dates between 1901 and 1920 and therefore may have been living before 1900.

Fire Scars

We were able to remove and crossdate fire-scarred samples from 19 trees. Three of these trees had only scars that were recorded on a single tree and so were excluded from further analyses. Of the remaining 16 trees, 8 were sampled in two of the four plots at this site. The eight other fire-scarred trees were sampled over an area of 4 acres, approximately 2.5 miles east of the plots (figs. E-1 and E-5). All of the 16 fire-scarred trees were ponderosa pine. Most were logs or stumps (63 percent) and the rest were live trees. They yielded 68 fire scars (figs. E-3 and E-6). However, 20 of these scar dates were eliminated from further analyses because they were recorded on only a single tree at the site. During the analysis period (1650 to 1900), we were able to assign an intra-ring position to 51 percent of the 45 fire scars. The fire scars were roughly equally distributed among intra-ring positions (fig. E-7).

Post-Fire Cohorts

We identified three cohorts of trees from estimated recruitment dates at two of the plots. All of these cohorts were recruited before 1900 (1580 to 1748) and were identified from 19 trees (5 to 9 trees per cohort), of which half was Colorado pinyon (53 percent) and half was ponderosa pine (47 percent; figs. E-5 and E-6). The cohorts that were recruited before 1900 occurred in two pinyon-juniper plots and one ponderosa pine plot.

Spatial Variation in Fire Regimes

We reconstructed too few fire intervals in plots during the analysis period (1650 to 1900) to compute plot-composite fire intervals by forest type at this site (fig. E-8). We assigned two plots to the mixed fire severity categories but we could not infer historical fire severity at the other two plots because they did not meet our requirements for any of the severity categories (table E-2). We sampled too few plots at this site to estimate fire extent.

Table E-1—Distribution of plots at RAY by historical (1860) and modern (2000) forest types (table 2).

Historical forest type (1860)	Modern forest type (2000)		
	Ponderosa pine	Pinyon-juniper	Total
Ponderosa pine	1		1
Pinyon-juniper		3	3
Total	1	3	4

Table E-2—Distribution of plots at RAY by historical forest type (1860; table 2) and fire severity (table 3).

Forest type	Mixed	Unclassified
Ponderosa pine	1	
Pinyon-juniper	1	2
Total	2	2

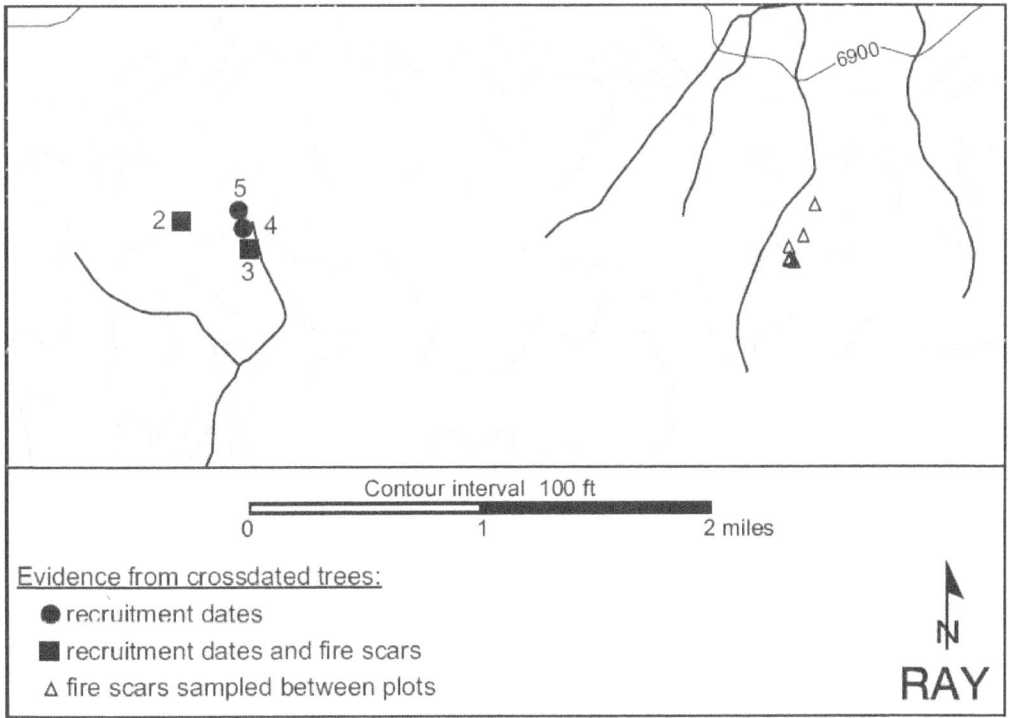

Contour interval 100 ft

0   1   2 miles

Evidence from crossdated trees:
● recruitment dates
■ recruitment dates and fire scars
△ fire scars sampled between plots

N

RAY

Figure E-1—Locations of plots and crossdated fire-scarred trees that were sampled outside of plots. Half the fire-scarred trees were sampled within plots and are not mapped individually. Plots at this site are identified by numbers only, as indicated on the map.

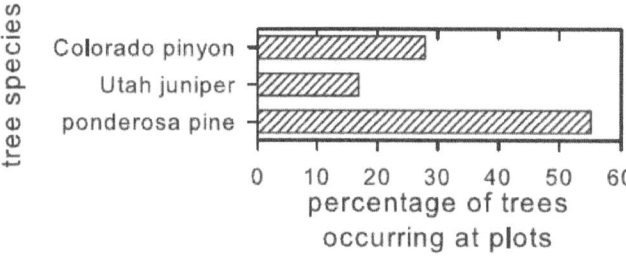

Figure E-2—Distribution by species of the 118 live and dead trees ≥8 inches DBH that occurred in plots at RAY, regardless of whether or not we removed wood samples and crossdated them.

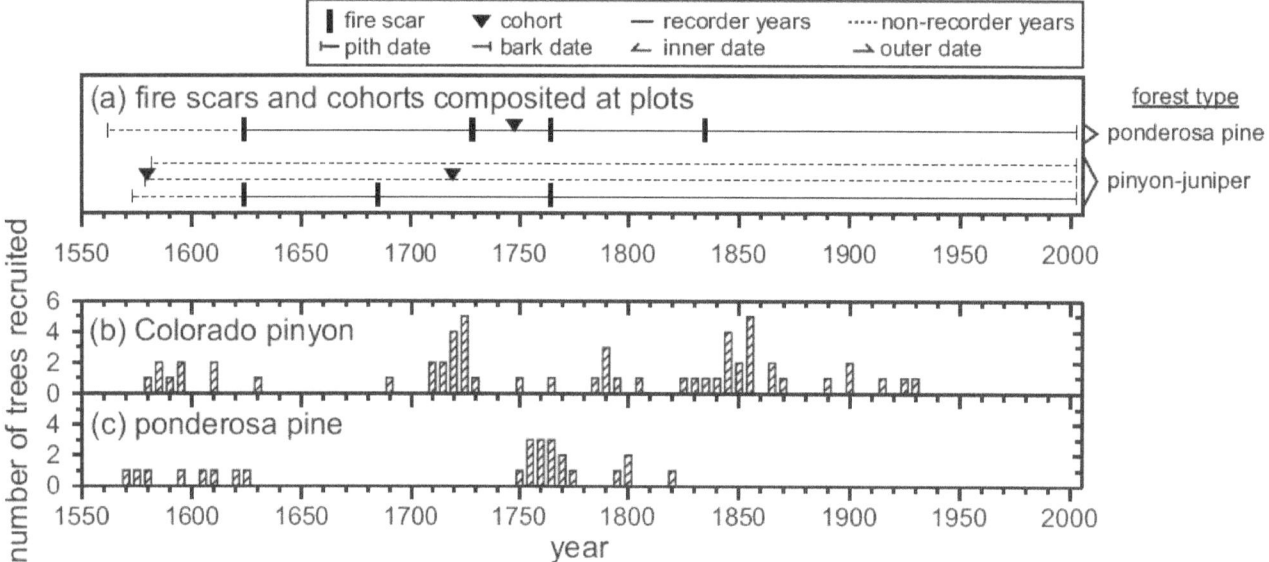

Figure E-3—Chronologies of fire and tree recruitment at RAY. In (a), horizontal lines show plot-composite dates of fire scars and cohorts by forest type. Non-recorder years precede the first scar at a plot, whereas recorder years generally follow it, but non-recorder years can also occur when the margin of the catface is consumed by subsequent fires or rot. In (b) and (c), recruitment dates are given for species comprising ≥10 percent of trees with such dates. Utah juniper is not given beause the samples from many trees of this species (10 percent) could not be crossdated. The latter part of the distribution is incomplete because we only cored trees that were ≥8 inches DBH.

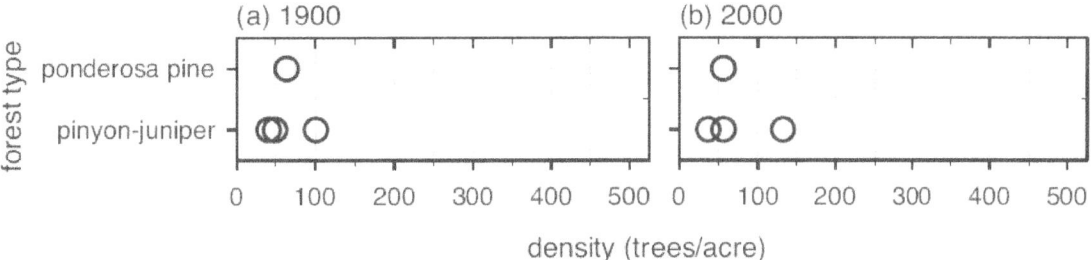

Figure E-4—Density of trees ≥8 inches DBH that were alive at each plot at RAY (a) in 1900 and (b) in 2000, by forest type (table 2).

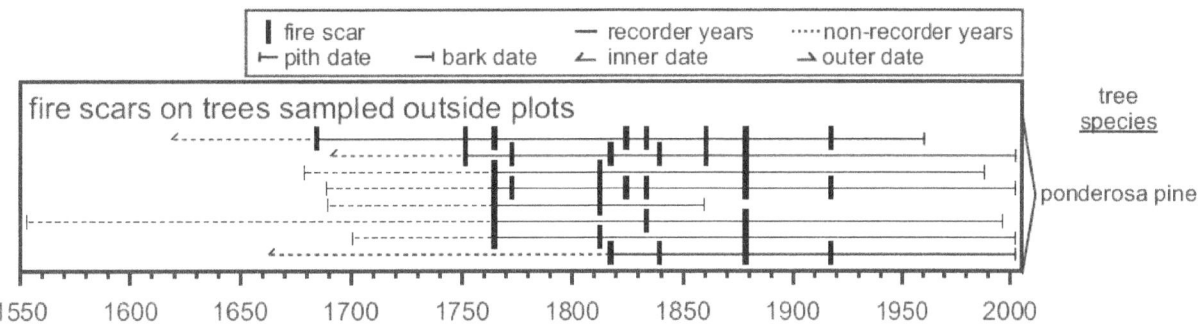

Figure E-5—Chronology of low-severity fires recorded on the eight trees sampled between plots over 4 acres east of the plots at RAY.

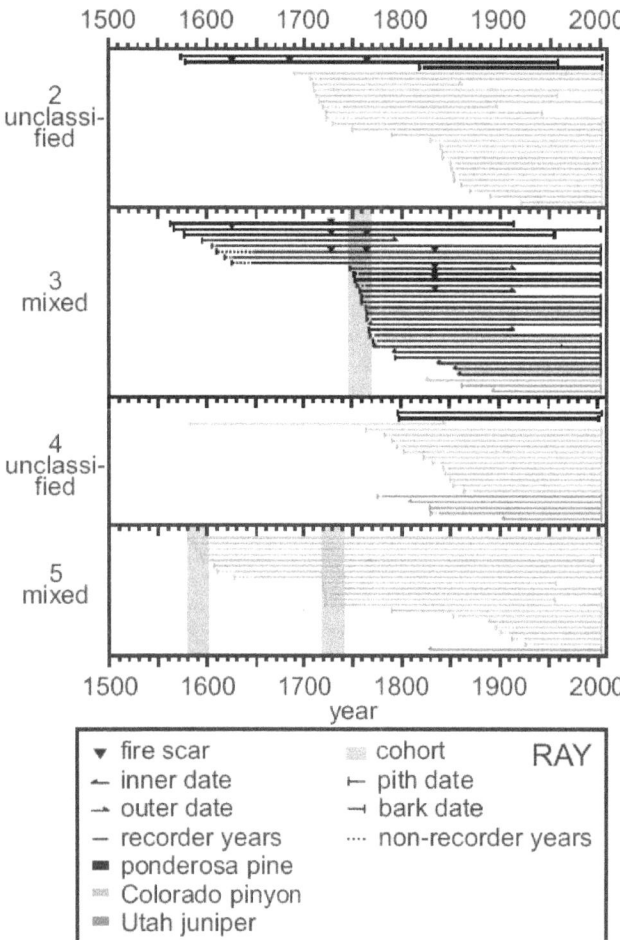

Figure E-6—Fire-demography diagrams (FDDs, Brown and others 2008b) showing chronologies of tree demography (recruitment and death), fire scars, and cohorts at each plot. Bark dates on four stumps are shown as outer dates. Not shown are eight fire-scarred trees that were sampled over 4 acres, approximately 2.5 miles east of the plots. Inferred fire severity (table 3) is indicated to the left of each panel.

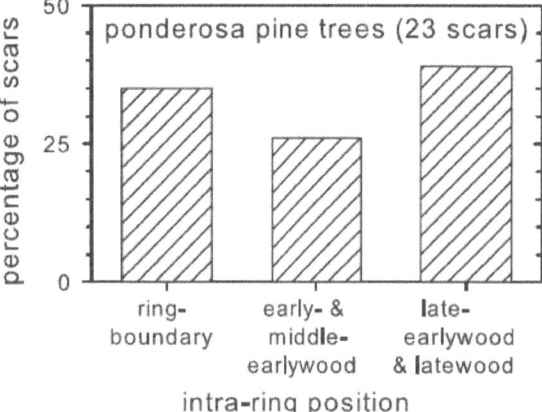

Figure E-7—Intra-ring position of fire scars on 16 trees sampled in and to the east of plots at RAY from 1650 to 1900, as a percentage of the number of scars for which the position could be determined (given in parentheses).

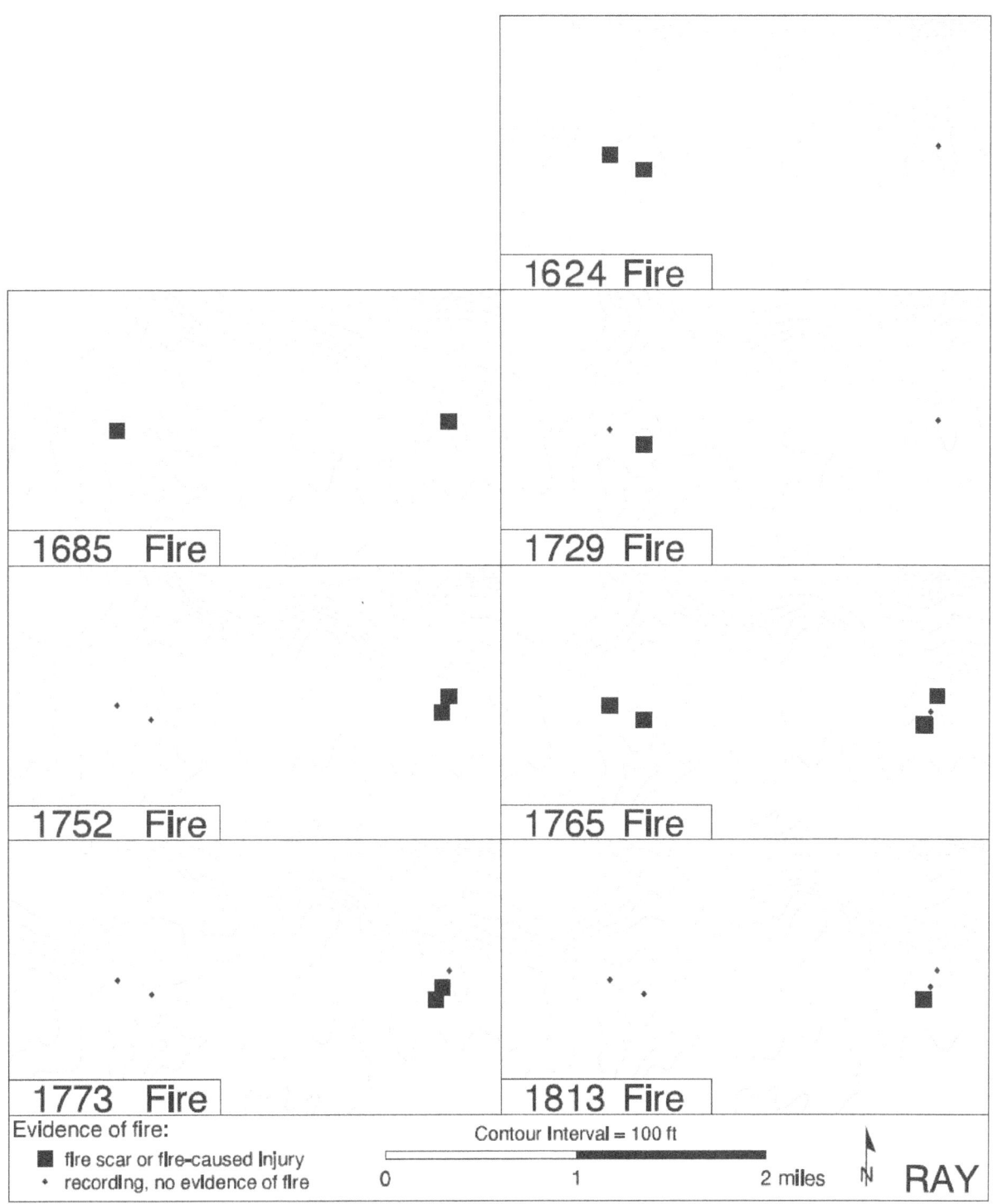

Figure E-8—Maps of years with evidence of low-severity fires in three or more cells at RAY. "Recording, no evidence of fire" indicates at least one tree was alive at that location during that year but did not have a fire scar or fire-caused injury. Empty cells indicate that no fire-scarred trees were recording in that cell during that year. Cohort dates are not mapped.

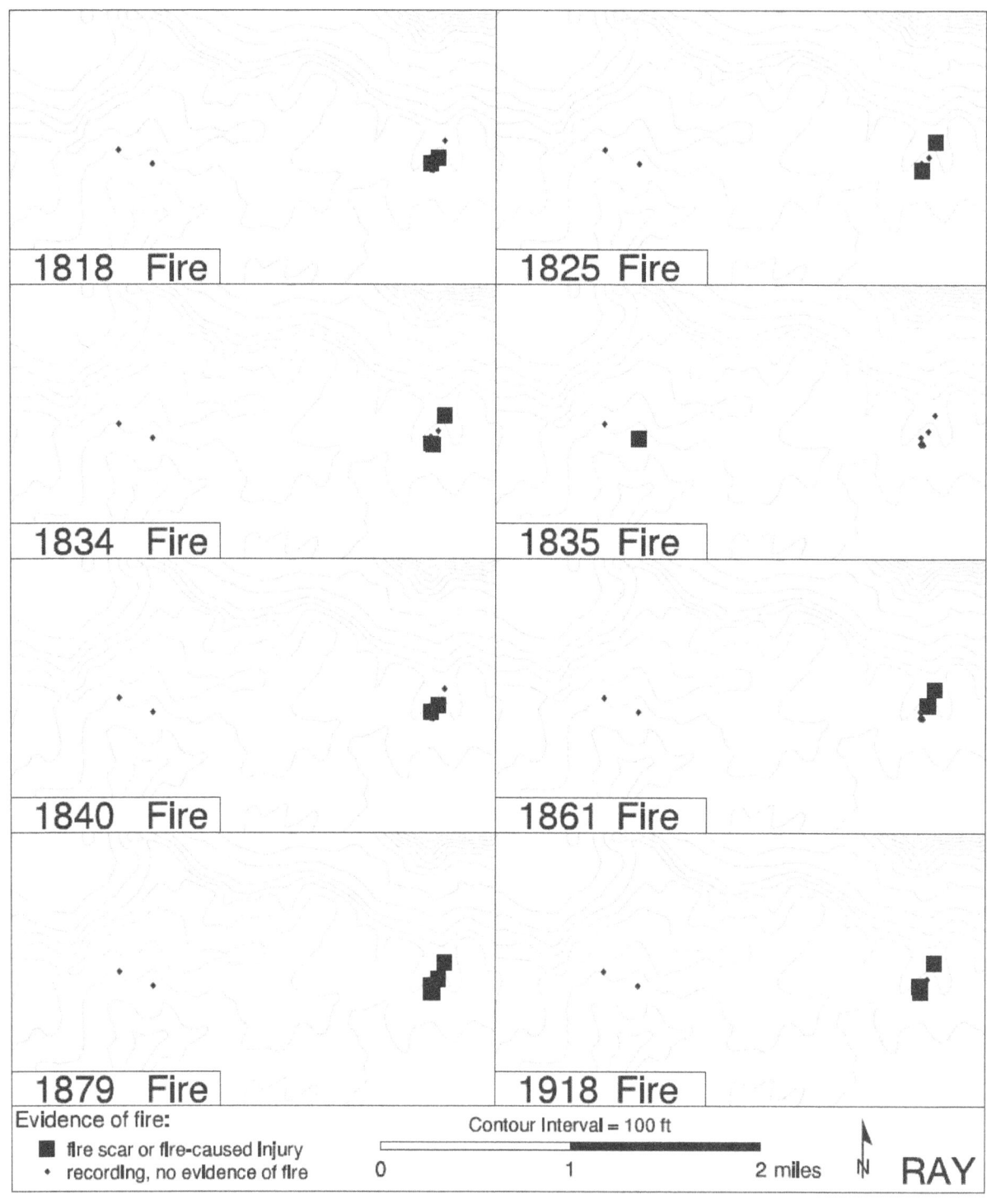

1818 Fire

1825 Fire

1834 Fire

1835 Fire

1840 Fire

1861 Fire

1879 Fire

1918 Fire

Evidence of fire:

■ fire scar or fire-caused injury
• recording, no evidence of fire

Contour Interval = 100 ft

0   1   2 miles

N

RAY

Figure E-8—*Continued.*

Appendix F. Snake Range, Great Basin National Park (BMC)

Topography

We sampled 24 plots over 1569 acres near Mill Creek in Great Basin National Park, White Pine County, Nevada (figs. 1 and F-1). The plots were separated by 0.30 miles on average (range 0.27 to 0.31 miles) and averaged 0.52 acres in area (range 0.10 to 1.18 acres). Plots were sampled within cells that averaged 61 acres and ranged from 49 to 75 acres. Plots ranged in elevation from 7757 to 10,596 ft (fig. F-2) and in slope from 19 to 57 percent. They were sampled on a range of aspects, but most were on north or east aspects (96 percent). The distribution of the plots by elevation, aspect, or slope differed from the distribution of the landscape by more than 10 percent only for moderate and steep slopes, which were over and under sampled, respectively (fig. F-2). We took between three and four photographs each at 18 of the plots.

Tree Demography

Of the 674 trees that occurred in the plots, most (99 percent) were singleleaf pinyon, curl-leaf mountain mahogany, ponderosa pine, white fir, Douglas-fir, limber pine, or Engelmann spruce, but 2 Utah juniper and 4 quaking aspen trees also occurred plus 3 trees we could not identify (fig. F-3). Most of these trees were living (79 percent) and the rest were snags (11 percent), logs (8 percent), or stumps (2 percent). We were able to remove and crossdate wood samples from most of these trees (507 trees or 75 percent), and we obtained actual or estimated pith dates for 470 of them. These pith dates ranged from 1154 to 1958, but many post-dated 1900 (119 trees; fig. F-4). The death dates we obtained for 52 logs and snags ranged from 1689 to 2003.

Historical and Current Forest Structure and Composition

The plots included a range of historical and modern forest types (sagebrush, shrubland, mountain mahogany, pinyon-juniper, ponderosa pine, mixed conifer, limber-bristlecone, and spruce-fir; table F-1). Some plots changed forest type between 1860 and 2000: one sagebrush plot converted to mountain mahogany; one sagebrush, one shrubland, and one mountain mahogany plot converted to pinyon-juniper; and two sagebrush, one mountain mahogany, and one ponderosa pine plot converted to mixed conifer. In 1900, tree density averaged 63 trees per acre and ranged from 0 to 242 trees per acre (fig. F-5). In 2000, tree density averaged 75 trees per acre and ranged from 5 to 235 trees per acre. However, we likely underestimated historical tree density because we could not obtain recruitment or earliest-ring dates for 167 of the 674 trees that occurred in the plots and only an earliest-ring date for another 37 trees.

Fire Scars

We were able to remove and crossdate fire-scarred samples from 110 trees, 7 of which had only scars that were recorded on a single tree and so were excluded from further analyses. Of the remaining 103 trees, 67 were sampled in 13 of the 24 plots at this site (1 to 16 trees per plot, average 5 trees). We sampled the 36 other fire-scarred trees as we encountered them between plots, over 614 acres throughout the site (fig. F-6). Most of the 103 fire-scarred trees were limber pine (45 percent) or ponderosa pine (30 percent) and the rest were white fir, Douglas-fir, singleleaf pinyon, and trees of unknown species. Most were live trees (59 percent) and the rest were logs, snags, or stumps. These 103 trees yielded 372 fire scars and 55 eroded fire scars or abrupt changes in ring width (figs. F-4 and F-7). However, 10 of the scar dates and 1 of the non-scar dates were eliminated from further analyses because they were recorded on only a single tree at the site. We were able to assign an intra-ring position to 79 percent of the 321 fire scars that occurred during the analysis period (1650 to

1900). Of the scars that occurred on ponderosa pine, Douglas-fir, and limber pine trees, many (39, 44, and 51 percent, respectively) occurred on the boundary between two rings (fig. F-8).

Post-Fire Cohorts

We identified 12 cohorts of trees from estimated recruitment dates at 12 of the plots. Nine of these cohorts were recruited before 1900 (1643 to 1826) and were identified from 64 trees (5 to 15 trees per cohort), which were ponderosa pine (23 percent), white fir (23 percent), singleleaf pinyon (22 percent), limber pine (16 percent), Douglas-fir (13 percent), and a few Engelmann spruce (figs. F-4 and F-7). The cohorts that were recruited before 1900 occurred in plots with a range of historical forest types: mixed conifer (56 percent of cohorts), pinyon-juniper (22 percent), ponderosa pine (11 percent), and spruce-fir (11 percent).

Spatial Variation in Fire Regimes

During the analysis period (1650 to 1900), plot-composite, low-severity fire intervals averaged 11 years (range 2 to 22 years) when pooled among ponderosa pine plots and averaged 19 years (range 1 to 62 years; fig. F-9) when pooled among mixed conifer plots. The tree-ring record before 1900 was less than 100 years long for 7 of the 24 plots at this site (fig. F-10).

Three plots were not historically forested and we could not infer historical fire severity at four others because they did not meet our requirements for any of the severity categories (table F-2). We assigned the remaining plots to the low, mixed, or high fire severity categories.

From 1650 to 1900, the 50 low-severity fires we reconstructed within our 1569-acre sampling area averaged 146 acres and ranged from 59 to 370 acres (fig. F-11), equivalent to 6 to 37 percent of the recording area (in other words, the combined area of cells containing recording, fire-scarred trees during a given year). Recording area varied among fire years, ranging from 619 to 990 acres. We likely underestimated the extent of low-severity fires because most fires intersected the boundary of the site (fig. F-12).

Table F-1—Distribution of plots at BMC by historical (1860) and modern (2000) forest types (table 2).

Historical forest type (1860)	Modern forest type (2000)					
	Spruce-fir	Limber-bristlecone	Mixed conifer	Pinyon-juniper	Mountain mahogany	Total plots in 1860
Spruce-fir	1					1
Limber-bristlecone		4				4
Mixed conifer			8			8
Ponderosa pine			1			1
Pinyon-juniper				2		2
Mountain mahogany			1	1	1	3
Shrubland				1		1
Sagebrush			2	1	1	4
Total plots in 2000	**1**	**4**	**12**	**5**	**2**	**24**

Table F-2—Distribution of plots at BMC by historical forest type (1860; table 2) and fire severity (table 3).

Forest type	High	Assumed high	Mixed	Assumed mixed	Low	Not historically forested	Unclassified
Spruce-fir			1				
Limber-bristlecone				1	3		
Mixed conifer	1	2	4		1		
Ponderosa pine			1				
Pinyon-juniper			2				
Mountain mahogany				1			2
Shrubland							1
Sagebrush						3	1
Total	**1**	**2**	**8**	**2**	**4**	**3**	**4**

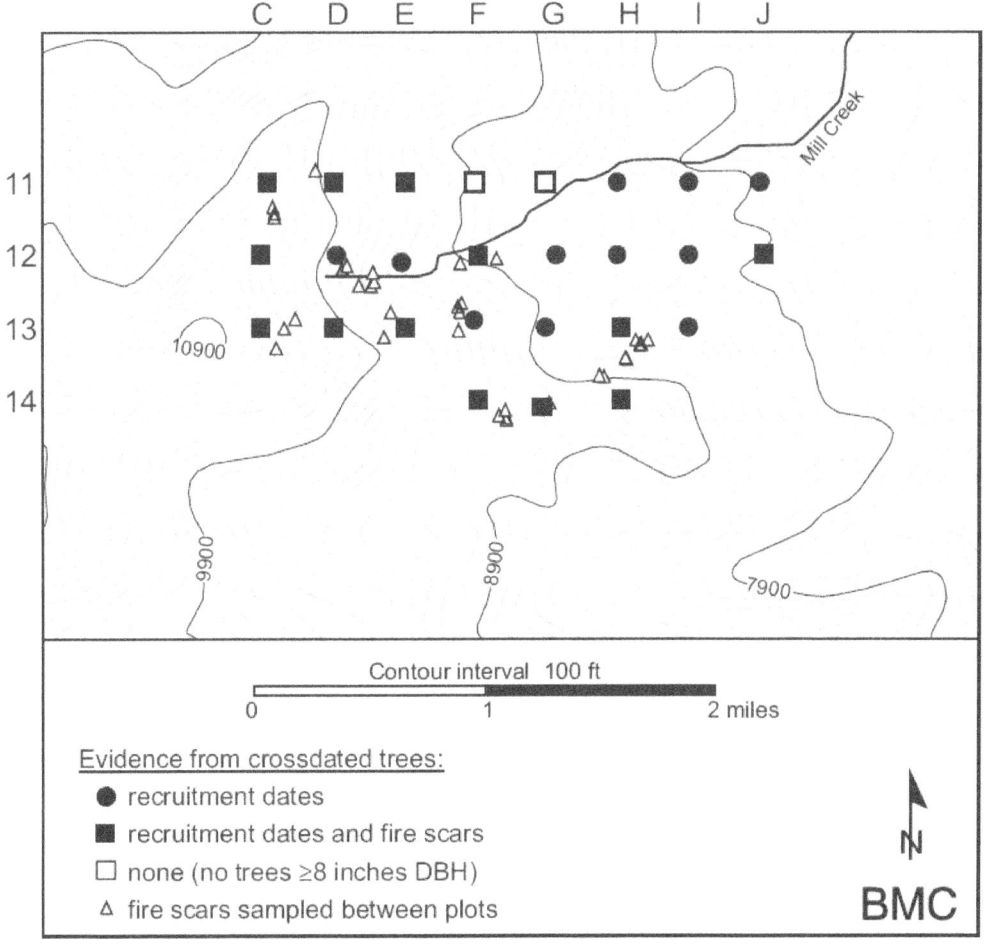

Figure F-1—Locations of plots and crossdated fire-scarred trees that were sampled outside of plots. More than half of the fire-scarred trees were sampled within plots and are not mapped individually. Plots are identified by column and row, in other words, the northwestern most plot is 11C, the next plot to the east is 11D, and so forth.

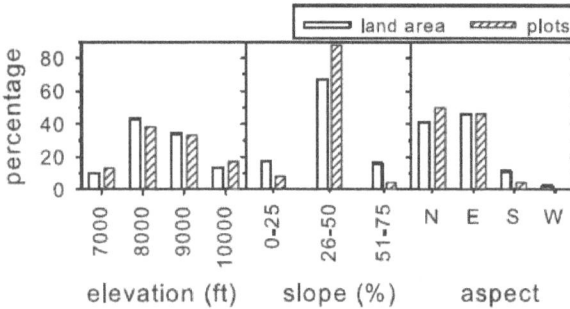

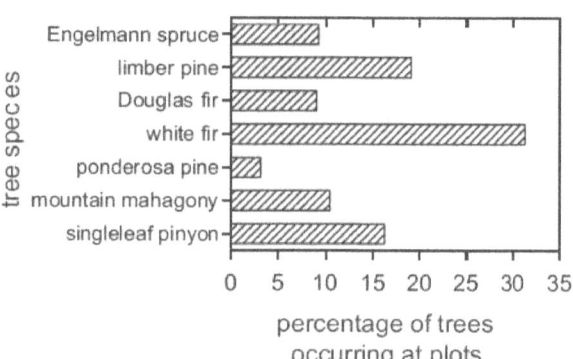

Figure F-2—Distribution of sampled plots and land area at BMC by topography. Aspect classes are 90° wide, beginning with 46° for east (E). Land area was derived from a digital elevation model (Utah AGRC 2004).

Figure F-3—Distribution by species of the 674 live and dead trees ≥8 inches DBH that occurred in plots at BMC, regardless of whether or not we removed wood samples and crossdated them. Not shown are two Utah juniper and four quaking aspen trees plus three trees of unknown species.

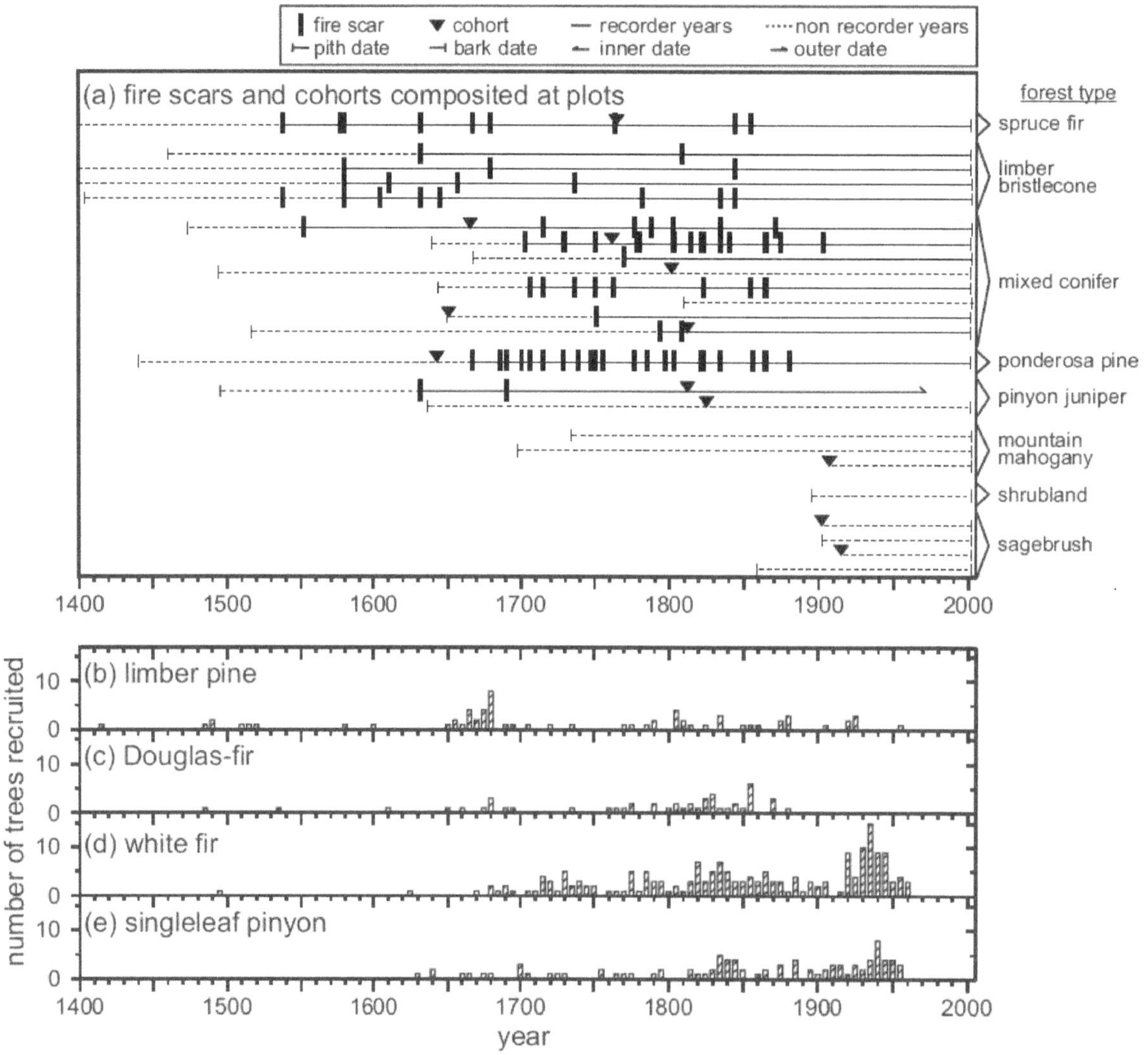

Figure F-4—Chronologies of fire and tree recruitment at BMC. In (a), horizontal lines are plot-composite fire-scar and cohort dates by forest type. Non-recorder years precede the first scar, whereas recorder years generally follow it, but non-recorder years can also occur when the catface margin is consumed by subsequent fires or rot. In (b) through (e), recruitment dates are given for species comprising ≥10 percent of trees with such dates. The latter part of the distribution is incomplete because we only cored trees that were ≥8 inches DBH.

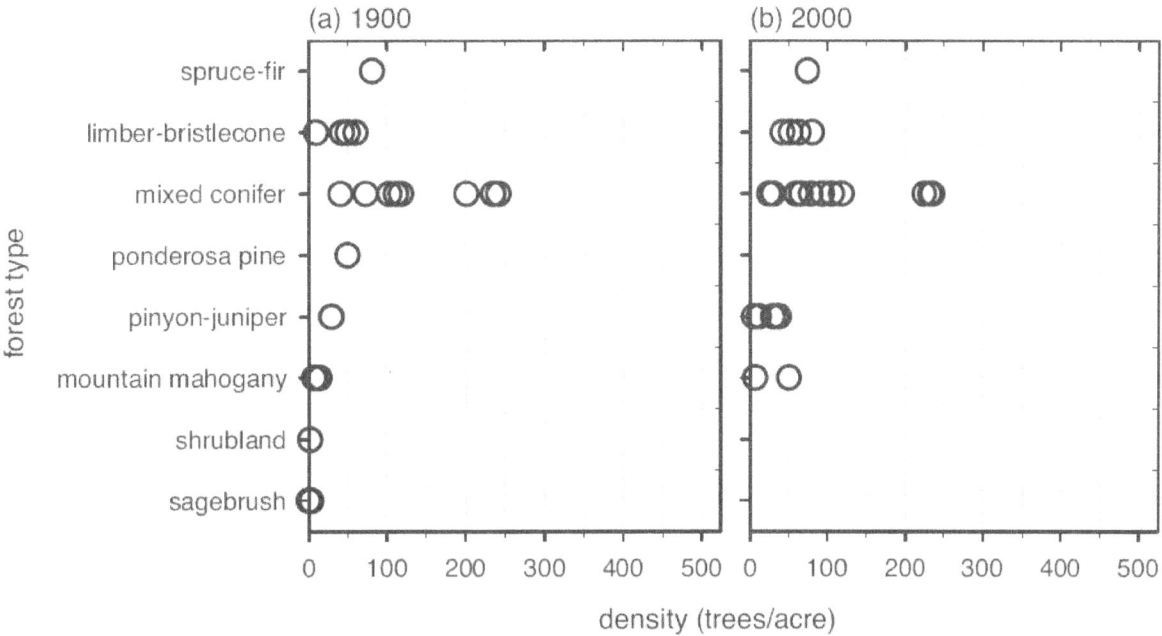

Figure F-5—Density of trees ≥8 inches DBH that were alive at each plot at BMC (a) in 1900 and (b) in 2000, by forest type (table 2).

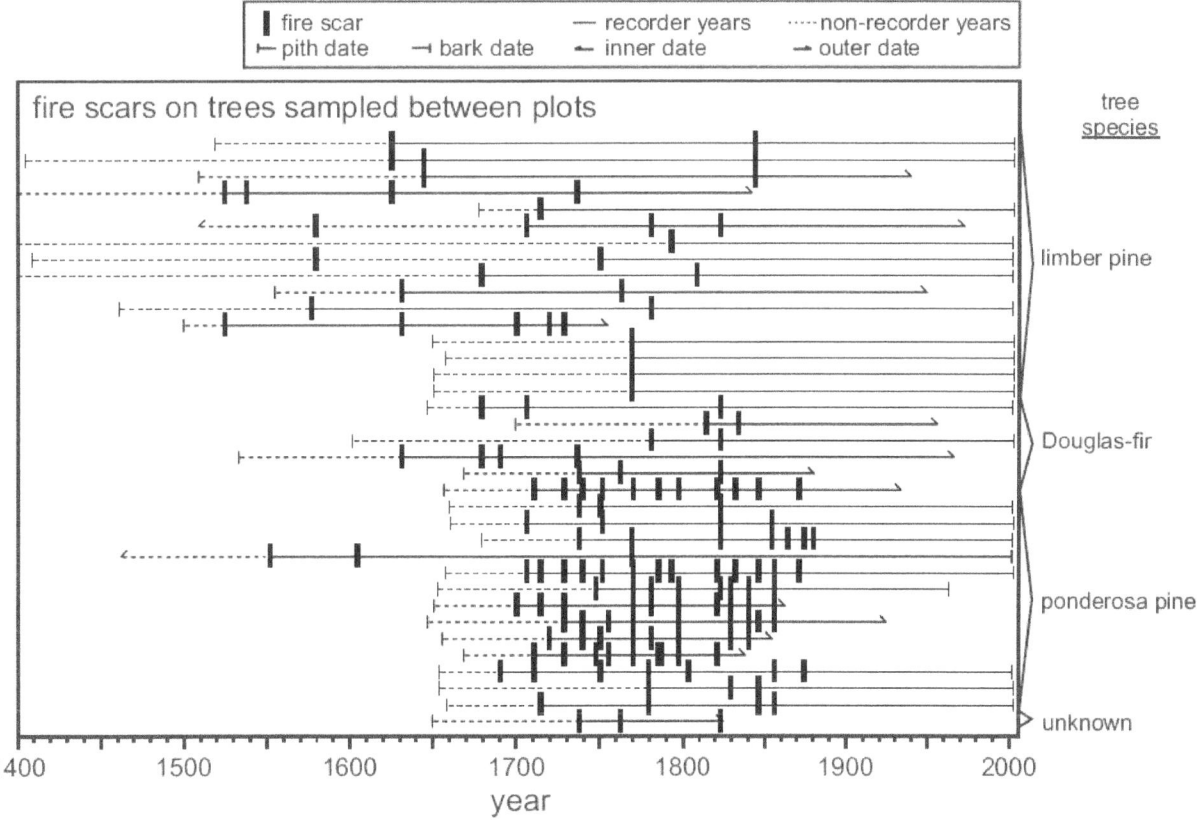

Figure F-6—Chronology of low-severity fires recorded on the 36 trees sampled between plots over approximately, 614 acres throughout the BMC site.

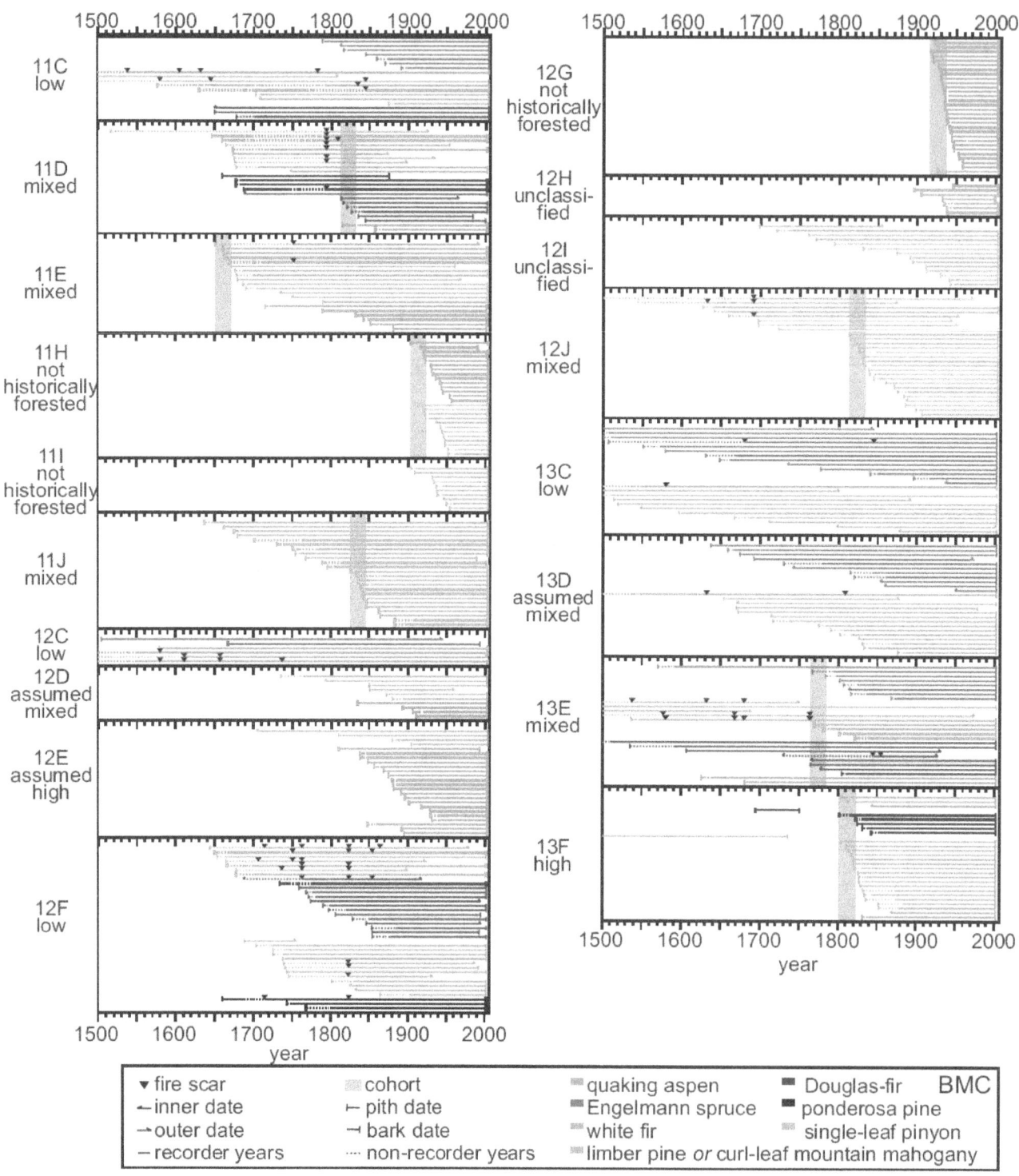

Figure F-7—Fire-demography diagrams (FDDs, Brown and others 2008b) showing chronologies of tree demography (recruitment and death), fire scars, and cohorts at each plot. Bark dates on 21 stumps are shown as outer dates. Not shown are 36 fire-scarred trees sampled between plots. Inferred fire severity (table 3) is indicated to the left of each panel. Most of the trees (92 percent) in the combined limber pine and curl-leaf mountain mahogany category are limber pine.

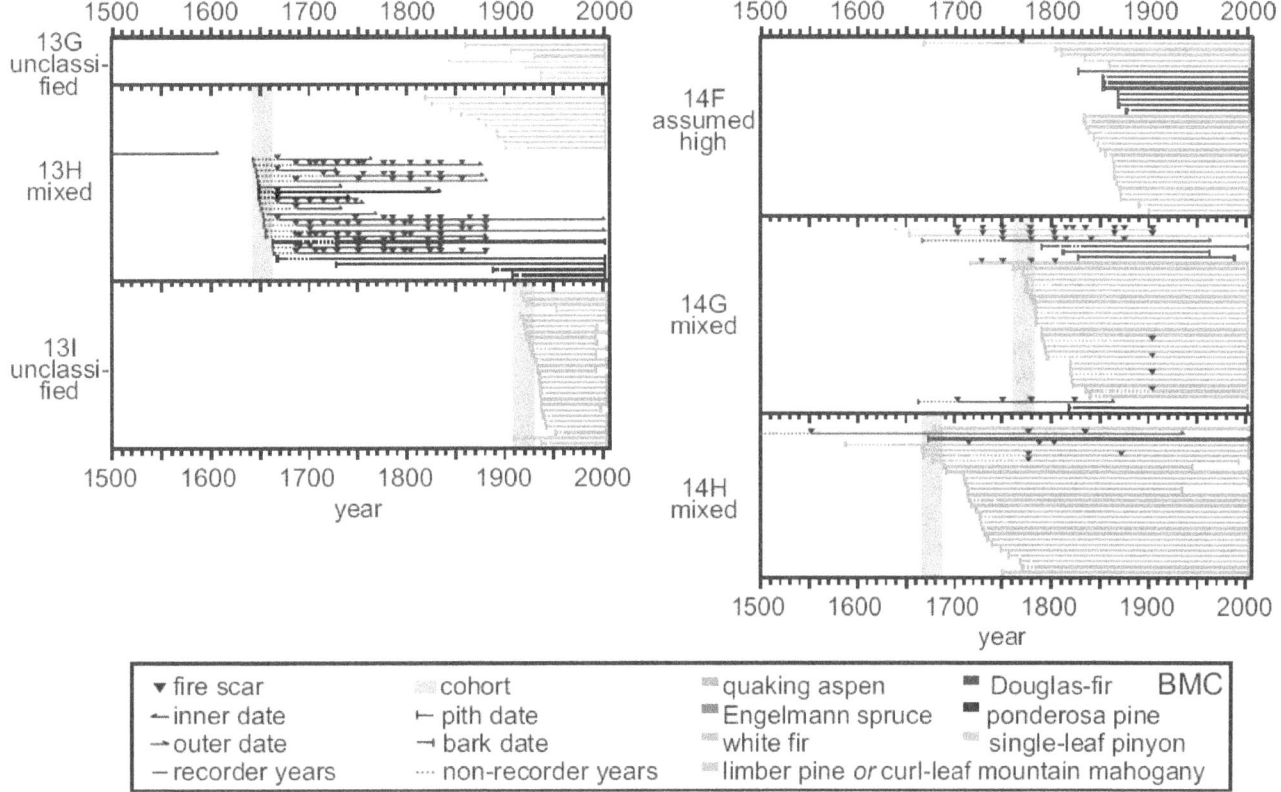

Figure F-7—Continued.

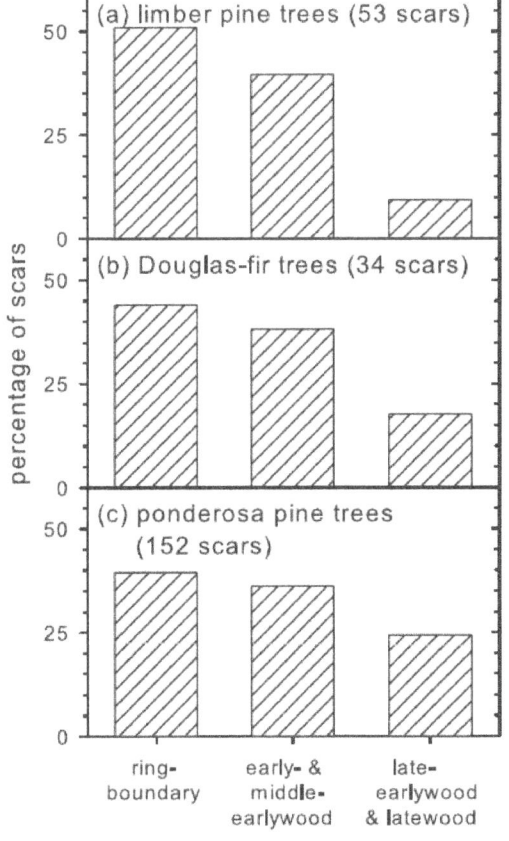

Figure F-8—Intra-ring position of fire scars sampled in and between plots at BMC from 1650 to 1900, as a percentage of the number of scars for which the position could be determined (given in parentheses). Not shown are intra-ring positions for 13 fire scars on singleleaf pinyon, white fir, and trees of unknown species.

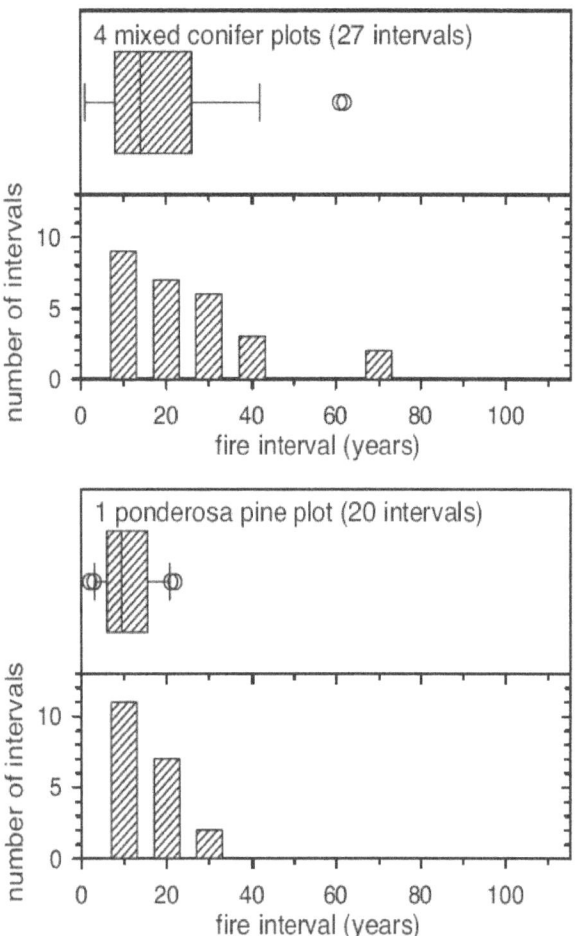

Figure F-9—Plot-composite intervals between low-severity fires in mixed conifer and ponderosa pine plots at BMC from 1650 to 1900. Plots averaged 0.52 acres. The boxes (top panels for each forest type) enclose the 25th to 75th percentiles and the whiskers enclose the 10th to 90th percentiles of the distribution of intervals. The vertical lines indicate the median fire interval, and all values falling outside the 10th to 90th percentiles are shown as circles. In the histogram (bottom panels for each forest type), the same intervals are plotted in 10-year bins (1 to 10 years, 11 to 20 years, and so forth).

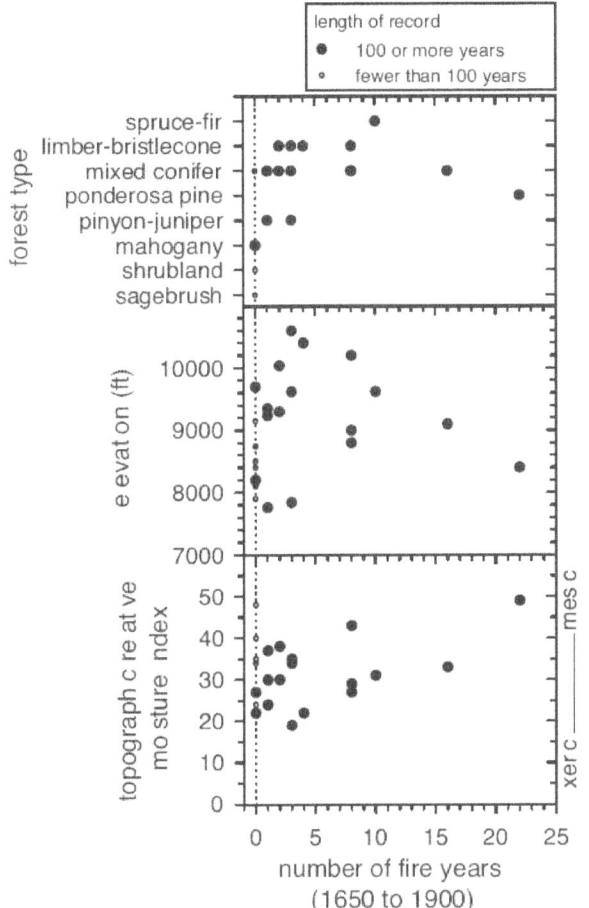

Figure F-10—Variation in fire among plots at BMC with topography, forest type, and relative soil moisture availability (Parker 1982). Number of fire years includes both fire-scar and cohort dates. Plots with no reconstructed fires during this period fall on the dotted line.

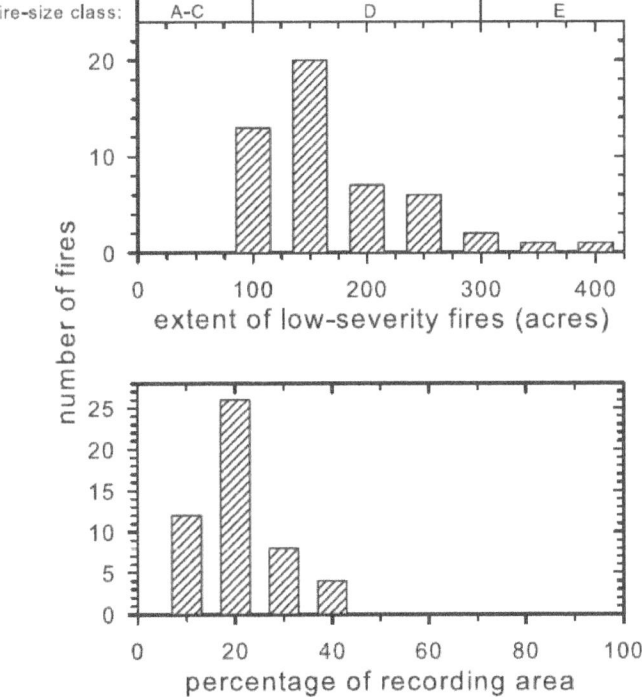

Figure F-11—Relative extent of low-severity fires within the 1569-acre BMC site, from 1650 to 1900, as area (top) and as a percentage of the recording area (in other words, the combined area of cells containing recording fire-scarred trees during each year; bottom). Commonly used fire-size classes are indicated at the top (NWCG 2007).

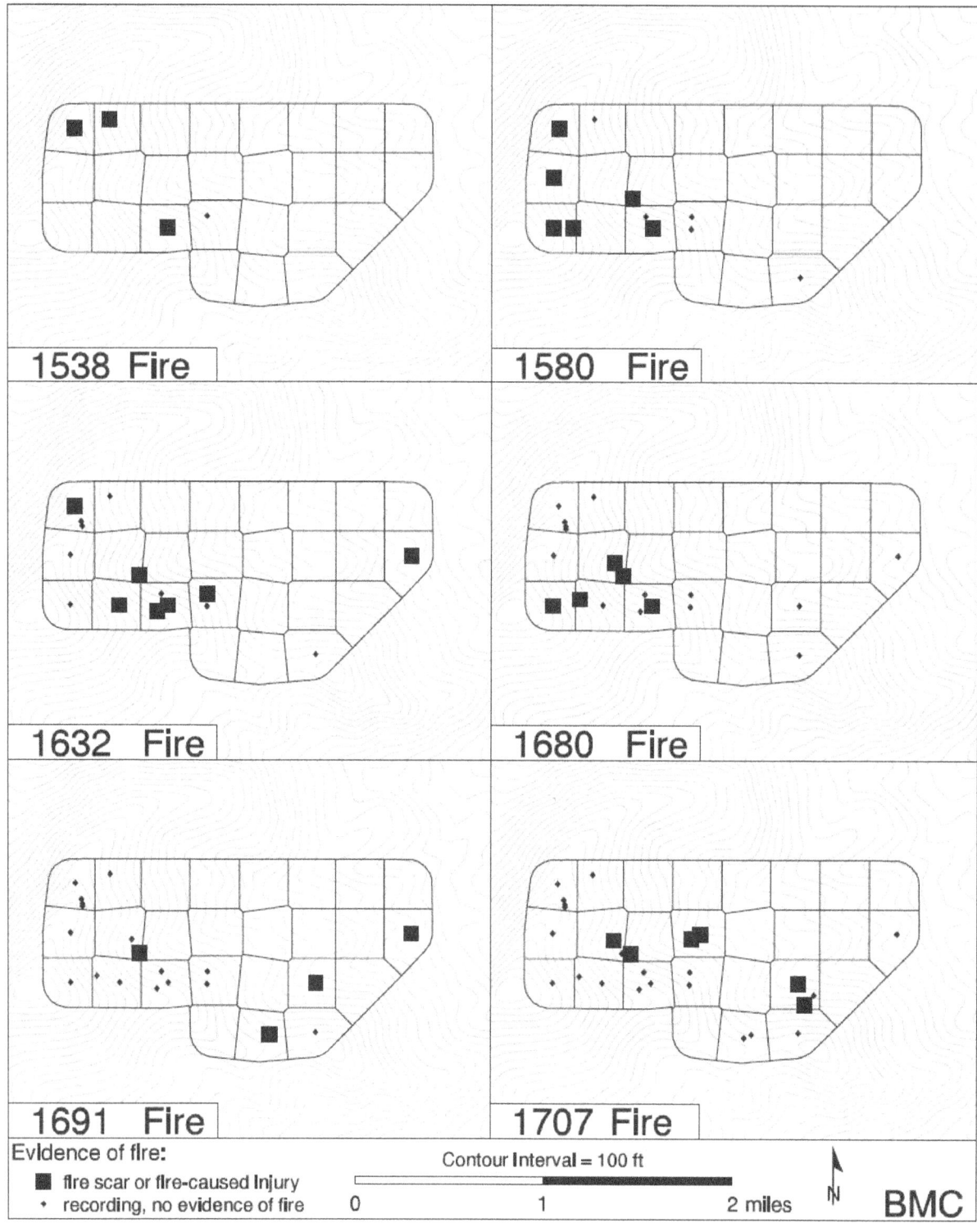

Figure F-12—Maps of years with evidence of low-severity fires in three or more cells at BMC. "Recording, no evidence of fire" indicates at least one tree was alive at that location during that year but did not have a fire scar or fire-caused injury. Empty cells indicate that no fire-scarred trees were recording in that cell during that year. Cohort dates are not mapped.

USDA Forest Service RMRS-GTR-261WWW. 2011.

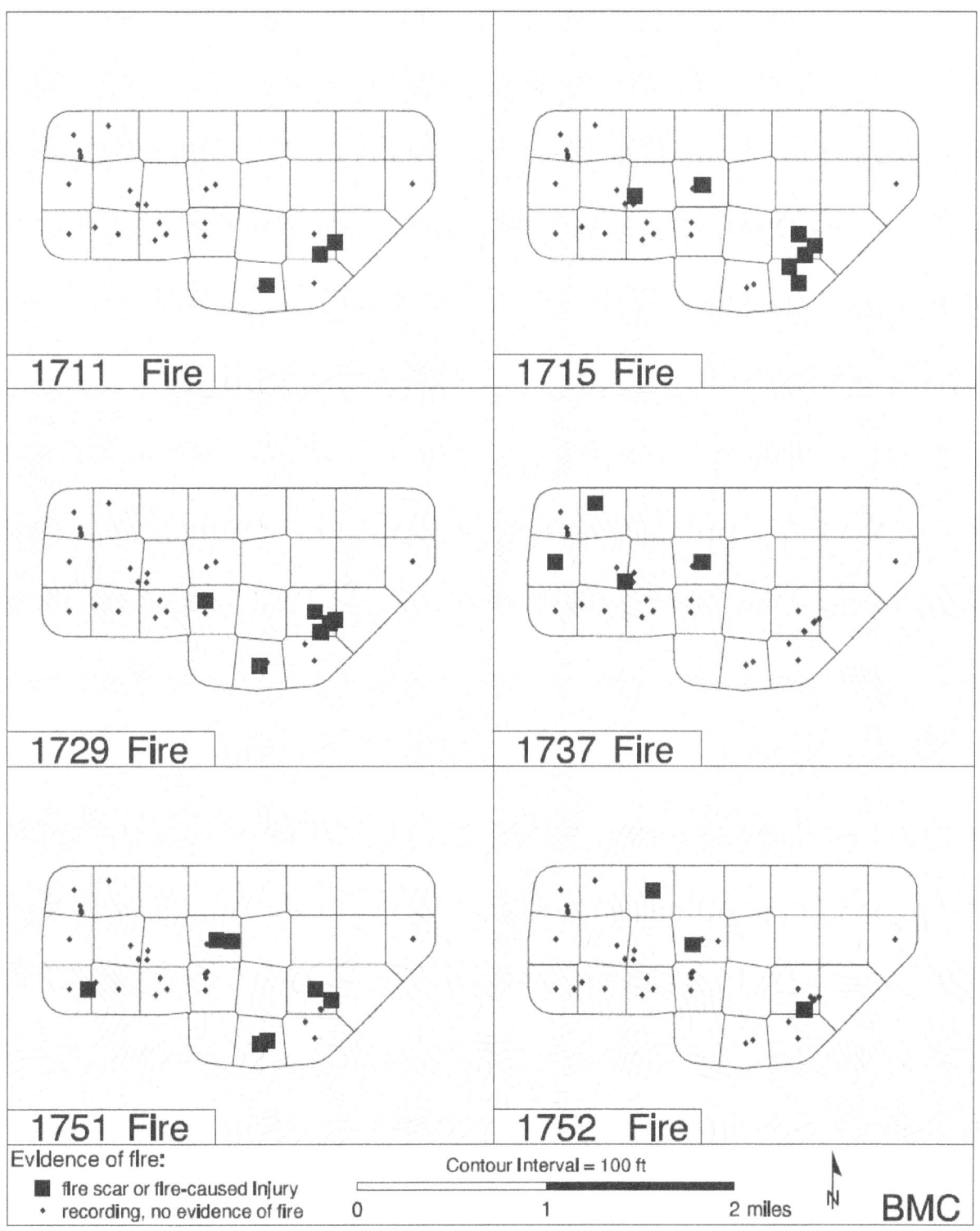

1711 Fire

1715 Fire

1729 Fire

1737 Fire

1751 Fire

1752 Fire

Evidence of fire:
■ fire scar or fire-caused injury
• recording, no evidence of fire

Contour Interval = 100 ft

0   1   2 miles

N

BMC

Figure F-12—*Continued.*

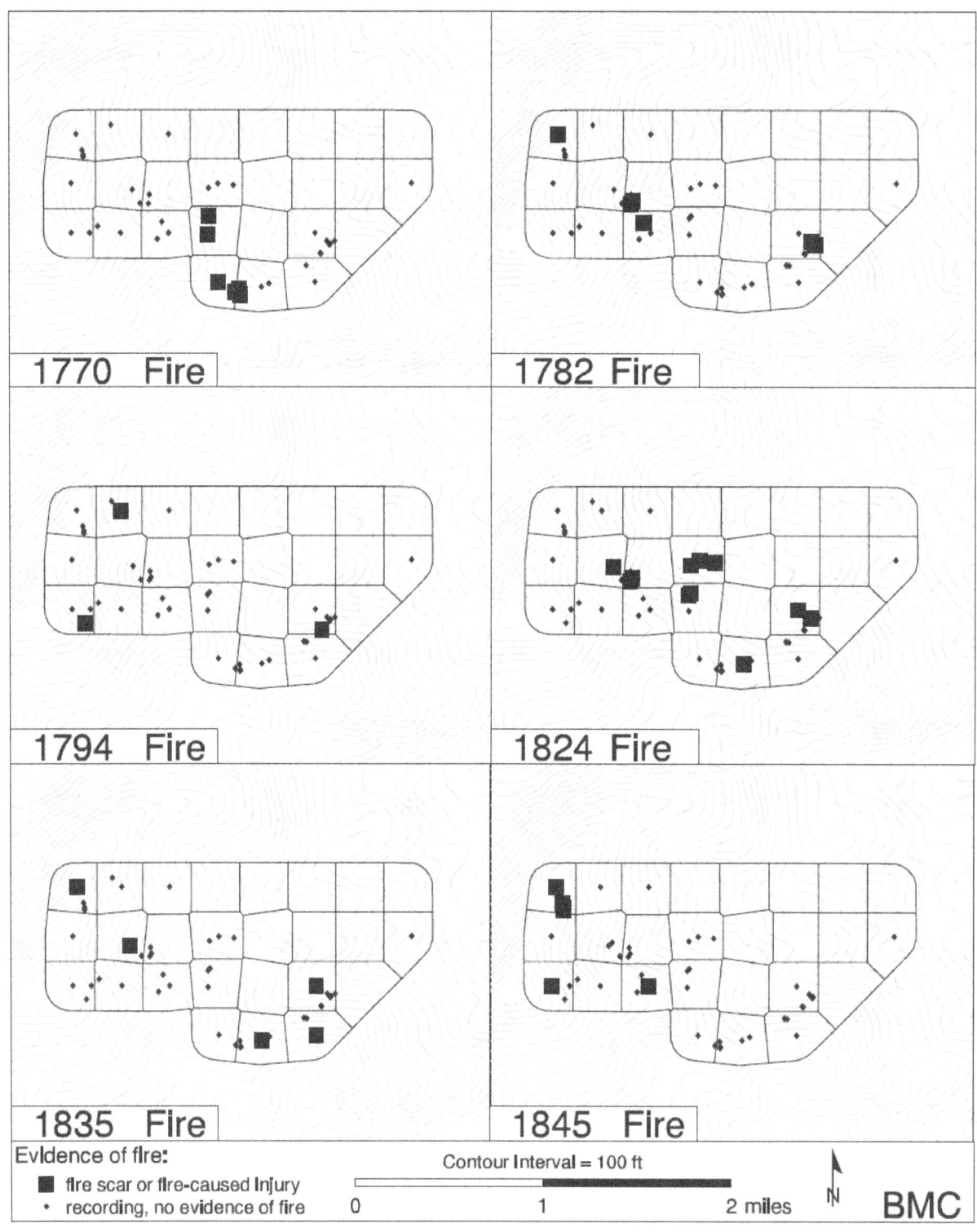

1770 Fire

1782 Fire

1794 Fire

1824 Fire

1835 Fire

1845 Fire

Evidence of fire:
- ■ fire scar or fire-caused injury
- ∙ recording, no evidence of fire

Contour Interval = 100 ft

0   1   2 miles

N

BMC

Figure F-12—*Continued.*

USDA Forest Service RMRS-GTR-261WWW. 2011.

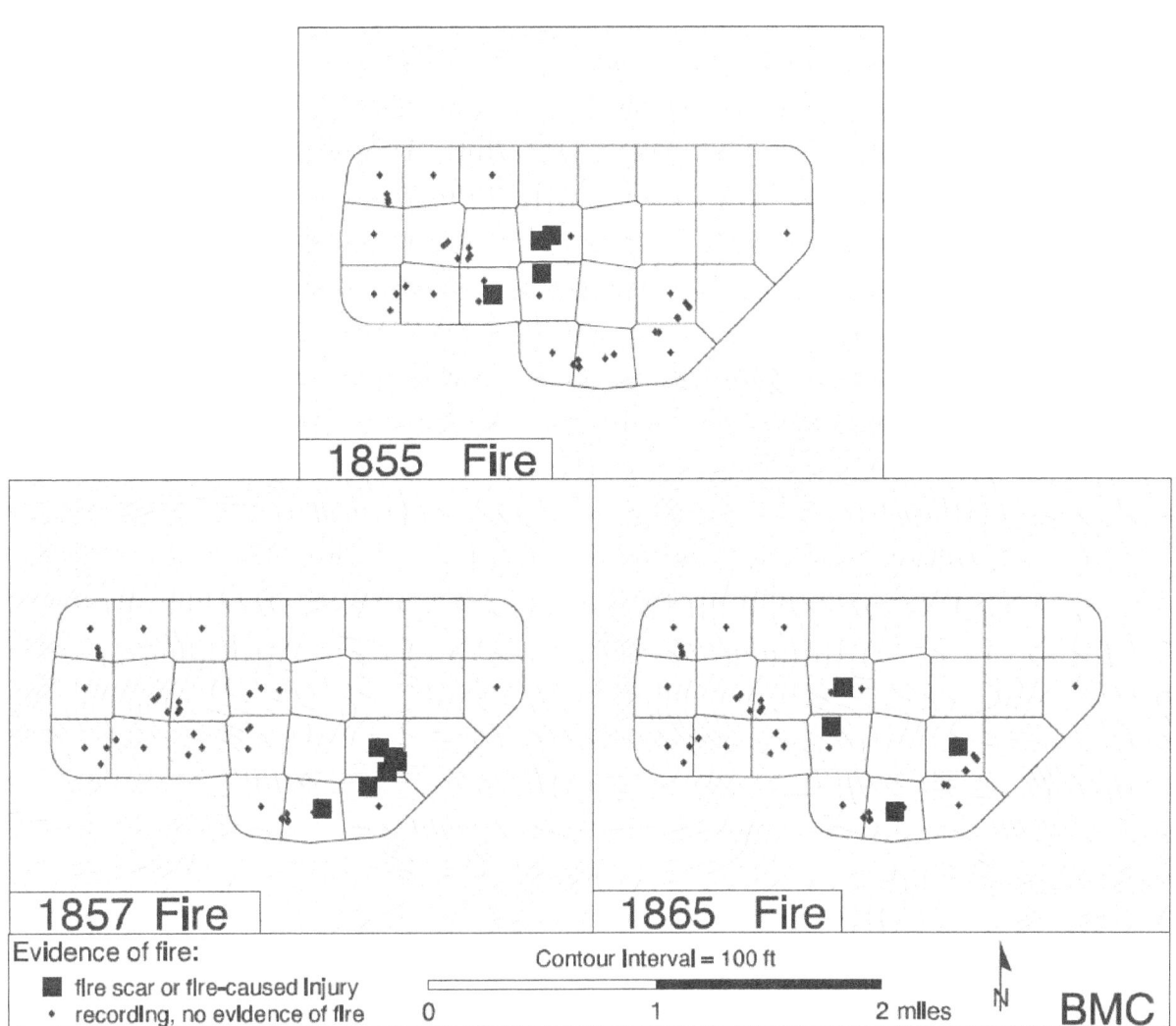

1855 Fire

1857 Fire

1865 Fire

Evidence of fire:
■ fire scar or fire-caused injury
• recording, no evidence of fire

Contour Interval = 100 ft

0   1   2 miles

N

BMC

Figure F-12—*Continued.*

Appendix G. Paunsaugunt Plateau, Dixie National Forest (PSG)

Topography

We sampled 29 plots over 2262 acres in Meadow and Pipeline Canyons on the Powell Ranger District of the Dixie National Forest in Kane County, Utah (figs. 1 and G-1). The plots were separated by 0.30 miles on average (range 0.23 to 0.33 miles) and averaged 0.69 acres in area (range 0.24 to 3.09 acres). Plots were sampled within cells that averaged 62 acres and ranged from 52 to 68 acres. Plots ranged in elevation from 7571 to 8972 ft (fig. G-2) and in slope from 4 to 75 percent. They were sampled on a range of aspects, but most were on south or east aspects (72 percent). The distribution of the plots by elevation, aspect, or slope differed from the distribution of the landscape by more than 10 percent only for moderate slopes, which were under sampled (fig. G-2). We took between three and four photographs each at five of the plots.

Tree Demography

Of the 844 trees that occurred in the plots, most (99 percent) were Utah juniper, Rocky Mountain juniper, ponderosa pine, white fir, Douglas-fir, quaking aspen, limber pine, or Engelmann spruce, but 9 Colorado pinyon trees also occurred plus 1 tree we could not identify (fig. G-3). Most of these trees were living (87 percent) and the rest were snags (6 percent), logs (2 percent), or stumps (5 percent). We were able to remove and crossdate wood samples from most of these trees (661 trees or 78 percent), and we obtained actual or estimated pith dates for 654 of them. These pith dates ranged from 1418 to 1974, but more than half of these post-dated 1900 (383 trees; fig. G-4). The death dates we obtained for 32 logs and snags ranged from 1939 to 2003.

Historical and Current Forest Structure and Composition

The plots included a range of historical and modern forest types (shrubland, pinyon-juniper, ponderosa pine, mixed conifer, aspen, and spruce-fir; table G-1). Nearly half the plots changed forest type between 1900 and 2000: nine shrubland, five ponderosa pine, and two aspen plots converted to mixed conifer. In 1900, tree density averaged 20 trees per acre and ranged from 0 to 81 trees per acre (fig. G-5). In 2000, tree density averaged 53 trees per acre and ranged from 6 to 121 trees per acre. However, we likely underestimated historical tree density because we could not obtain recruitment or earliest-ring dates for 183 of the 844 trees that occurred in the plots and only an earliest-ring date for another 7 trees. One of these had an earliest-ring date between 1901 and 1920 and therefore may have been living before 1900.

Fire Scars

We were able to remove and crossdate fire-scarred samples from 52 trees, 6 of which had only scars that were recorded on a single tree and so were excluded from further analyses. Of the remaining 46 trees, about 18 were sampled in 11 of the 29 plots at this site (1 to 3 trees per plot). We sampled the 28 other fire-scarred trees as we encountered them between plots over 1126 acres throughout the site (fig. G-6). Most of the 46 fire-scarred trees were ponderosa pine (76 percent) and the rest were Douglas-fir, limber pine, white fir, and Engelmann spruce. Most were logs, snags, or stumps (67 percent) and the rest were live trees. These 46 trees yielded 147 fire scars and 11 eroded fire scars or abrupt changes in ring width (figs. G-4 and G-7). However, six of these scar dates were eliminated from further analyses because they were recorded on only a single tree at the site. We were able to assign an intra-ring position to 81 percent of the 134 fire scars that occurred during the analysis period (1650 to 1900). Of the scars that occurred on ponderosa pine trees, over half (62 percent) occurred on the boundary between two rings (fig. G-8).

Post-Fire Cohorts

We identified 16 cohorts of trees from estimated recruitment dates at 15 of the plots. Eight of these cohorts were recruited before 1900 (1809 to 1897) and were identified from 58 trees (5 to 15 trees per cohort) composed of white fir (41 percent), ponderosa pine (24 percent), Rocky Mountain juniper (13 percent), limber pine (10 percent), and Douglas-fir (10 percent; figs. G-4 and G-7). The cohorts recruited before 1900 occurred in plots with a range of forest types: mixed conifer (38 percent of cohorts), aspen (25 percent), shrubland (25 percent), and ponderosa pine (13 percent).

Spatial Variation in Fire Regimes

We reconstructed too few fire intervals in plots during the analysis period (1650 to 1900) to compute plot-composite fire intervals by forest type at this site. The tree-ring record before 1900 was less than 100 years long for 12 of the 29 plots (fig. G-9).

We inferred that one shrubland plot did not sustain fire over the period of record (table G-2). Four plots were not historically forested, and we could not infer historical fire severity at four others because they did not meet our requirements for any of the severity categories. We assigned the remaining plots to the low, mixed, or high fire severity categories.

From 1650 to 1900, the 26 low-severity fires we reconstructed within our 2262-acre sampling area averaged 213 acres and ranged from 62 to 743 acres (fig. G-10), equivalent to 8 to 74 percent of the recording area (in other words, the combined area of cells containing recording, fire-scarred trees during a given year). Recording area varied among fire years, ranging from 244 to 1001 acres. We likely underestimated the extent of low-severity fires because most fires intersected the boundary of the site (fig. G-11).

Table G-1—Distribution of plots at PSG by historical (1860) and modern (2000) forest types (table 2).

Historical forest type (1860)	Modern forest type (2000)				Total plots in 1860
	Spruce-fir	Mixed conifer	Ponderosa pine	Pinyon-juniper	
Spruce-fir	2				2
Aspen		2			2
Mixed conifer		8			8
Ponderosa pine		5	2		7
Pinyon-juniper				1	1
Shrubland		9			9
Total plots in 2000	**2**	**24**	**2**	**1**	**29**

Table G-2—Distribution of plots at PSG by historical forest type (1860; table 2) and fire severity (table 3).

Forest type	High	Assumed high	Mixed	Assumed mixed	Low	Assumed no fire	Not historically forested	Unclassified
Spruce-fir		2						
Aspen	2							
Mixed conifer	1	1	2	3	1			
Ponderosa pine			1	2	2		1	1
Pinyon-juniper								1
Shrubland			2	1		1	3	2
Total	**3**	**3**	**5**	**6**	**3**	**1**	**4**	**4**

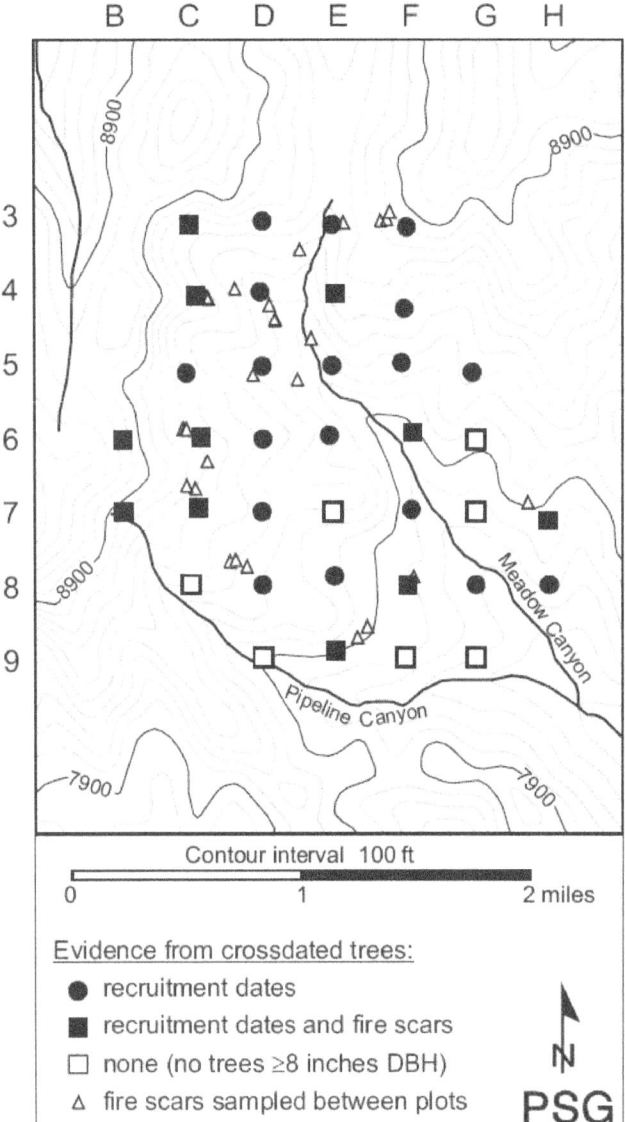

Figure G-1—Locations of plots and crossdated fire-scarred trees that were sampled outside of plots. About one-third of the fire-scarred trees were sampled within plots and are not mapped individually. Plots are identified by column and row, in other words, the northwestern most plot is 3C, the next plot to the east is 3D, and so forth.

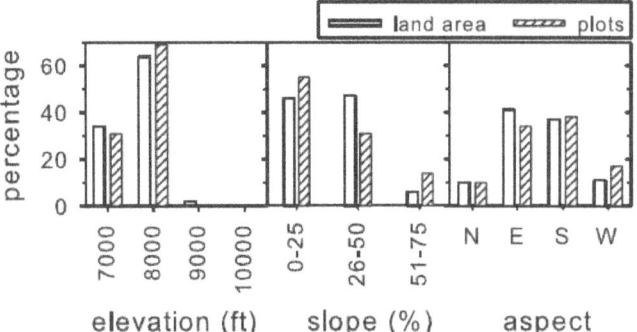

Figure G-2—Distribution of sampled plots and land area at PSG by topography. Aspect classes are 90° wide, beginning with 46° for east (E). Land area was derived from a digital elevation model (Utah AGRC 2004).

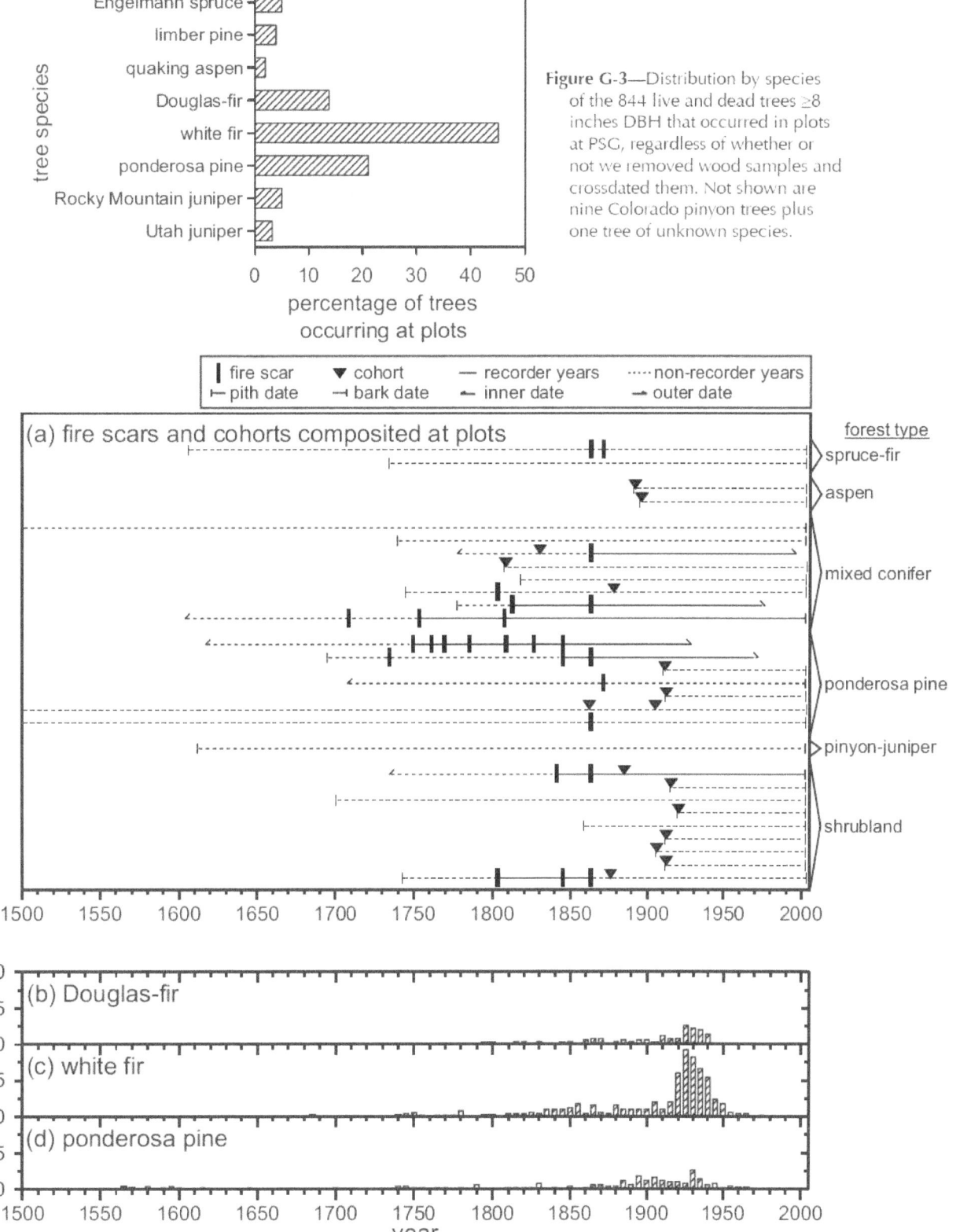

Figure G-3—Distribution by species of the 844 live and dead trees ≥8 inches DBH that occurred in plots at PSG, regardless of whether or not we removed wood samples and crossdated them. Not shown are nine Colorado pinyon trees plus one tree of unknown species.

Figure G-4—Chronologies of fire and tree recruitment at PSG. In (a), horizontal lines are plot-composite fire-scar and cohort dates by forest type. Non-recorder years precede the first scar, whereas recorder years generally follow it, but non-recorder years can also occur when the catface margin is consumed by subsequent fires or rot. In (b) through (d), recruitment dates are given for species comprising ≥10 percent of trees with such dates. The latter part of the distribution is incomplete because we only cored trees that were ≥8 inches DBH.

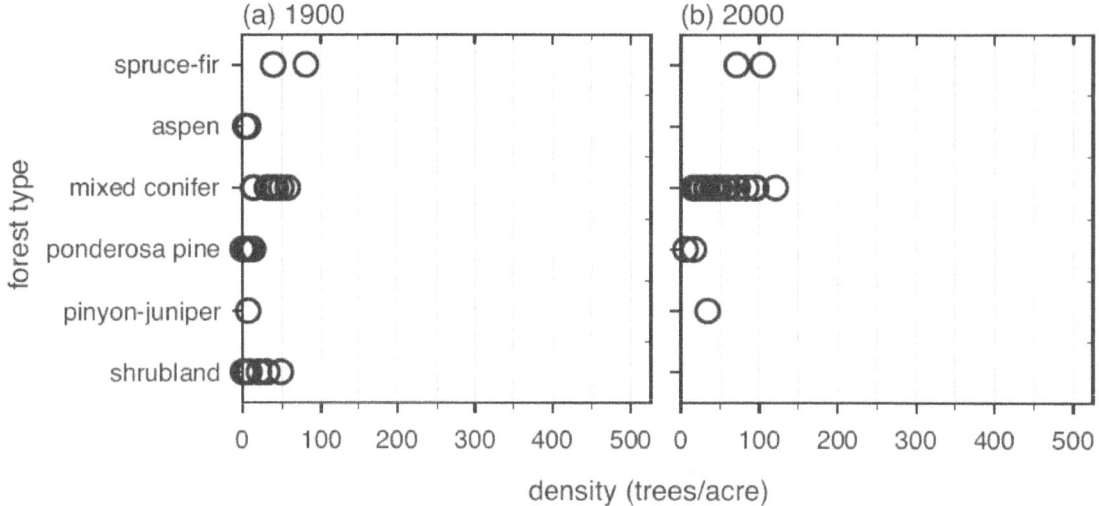

Figure G-5—Density of trees ≥8 inches DBH that were alive at each plot at PSG (a) in 1900 and (b) in 2000, by forest type (table 2).

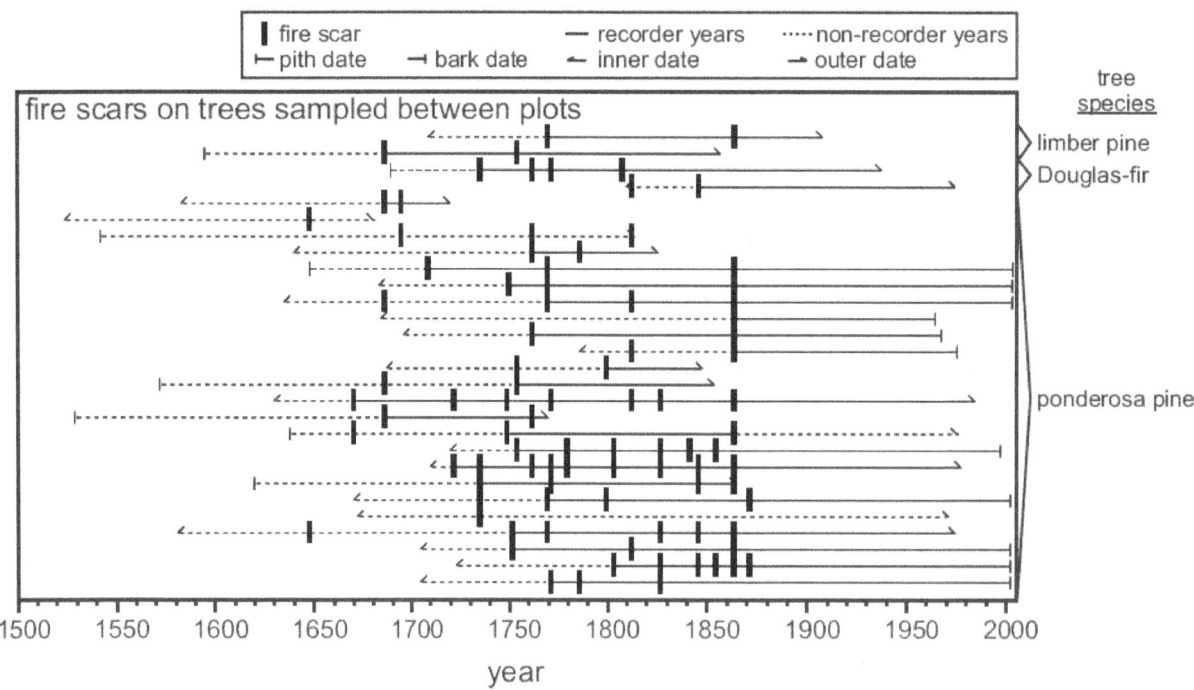

Figure G-6—Chronology of low-severity fires recorded on the 28 trees sampled between plots over approximately, 1126 acres throughout the PSG site.

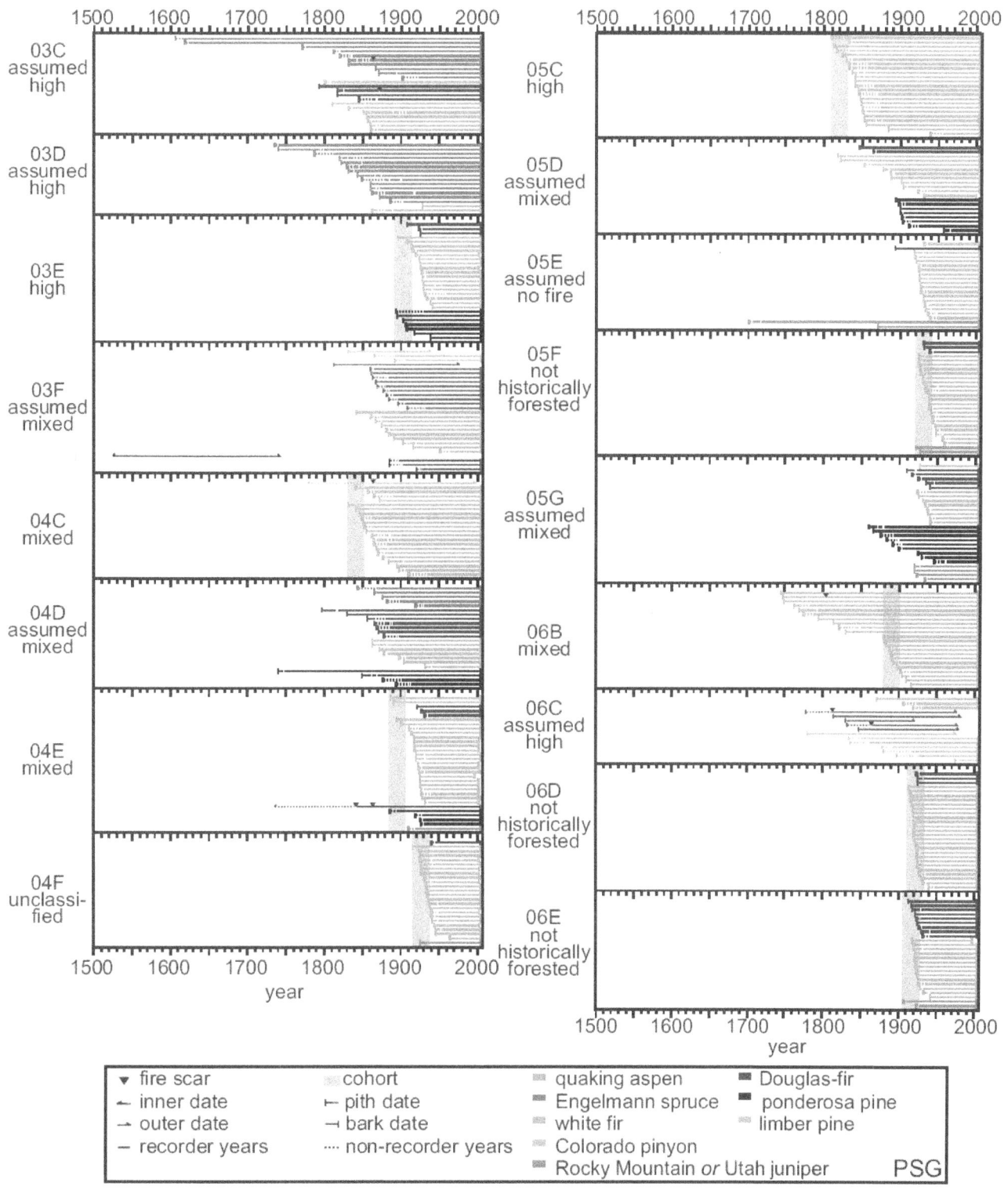

Figure G-7—Fire-demography diagrams (FDDs, Brown and others 2008b) showing chronologies of tree demography (recruitment and death), fire scars, and cohorts at each plot. Bark dates on 34 stumps are shown as outer dates. Not shown are 28 fire-scarred trees sampled between plots. Inferred fire severity (table 3) is indicated to the left of each panel. Most of the trees (81 percent) in the combined Rocky Mountain and Utah juniper category are Rocky Mountain juniper.

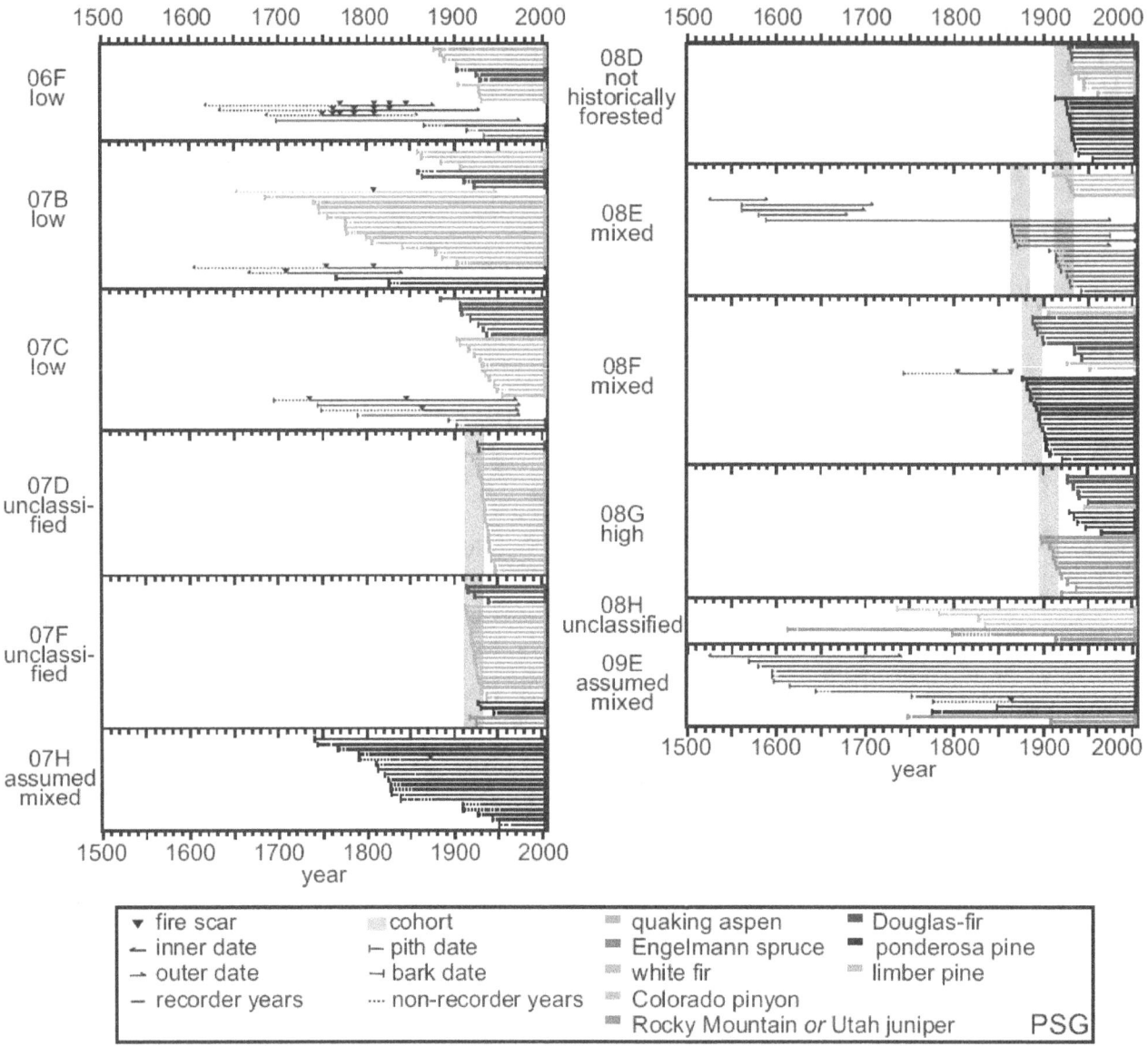

Figure G-7—*Continued.*

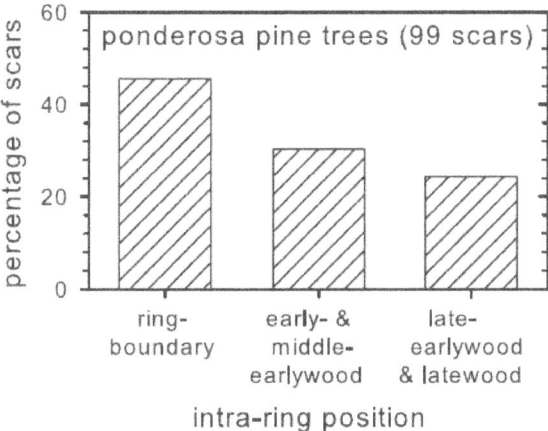

Figure G-8—Intra-ring position of fire scars sampled in and between plots at PSG from 1650 to 1900, as a percentage of the number of scars for which the position could be determined (given in parentheses). Not shown are intra-ring positions for nine fire scars on white fir, Douglas-fir, and limber pine trees.

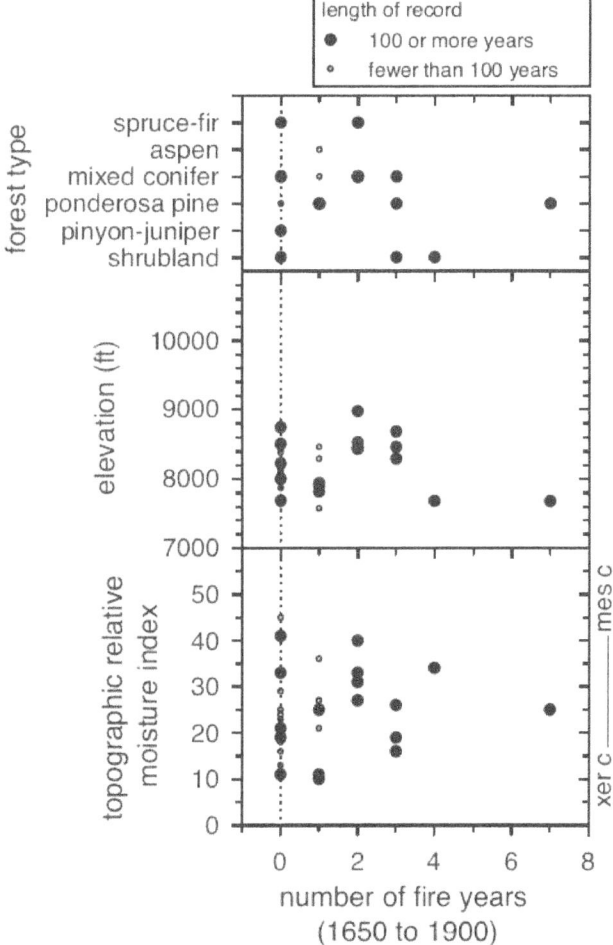

Figure G-9—Variation in fire among plots at PSG with topography, forest type, and relative soil moisture availability (Parker 1982). Number of fire years includes both fire-scar and cohort dates. Plots with no reconstructed fires during this period fall on the dotted line.

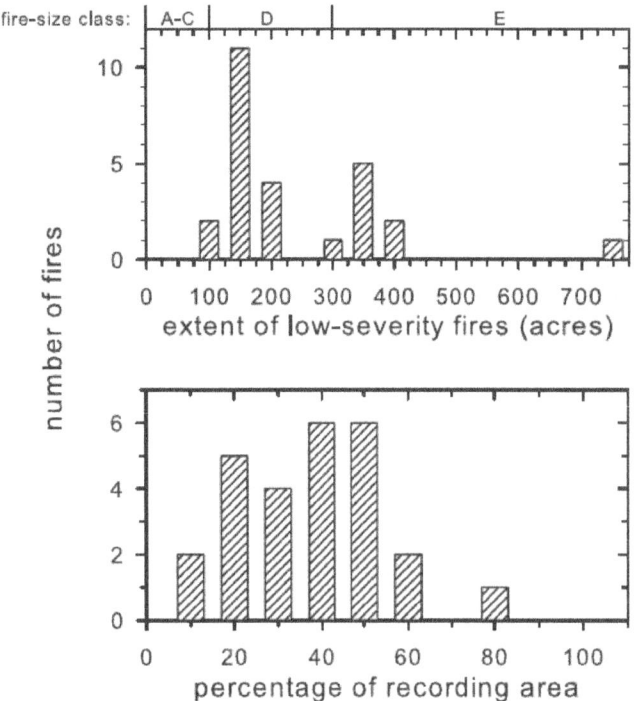

Figure G-10—Relative extent of low-severity fires within the 2262-acre PSG site, from 1650 to 1900, as area (top) and as a percentage of the recording area (in other words, the combined area of cells containing recording, fire-scarred trees during each year; bottom). Commonly used fire-size classes are indicated at the top (NWCG 2007).

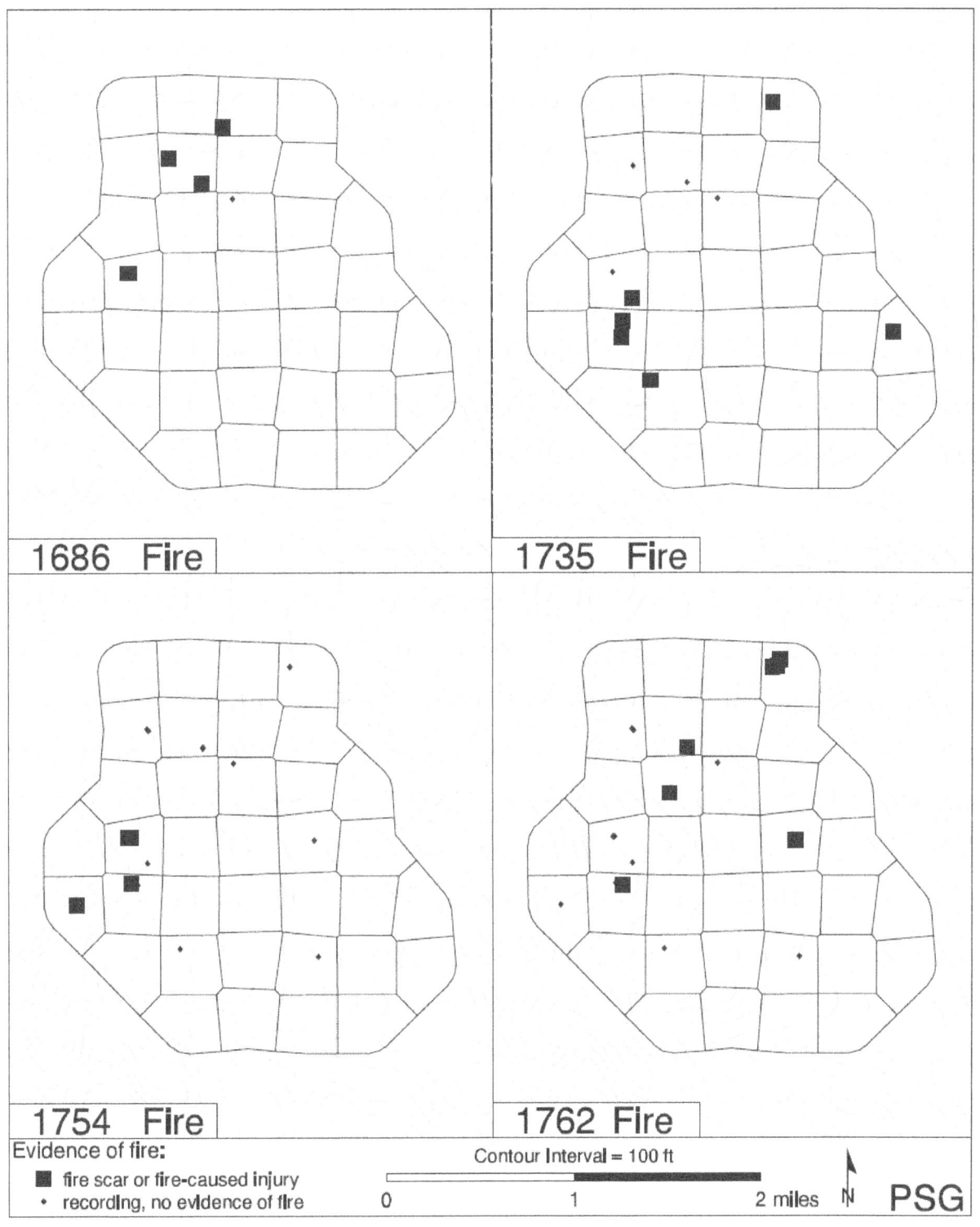

Figure G-11—Maps of years with evidence of low-severity fires in three or more cells at PSG. "Recording, no evidence of fire" indicates at least one tree was alive at that location during that year but did not have a fire scar or fire-caused injury. Empty cells indicate that no fire-scarred trees were recording in that cell during that year. Cohort dates are not mapped.

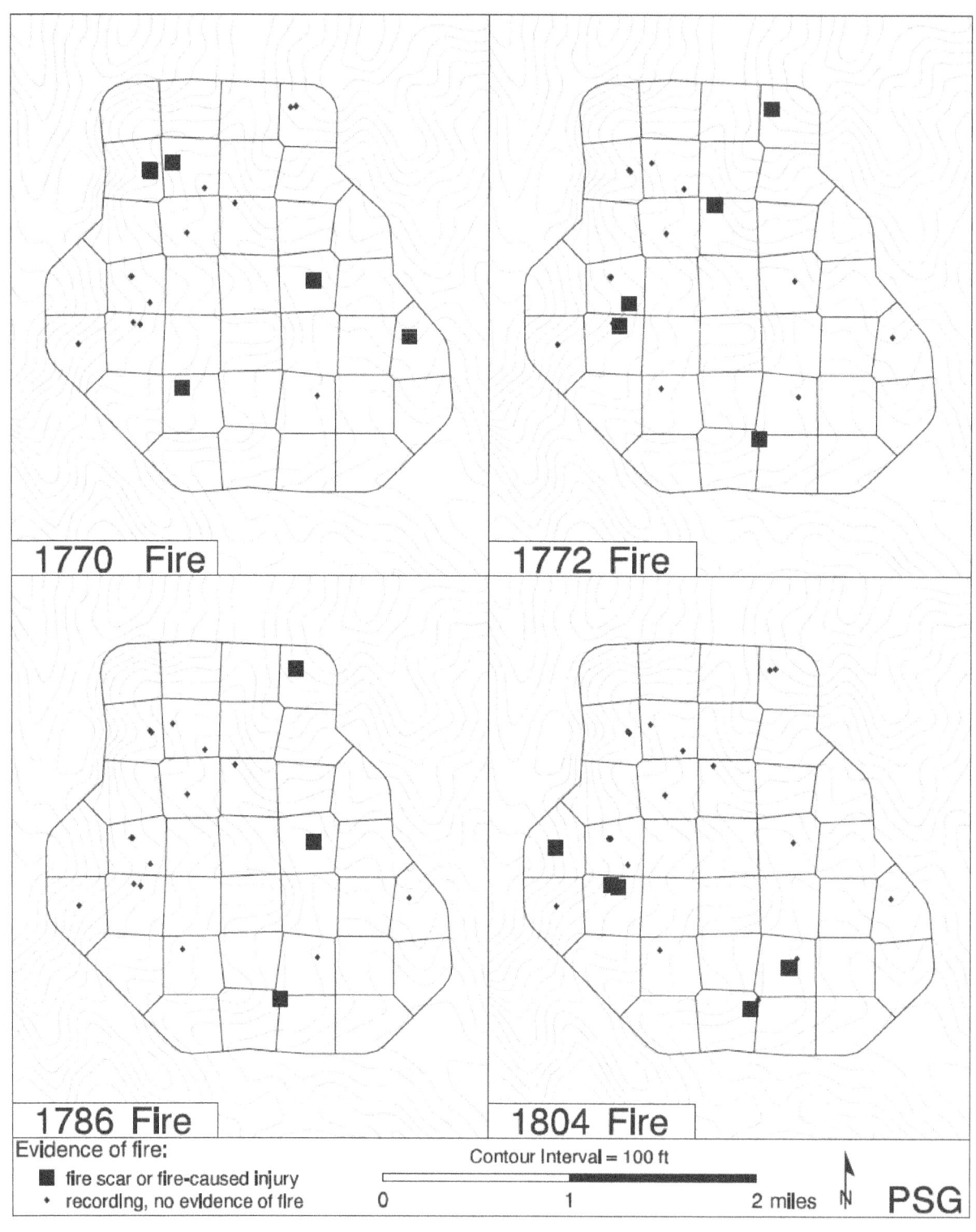

1770 Fire

1772 Fire

1786 Fire

1804 Fire

Evidence of fire:
■ fire scar or fire-caused injury
• recording, no evidence of fire

Contour Interval = 100 ft

0   1   2 miles   N   PSG

Figure G-11—*Continued*.

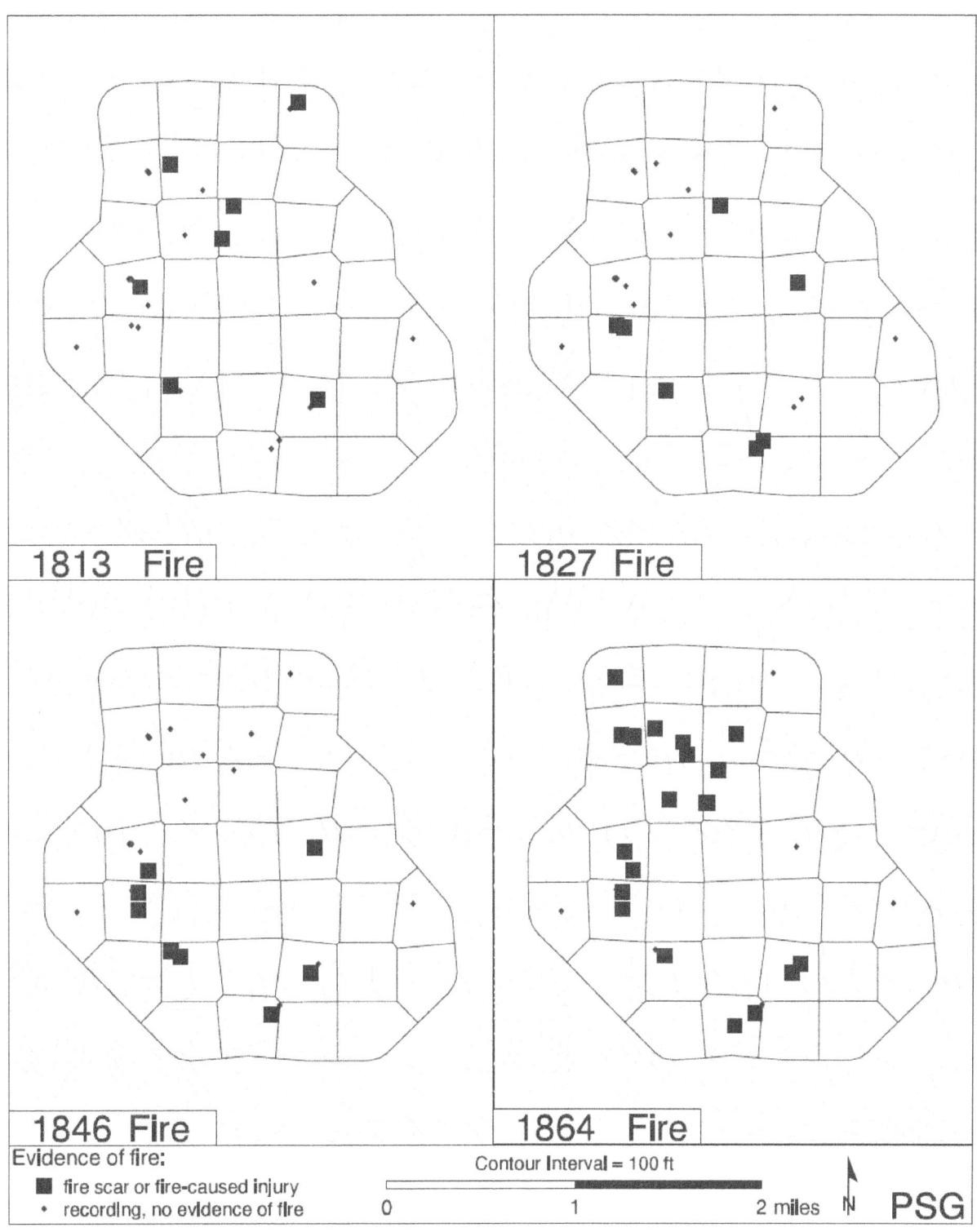

1813 Fire

1827 Fire

1846 Fire

1864 Fire

Evidence of fire:
■ fire scar or fire-caused injury
• recording, no evidence of fire

Contour Interval = 100 ft

0   1   2 miles   N   PSG

Figure G-11—*Continued.*

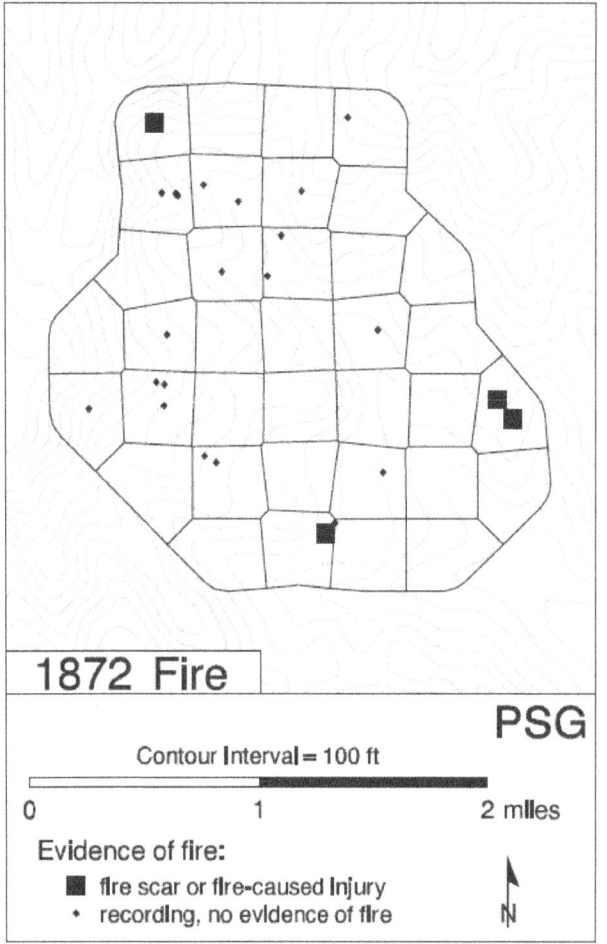

1872 Fire

PSG

Contour Interval = 100 ft

0   1   2 miles

Evidence of fire:
■ fire scar or fire-caused injury
• recording, no evidence of fire

N

Figure G-11—*Continued.*

Appendix H. Boulder Mountain, Dixie National Forest (BOM)

Topography

We sampled 30 plots over 1963 acres near Spring Creek on the Teasdale Ranger District of the Dixie National Forest in Wayne County, Utah (figs. 1 and H-1). The plots were separated by 0.31 miles on average (range 0.27 to 0.31 miles) and averaged 0.35 acres in area (range 0.08 to 0.90 acres). Plots were sampled within cells that averaged 65 acres and ranged from 58 to 74 acres. Plots ranged in elevation from 7887 to 11,071 ft (fig. H-2) and in slope from 0 to 47 percent. They were sampled on a range of aspects, but most were on north and east aspects (77 percent). The distribution of the plots by elevation, aspect, or slope did not differ from the distribution of the landscape by more than 10 percent in any category except gentle and moderate slopes, which were under and over sampled, respectively (fig. H-2). We took four photographs each at three of the plots.

Tree Demography

All of the 892 trees that occurred in the plots were Utah juniper, Colorado pinyon, Rocky Mountain juniper, ponderosa pine, Douglas-fir, quaking aspen, subalpine fir, or Engelmann spruce (fig. H-3). Most of these trees were living (75 percent) and the rest were snags (11 percent), logs (7 percent), or stumps (8 percent). We were able to remove and crossdate wood samples from most of these trees (788 trees or 88 percent), and we obtained actual or estimated pith dates for 696 of these. These pith dates ranged from 1346 to 1971 and many of these post-dated 1900 (244 trees; fig. H-4). The death dates we obtained for 117 logs and snags ranged from 1510 to 2004.

Historical and Current Forest Structure and Composition

The plots included a range of historical and modern forest types (pinyon-juniper, ponderosa pine, mixed conifer, aspen-mixed conifer, aspen, and spruce-fir; table H-1). Some plots changed forest type between 1860 and 2000: one ponderosa pine and two aspen plots converted to aspen-mixed conifer. In 1900, tree density averaged 86 trees per acre and ranged from 2 to 290 trees per acre (fig. H-5). In 2000, tree density averaged 110 trees per acre and ranged from 19 to 322 trees per acre. However, we likely underestimated historical tree density because we could not obtain recruitment or earliest-ring dates for 104 of the 892 trees that occurred in the plots and only an earliest-ring date for another 92 trees. Twelve of these trees had earliest-ring dates between 1901 and 1920 and therefore may have been living before 1900.

Fire Scars

We were able to remove and crossdate fire-scarred samples from 104 trees, 9 of which had only scars that were recorded on a single tree and so were excluded from further analyses. Of the remaining 95 trees, most (68 trees) were sampled in 22 of the 30 plots at this site (1 to 7 trees per plot, average 3 trees). We sampled the 27 other fire-scarred trees as we encountered them between plots over 1344 acres throughout the site (fig. H-6). Most of the 95 fire-scarred trees were ponderosa pine (60 percent) or Engelmann spruce (20 percent) and the rest were Douglas-fir, Colorado pinyon, quaking aspen, and Utah juniper. Most were logs, snags or stumps (80 percent) and the rest were live trees. These 95 trees yielded 441 fire scars and 3 eroded fire scars or abrupt changes in ring width (figs. H-4 and H-7). However, 10 of these scar dates were eliminated from further analyses because they were recorded on only a single tree at the site. We were able to assign an intra-ring position to 60 percent of the 380 fire scars that occurred during the analysis period (1650 to 1900). Of the scars that occurred on ponderosa pine trees, many (42 percent) occurred in the early- or middle-earlywood (fig. H-8).

Post-Fire Cohorts

We identified 19 cohorts of trees from estimated recruitment dates at 17 of the plots. Sixteen of these cohorts were recruited before 1900 (1605 to 1875) and were identified from 112 trees (5 to 11 trees per cohort), most of which were quaking aspen (35 percent), Engelmann spruce (29 percent), ponderosa pine (24 percent), or Douglas-fir (6 percent), but there were also a few Utah juniper, Colorado pinyon, and Rocky Mountain juniper (figs. H-4 and H-7). The cohorts that were recruited before 1900 occurred in plots with a range of forest types: spruce-fir (44 percent of cohorts), pinyon-juniper (6 percent of cohorts) and ponderosa pine, mixed conifer, aspen-mixed conifer, and aspen forest types (each 13 percent of cohorts).

Spatial Variation in Fire Regimes

During the analysis period (1650 to 1900), plot-composite, low-severity fire intervals averaged 26 years (range 7 to 26 years) when pooled among pinyon-juniper plots; 16 years (range 1 to 64 years) when pooled among ponderosa pine plots; 30 years (range 5 to 110 years) when pooled among mixed conifer plots; and 13 years (range 3 to 40 years) when pooled among aspen plots (fig. H-9). More fires occurred in mixed conifer, ponderosa pine, and pinyon-juniper plots than in spruce-fir, aspen, and aspen-mixed conifer plots (fig. H-10). The tree-ring record before 1900 was less than 100 years long for 4 of the 30 plots at this site.

We inferred that one ponderosa pine plot did not sustain fire over the period of record (table H-2). We could not infer historical fire severity at two plots because they did not meet our requirements for any of the severity categories. We assigned the remaining plots to the low, mixed, or high fire severity categories.

From 1650 to 1900, the 50 low-severity fires we reconstructed within our 1963-acre sampling area averaged 258 acres and ranged from 62 to 795 acres (fig. H-11), equivalent to 5 to 75 percent of the recording area (in other words, the combined area of cells containing recording, fire-scarred trees during a given year). Recording area varied among fire years, ranging from 784 to 1453 acres. We likely underestimated the extent of low-severity fires because most fires intersected the boundary of the site (fig. H-12).

Table H-1—Distribution of plots at BOM by historical (1860) and modern (2000) forest types (table 2).

Historical forest type (1860)	Modern forest type (2000)						
	Spruce-fir	Aspen	Aspen-mixed conifer	Mixed conifer	Ponderosa pine	Pinyon-juniper	Total plots in 1860
Spruce-fir	6						6
Aspen		1	2				3
Aspen-mixed conifer			3				3
Mixed conifer				6			6
Ponderosa pine			1		7		8
Pinyon-juniper						4	4
Total plots in 2000	**6**	**1**	**6**	**6**	**7**	**4**	**30**

Table H-2—Distribution of plots at BOM by historical forest type (1860; table 2) and fire severity (table 3).

Forest type	High	Assumed high	Mixed	Assumed mixed	Low	Assumed no fire	Unclassified
Spruce-fir	1		4		1		
Aspen	2	1					
Aspen-mixed conifer			2		1		
Mixed conifer			2	2	2		
Ponderosa pine			2	1	4	1	
Pinyon-juniper			1		1		2
Total	3	1	11	3	9	1	2

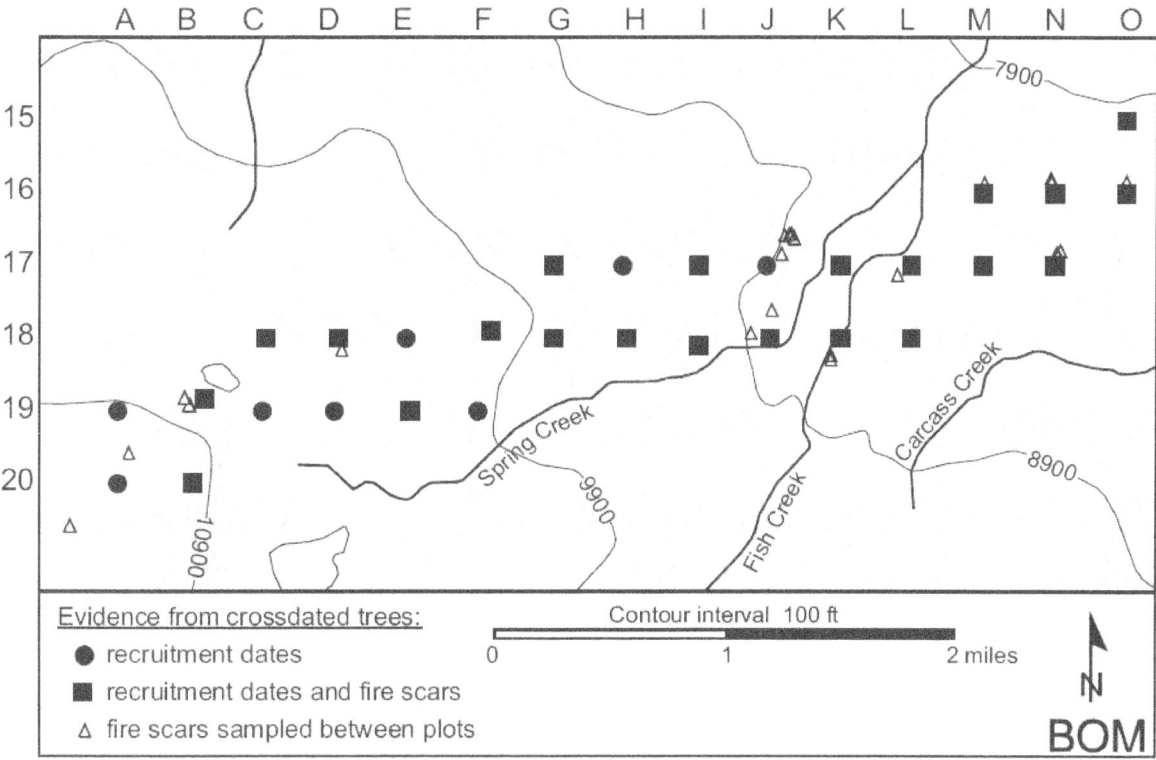

Figure H-1—Locations of plots and crossdated fire-scarred trees that were sampled outside of plots. About three-fourths of the fire-scarred trees were sampled within plots and are not mapped individually. Plots are identified by column and row, in other words, the southwestern most plot is 20A, the next plot to the east is 20B, and so forth.

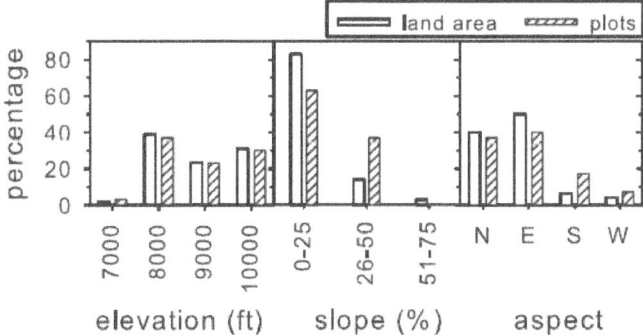

Figure H-2—Distribution of sampled plots and land area at BOM by topography. Aspect classes are 90° wide, beginning with 46° for east (E). Land area was derived from a digital elevation model (Utah AGRC 2004). Five percent of the land area and 7 percent of the plots were sampled above 11,000 ft and are not shown here.

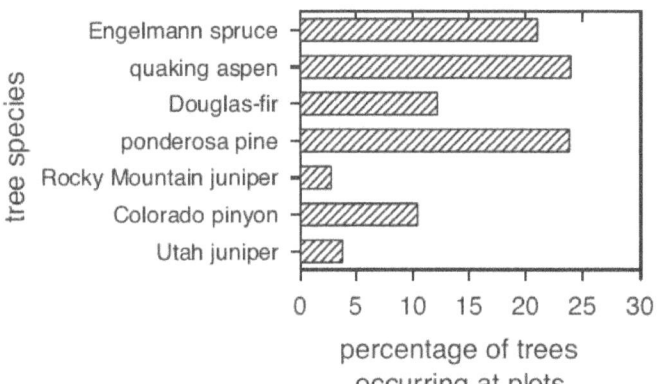

Figure H-3—Distribution by species of the 892 live and dead trees ≥8 inches DBH that occurred in plots at BOM, regardless of whether or not we removed wood samples and crossdated them. Not shown are 16 subalpine fir trees.

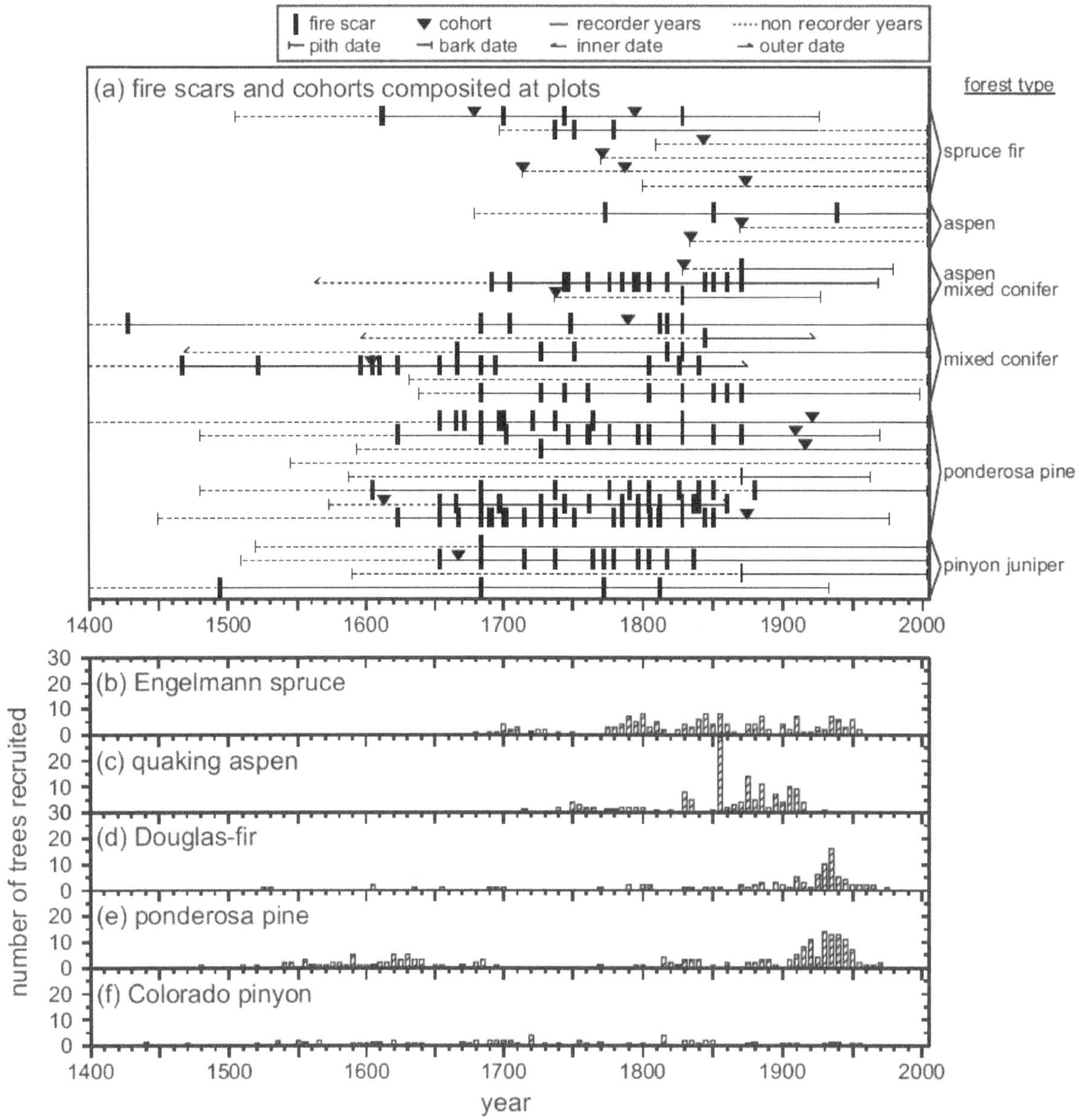

| fire scar | ▼ cohort | — recorder years | ······ non recorder years |
| ⊢ pith date | ⊣ bark date | ⊢ inner date | → outer date |

(a) fire scars and cohorts composited at plots

forest type
- spruce fir
- aspen
- aspen mixed conifer
- mixed conifer
- ponderosa pine
- pinyon juniper

1400   1500   1600   1700   1800   1900   2000

(b) Engelmann spruce

(c) quaking aspen

(d) Douglas-fir

(e) ponderosa pine

(f) Colorado pinyon

number of trees recruited

1400   1500   1600   1700   1800   1900   2000

year

Figure H-4—Chronologies of fire and tree recruitment at BOM. In (a), horizontal lines are plot-composite fire-scar and cohort dates by forest type. Non-recorder years precede the first scar, whereas recorder years generally follow it, but non-recorder years can also occur when the catface margin is consumed by subsequent fires or rot. In (b) through (f), recruitment dates are given for species comprising ≥10 percent of trees with such dates. The latter part of the distribution is incomplete because we only cored trees that were ≥8 inches DBH.

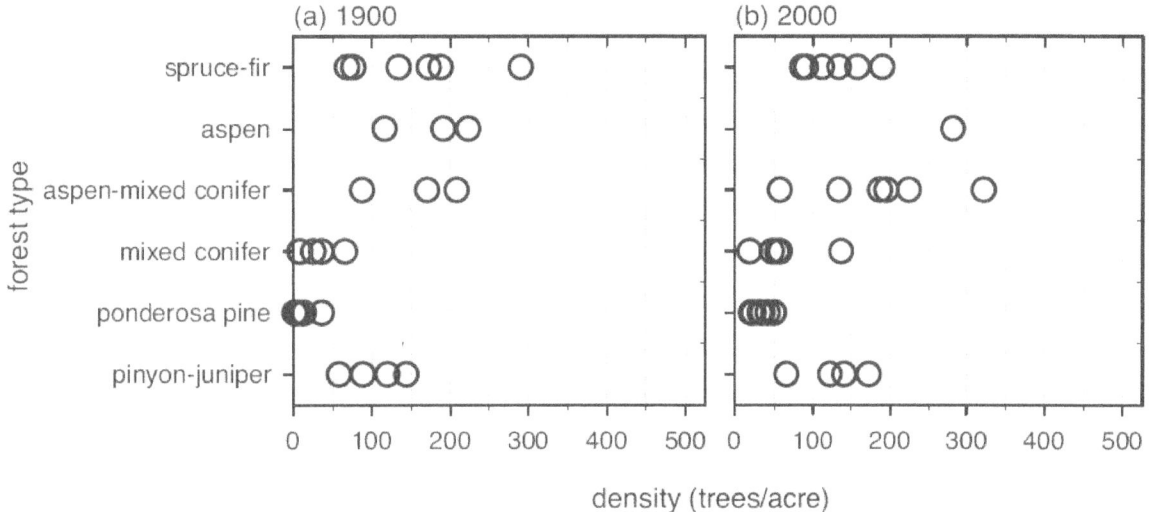

Figure H-5—Density of trees ≥8 inches DBH that were alive at each plot at BOM (a) in 1900 and (b) in 2000, by forest type (table 2).

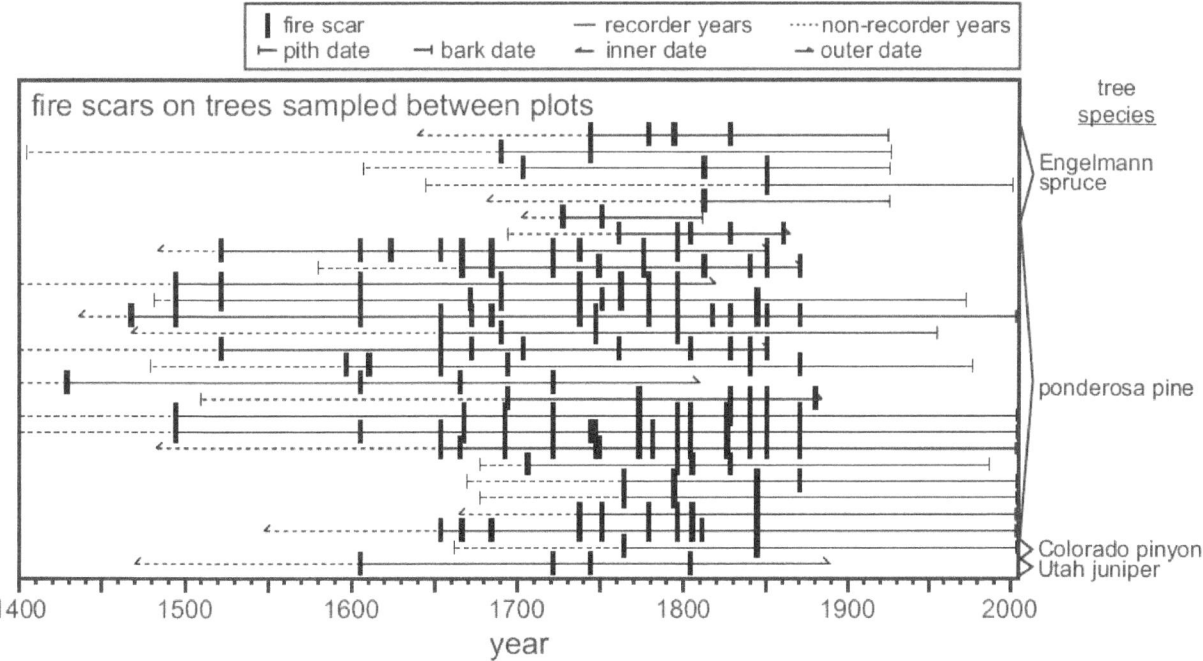

Figure H-6—Chronology of low-severity fires recorded on the 27 trees sampled between plots over approximately 1344 acres throughout the BOM site.

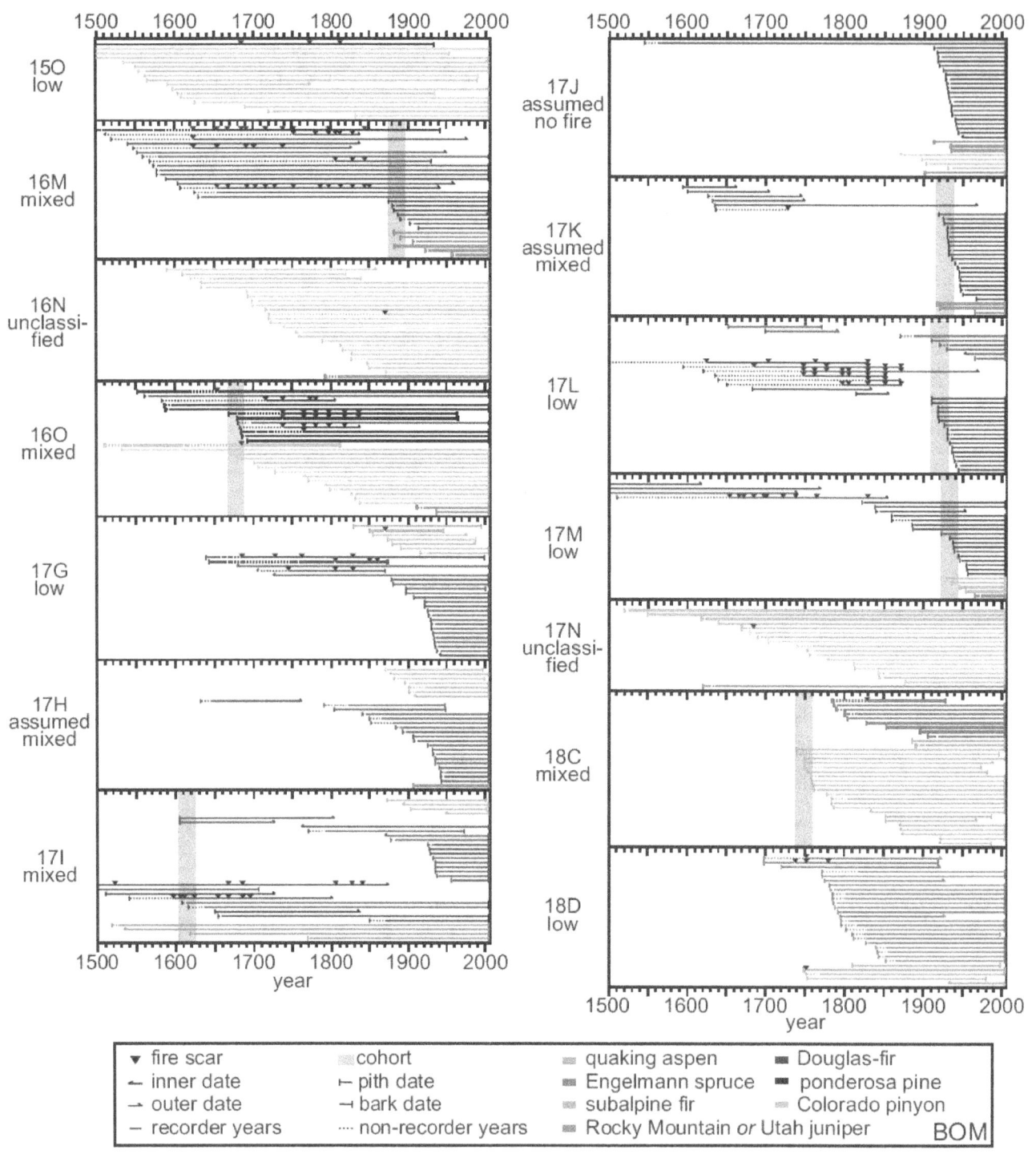

Figure H-7—Fire-demography diagrams (FDDs, Brown and others 2008b) showing chronologies of tree demography (recruitment and death), fire scars, and cohorts at each plot. Bark dates on 73 stumps are shown as outer dates. Not shown are 27 fire-scarred trees sampled between plots. Inferred fire severity (table 3) is indicated to the left of each panel. Most of the trees (74 percent) in the combined Rocky Mountain and Utah juniper category are Utah juniper.

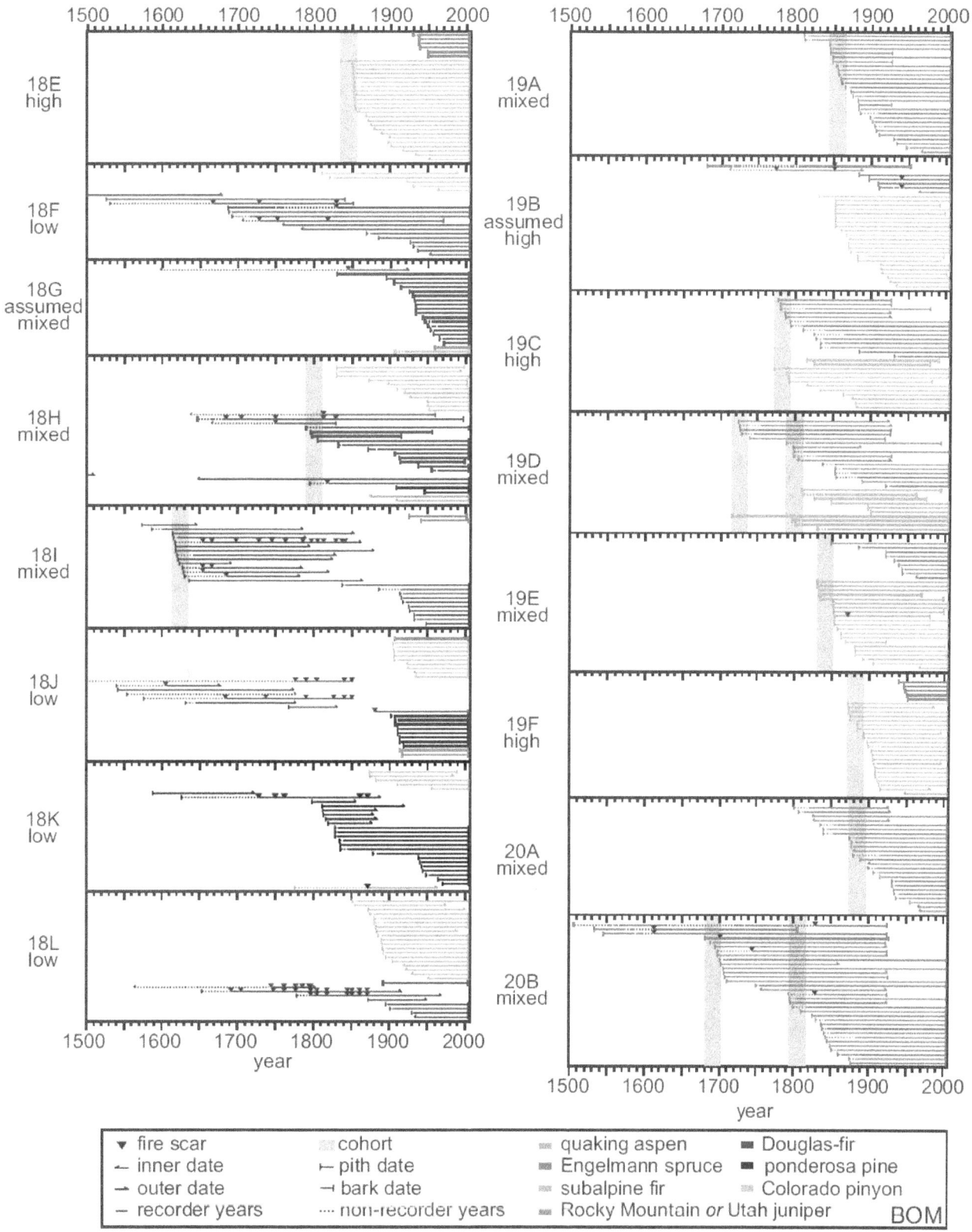

Figure H-7—*Continued.*

Figure H-8—Intra-ring position of fire scars sampled in and between plots at BOM from 1650 to 1900, as a percentage of the number of scars for which the position could be determined (given in parentheses). Not shown are intra-ring positions for 36 fire scars on Utah juniper, Colorado pinyon, Douglas-fir, aspen, and Engelmann spruce trees.

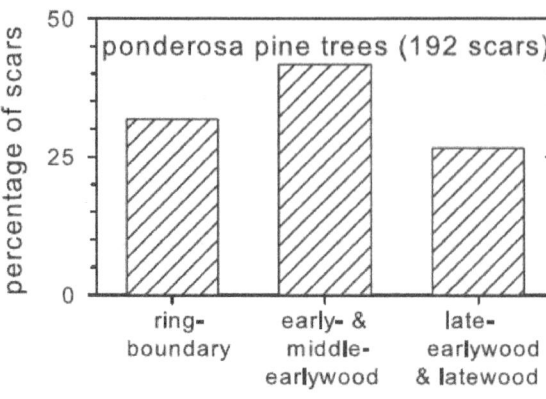

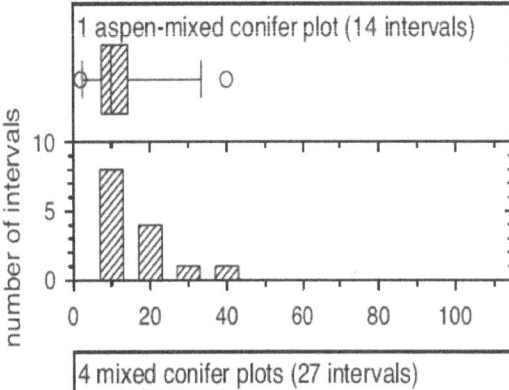

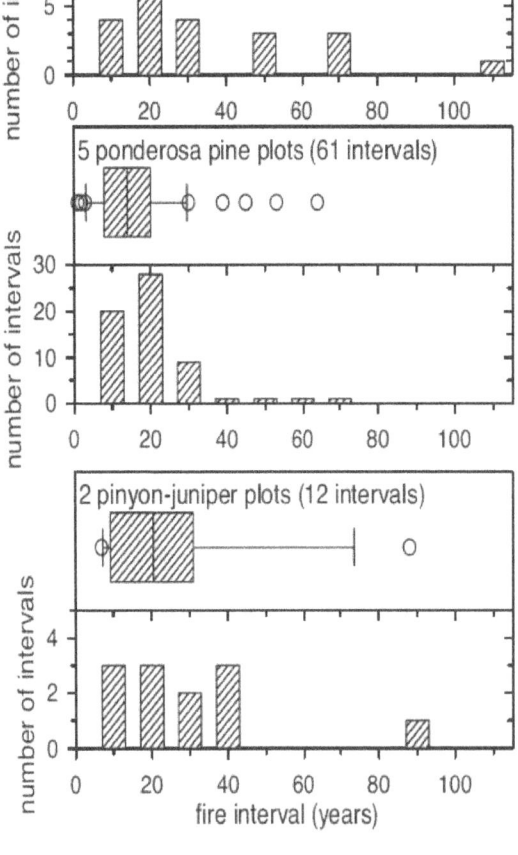

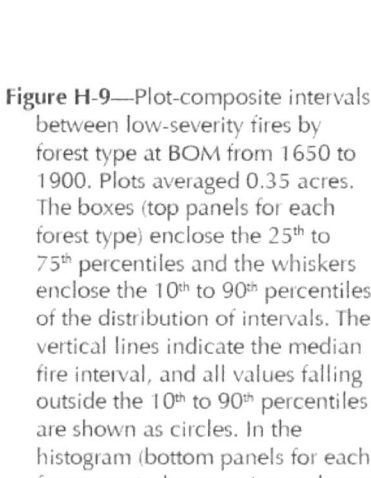

Figure H-9—Plot-composite intervals between low-severity fires by forest type at BOM from 1650 to 1900. Plots averaged 0.35 acres. The boxes (top panels for each forest type) enclose the 25th to 75th percentiles and the whiskers enclose the 10th to 90th percentiles of the distribution of intervals. The vertical lines indicate the median fire interval, and all values falling outside the 10th to 90th percentiles are shown as circles. In the histogram (bottom panels for each forest type), the same intervals are plotted in 10-year bins (1 to 10 years, 11 to 20 years, and so forth).

USDA Forest Service RMRS-GTR-261WWW. 2011.

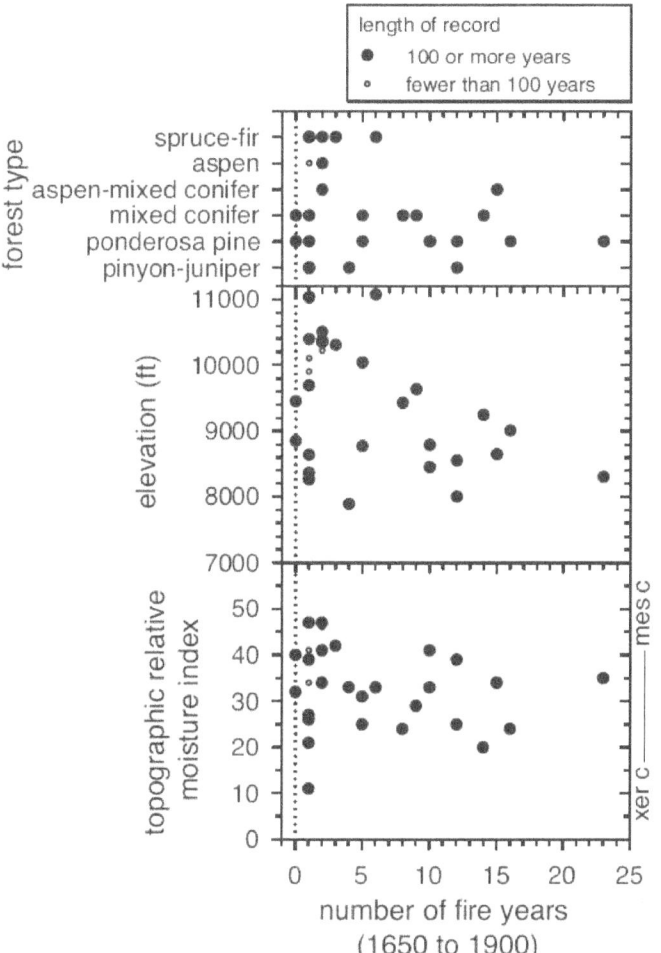

Figure H-10—Variation in fire among plots at BOM with topography, forest type, and relative soil moisture availability (Parker 1982). Number of fire years includes both fire-scar and cohort dates. Plots with no reconstructed fires during this period fall on the dotted line.

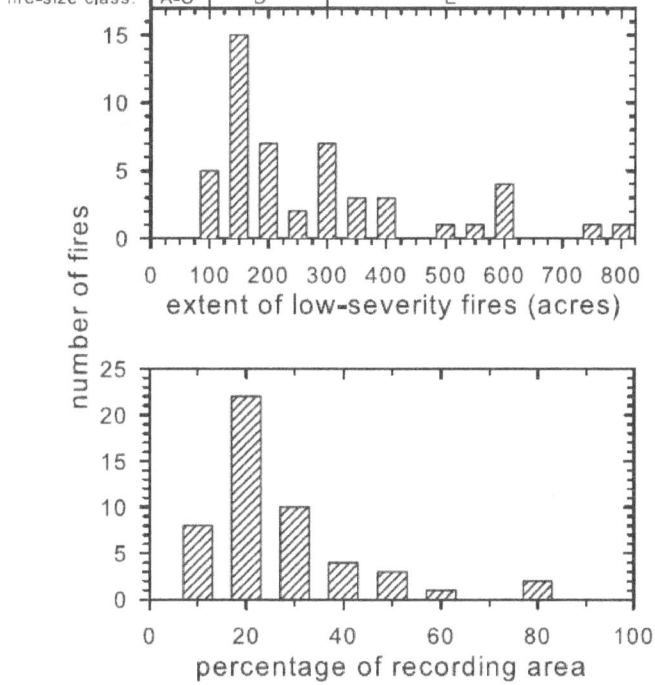

Figure H-11—Relative extent of low-severity fires within the 1963-acre BOM site, from 1650 to 1900, as area (top) and as a percentage of the recording area (in other words, the combined area of cells containing recording, fire-scarred trees during each year; bottom). Commonly used fire-size classes are indicated at the top (NWCG 2007).

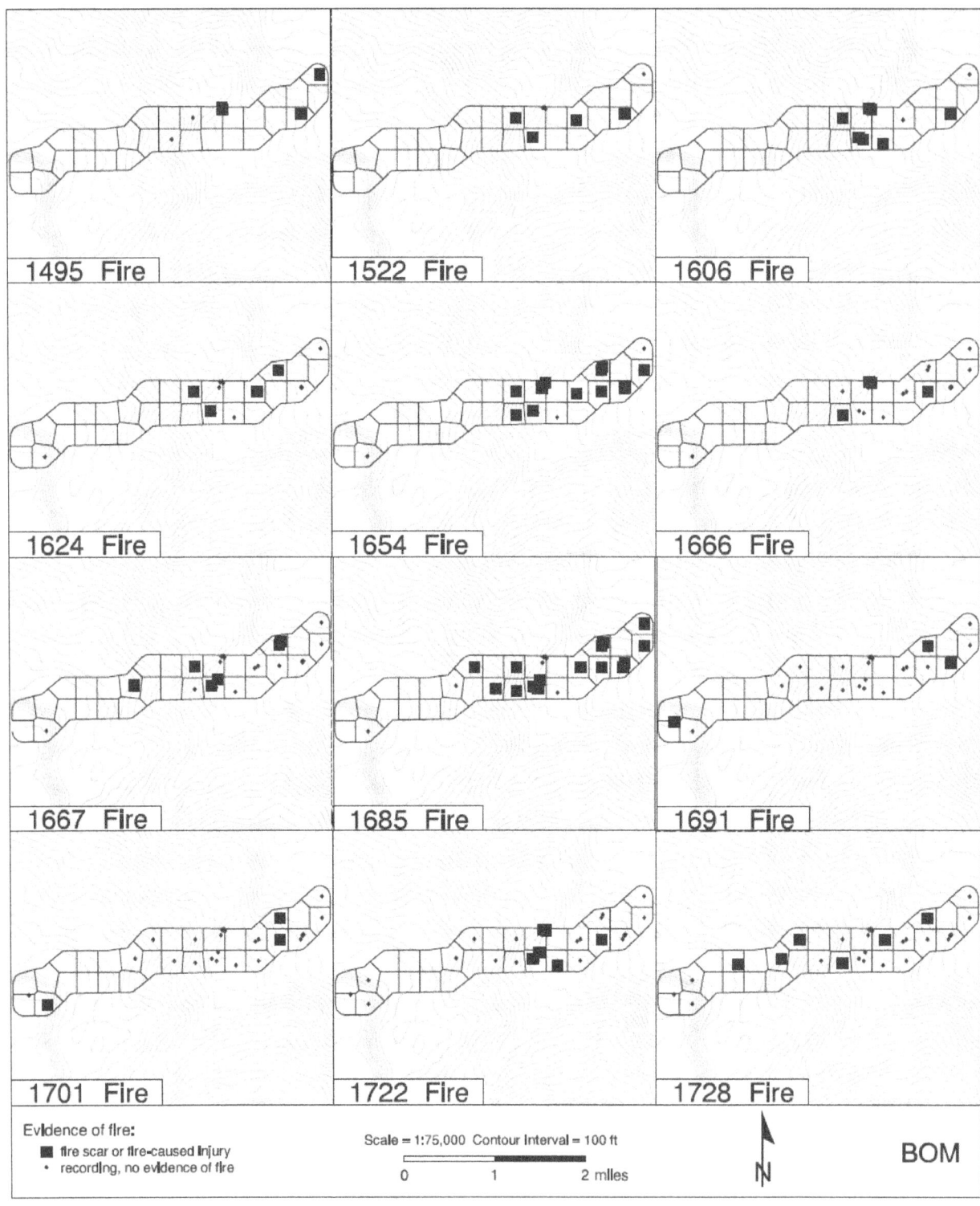

Figure H-12—Maps of years with evidence of low-severity fires in three or more cells at BOM. "Recording, no evidence of fire" indicates at least one tree was alive at that location during that year but did not have a fire scar or fire-caused injury. Empty cells indicate that no fire-scarred trees were recording in that cell during that year. Cohort dates are not mapped.

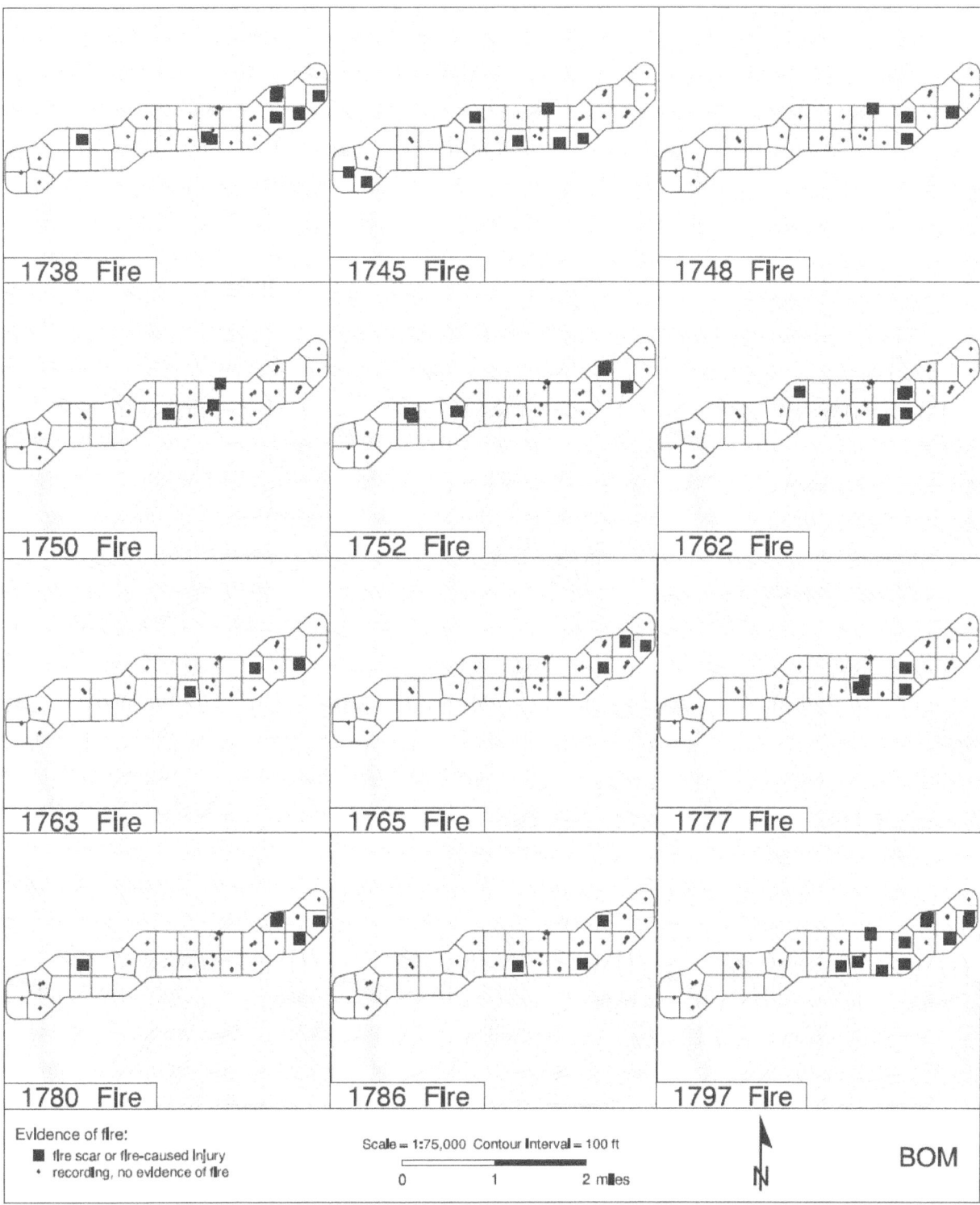

Figure H-12—*Continued.*

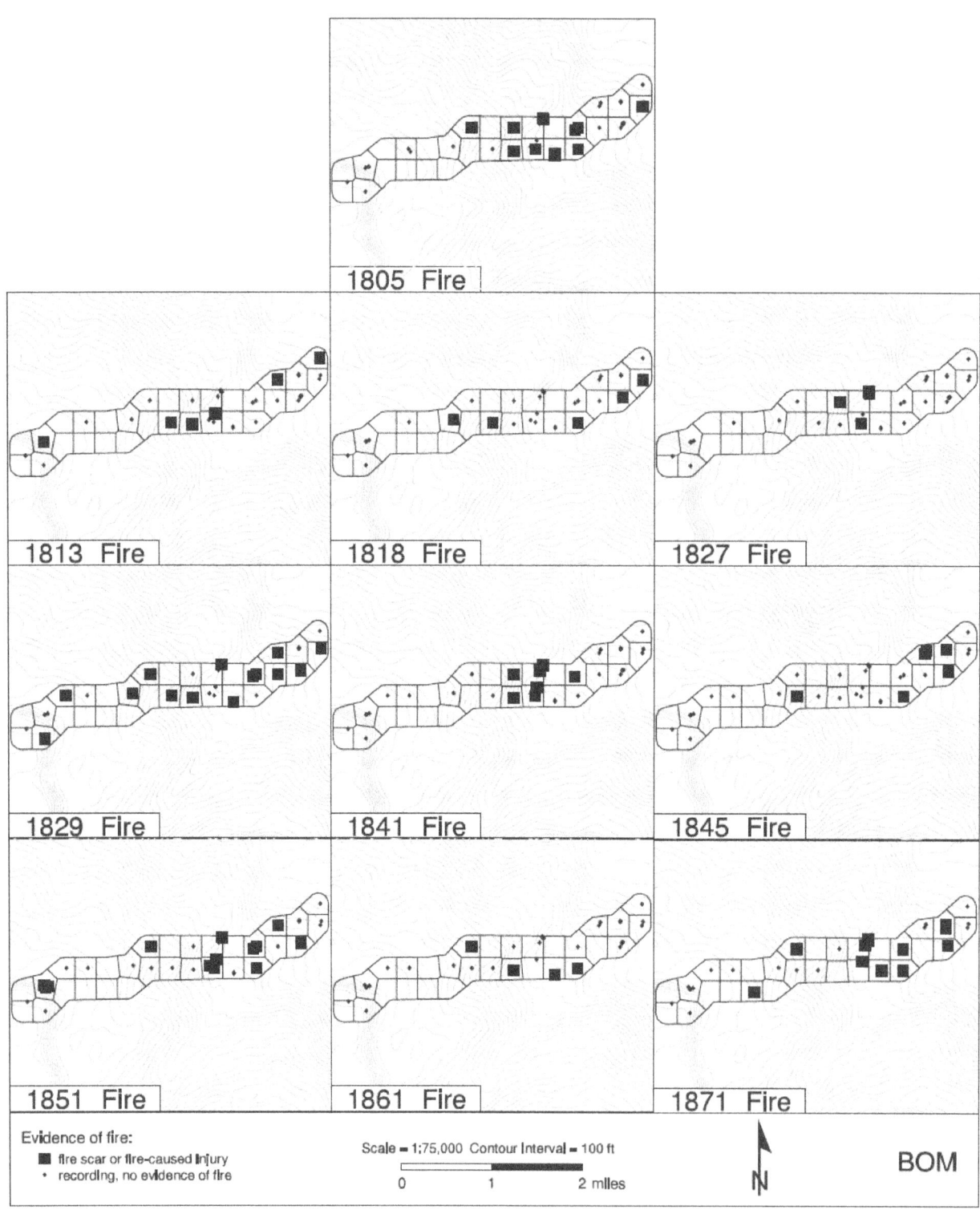

1805 Fire

1813 Fire

1818 Fire

1827 Fire

1829 Fire

1841 Fire

1845 Fire

1851 Fire

1861 Fire

1871 Fire

Evidence of fire:
■ fire scar or fire-caused injury
• recording, no evidence of fire

Scale = 1:75,000 Contour Interval = 100 ft

0   1   2 miles

N

BOM

Figure H-12—*Continued.*

Appendix I. Beaver River, Tushar Mountains, Fishlake National Forest (RBC)

Topography

We sampled 44 plots (half again as many plots as we sampled at the other gridded sites) over 2837 acres along the Beaver River, on the Beaver Ranger District of the Fishlake National Forest in Beaver County, Utah (figs. 1 and I-1). The plots were separated by 0.30 miles on average (range 0.27 to 0.33 miles) and averaged 0.24 acres in area (range 0.07 to 0.82 acres). Plots were sampled within cells that averaged 63 acres and ranged from 55 to 76 acres. Plots ranged in elevation from 7732 to 10,091 ft and in slope from 2 to 56 percent (fig. I-2). They were sampled on a range of aspects, but most were on north and east aspects (70 percent). The distribution of the plots by elevation, aspect, or slope did not differ from the distribution of the landscape by more than 10 percent in any category except west aspects, which were under sampled (fig. I-2). We took two to four photographs each at 41 of the plots.

Tree Demography

Of the 1332 trees that occurred in the plots, most were ponderosa pine, white fir, Douglas-fir, quaking aspen, subalpine fir, or Engelmann spruce, but 5 Rocky Mountain juniper also occurred (fig. I-3). Most of these trees were living (77 percent) and the rest were snags (14 percent), logs (8 percent), or stumps (2 percent). We were able to remove and crossdate wood samples from most of these trees (913 trees or 69 percent) and we obtained actual or estimated pith dates for 881 of them. These pith dates ranged from 1535 to 1955, but many post-dated 1900 (252 trees; fig. I-4). The death dates we obtained for 128 logs and snags ranged from 1830 to 2002.

Historical and Current Forest Structure and Composition

The plots included a range of historical and modern forest types (ponderosa pine, mixed conifer, aspen-mixed conifer, aspen, and spruce-fir; table I-1). Nearly half the plots changed forest type between 1860 and 2000: five ponderosa pine and four aspen plots converted to mixed conifer; one mixed conifer, five aspen, and four spruce fir plots converted to aspen-mixed conifer; and one aspen-mixed conifer plot converted to spruce-fir. In 1900, tree density averaged 82 trees per acre and ranged from 0 to 242 trees per acre (fig. I-5). In 2000, tree density averaged 127 trees per acre and ranged from 28 to 349 trees per acre. However, we likely underestimated historical tree density because we could not obtain recruitment or earliest-ring dates for 419 of the 1332 trees that occurred in the plots and only an earliest-ring date for another 32 trees. Five of these trees had earliest-ring dates between 1901 and 1920 and therefore may have been living before 1900.

Fire Scars

We were able to remove and crossdate fire-scarred samples from 164 trees. We sampled 112 of these trees in 24 of the 44 plots at this site (1 to 16 trees per plot, average 5 trees). We sampled the 52 other fire-scarred trees as we encountered them between plots over 2005 acres throughout the site (fig. I-6). Most of the 164 fire-scarred trees were ponderosa pine (41 percent) or Douglas-fir (38 percent), and the rest were Engelmann spruce, subalpine fir, white fir, quaking aspen, or trees we could not identify. Most were logs, snags or stumps (65 percent), and the rest were live trees. These 164 trees yielded 620 fire scars and 46 eroded fire scars or abrupt changes in ring width (figs. I-4 and I-7). However, two of the non-scar dates were eliminated from further analyses because they were recorded on only a single tree at the site. We were able to assign an intra-ring position to 69 percent of the 568 fire scars that occurred during the analysis period (1650 to 1900). Of the scars that occurred on ponderosa pine trees, most (44 percent) occurred in the late-earlywood or latewood. In contrast, most of those that occurred on Douglas-fir trees (60 percent) were on the boundary between two rings (fig. I-8).

Post-Fire Cohorts

We identified 28 cohorts of trees from estimated recruitment dates at 25 of the plots. Twenty-four of these cohorts were recruited before 1900 (1619 to 1897) and were identified from 191 trees (5 to 15 trees per cohort), most of which were quaking aspen (25 percent), Douglas-fir (24 percent), sub-alpine fir (16 percent), Engelmann spruce (15 percent), or ponderosa pine (12 percent) but included a few Rocky Mountain juniper and white fir (figs. I-4 and I-7). The cohorts that were recruited before 1900 occurred in plots with a range of forest types: aspen (33 percent of cohorts), mixed conifer (29 percent), spruce-fir (21 percent), and ponderosa pine (17 percent).

Spatial Variation in Fire Regimes

During the analysis period (1650 to 1900), plot-composite, low-severity fire intervals averaged 12 years (range 1 to 31 years) when pooled among ponderosa pine plots; 34 years (range 2 to 100 years) when pooled among mixed conifer plots; 18 years (range 7 to 49 years) when pooled among aspen-mixed conifer plots; and 32 years (range 4 to 116 years) when pooled among spruce-fir plots (fig. I-9). There were more fire years in ponderosa pine and aspen-mixed conifer plots than in plots of other forest types (fig. I-10). There were also more fire years in low-elevation plots than in high-elevation plots. The tree-ring record before 1900 was less than 100 years long for 19 of the 44 plots.

We could not infer historical fire severity at one plot because it did not meet our requirements for any of the severity categories (table I-2). We assigned the remaining plots to the low, mixed, or high fire severity categories.

From 1650 to 1900, the 59 low-severity fires we reconstructed within our 2837-acre sampling area averaged 220 acres and ranged from 58 to 1209 acres (fig. I-11), equivalent to 5 to 86 percent of the recording area (in other words, the combined area of cells containing recording, fire-scarred trees during a given year). Recording area varied among fire years, ranging from 380 to 1419 acres. We likely underestimated the extent of low-severity fires because most fires intersected the boundary of the site (fig. I-12).

Table I-1—Distribution of plots at RBC by historical (1860) and modern (2000) forest types (table 2).

Historical forest type (1860)	Modern forest type (2000)					
	Spruce-fir	Aspen	Aspen-mixed conifer	Mixed conifer	Ponderosa pine	Total plots in 1860
Spruce-fir	10		4			14
Aspen		1	5	4		10
Aspen-mixed conifer	1		2			3
Mixed conifer			1	10		11
Ponderosa pine				5	1	6
Total plots in 2000	**11**	**1**	**12**	**19**	**1**	**44**

Table I-2—Distribution of plots at RBC by historical forest type (1860; table 2) and fire severity (table 3).

Forest type	High	Assumed high	Mixed	Assumed mixed	Low	Unclassified
Spruce-fir	2	8	3		1	
Aspen	5	2	3			
Aspen-mixed conifer		2			1	
Mixed conifer		1	6	1	2	1
Ponderosa pine			3		3	
Total	**7**	**13**	**15**	**1**	**7**	**1**

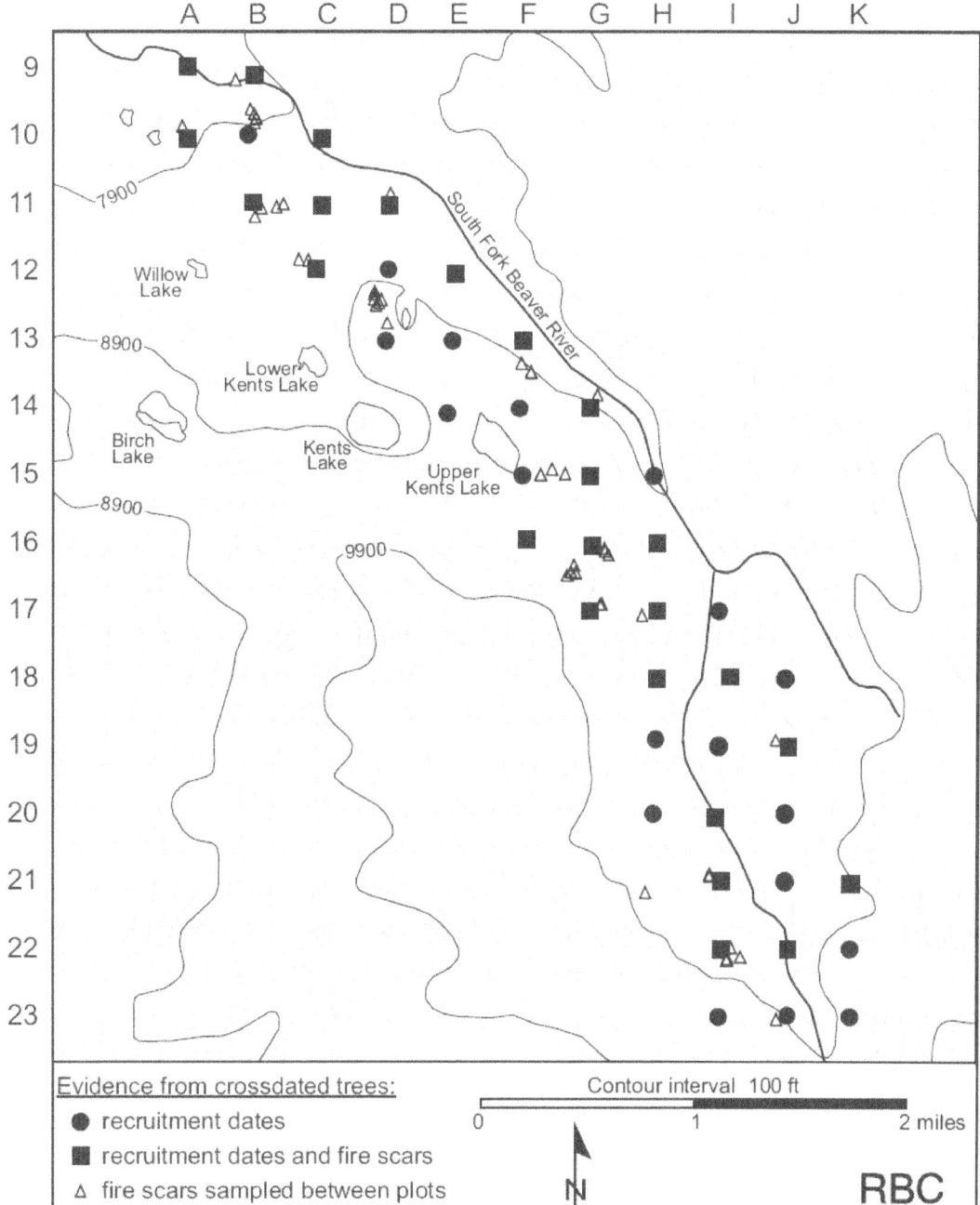

Figure I-1—Locations of plots and crossdated fire-scarred trees that were sampled outside of plots. More than half of the fire-scarred trees were sampled within plots and are not mapped individually. Plots are identified by column and row, in other words, the northwestern most plot is 9A, the next plot to the east is 9B, and so forth.

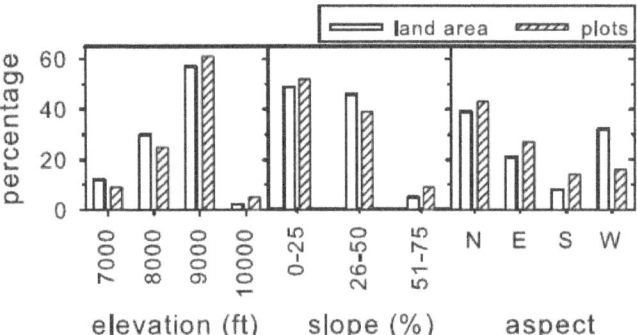

Figure I-2—Distribution of sampled plots and land area at RBC by topography. Aspect classes are 90° wide, beginning with 46° for east (E). Land area was derived from a digital elevation model (Utah AGRC 2004).

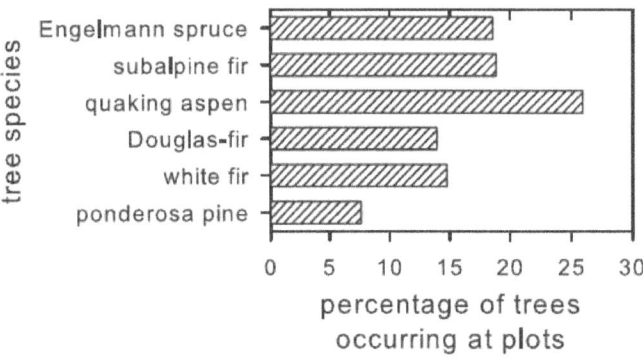

Figure I-3—Distribution by species of the 1332 live and dead trees ≥8 inches DBH that occurred in plots at RBC, regardless of whether or not we removed wood samples and crossdated them. Not shown are five Rocky Mountain juniper trees.

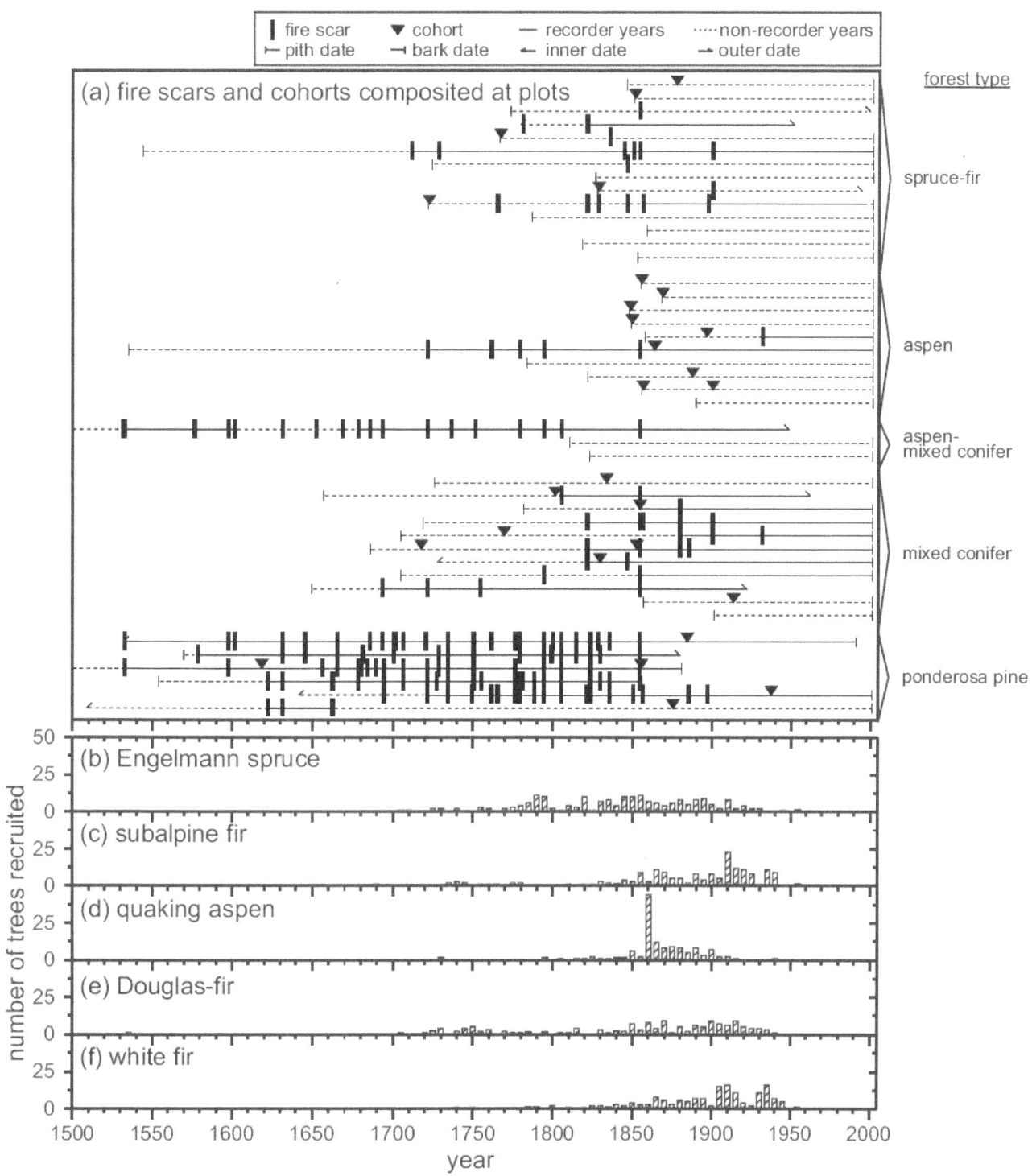

Figure I-4—Chronologies of fire and tree recruitment at RBC. In (a), horizontal lines are plot-composite fire-scar and cohort dates by forest type. Non-recorder years precede the first scar, whereas recorder years generally follow it, but non-recorder years can also occur when the catface margin is consumed by subsequent fires or rot. In (b) through (f), recruitment dates are given for species comprising ≥10 percent of trees with such dates. The latter part of the distribution is incomplete because we only cored trees that were ≥8 inches DBH.

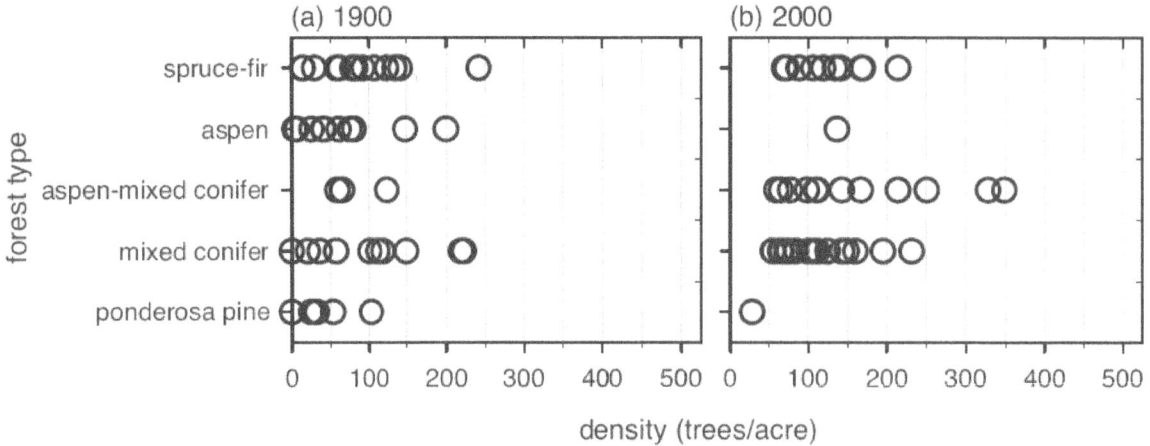

Figure I-5—Density of trees ≥8 inche DBH that were alive at each plot at RBC (a) in 1900 and (b) in 2000, by forest type (table 2).

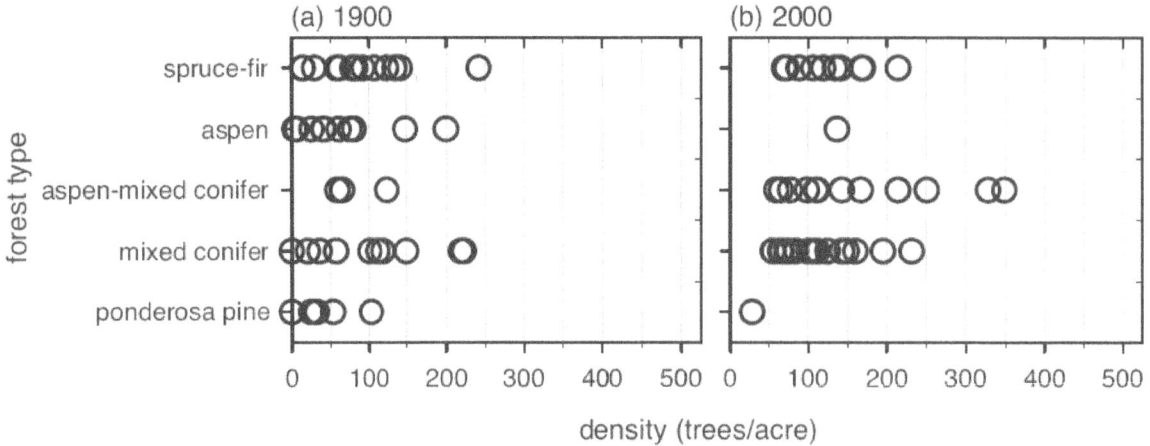

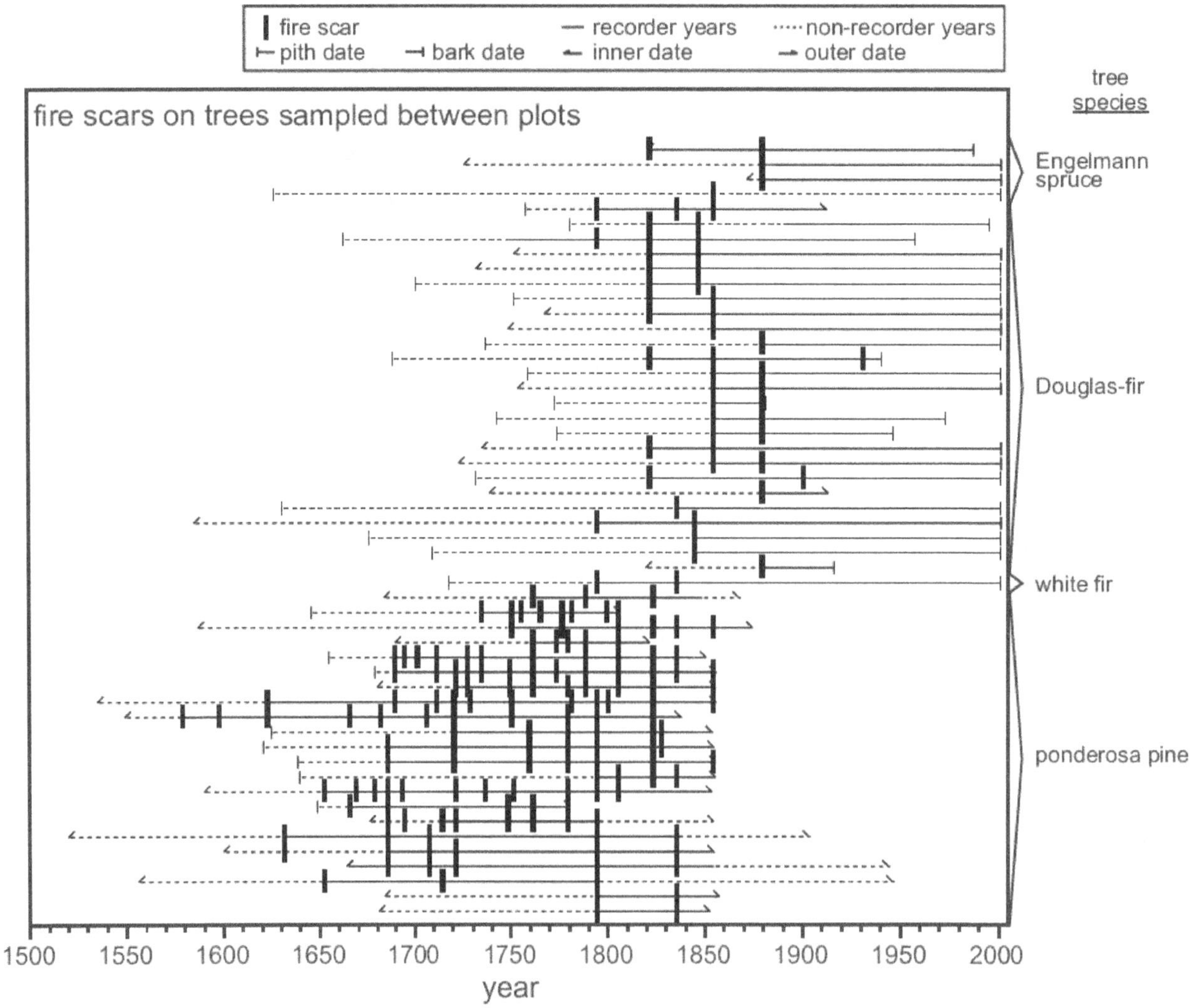

Figure I-6—Chronology of low-severity fires recorded on the 52 trees sampled between plots over approximately 2005 acres throughout the RBC site.

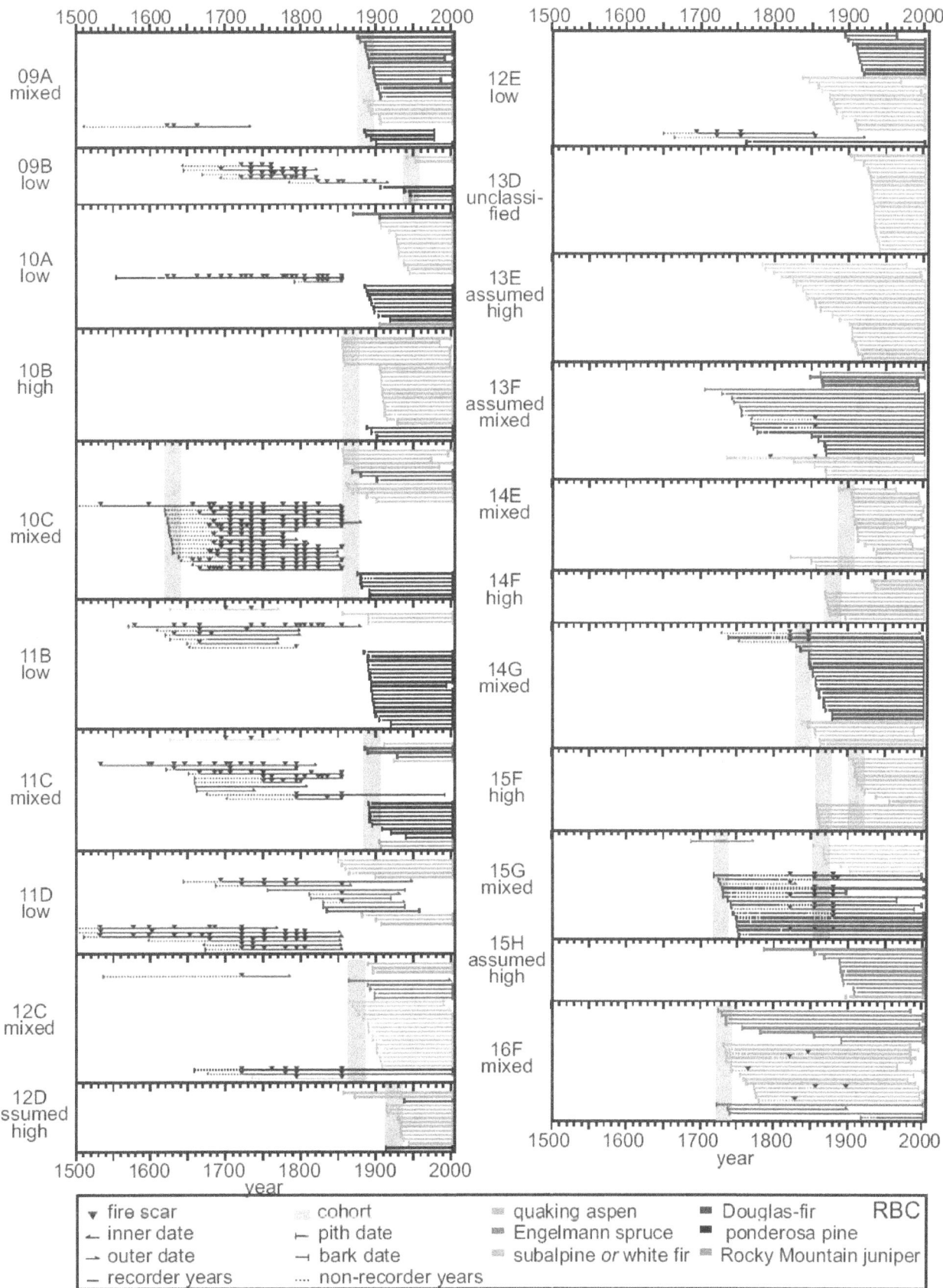

Figure I-7—Fire-demography diagrams (FDDs, Brown and others 2008b) showing chronologies of tree demography (recruitment and death), fire scars, and cohorts at each plot. Bark dates on 55 stumps are shown as outer dates. Not shown are 52 fire-scarred trees sampled between plots. Inferred fire severity (table 3) is indicated to the left of each panel. The trees in the combined subalpine/white fir category are evenly divided between those two species.

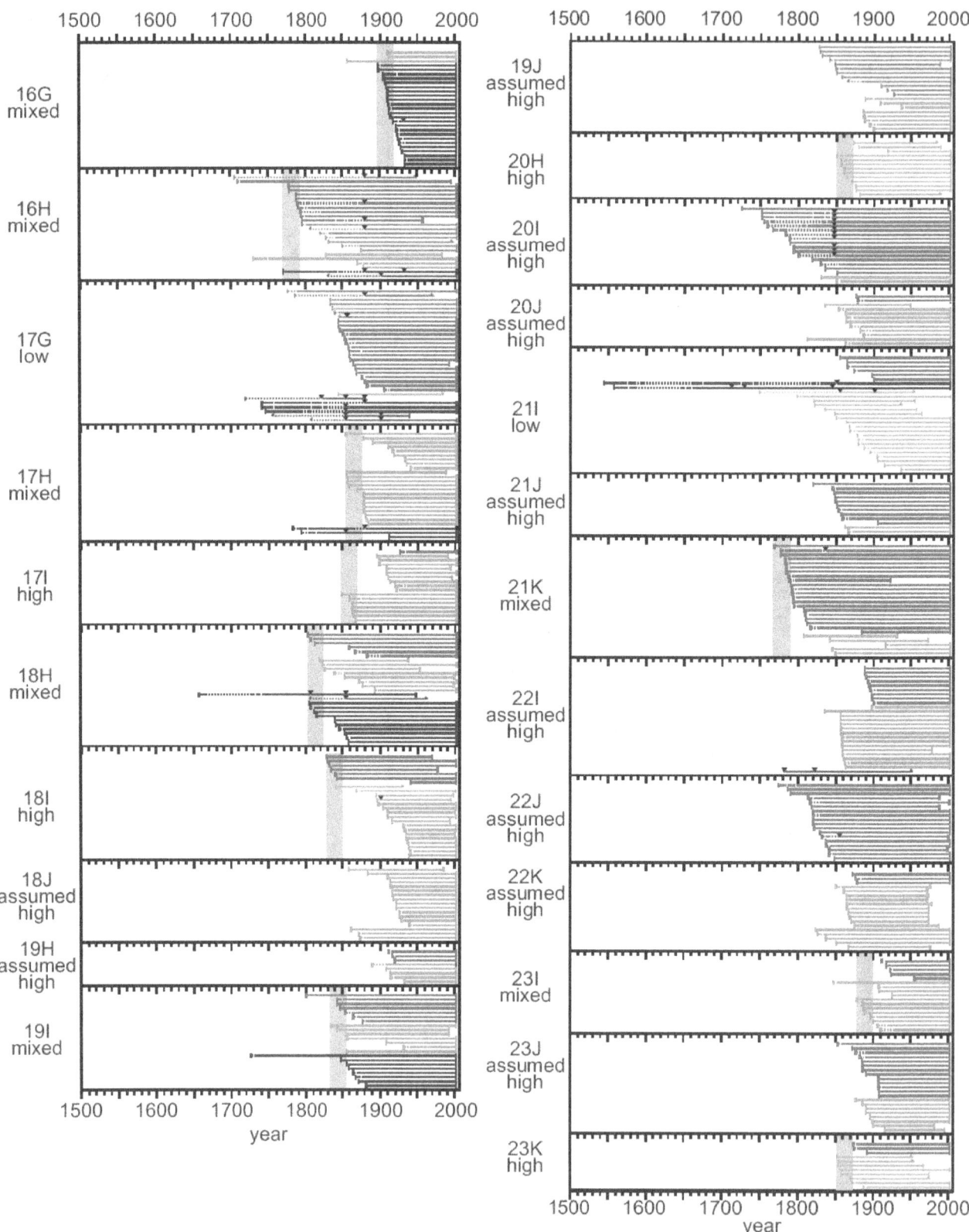

Figure I-7—*Continued.*

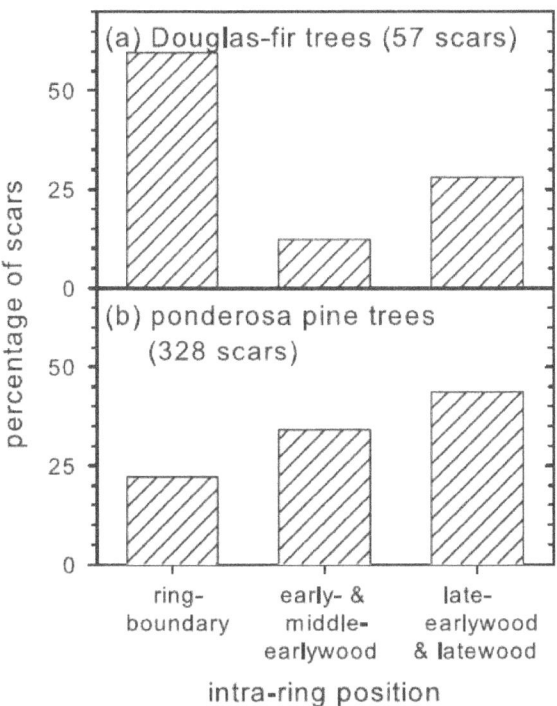

(a) Douglas-fir trees (57 scars)

(b) ponderosa pine trees (328 scars)

percentage of scars

intra-ring position

ring-boundary / early- & middle-earlywood / late-earlywood & latewood

Figure I-8—Intra-ring position of fire scars sampled in and between plots at RBC from 1650 to 1900, as a percentage of the number of scars for which the position could be determined (given in parentheses). Not shown are intra-ring positions for nine fire scars on Engelmann spruce, subalpine fir, white fir, and trees of unknown species.

Figure I-9—Plot-composite intervals between low-severity fires by forest type at RBC from 1650 to 1900. Plots averaged 0.24 acres. The boxes (top panels for each forest type) enclose the 25th to 75th percentiles and the whiskers enclose the 10th to 90th percentiles of the distribution of intervals. The vertical lines indicate the median fire interval and all values falling outside the 10th to 90th percentiles are shown as circles. In the histogram (bottom panels for each forest type), the same intervals are plotted in 10-year bins (1 to 10 years, 11 to 20 years, and so forth).

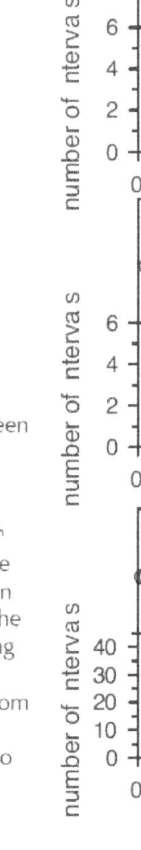
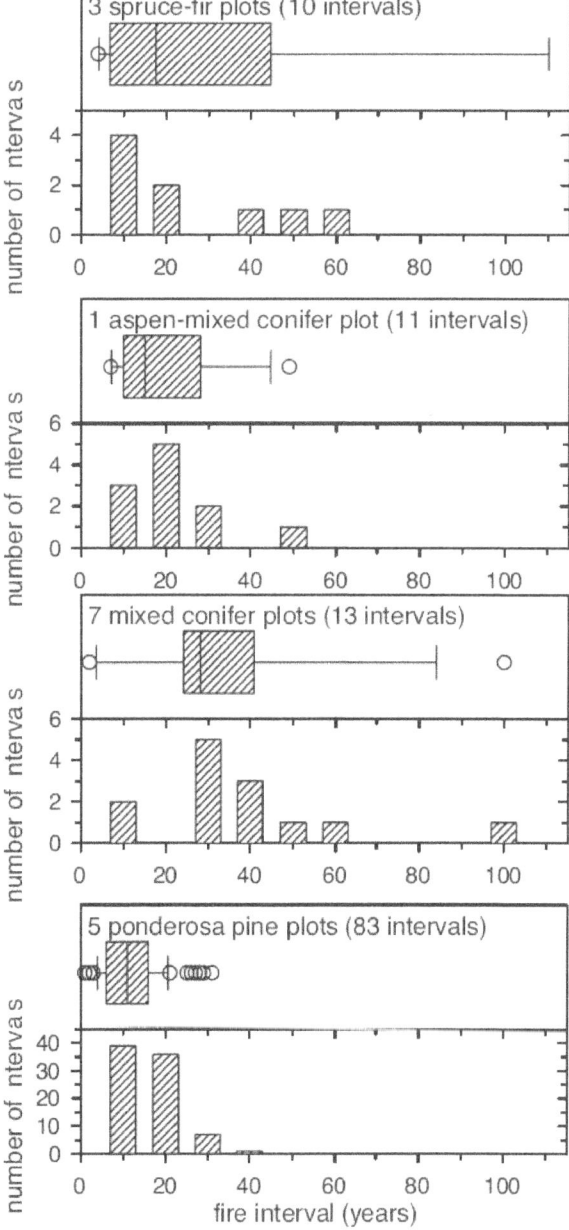

3 spruce-fir plots (10 intervals)

1 aspen-mixed conifer plot (11 intervals)

7 mixed conifer plots (13 intervals)

5 ponderosa pine plots (83 intervals)

number of intervals

fire interval (years)

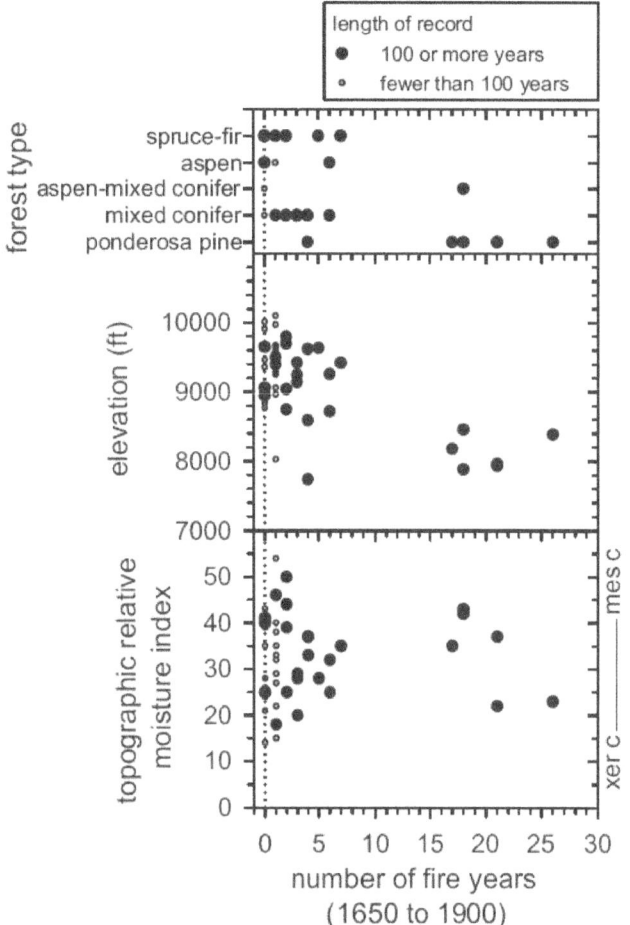

Figure I-10—Variation in fire among plots at RBC with topography, forest type, and relative soil moisture availability (Parker 1982). Number of fire years includes both fire-scar and cohort dates. Plots with no reconstructed fires during this period fall on the dotted line.

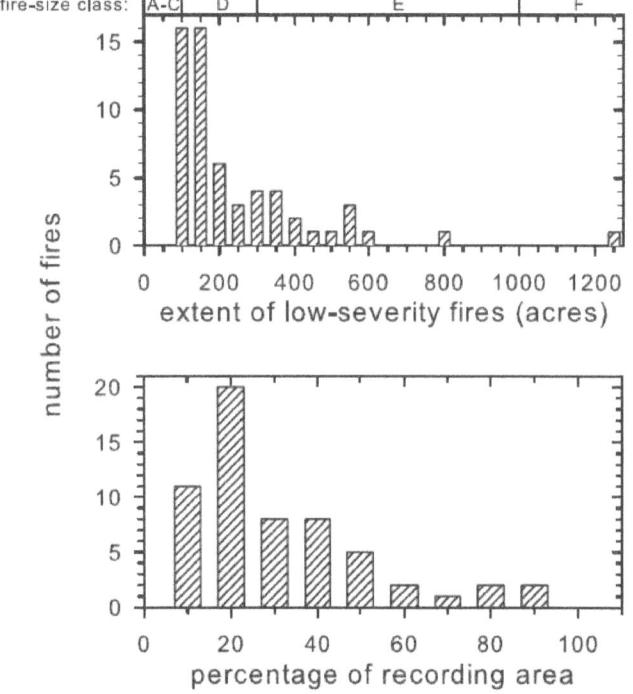

Figure I-11—Relative extent of low-severity fires within the 2837-acre RBC site, from 1650 to 1900, as area (top) and as a percentage of the recording area (in other words, the combined area of cells containing recording, fire-scarred trees during each year; bottom). Commonly used fire-size classes are indicated at the top (NWCG 2007).

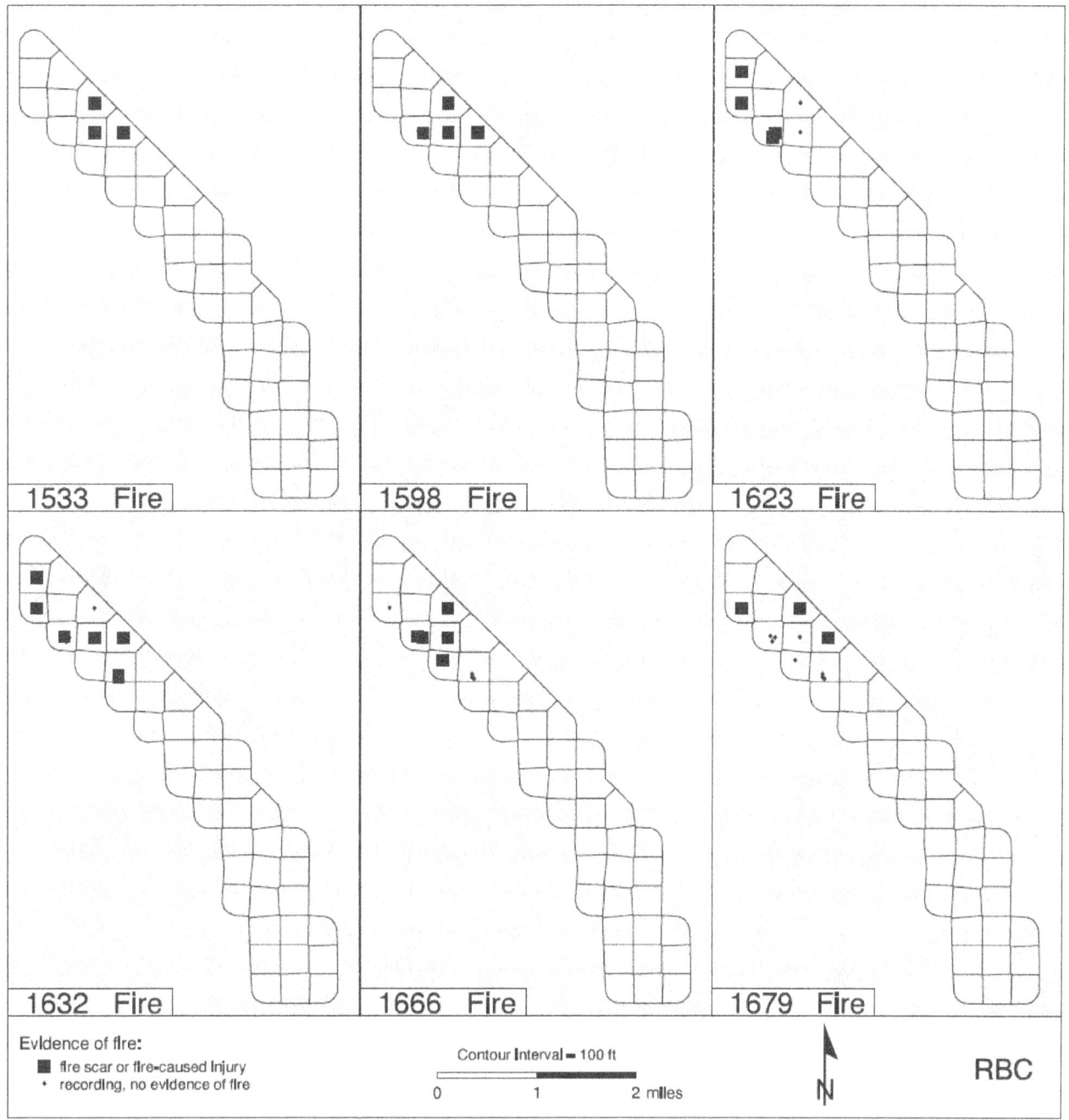

Figure I-12—Maps of years with evidence of low-severity fires in three or more cells at RBC. "Recording, no evidence of fire" indicates at least one tree was alive at that location during that year but did not have a fire scar or fire-caused injury. Empty cells indicate that no fire-scarred trees were recording in that cell during that year. Cohort dates are not mapped.

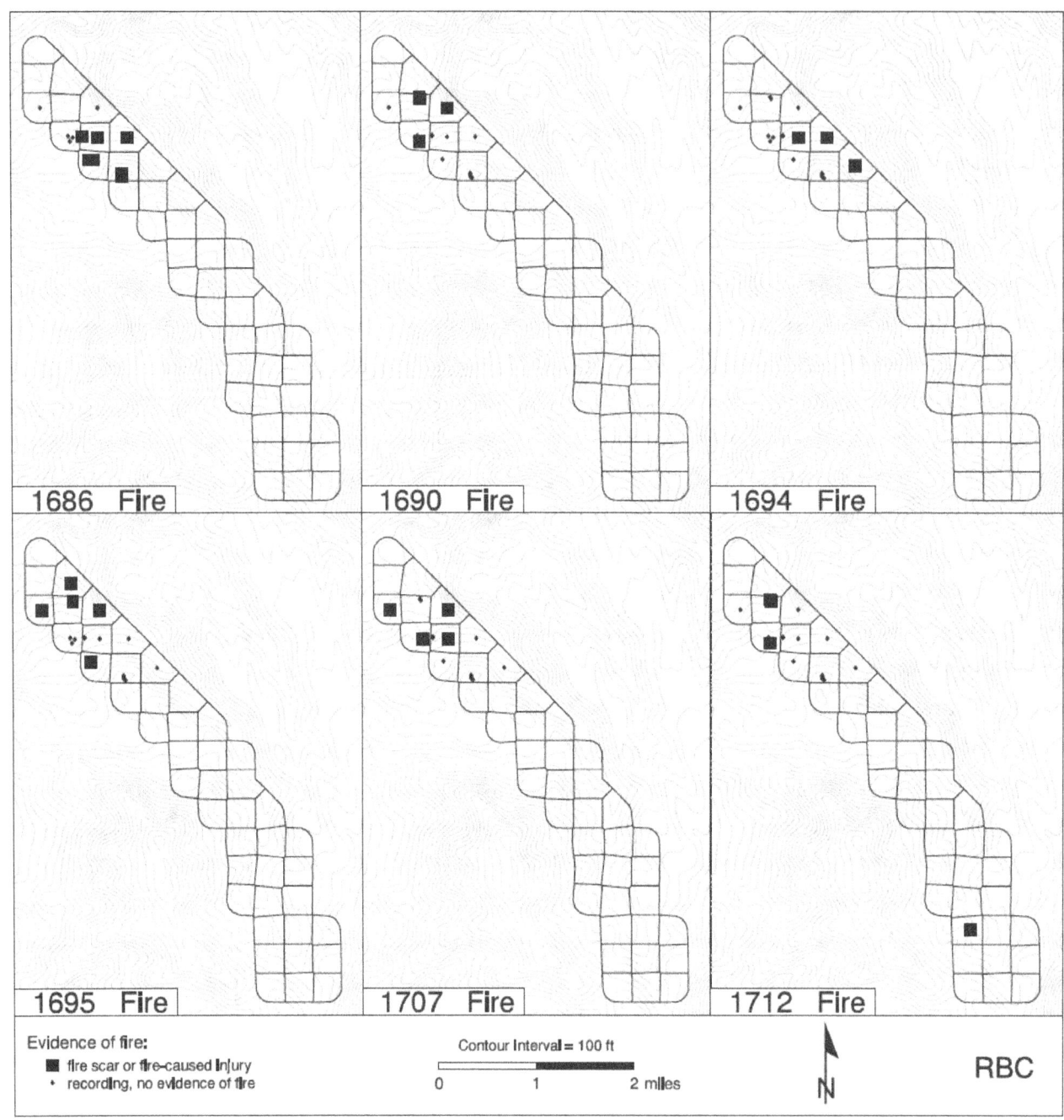

Figure I-12—*Continued.*

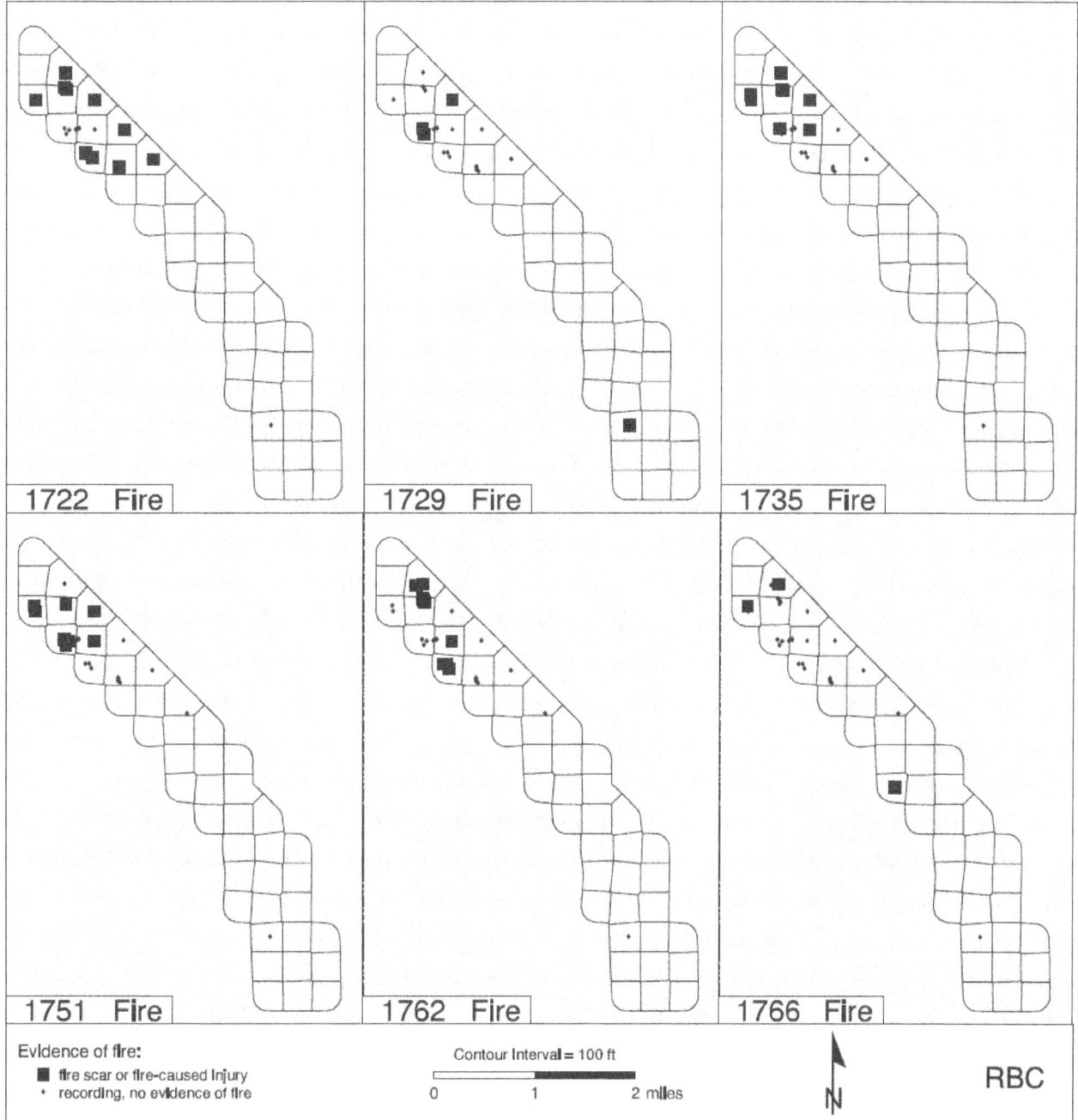

Figure I-12—*Continued.*

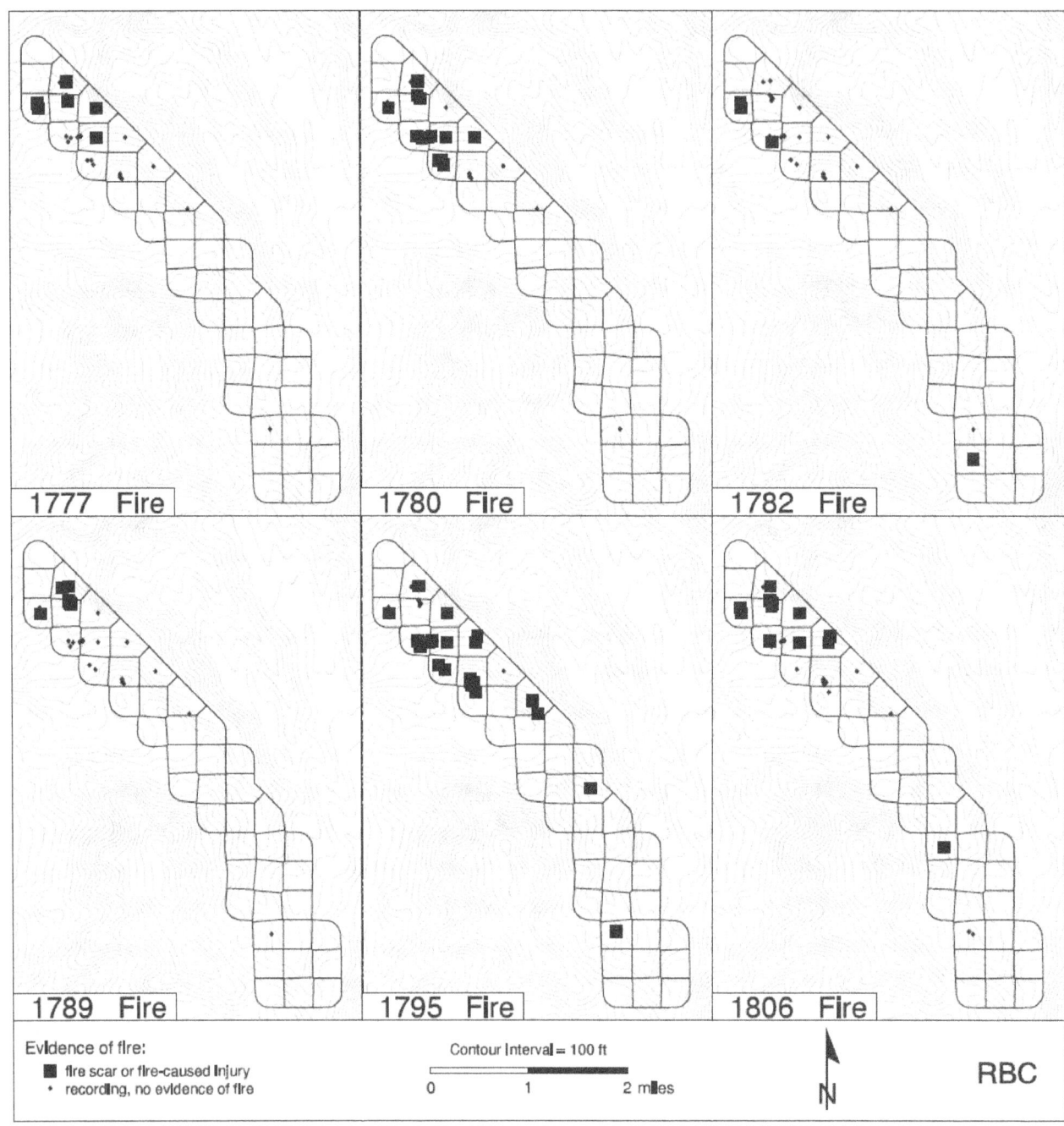

Figure I-12—*Continued.*

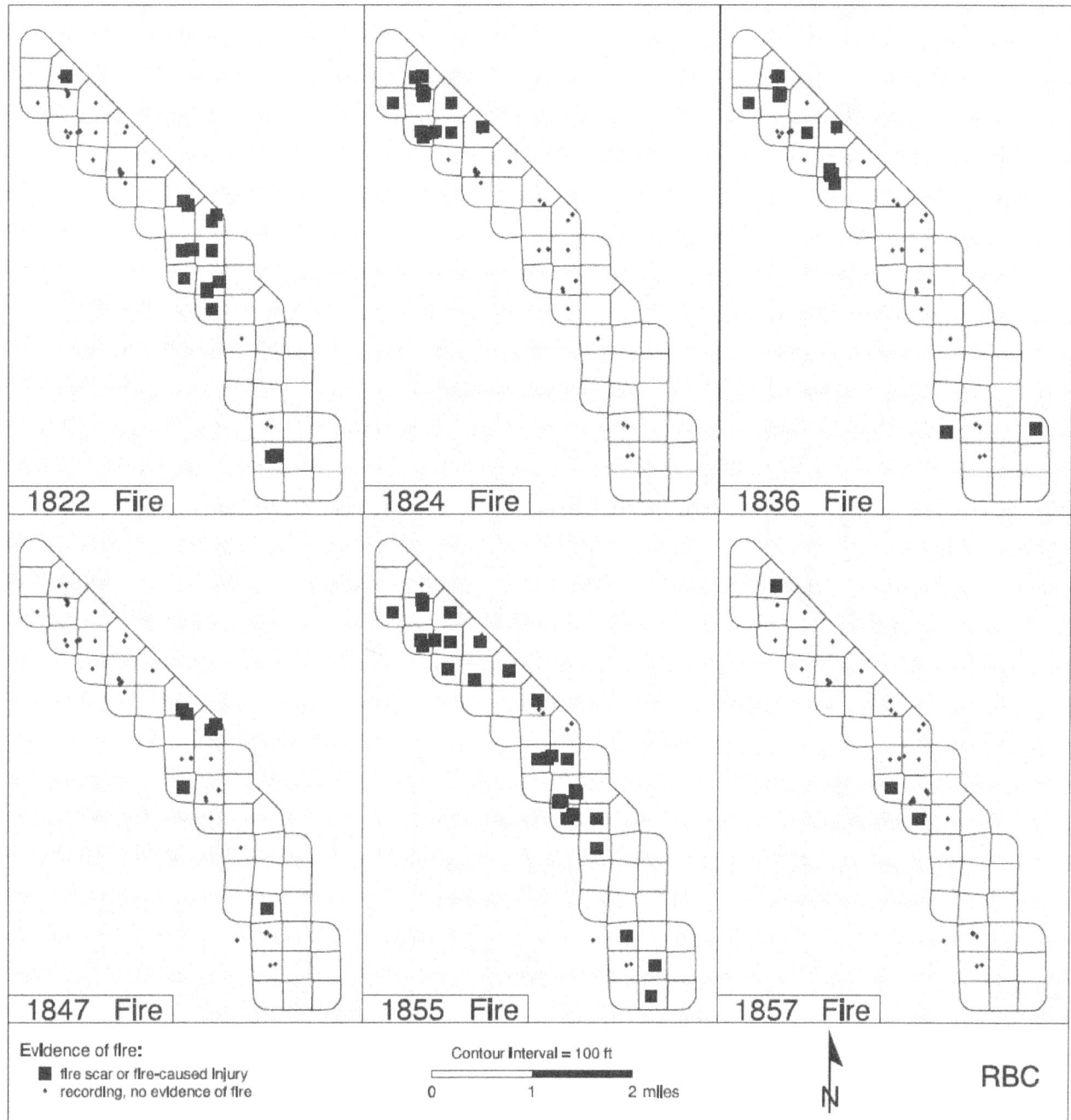

1822 Fire

1824 Fire

1836 Fire

1847 Fire

1855 Fire

1857 Fire

Evidence of fire:
■ fire scar or fire-caused injury
• recording, no evidence of fire

Contour interval = 100 ft

0   1   2 miles

N

RBC

Figure I-12—*Continued.*

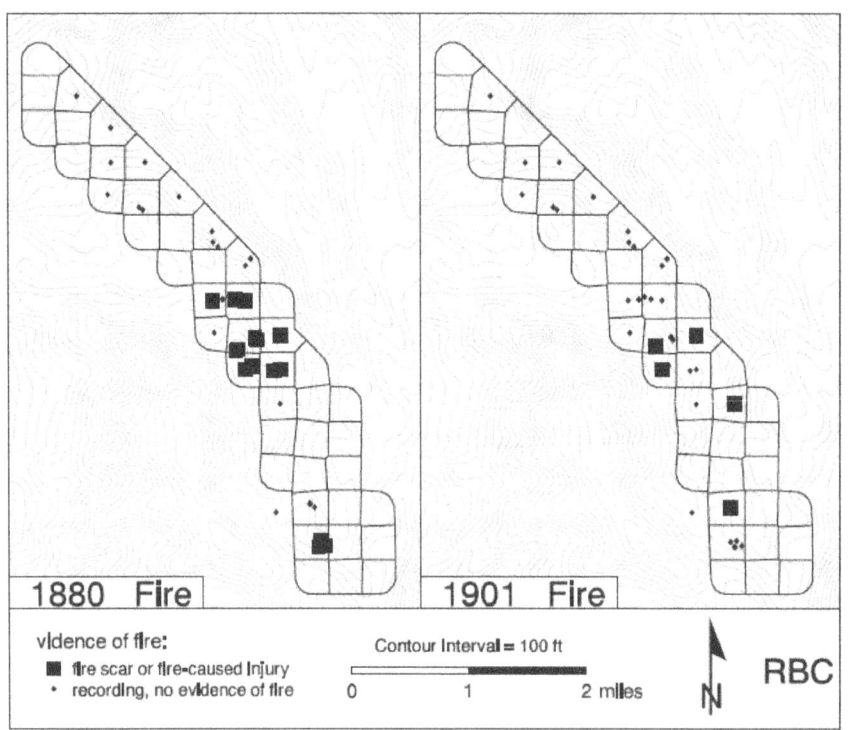

Figure I-12—*Continued.*

USDA Forest Service RMRS-GTR-261WWW. 2011.

Appendix J. Indian Creek, Tushar Mountains, Fishlake National Forest (INC)

Topography

We sampled only six plots over 624 acres along Indian Creek, on the Beaver Ranger District of the Fishlake National Forest in Beaver County, Utah (figs. 1 and J-1). The plots were separated by 0.30 miles on average (range 0.28 to 0.33 miles) and averaged 0.42 acres in area (range 0.22 to 0.57 acres). Plots were sampled within cells that averaged 104 acres and ranged from 55 to 167 acres. Plots ranged in elevation from 7752 to 8257 ft. They ranged in slope from 7 to 60 percent and were sampled on a range of aspects. There were too few plots to compare with the distribution of land area by topography. We took four photographs at each of the six plots.

Tree Demography

Of the 182 trees that occurred in the plots, most (96 percent) were ponderosa pine, white fir, Douglas-fir, and quaking aspen, but two Rocky Mountain juniper, one curl-leaf mountain mahogany, and five limber pine also occurred (fig. J-2). Most of these trees were living (84 percent) and the rest were snags (5 percent), logs (3 percent), or stumps (7 percent). We were able to remove and crossdate wood samples from most of these trees (146 trees or 80 percent), and we obtained actual or estimated pith dates for 140 of them. These pith dates ranged from 1479 to 1947 and 26 of them post-dated 1900 (fig. J-3). The death dates we obtained for four logs and snags ranged from 1986 to 1999.

Historical and Current Forest Structure and Composition

The plots included three historical and modern forest types (ponderosa pine, mixed conifer, and aspen-mixed conifer; table J-1). Half the plots changed forest type between 1860 and 2000: one of the ponderosa pine plots converted to mixed conifer and two others converted to aspen-mixed conifer. In 1900, tree density averaged 49 trees per acre and ranged from 30 to 95 trees per acre (fig. J-4). In 2000, tree density averaged 70 trees per acre and ranged from 35 to 114 trees per acre. However, we likely underestimated historical tree density because we could not obtain recruitment or earliest-ring dates for 36 of the 182 trees that occurred in the plots and only an earliest-ring date for another 6 trees, 1 of which had an earliest-ring date between 1901 and 1920 and therefore may have been living before 1900.

Fire Scars

We were able to remove and crossdate fire-scarred samples from 35 trees, 1 of which had only scars that were recorded on a single tree and so was excluded from further analyses. Of the remaining 34 trees, 14 were sampled in five of the six plots at this site (1 to 5 trees per plot). We sampled the 20 other fire-scarred trees as we encountered them between plots, over 359 acres throughout the site (fig. J-5). Most of the 34 fire-scarred trees were ponderosa pine (88 percent), and the rest were Douglas-fir and white fir. Most were logs, snags or stumps (59 percent), and the rest were live trees. These 34 trees yielded 153 fire scars and 28 eroded fire scars or abrupt changes in ring width (figs. J-3 and J-6). However, five of these scar dates were eliminated from further analyses because they were recorded on only a single tree at the site. We were able to assign an intra-ring position to 76 percent of the 128 fire scars that occurred during the analysis period (1650 to 1900). Of the scars that occurred on ponderosa pine trees, most (58 percent) occurred in the early- and middle-earlywood (fig. J-7).

Post-Fire Cohorts

We identified three cohorts of trees from estimated recruitment dates at three of the plots. All of these cohorts were recruited before 1900 (1838 to 1866) and were identified from 22 trees (5 to 16 trees per cohort), most of which were quaking aspen (32 percent), ponderosa pine (32 percent), white fir (18 percent), Douglas-fir (14 percent), and limber pine trees (5 percent, figs. J-3 and J-6). The cohorts occurred in plots of two forest types: ponderosa pine (67 percent of cohorts) and mixed conifer (33 percent).

Spatial Variation in Fire Regimes

During the analysis period (1650 to 1900), plot-composite, low-severity fire intervals averaged 30 years (range 6 to 81 years) when pooled among ponderosa plots and 28 years (range 6 to 75 years) when pooled among mixed-conifer plots (fig. J-8). The tree-ring record before 1900 was longer than 100 years for all six plots at this site (fig. J-9). We assigned half of the six plots to the low fire severity category and half to the mixed fire severity category (table J-2).

From 1650 to 1900, the 27 low-severity fires we reconstructed within our 624-acre sampling area averaged 240 acres and ranged from 61 to 568 acres (fig. J-10), equivalent to 11 to 100 percent of the recording area (in other words, the combined area of cells containing recording, fire-scarred trees during a given year). Recording area varied among fire years, ranging from 507 to 568 acres. We likely underestimated the extent of low-severity fires because most fires intersected the boundary of the site (fig. J-11).

Table J-1—Distribution of plots at INC by historical (1860) and modern (2000) forest types (table 2).

Historical forest type (1860)	Modern forest type (2000)			Total plots in 1860
	Aspen-mixed conifer	Mixed conifer	Ponderosa pine	
Mixed conifer		2		2
Ponderosa pine	1	2	1	4
Total plots in 2000	**1**	**4**	**1**	**6**

Table J-2—Distribution of plots at INC by historical forest type (1860; table 2) and fire severity (table 3).

Forest type	Mixed	Low
Mixed conifer	1	1
Ponderosa pine	2	2
Total	**3**	**3**

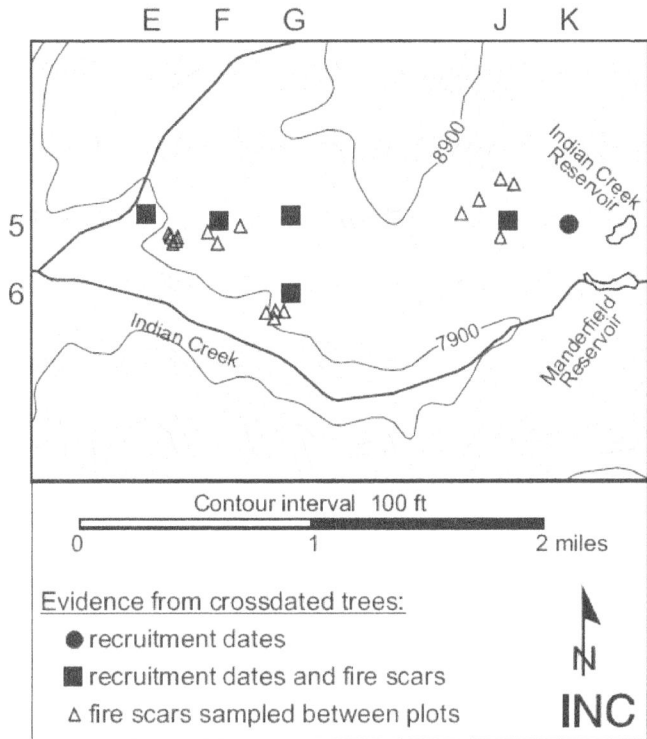

Figure J-1—Locations of plots and crossdated fire-scarred trees that were sampled outside of plots. Nearly half of the fire-scarred trees were sampled within plots and are not mapped individually. Plots are identified by column and row, in other words, the northwestern most plot is 5E, the next plot to the east is 5F, and so forth.

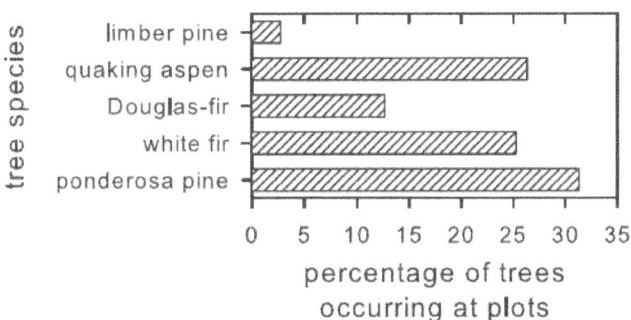

Figure J-2—Distribution by species of the 182 live and dead trees ≥8 inches DBH that occurred in plots at INC, regardless of whether or not we removed wood samples and crossdated them. Not shown are two Rocky Mountain juniper and one curl-leaf mountain mahogany tree.

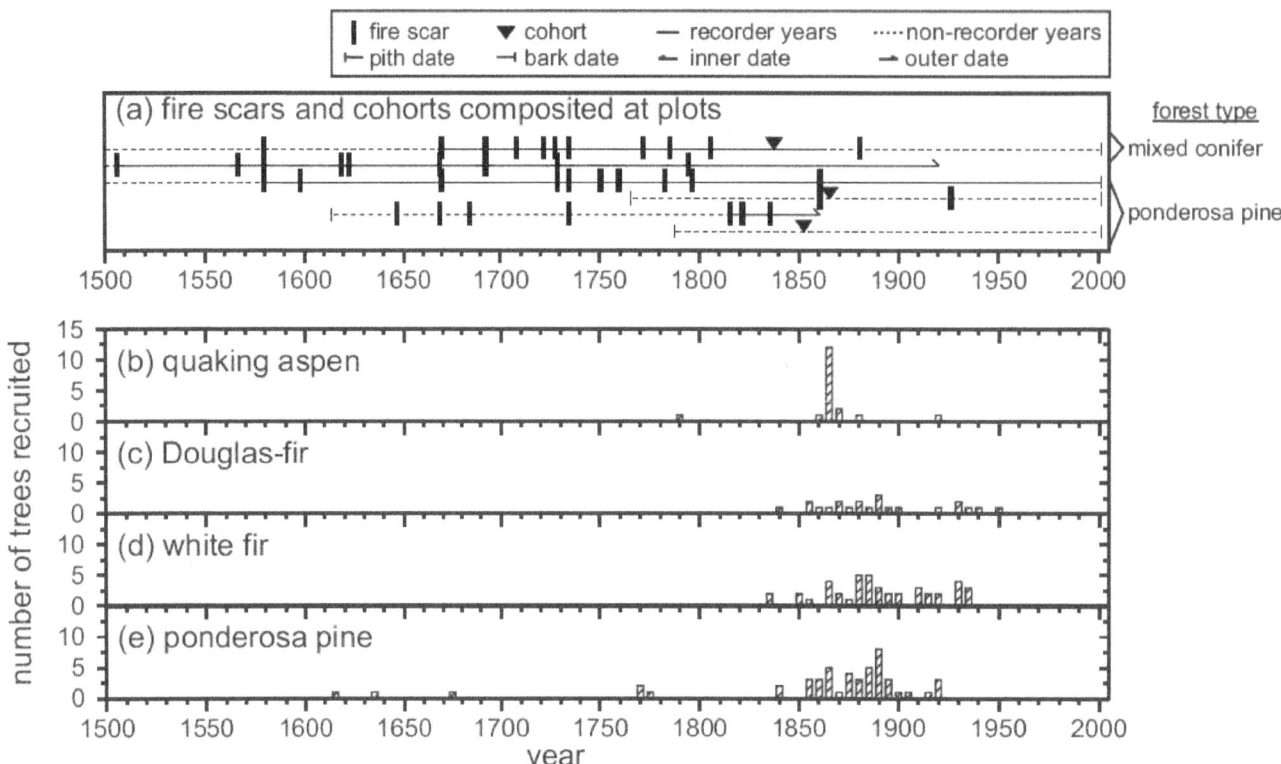

Figure J-3—Chronologies of fire and tree recruitment at INC. In (a), horizontal lines are plot-composite fire-scar and cohort dates by forest type. Non-recorder years precede the first scar, whereas recorder years generally follow it, but non-recorder years can also occur when the catface margin is consumed by subsequent fires or rot. In (b) through (e), recruitment dates are given for species comprising ≥10 percent of trees with such dates. The latter part of the distribution is incomplete because we only cored trees that were ≥8 inches DBH.

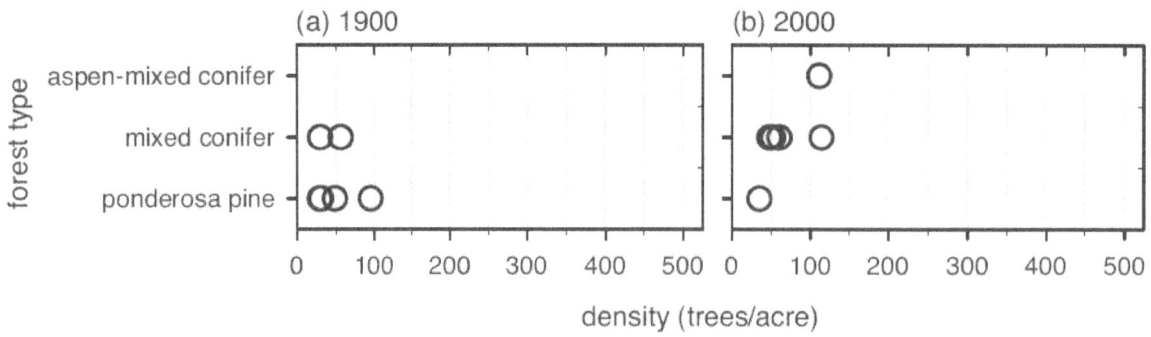

Figure J-4—Density of trees ≥8 inches DBH that were alive at each plot at INC (a) in 1900 and (b) in 2000, by forest type (table 2).

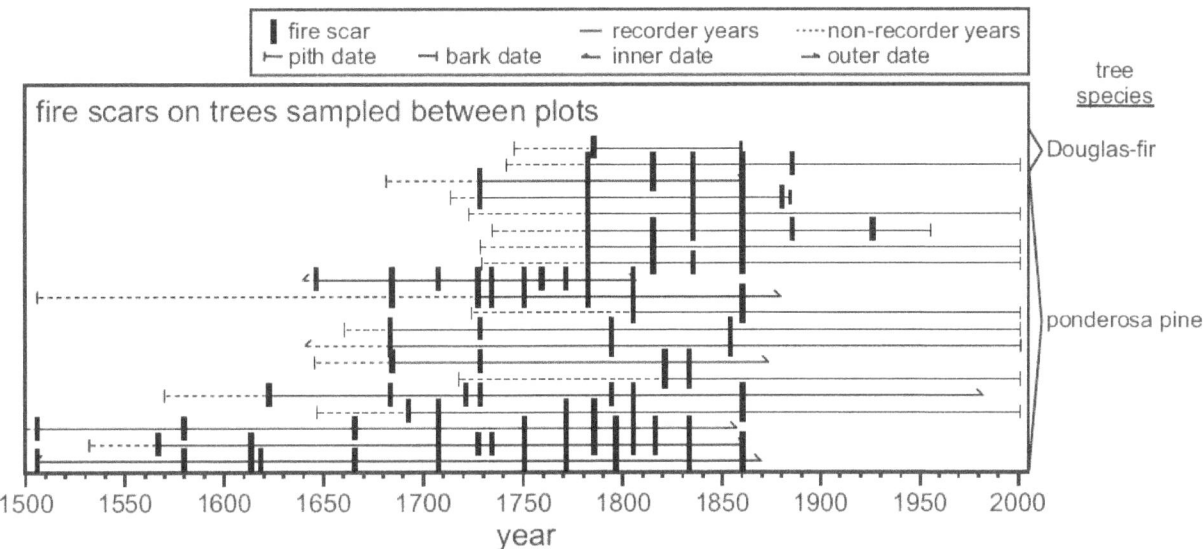

Figure J-5—Chronology of low-severity fires recorded on the 20 trees sampled between plots over approximately, 359 acres throughout the INC site.

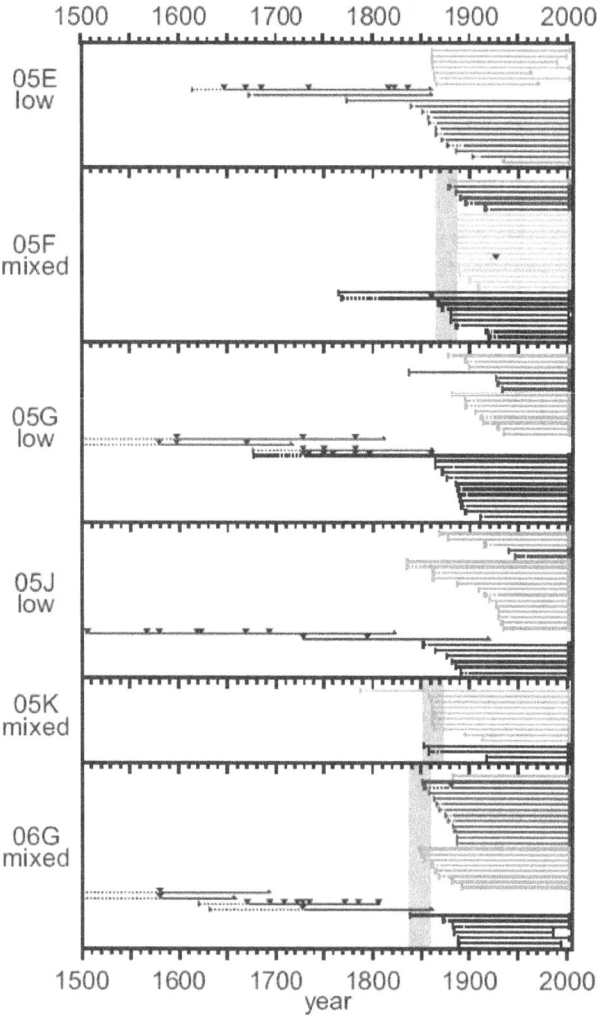

Figure J-6—Fire-demography diagrams (FDDs, Brown and others 2008b) showing chronologies of tree demography (recruitment and death), fire scars, and cohorts at each plot. Bark dates on 19 stumps are shown as outer dates. Not shown are 20 fire-scarred trees sampled between plots. Inferred fire severity (table 3) is indicated to the left of each panel.

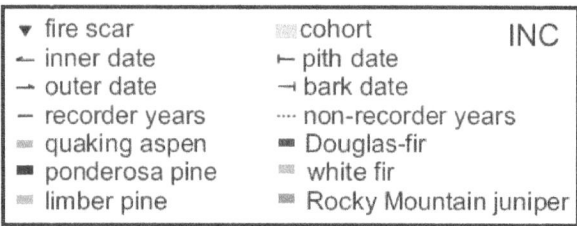

▼ fire scar	▨ cohort INC
⊢ inner date	⊣ pith date
⊣ outer date	⊣ bark date
— recorder years	···· non-recorder years
▥ quaking aspen	▪ Douglas-fir
▪ ponderosa pine	▨ white fir
▨ limber pine	▨ Rocky Mountain juniper

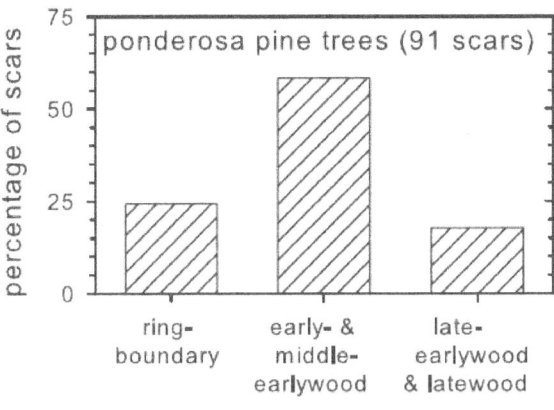

Figure J-7—Intra-ring position of fire scars sampled in and between plots at INC from 1650 to 1900, as a percentage of the number of scars for which the position could be determined (given in parentheses). Not shown are intra-ring positions for six fire scars on Douglas-fir trees.

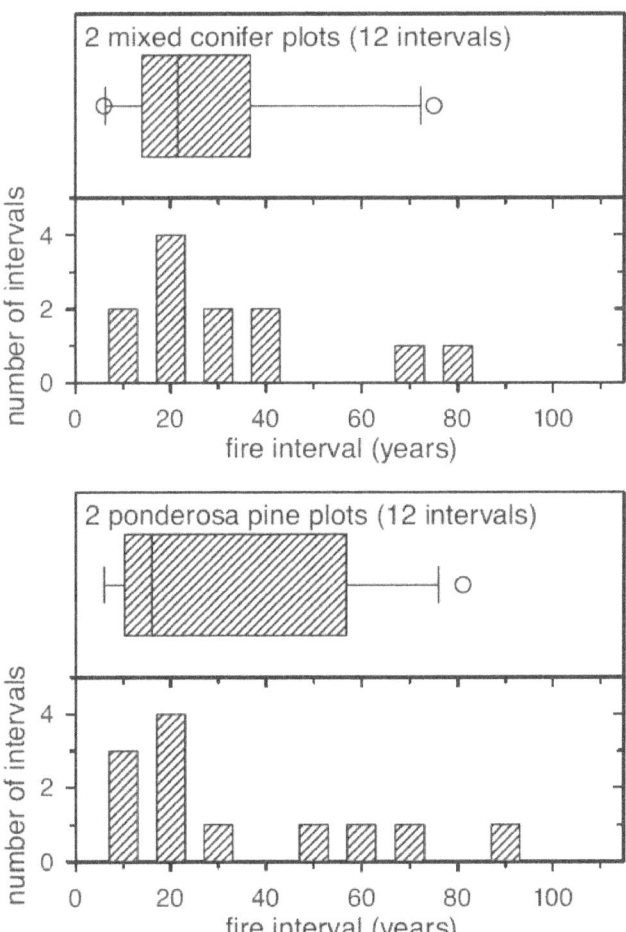

Figure J-8—Plot-composite intervals between low-severity fires by forest type at INC from 1650 to 1900. Plots averaged 0.42 acres. The boxes (top panels for each forest type) enclose the 25th to 75th percentiles and the whiskers enclose the 10th to 90th percentiles of the distribution of intervals. The vertical lines indicate the median fire interval, and all values falling outside the 10th to 90th percentiles are shown as circles. In the histogram (bottom panels for each forest type), the same intervals are plotted in 10-year bins (1 to 10 years, 11 to 20 years, and so forth).

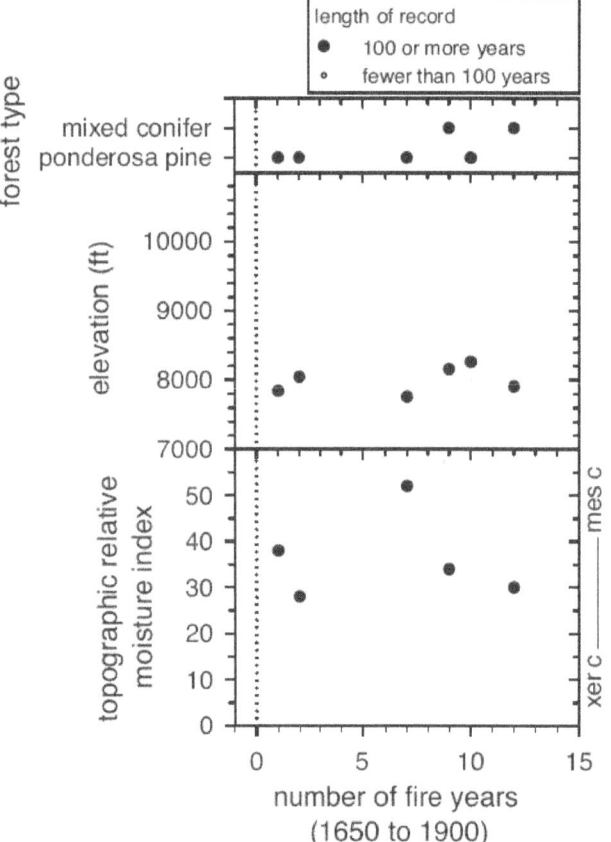

Figure J-9—Variation in fire among plots at INC with topography, forest type, and relative soil moisture availability (Parker 1982). Number of fire years includes both fire-scar and cohort dates. The dotted line indicates no fires from 1650 to 1900.

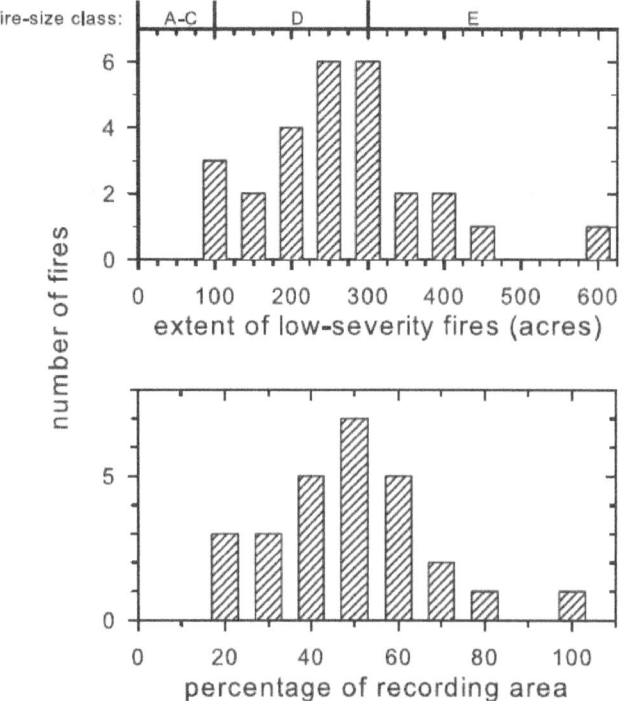

Figure J-10—Relative extent of low-severity fires within the 624-acre INC site, from 1650 to 1900, as area (top) and as a percentage of the recording area (in other words, the combined area of cells containing recording, fire-scarred trees during each year; bottom). Commonly used fire-size classes are indicated at the top (NWCG 2007).

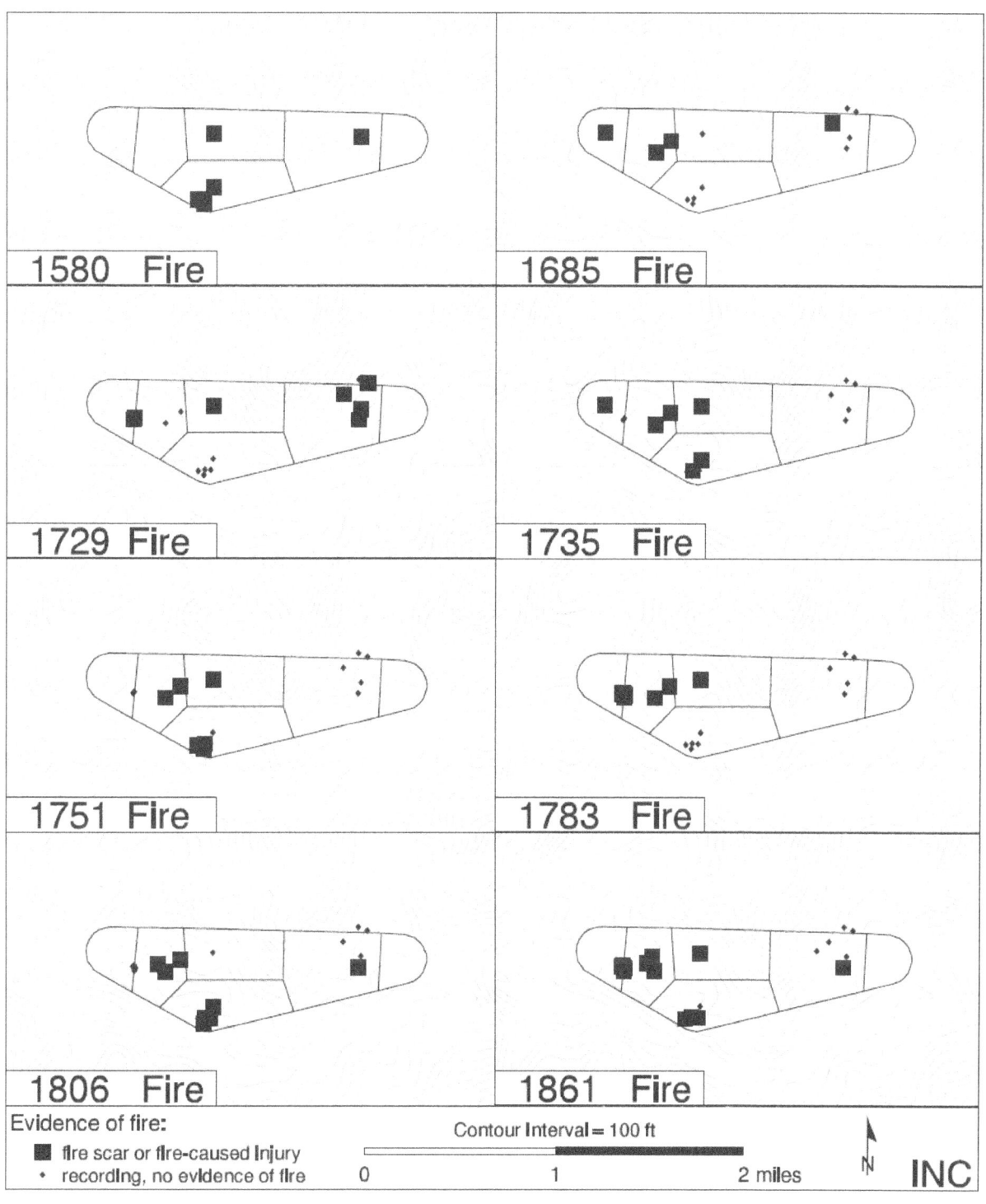

Figure J-11—Maps of years with evidence of low-severity fires in three or more cells at INC. "Recording, no evidence of fire" indicates at least one tree was alive at that location during that year but did not have a fire scar or fire-caused injury. Empty cells indicate that no fire-scarred trees were recording in that cell during that year. Cohort dates are not mapped.

Appendix K. Upper Fremont River, Mytoge Mountains, Fishlake National Forest (UFR)

Topography

We sampled 15 plots over 1391 acres surrounding the northern Crater Lake, near the north end of Fish Lake, on the Loa Ranger District of the Fishlake National Forest in Sevier County, Utah (figs. 1 and K-1). We sampled half as many plots here as at the other gridded sites because the Fishlake National Forest managers needed data from this area to address wildland-urban interface issues near Fish Lake, but the area lacked strong gradients in elevation or forest type. The plots were separated by 0.31 miles on average (range 0.28 to 0.31 miles) and averaged 0.25 acres in area (range 0.12 to 0.55 acres). Plots were sampled within cells that averaged 71 acres and ranged from 56 to 101 acres. Plots ranged in elevation from 9180 to 9964 ft (fig. K-2). They ranged in slope from 4 to 65 percent, but most had slopes less than 20 percent (87 percent of plots). They were sampled on a range of aspects. The distribution of the plots by elevation, aspect, or slope did not differ from the distribution of the landscape by more than 10 percent except for gentle and moderate slopes (over and under sampled, respectively) and north aspects, which were over sampled (fig. K-2). We took two photographs at one of the plots.

Tree Demography

Of the 447 trees that occurred in the plots, most (99 percent) were Douglas-fir, quaking aspen, subalpine fir, or Engelmann spruce, but 1 curl-leaf mountain mahogany also occurred as well as 2 trees we could not identify (fig. K-3). Most of these trees were living (73 percent) and the rest were snags (15 percent) and logs (12 percent). We were able to remove and crossdate wood samples from most of these trees (402 trees or 90 percent), and we obtained actual or estimated pith dates for 299 of them. These pith dates ranged from 1511 to 1964 and 62 of these post-dated 1900 (fig. K-4). The death dates we obtained for 83 logs and snags ranged from 1853 to 2003.

Historical and Current Forest Structure and Composition

The plots included a range of historical and modern forest types (mixed conifer, aspen-mixed conifer, aspen, and spruce-fir; table K-1). Some plots changed forest type between 1860 and 2000: three mixed conifer, one aspen, and one spruce-fir plot converted to aspen-mixed conifer. In 1900, tree density averaged 87 trees per acre and ranged from 22 to 204 trees per acre (fig. K-5). In 2000, tree density averaged 112 trees per acre and ranged from 40 to 219 trees per acre. However, we likely underestimated historical tree density because we could not obtain recruitment or earliest-ring dates for 45 of the 447 trees that occurred in the plots and only an earliest-ring date for another 103 trees. Twenty of these trees had earliest-ring dates between 1901 and 1920 and therefore may have been living before 1900.

Fire Scars

We were able to remove and crossdate fire-scarred samples from 16 trees, 3 of which had only scars that were recorded on a single tree and so were excluded from further analyses. Of the remaining 13 trees, 6 were sampled in 5 of the 15 plots at this site (1 to 2 trees per plot). We sampled the seven other fire-scarred trees as we encountered them between plots over 225 acres throughout the site (fig. K-6). Most of the 13 fire-scarred trees were ponderosa pine (92 percent) and the rest were Engelmann spruce. They were nearly equally divided among snags (38 percent), logs (31 percent), and live trees (31 percent). The fire-scarred trees yielded 24 fire scars and 1 abrupt change in ring width (figs. K-4 and K-7). However, five of these scar dates were eliminated from further analyses because they were recorded on only a single tree at the site. We were able to assign an intra-ring position to 42 percent of the 12 fire scars that occurred during the analysis period (1650 to 1900).

Post-Fire Cohorts

We identified eight cohorts of trees from estimated recruitment dates at seven of the plots. All of these cohorts were recruited before 1900 (1730 to 1890) and were identified from 59 trees (5 to 12 trees per cohort), most of which were Douglas-fir (46 percent), aspen (39 percent), or subalpine fir (12 percent), but there were also a few Engelmann spruce (figs. K-4 and K-7). The cohorts occurred in plots with a range of forest types: mixed conifer (63 percent of cohorts), aspen (25 percent), and spruce-fir (13 percent).

Spatial Variation in Fire Regimes

We reconstructed too few fire intervals in plots during the analysis period (1650 to 1900) to compute plot-composite fire intervals by forest type at this site. The tree-ring record before 1900 was less than 100 years long for 1 of the 15 plots at this site (fig. K-8). We assigned the remaining plots to the mixed or high fire severity categories (table K-2).

From 1650 to 1900, the three low-severity fires we reconstructed within our 1391-acre sampling area averaged 137 acres and ranged from 62 to 230 acres, equivalent to 33 to 65 percent of the recording area (in other words, the combined area of cells containing recording, fire-scarred trees during a given year). Recording area varied among fire years, ranging from 185 to 353 acres. We likely underestimated the extent of low-severity fires because most fires intersected the boundary of the site (fig. K-9).

Table K-1—Distribution of plots at UFR by historical (1860) and modern (2000) forest types (table 2).

| Historical forest type (1860) | Modern forest type (2000) | | | |
	Spruce-fir	Aspen-mixed conifer	Mixed conifer	Total plots in 1860
Spruce-fir	2	1		3
Aspen		1		1
Aspen-mixed conifer		2		2
Mixed conifer		3	6	9
Total plots in 2000	**2**	**7**	**6**	**15**

Table K-2—Distribution of plots at UFR by historical forest type (1860; table 2) and fire severity (table 3).

Forest type	High	Assumed high	Mixed
Spruce-fir		2	1
Aspen			1
Aspen-mixed conifer		2	
Mixed conifer	3	4	2
Total	**3**	**8**	**4**

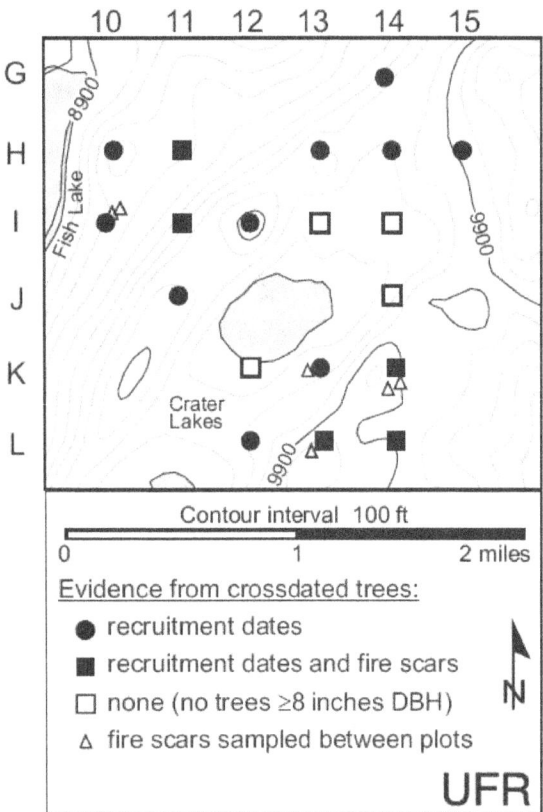

Figure K-1—Locations of plots and crossdated fire-scarred trees that were sampled outside plots. About half of the fire-scarred trees were sampled within plots and are not mapped individually. Plots are identified by column and row, in other words, the northwestern most plot is 10H, the next plot to the east is 11H, and so forth. Note that at most other sites, the rows are identified by number and the columns by letter.

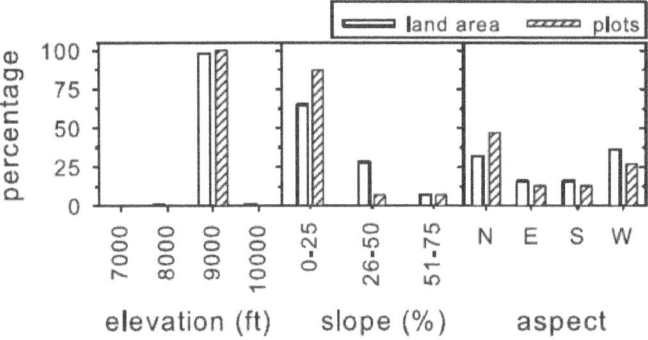

Figure K-2—Distribution of sampled plots and land area at UFR by topography. Aspect classes are 90° wide, beginning with 46° for east (E). Land area was derived from a digital elevation model (Utah AGRC 2004).

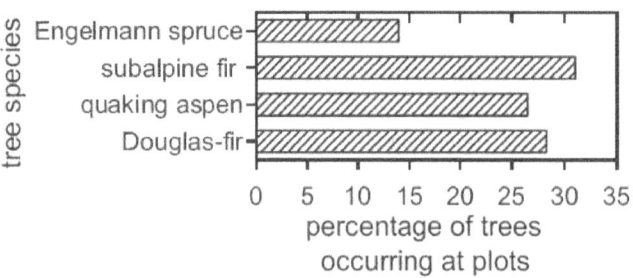

Figure K-3—Distribution by species of the 447 live and dead trees ≥8 inches DBH that occurred in plots at UFR, regardless of whether or not we removed wood samples and crossdated them. Not shown are one curl-leaf mountain mahogany and two trees of unknown species.

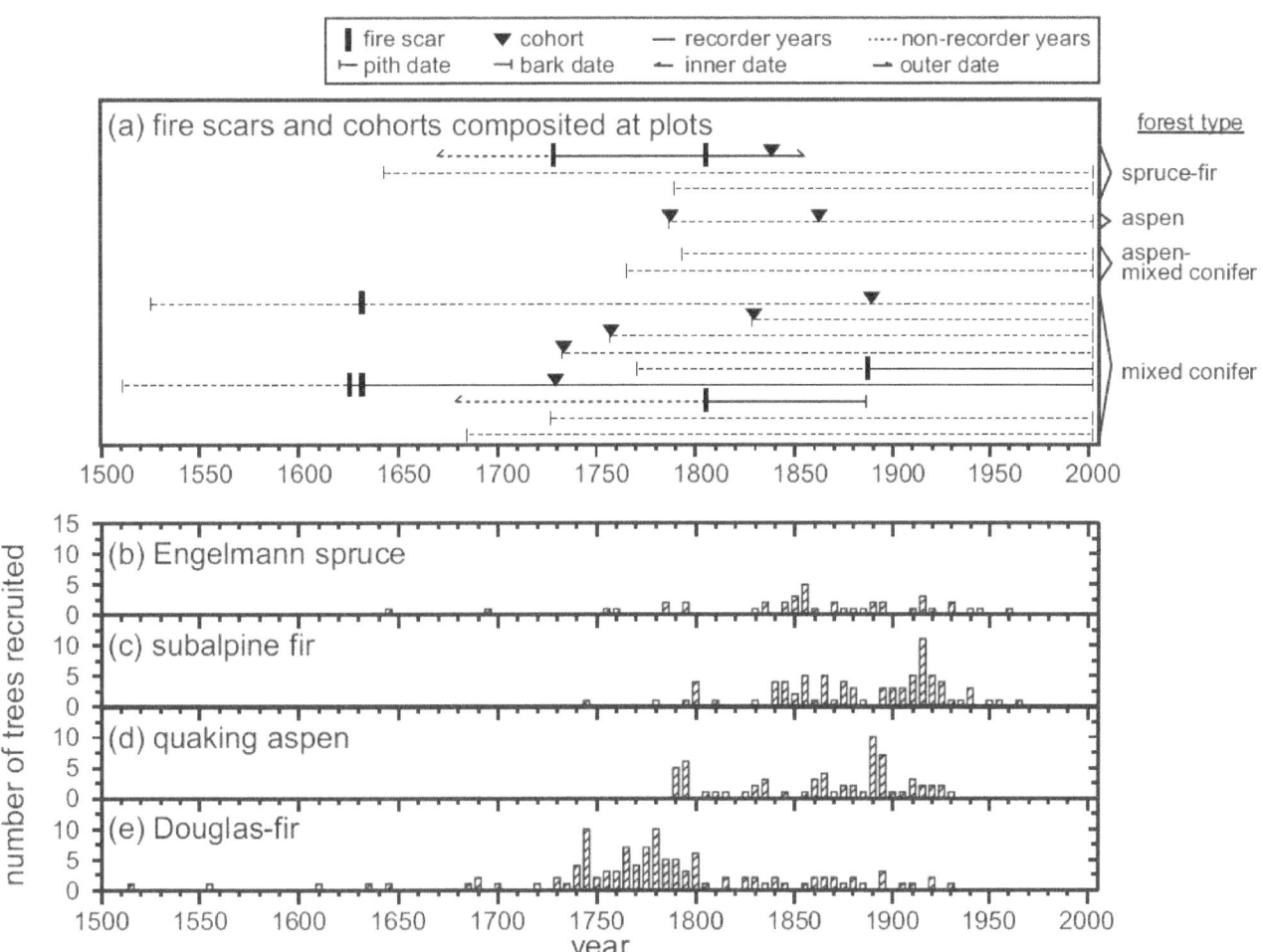

Figure K-4—Chronologies of fire and tree recruitment at UFR. In (a), horizontal lines are plot-composite fire-scar and cohort dates by forest type. Non-recorder years precede the first scar, whereas recorder years generally follow it, but non-recorder years can also occur when the catface margin is consumed by subsequent fires or rot. In (b) through (e), recruitment dates are given for species comprising ≥10 percent of trees with such dates. The latter part of the distribution is incomplete because we only cored trees that were ≥8 inches DBH.

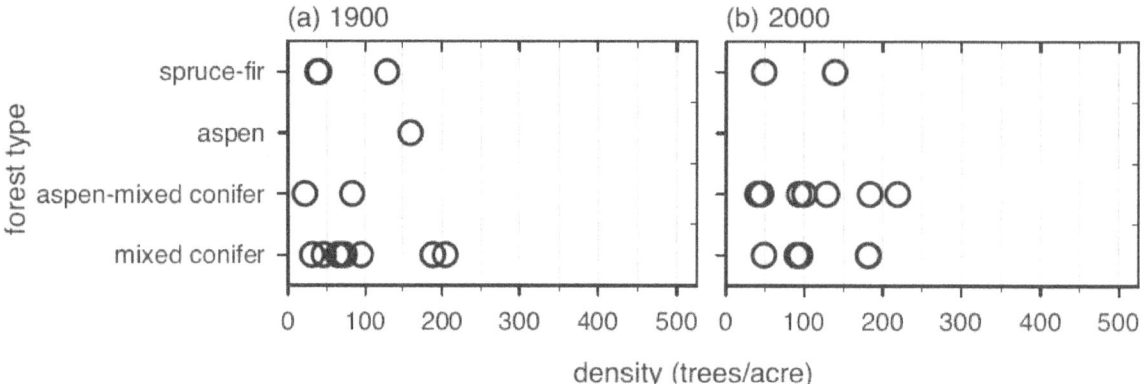

Figure K-5—Density of trees ≥8 inches DBH that were alive at each plot at UFR (a) in 1900 and (b) in 2000, by forest type (table 2).

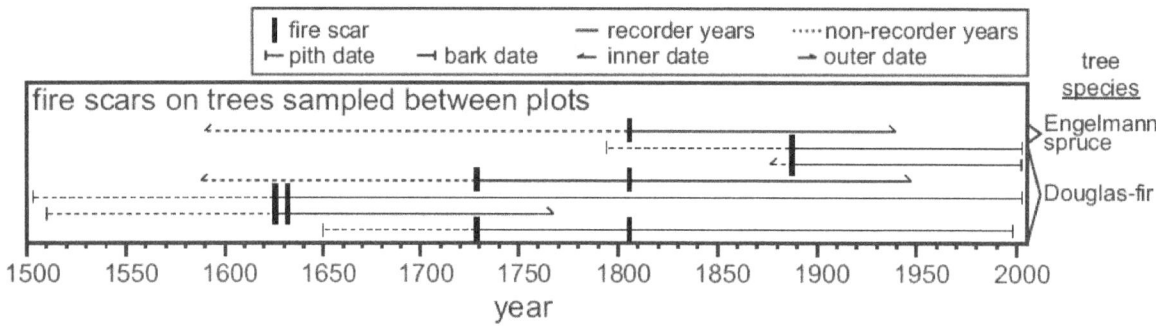

Figure K-6—Chronology of low-severity fires recorded on the seven trees sampled between plots over approximately, 225 acres at southern and western edges of the UFR site.

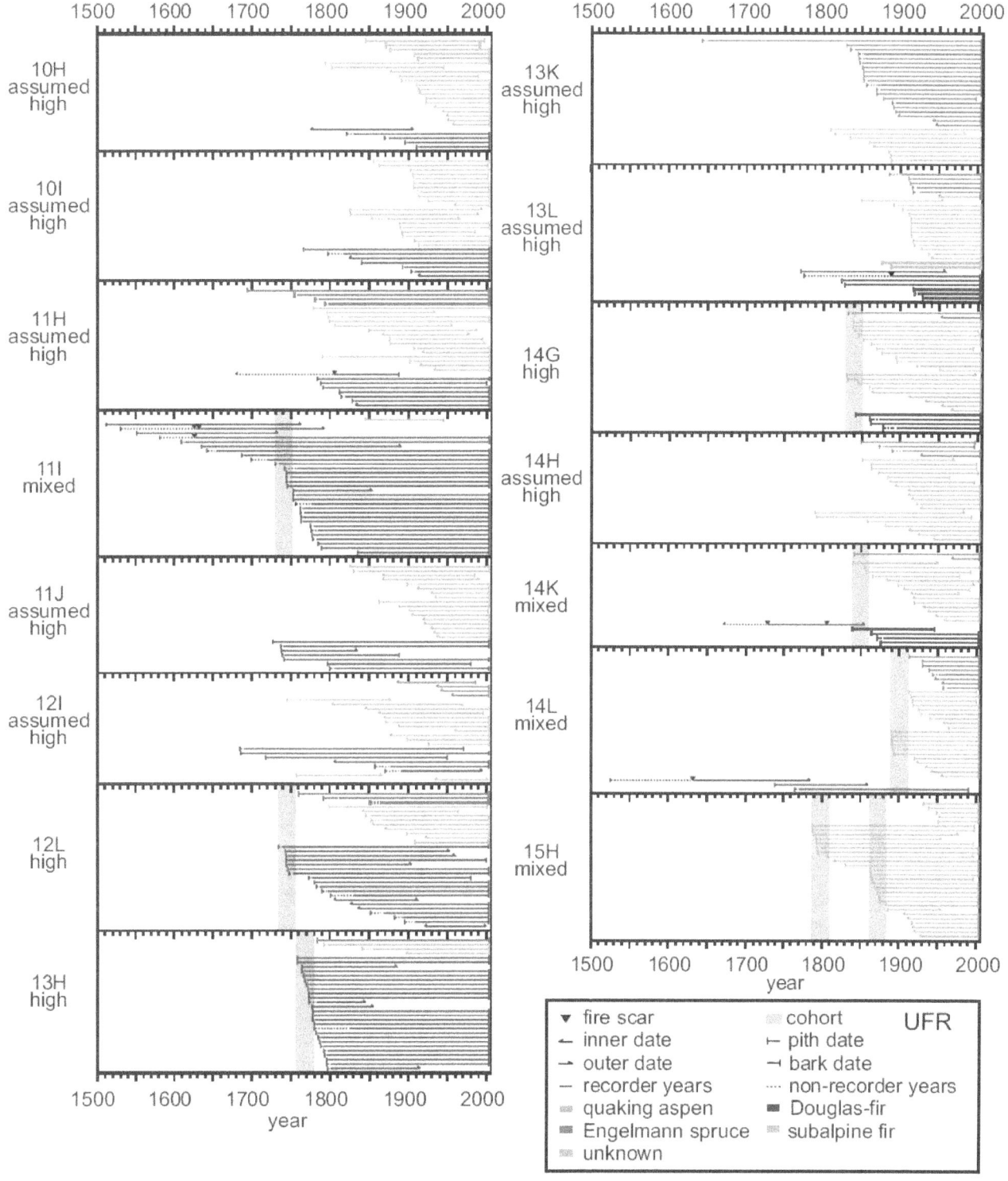

Figure K-7—Fire-demography diagrams (FDDs, Brown and others 2008b) showing chronologies of tree demography (recruitment and death), fire scars, and cohorts at each plot. Not shown are seven fire-scarred trees sampled between plots. Inferred fire severity (table 3) is indicated to the left of each panel. There is only one tree for which the species is unknown.

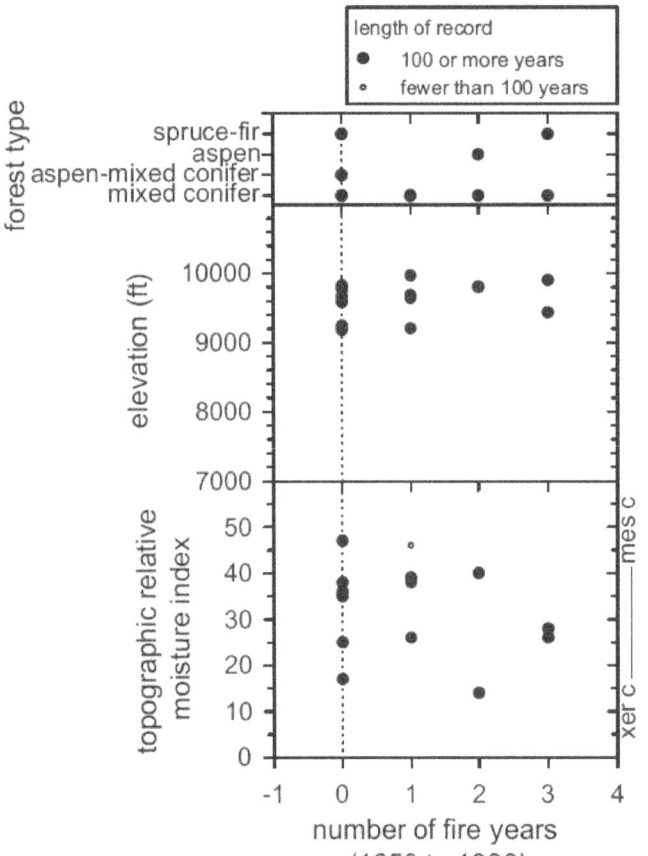

Figure K-8—Variation in fire among plots at UFR with topography, forest type, and relative soil moisture availability (Parker 1982). Number of fire years includes both fire-scar and cohort dates. Plots with no reconstructed fires during this period fall on the dotted line.

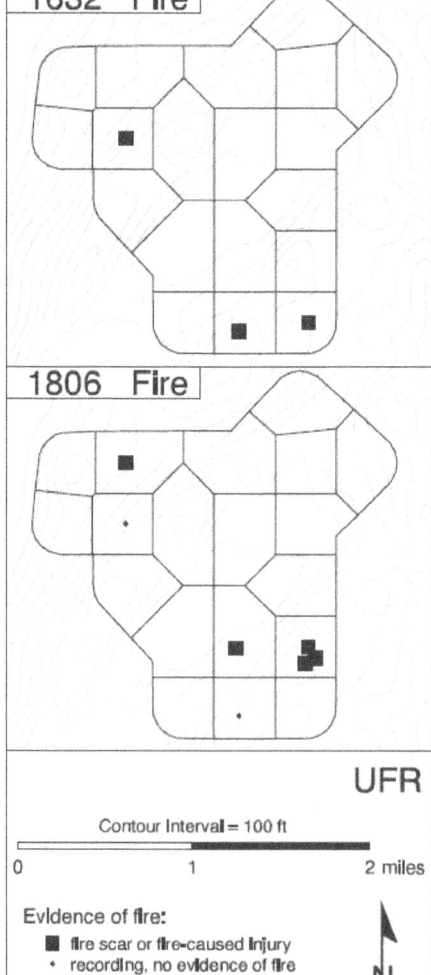

Figure K-9—Maps of years with evidence of low-severity fires in three or more cells at UFR. "Recording, no evidence of fire" indicates at least one tree was alive at that location during that year but did not have a fire scar or fire-caused injury. Empty cells indicate that no fire-scarred trees were recording in that cell during that year. Cohort dates are not mapped.

Appendix L. Wasatch Plateau, Fishlake National Forest (OWP)

In 2003, we removed fire-scarred partial cross sections from 17 ponderosa pine trees over an area of 49 acres on Old Woman Plateau on the Richfield Ranger District of the Fishlake National Forest in Sevier County, Utah (fig. 1). The forest was a relatively open ponderosa pine/sagebrush ecosystem on a flat sandy bench. We sampled here at the request of the Fishlake National Forest because it is near both the wildland-urban interface (it is close to a summer cabin subdivision and other developed areas) and a Research Natural Area (approximately 6 miles to the southeast). All of the trees were dead when sampled (nine stumps, two logs, and six snags). We were able to crossdate samples from all but one of them, from which we identified 96 fire scars and no fire-caused injuries (fig. L-1). From the composite fire-scar record of 12 intervals over the analysis period (1650 to 1900), a fire occurred somewhere in the 49-acre sampling area every 20 years on average (range 4 to 39 years; fig. L-2) and these fires scarred an average of 52 percent of the sampled trees that were recording (range 18 to 89 percent). We were able to assign an intra-ring position to most (62 percent) of the scars that were formed during the analysis period (1650 to 1990). Of the scars to which we could assign an intra-ring position, about half were created by fires that burned when the cambium was dormant (58 percent ring-boundary scars; fig. L-3). The rest were created during the growing season (18 percent in early- plus middle-earlywood versus 24 percent in late-earlywood plus latewood).

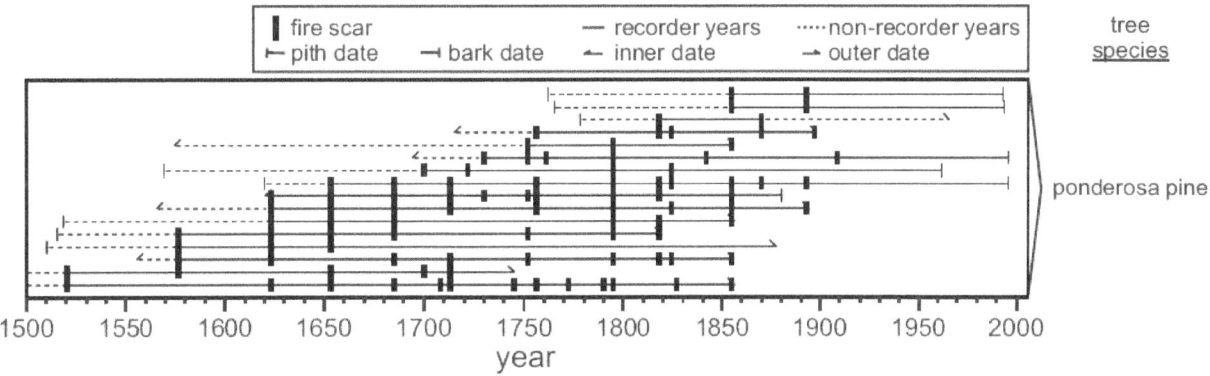

Figure L-1—Chronology of surface fires from trees sampled over 49 acres at OWP. Each horizontal line indicates the length of record for a single tree. Non-recorder years precede the first scar at a plot, whereas recorder years generally follow it. However, non-recorder years also occur when the margin of the catface is consumed by subsequent fires or rot.

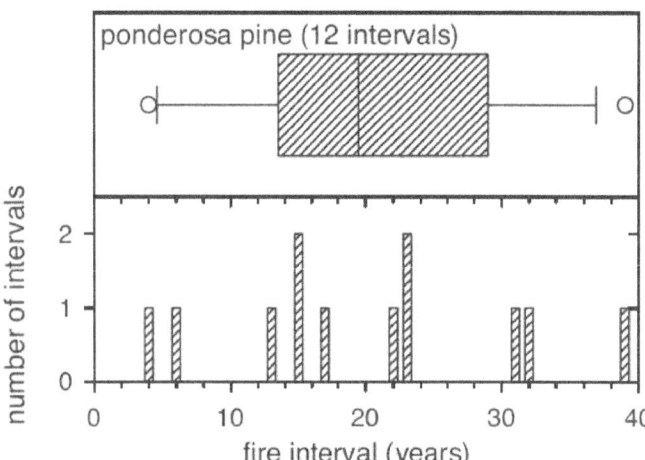

Figure L-2—Composite fire intervals at OWP, determined as the intervals between years with fire scars on two or more ponderosa pine trees over the 49-acre sampling area during the period from 1650 to 1900. The box (top) encloses the 25th to 75th percentiles and the whiskers enclose the 10th to 90th percentiles of the distribution of intervals. The vertical line across the box indicates the median fire interval, and all values falling outside the 10th to 90th percentiles are shown as circles. In the histogram (bottom), the same intervals are plotted in 2-year bins.

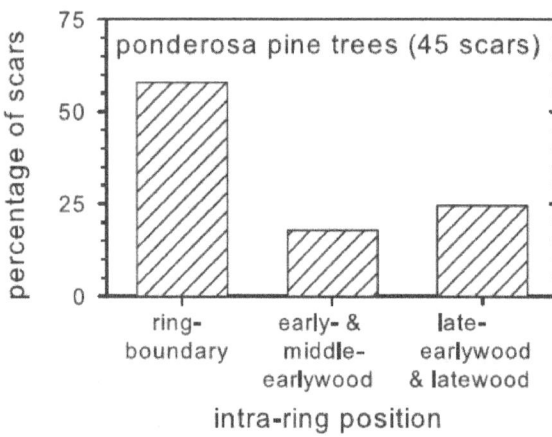

Figure L-3—Intra-ring position of fire scars on ponderosa pine trees at OWP from 1650 to 1900, as a percentage of the number of scars for which the position could be determined (given in parentheses).

Appendix M. Monroe Mountain, Fishlake National Forest (MON)

We crossdated fire-scarred sections from 10 trees that had been sampled on Monroe Mountain on the Richfield Ranger District of the Fishlake National Forest in Sevier and Paiute Counties, Utah (fig. 1). The trees were sampled along an approximately 35-mile north-south transect for a previous study (Chappell 1997). Although we lack exact locations for each tree, they occurred between 8350 and 9600 ft on easterly to northerly slopes. All, but one was living when sampled. We identified 36 fire scars and 4 fire-caused injuries (fig. M-1). We were able to assign an intra-ring position to all, but 2 of the 26 scars that formed on the six ponderosa pine trees during the analysis period (1650 to 1900). We did not compute fire intervals for this site because the trees were sampled over a very large area of unknown size. Of the scars to which we could assign an intra-ring position, over half were created by fires burning when the cambium was dormant (59 percent ring-boundary scars; fig. M-2). The remaining scars were created during the growing season (29 percent in early- plus middle-earlywood versus 13 percent in late-earlywood plus latewood).

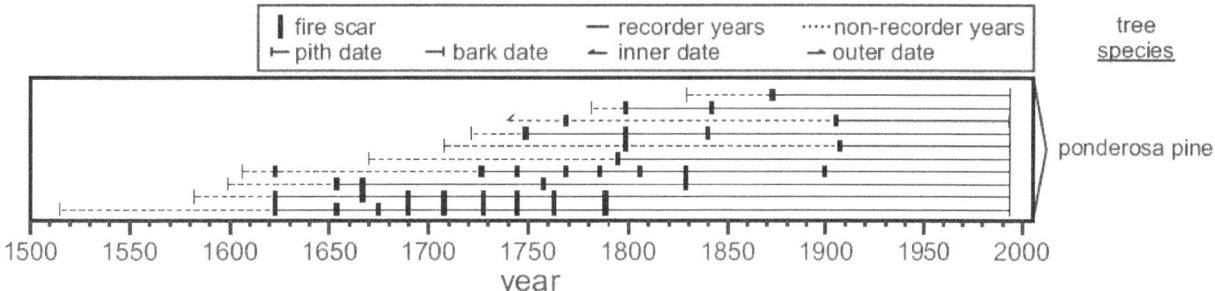

Figure M-1—Chronology of surface fires at MON, sampled over an approximately 35-mile north-south transect. Each horizontal line indicates the length of record for a single tree. Non-recorder years precede the first scar at a plot, whereas recorder years generally follow it. However, non-recorder years also occur when the margin of the catface is consumed by subsequent fires or rot.

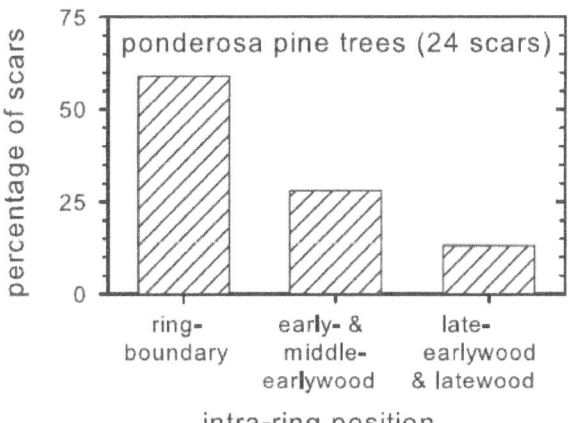

Figure M-2—Intra-ring position of fire scars on ponderosa pine trees at MON from 1650 to 1900, as a percentage of the number of scars for which the position could be determined (given in parentheses).

Appendix N. Abajo Mountains, Manti-La Sal National Forest (ABM)

Topography

We sampled 26 plots over 2223 acres along North Canyon Creek and Pine Ridge on the east side of the Abajo Mountains, on the Monticello Ranger District of the Manti-La Sal National Forest in San Juan County, Utah (figs. 1 and N-1). The plots were separated by 0.31 miles on average (range 0.27 to 0.44 miles) and averaged 0.41 acres in area (range 0.06 to 1.64 acres). Plots were sampled within cells that averaged 68 acres and ranged from 54 to 86 acres. Plots ranged in elevation from 8387 to 10,598 ft, but most (77 percent) were below 9500 ft (fig. N-2). They ranged in slope from 1 to 69 percent and were sampled on a range of aspects, but most were on north or east aspects (77 percent). The distribution of the plots by elevation, aspect, or slope did not differ from the distribution of the landscape by more than 10 percent in any category (fig. N-2). We took between one and four photographs each at 10 of the plots.

Tree Demography

Of the 737 trees that occurred in the plots, most (98 percent) were Gambel oak, ponderosa pine, Douglas-fir, quaking aspen, subalpine fir, or Engelmann spruce, but 3 white fir and 2 Colorado pinyon also occurred (fig. N-3). Most of these trees were living (76 percent) and the rest were snags (15 percent), logs (7 percent), or stumps (2 percent). We were able to remove and crossdate wood samples from most of these trees (697 trees or 95 percent), and we obtained actual or estimated pith dates for 559 of them. These pith dates ranged from 1326 to 1973, but many post-dated 1900 (208 trees; fig. N-4). The death dates we obtained for 109 logs and snags ranged from 1825 to 2003.

Historical and Current Forest Structure and Composition

The plots included a range of historical and modern forest types (oak, ponderosa pine, mixed conifer, aspen-mixed conifer, aspen, and spruce-fir; table N-1). Some plots changed forest type between 1860 and 2000: one aspen-mixed conifer and two aspen plots converted to mixed conifer; and one ponderosa pine and two aspen plots converted to aspen-mixed conifer. In 1900, tree density averaged 80 trees per acre and ranged from 6 to 250 trees per acre (fig. N-5). In 2000, tree density averaged 126 trees per acre and ranged from 18 to 511 trees per acre. However, we likely underestimated historical tree density because we could not obtain recruitment or earliest-ring dates for 40 of the 737 trees that occurred in the plots and only an earliest-ring date for another 138 trees. Some of these trees (24 trees) had earliest-ring dates between 1901 and 1920 and therefore may have been living before 1900.

Fire Scars

We were able to remove and crossdate fire-scarred samples from 68 trees, 13 of which had only scars that were recorded on a single tree and so were excluded from further analyses. Of the remaining 55 trees, about half (28 trees) were sampled in 10 of the 26 plots at this site (1 to 10 trees per plot, average 3 trees). We sampled the 27 other fire-scarred trees as we encountered them between plots, over 547 acres, at the north end of the site (fig. N-6). Most of the 55 fire-scarred trees were ponderosa pine (96 percent) and the rest were Engelmann spruce and Gambel oak. Most were logs, snags, or stumps (70 percent) and the rest were live trees. These 55 trees yielded 198 fire scars and 3 eroded fire scars or abrupt changes in ring width (figs. N-4 and N-7). However, 15 of these scar dates were eliminated from further analyses because they were recorded on only a single tree at the site. We were able to assign an intra-ring position to 57 percent of the 151 fire scars that occurred during the analysis period (1650 to 1900). Of the scars that occurred on ponderosa pine trees, half (48 percent) occurred on the boundary between two rings (fig. N-8).

Post-Fire Cohorts

We identified 17 cohorts of trees from estimated recruitment dates at 16 of the plots. Thirteen of these cohorts were recruited before 1900 (1326 to 1896) and were identified from 101 trees (5 to 15 trees per cohort), most of which were quaking aspen (56 percent), ponderosa pine (26 percent), Engelmann spruce (8 percent), or subalpine fir (6 percent), but there were also a few Douglas-fir and white fir (figs. N-4 and N-7). The cohorts that were recruited before 1900 occurred in plots with a range of forest types: aspen (38 percent of cohorts), ponderosa pine (38 percent), spruce-fir (15 percent), and mixed conifer (8 percent).

Spatial Variation in Fire Regimes

During the analysis period (1650 to 1900), plot-composite low-severity fire intervals pooled among ponderosa pine plots averaged 31 years (range 3 to 107 years; fig. N-9). There were more fire years in plots below versus above 9000 ft in ponderosa pine than in other forest types, and with higher relative soil moisture (fig. N-10). The tree-ring record before 1900 was less than 100 years long for 7 of the 26 plots at this site.

We could not infer historical fire severity at one plot because it did not meet our requirements for any of the severity categories (table N-2). We assigned the remaining plots to the low, mixed, or high fire severity categories.

From 1650 to 1900, the 30 low-severity fires we reconstructed within our 2223-acre sampling area averaged 187 acres and ranged from 71 to 398 acres (fig. N-11), equivalent to 14 to 75 percent of the recording area (in other words, the combined area of cells containing recording, fire-scarred trees during a given year). Recording area varied among fire years, ranging from 384 to 628 acres. We likely underestimated the extent of low-severity fires because most fires intersected the boundary of the site (fig. N-12).

Table N-1—Distribution of plots at ABM by historical (1860) and modern (2000) forest types (table 2).

Historical forest type (1860)	Modern forest type (2000)						Total plots in 1860
	Spruce-fir	Aspen	Aspen-mixed conifer	Mixed conifer	Ponderosa pine	Oak	
Spruce-fir	5						5
Aspen		3	2	2			7
Aspen-mixed conifer				1			1
Mixed conifer				2			2
Ponderosa pine			1		9		10
Oak						1	1
Total plots in 2000	**5**	**3**	**3**	**5**	**9**	**1**	**26**

Table N-2—Distribution of plots at ABM by historical forest type (1860; table 2) and fire severity (table 3).

Forest type	High	Assumed high	Mixed	Assumed mixed	Low	Unclassified
Spruce-fir		3	2			
Aspen	5	2				
Aspen-mixed conifer		1				
Mixed conifer		1	1			
Ponderosa pine			4	2	4	
Oak						1
Total	**5**	**7**	**7**	**2**	**4**	**1**

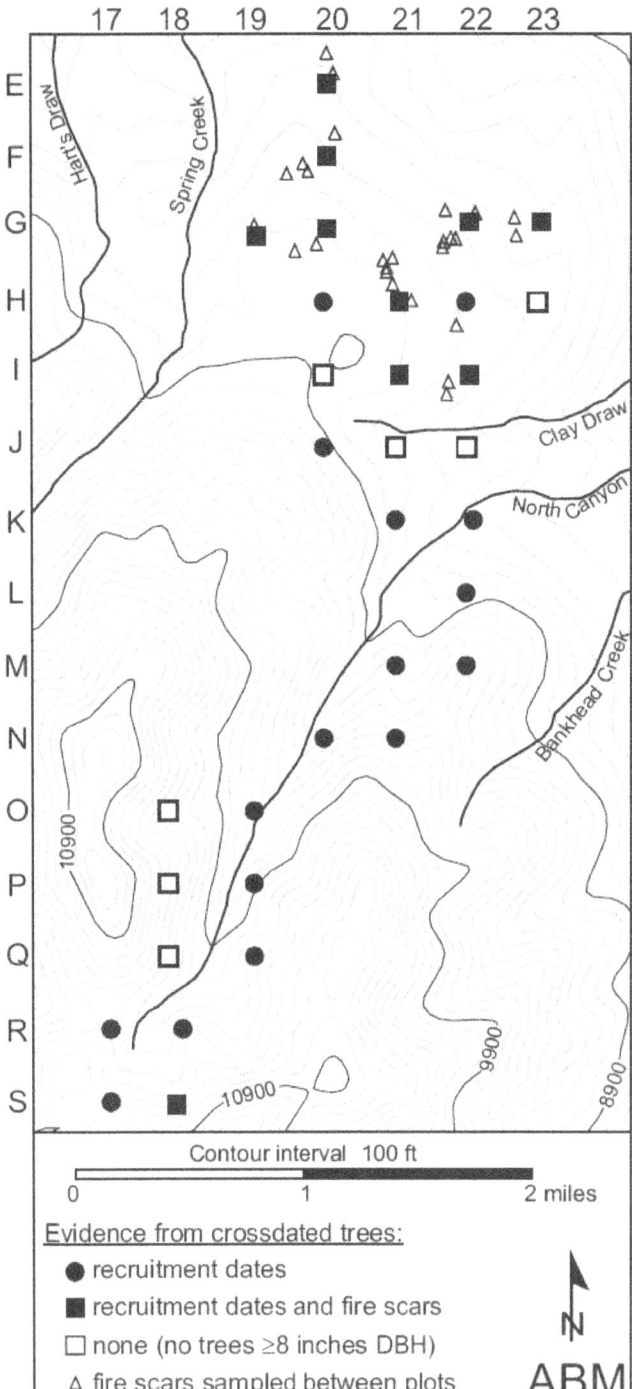

Figure N-1—Locations of plots and crossdated fire-scarred trees that were sampled outside plots. About half of the fire-scarred trees were sampled within plots and are not mapped individually. Plots are identified by column and row, in other words, the southwestern most plot is S17, the next plot to the east is S18, and so forth. Note that at most other sites, the rows are identified by number and the columns by letter.

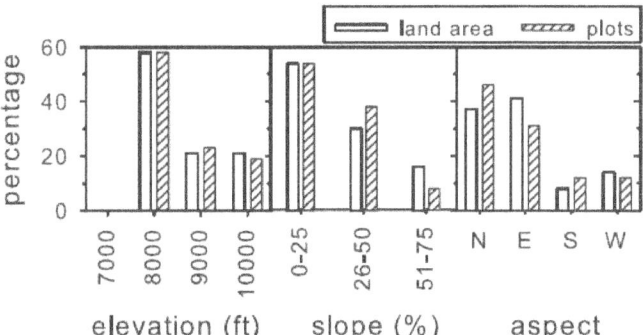

Figure N-2—Distribution of sampled plots and land area at ABM by topography. Aspect classes are 90° wide, beginning with 46° for east (E). Land area was derived from a digital elevation model (Utah AGRC 2004).

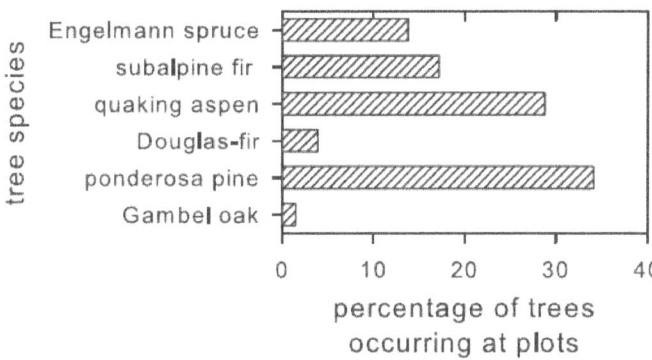

Figure N-3—Distribution by species of the 737 live and dead trees ≥8 inches DBH that occurred in plots at ABM, regardless of whether or not we removed wood samples and crossdated them. Not shown are two Colorado pinyon and three white fir trees.

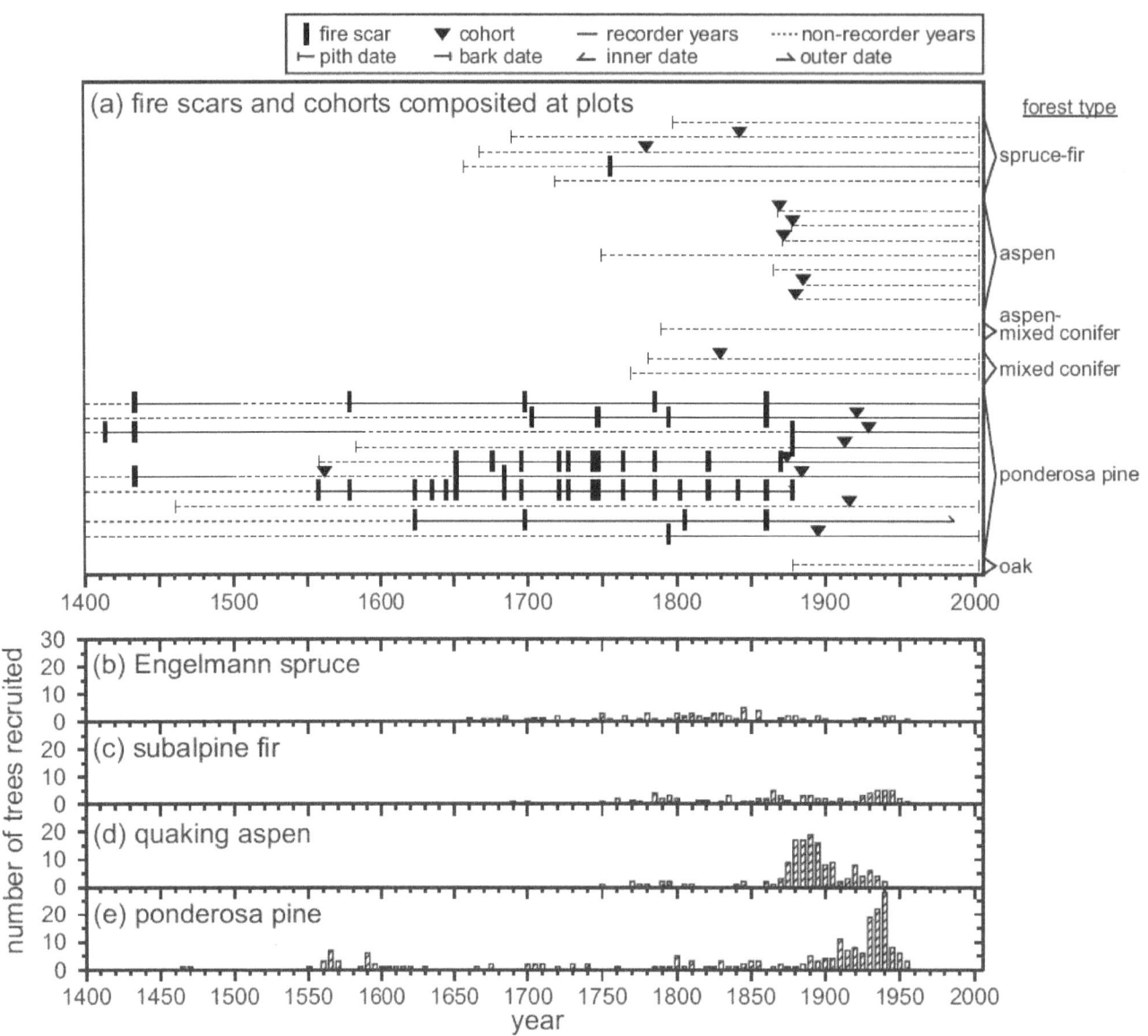

Figure N-4—Chronologies of fire and tree recruitment at ABM. In (a), horizontal lines are plot-composite fire-scar and cohort dates by forest type. Non-recorder years precede the first scar, whereas recorder years generally follow it, but non-recorder years can also occur when the catface margin is consumed by subsequent fires or rot. In (b) through (e), recruitment dates are given for species comprising ≥10 percent of trees with such dates. The latter part of the distribution is incomplete because we only cored trees that were ≥8 inches DBH.

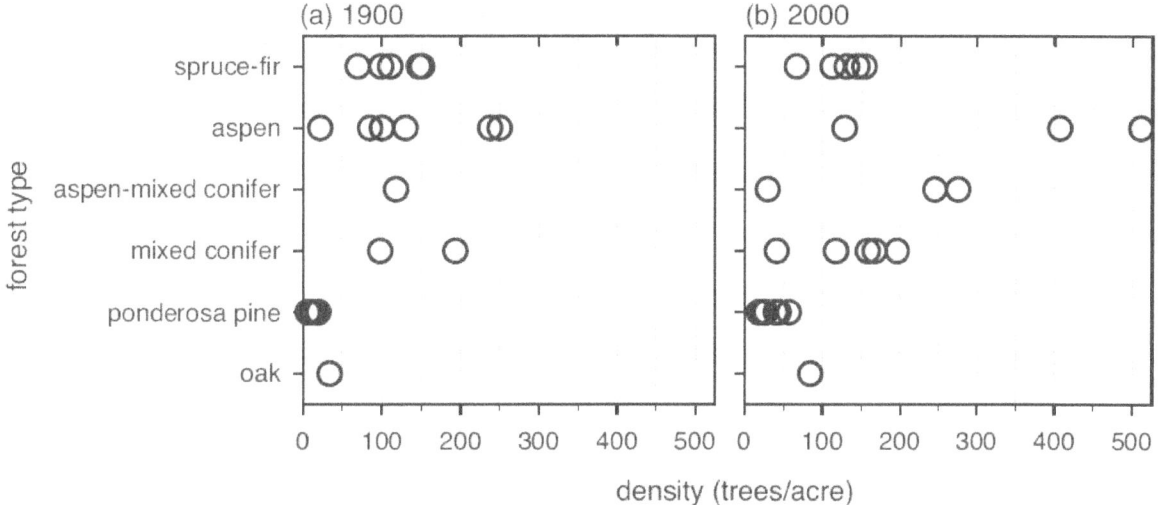

Figure N-5—Density of trees ≥8 inches DBH that were alive at each plot at ABM (a) in 1900 and (b) in 2000, by forest type (table 2).

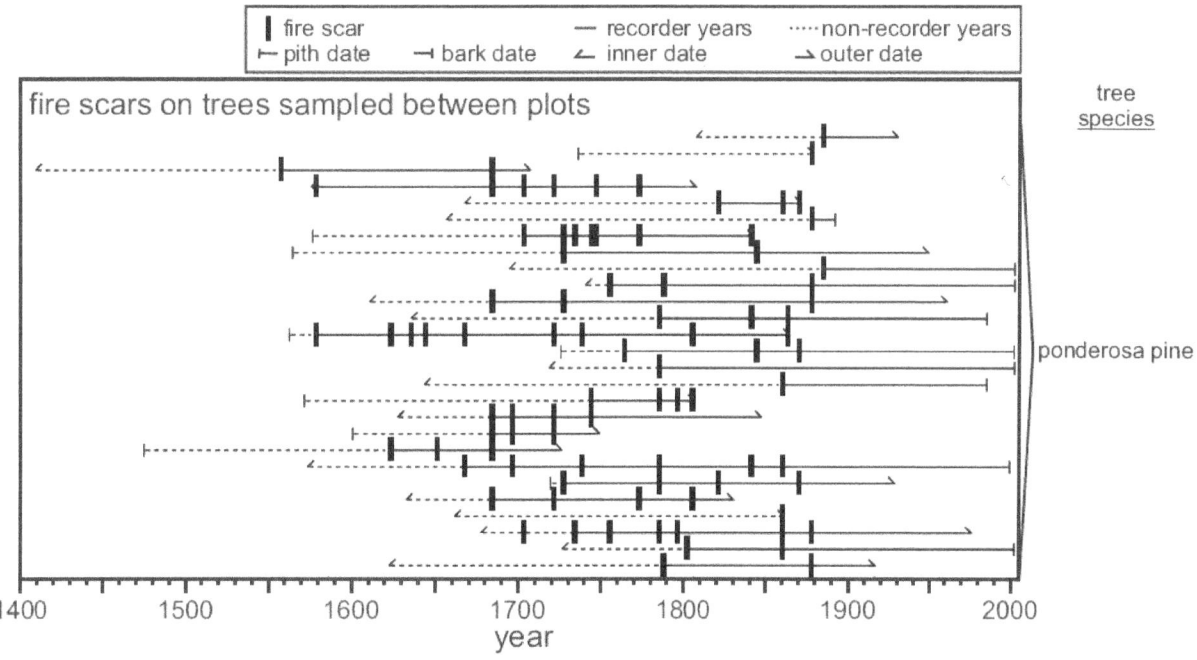

Figure N-6—Chronology of low-severity fires recorded on the 27 trees sampled between plots over approximately, 547 acres at the northern end of the ABM site.

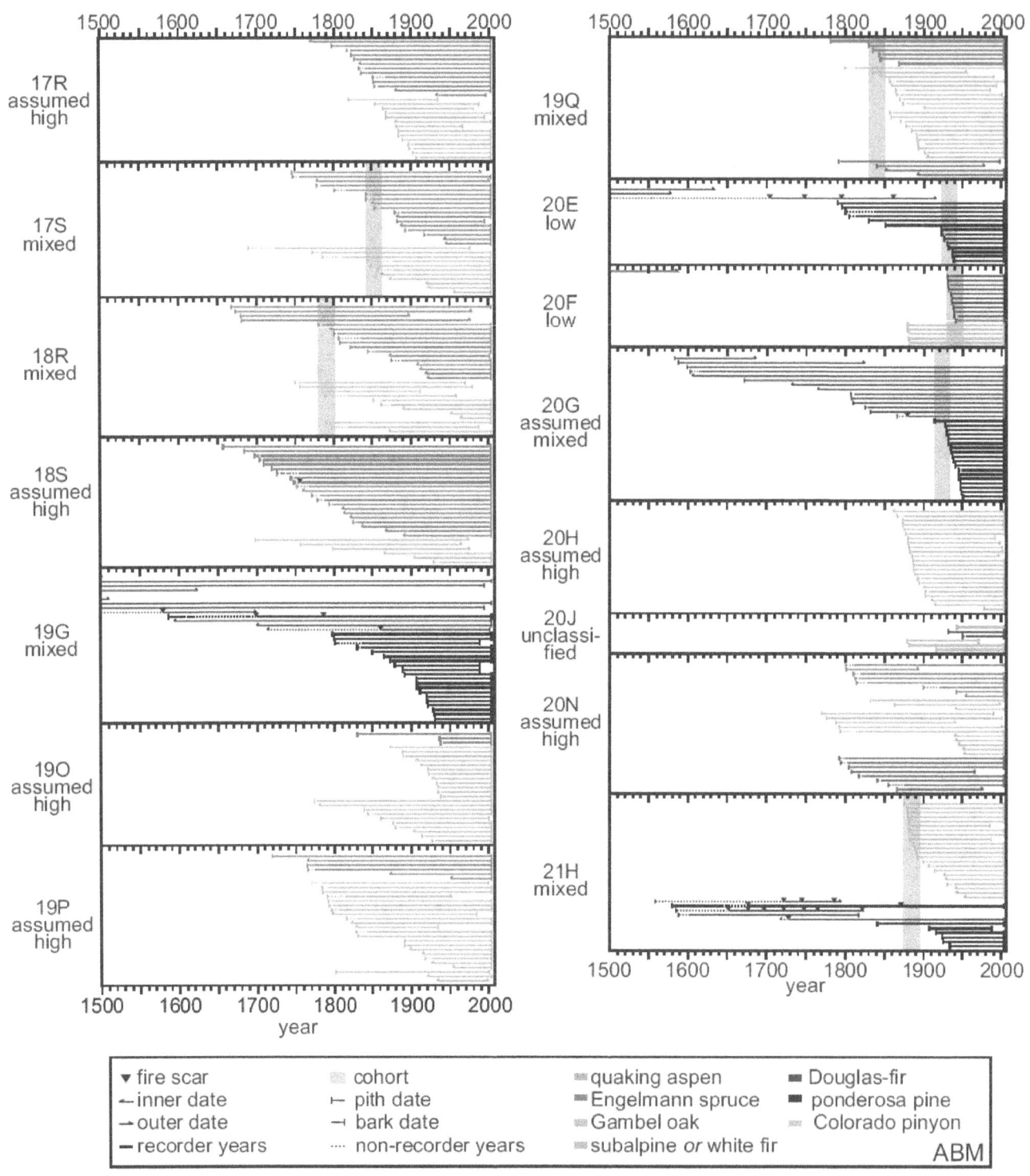

Figure N-7—Fire-demography diagrams (FDDs, Brown and others 2008b) showing chronologies of tree demography (recruitment and death), fire scars, and cohorts at each plot. Bark dates on 16 stumps are shown as outer dates. Not shown are 27 fire-scarred trees sampled between plots. Plot identifier and inferred fire severity (table 3) are indicated to the left of each panel. Most of the trees (96 percent) in the combined subalpine/white fir category are subalpine fir.

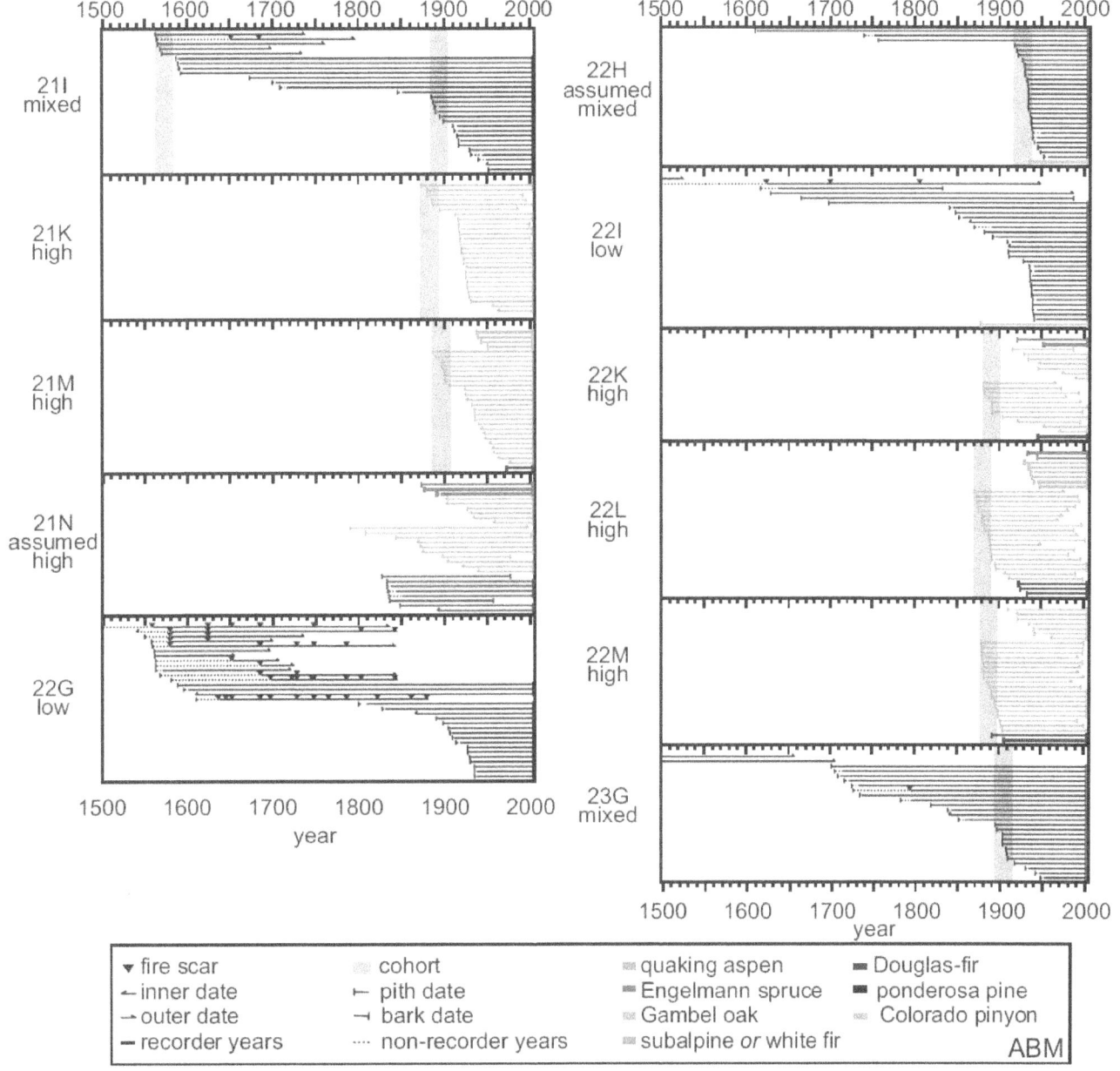

Figure N-7—*Continued.*

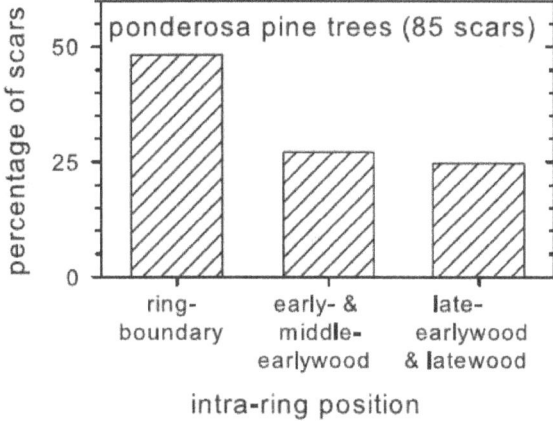

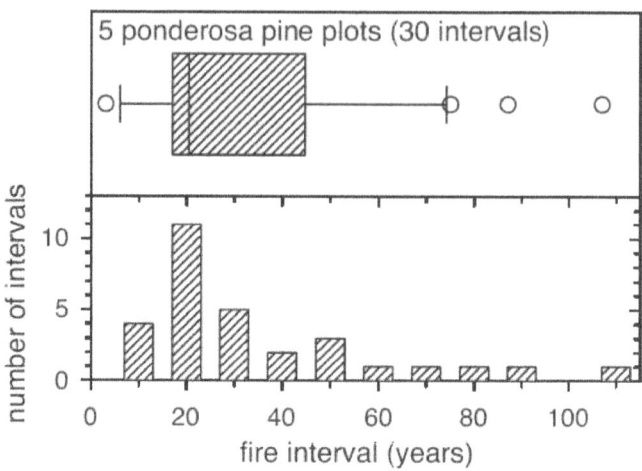

Figure N-8—Intra-ring position of fire scars on trees sampled in and between plots at ABM from 1650 to 1900, as a percentage of the number of scars for which the position could be determined (given in parentheses). Not shown is the intra-ring position for one fire scar on an Engelmann spruce tree.

Figure N-9—Plot-composite intervals between low-severity fires in ponderosa pine plots at ABM from 1650 to 1900. Plots averaged 0.41 acres. The box (top) encloses the 25th to 75th percentiles and the whiskers enclose the 10th to 90th percentiles of the distribution of intervals. The vertical line indicates the median fire interval, and all values falling outside the 10th to 90th percentiles are shown as circles. In the histogram (bottom), the same intervals are plotted in 10-year bins (1 to 10 years, 11 to 20 years, and so forth).

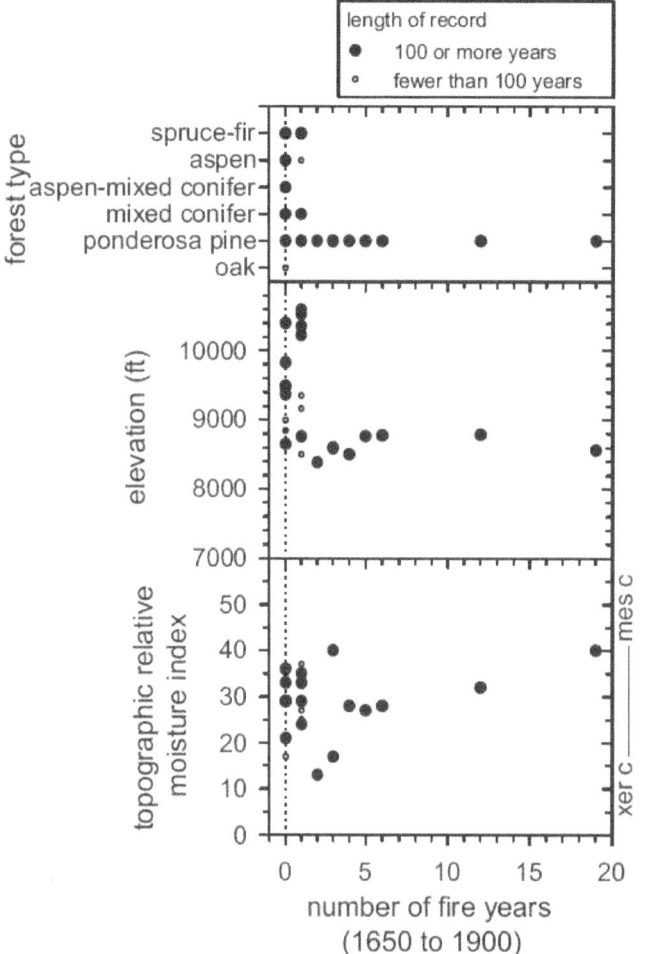

Figure N-10—Variation in fire among plots at ABM with topography, forest type, and relative soil moisture availability (Parker 1982). Number of fire years includes both fire-scar and cohort dates. Plots with no reconstructed fires during this period fall on the dotted line.

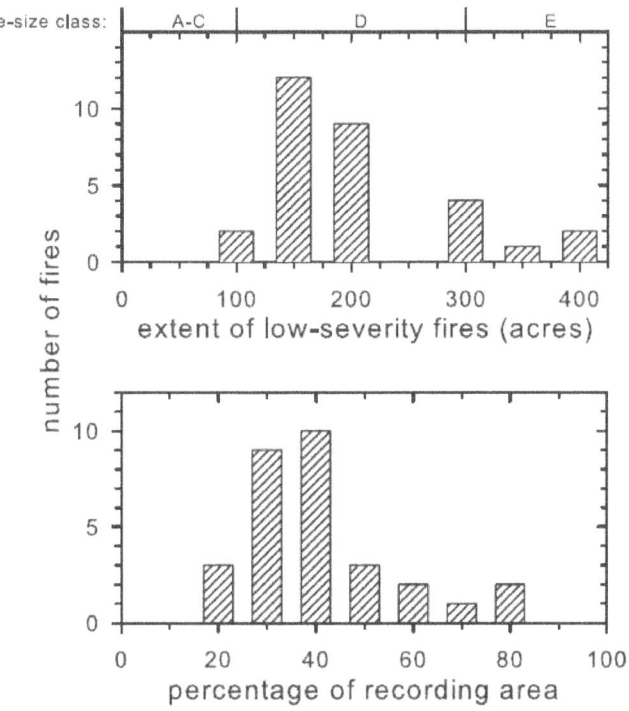

Figure N-11—Relative extent of low-severity fires within the 2223-acre ABM site, from 1650 to 1900, as area (top) and as a percentage of the recording area (in other words, the combined area of cells containing recording fire-scarred trees during each year; bottom). Commonly used fire-size classes are indicated at the top (NWCG 2007).

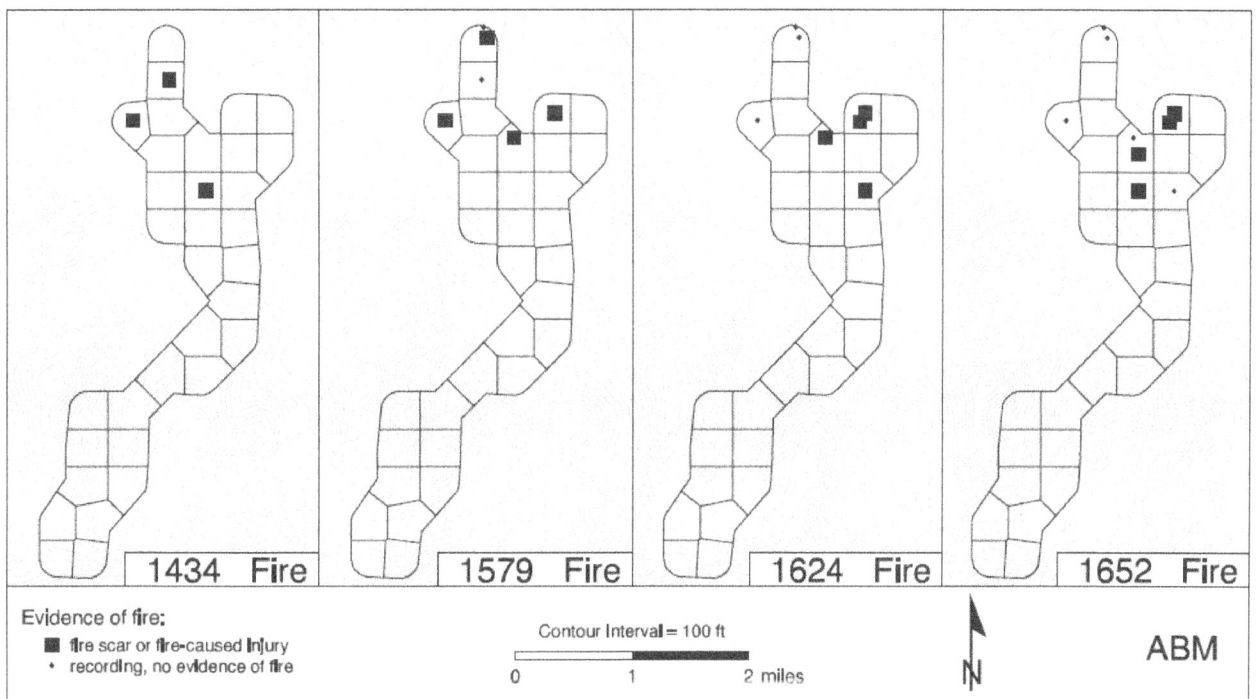

Figure N-12—Maps of years with evidence of low-severity fires in three or more cells at ABM. "Recording, no evidence of fire" indicates at least one tree was alive at that location during that year but did not have a fire scar or fire-caused injury. Empty cells indicate that no fire-scarred trees were recording in that cell during that year. Cohort dates are not mapped.

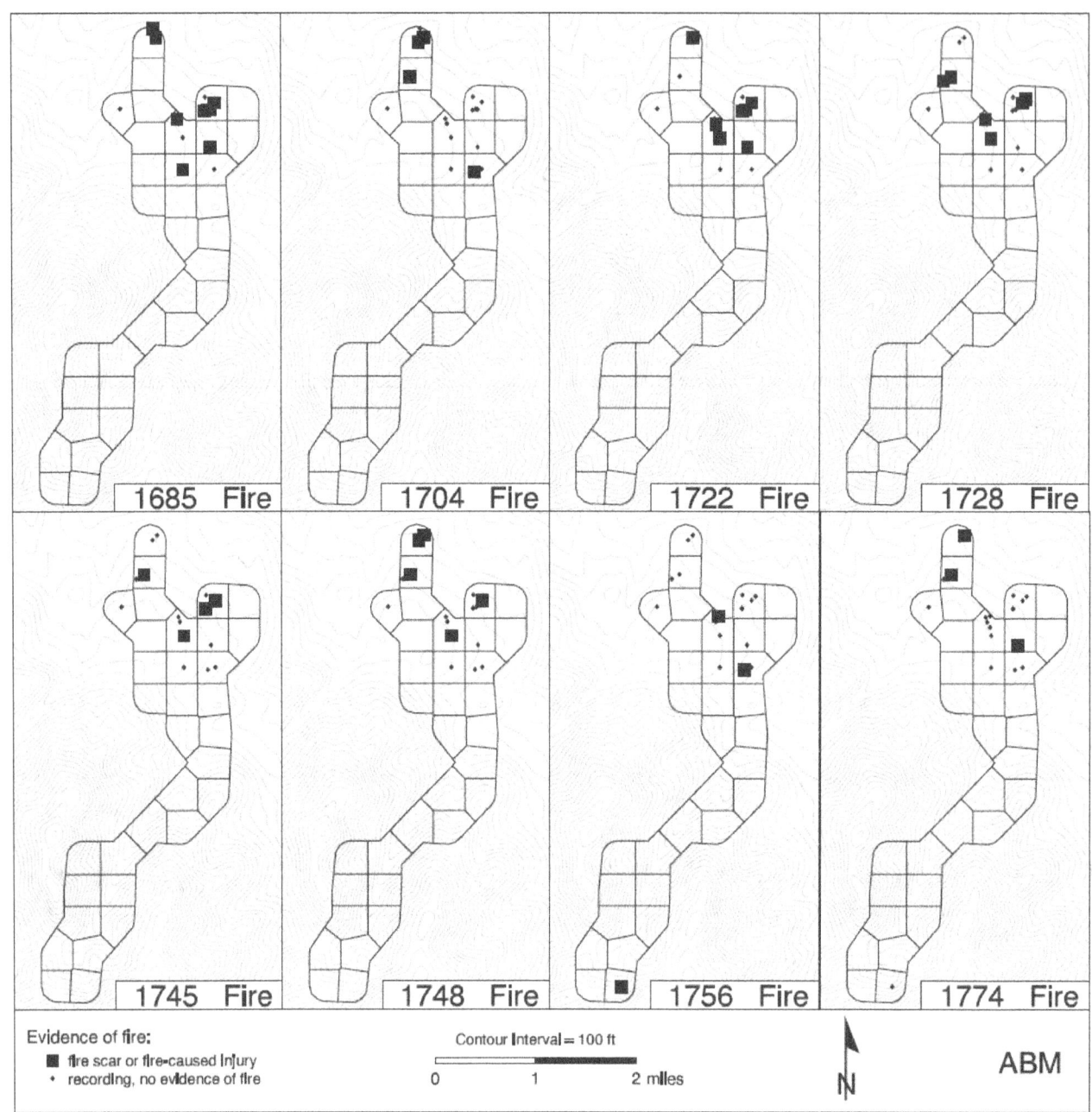

Figure N-12—*Continued.*

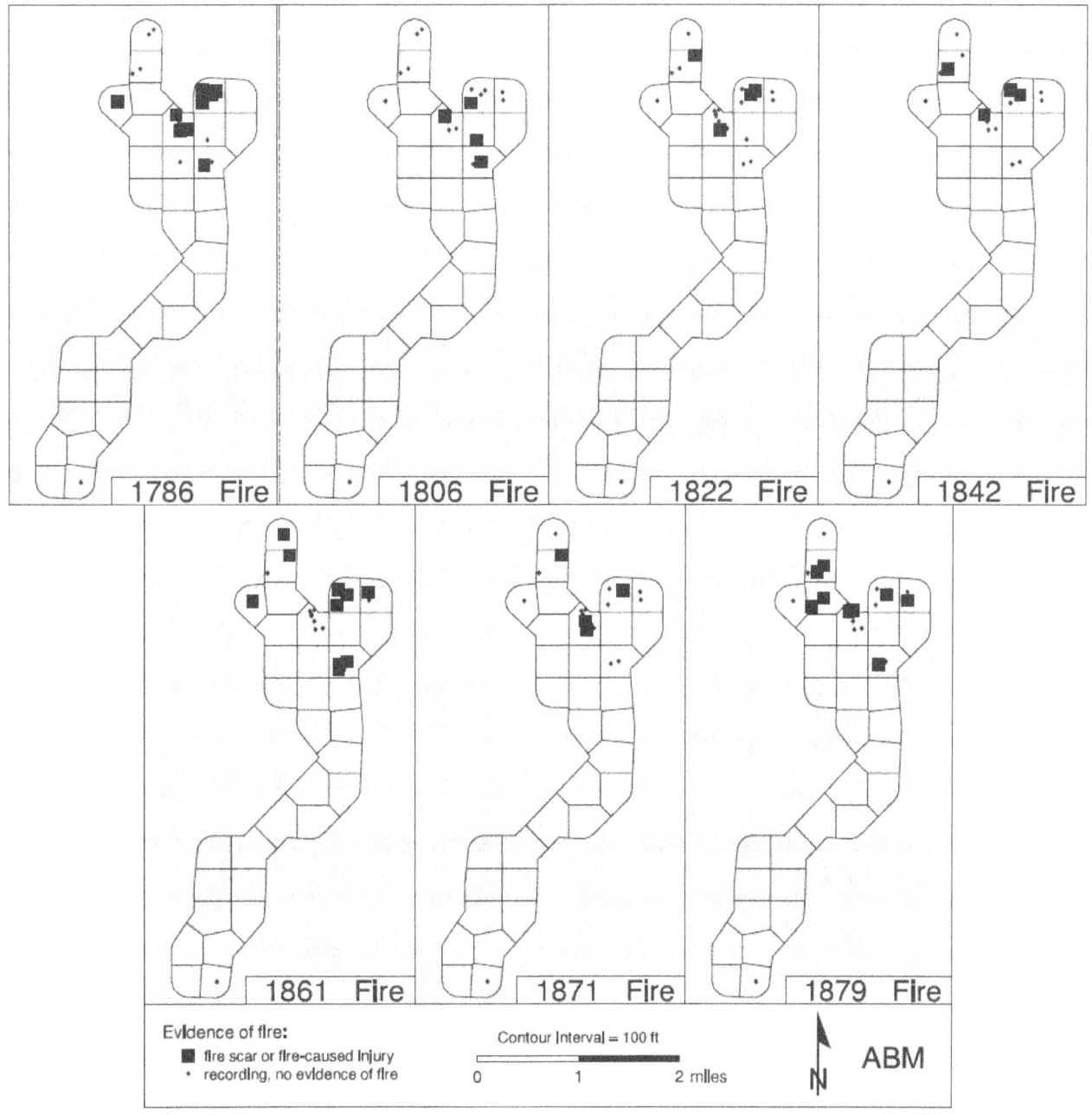

Figure N-12—*Continued.*

Appendix O. Wasatch Plateau, Manti-La Sal National Forest (EPH)

Topography

We sampled 29 plots over 1876 acres near Maple and Cottonwood Creeks on the Sanpete Ranger District of the Manti-La Sal National Forest in Sanpete County, Utah (figs. 1 and O-1). The plots were separated by 0.30 miles on average (range 0.25 to 0.31 miles) and averaged 0.43 acres in area (range 0.07 to 1.16 acres). Plots were sampled within cells that averaged 63 acres and ranged from 54 to 72 acres. Plots ranged in elevation from 7601 to 9196 ft (fig. O-2) and in slope from 3 to 63 percent. They were sampled on a range of aspects, but most were on north and west aspects (79 percent). The distribution of the plots by elevation, aspect, or slope did not differ from the distribution of the landscape by more than 10 percent in any category (fig. O-2). We took four photographs each at 28 of the plots.

Tree Demography

Of the 856 trees that occurred in the plots, most (99 percent) were Rocky Mountain juniper, Gambel oak, white fir, Douglas-fir, quaking aspen, subalpine fir, or Engelmann spruce, but 2 bigtooth maple, 1 ponderosa pine, and 5 limber pine also occurred (fig. O-3). Most of these trees were living (85 percent) and the rest were snags (11 percent), logs (3 percent), or stumps (1 percent). We were able to remove and crossdate wood samples from most of these trees (724 trees or 85 percent), and we obtained actual or estimated pith dates for 680 of them. These pith dates ranged from 1593 to 1983 and many post-dated 1900 (310 trees; fig. O-4). The death dates we obtained for 72 logs and snags ranged from 1962 to 2004.

Historical and Current Forest Structure and Composition

The plots included a range of historical and modern forest types (oak, mixed conifer, aspen-mixed conifer, aspen, and spruce-fir; table O-1). Most plots changed forest type between 1860 and 2000: one oak plot converted to pinyon-juniper; three oak and eight aspen-mixed conifer plots converted to mixed conifer; six aspen plots converted to aspen-mixed conifer; and two mixed conifer and one aspen plot converted to spruce-fir. In 1900, tree density averaged 57 trees per acre and ranged from 4 to 200 trees per acre (fig. O-5). In 2000, tree density averaged 92 trees per acre and ranged from 18 to 400 trees per acre. However, we likely underestimated historical tree density because we could not obtain recruitment or earliest-ring dates for 132 of the 856 trees that occurred in the plots and only an earliest-ring date for another 44 trees. Eleven of these trees had earliest-ring dates between 1901 and 1920 and therefore may have been living before 1900.

Fire Scars

We were able to remove and crossdate fire-scarred samples from 30 trees, 4 of which had only scars that were recorded on a single tree and so were excluded from further analyses. Of the remaining 26 trees, 11 were sampled in 5 of the 29 plots at this site (1 to 4 trees per plot). We sampled the 15 other fire-scarred trees as we encountered them between plots, over 453 acres at the southeastern end of the site (fig. O-6). Most of the 26 fire-scarred trees were white fir (35 percent), limber pine (31 percent), or Douglas-fir (27 percent) and the rest were Engelmann spruce or subalpine fir. Most were live trees (62 percent) and the rest were snags (27 percent), stumps (8 percent), or logs (4 percent). These 26 trees yielded 48 fire scars and 12 eroded fire scars or abrupt changes in ring width (figs. O-4 and O-7). However, six of these scar dates were eliminated from further analyses because they were recorded on only a single tree at the site. We were able to assign an intra-ring position to 76 percent of the 33 fire scars that occurred during the analysis period (1650 to 1900).

Post-Fire Cohorts

We identified 17 cohorts of trees from estimated recruitment dates at 16 of the plots. All of these cohorts were recruited before 1900 (1794 to 1896) and were identified from 158 trees (5 to 17 trees per cohort), most of which were quaking aspen (55 percent), white fir (20 percent), Douglas-fir (11 percent), as well as a few Gambel oak, subalpine fir, and Engelmann spruce (figs. O-4 and O-7). The cohorts that were recruited before 1900 occurred in plots with a range of forest types: aspen (29 percent of cohorts), aspen-mixed conifer (29 percent), mixed conifer (29 percent), and oak (12 percent).

Spatial Variation in Fire Regimes

We reconstructed too few fire intervals in plots during the analysis period (1650 to 1900) to compute plot-composite fire intervals by forest type at this site. The tree-ring record before 1900 was less than 100 years long for 21 of the 29 plots at this site (fig. O-8).

We could not infer historical fire severity at two plots because they did not meet our requirements for any of the severity categories (table O-2). We assigned the remaining plots to the low, mixed, or high fire severity categories.

From 1650 to 1900, the 12 low-severity fires we reconstructed within our 1876-acre sampling area averaged 126 acres and ranged from 61 to 199 acres (fig. O-9), equivalent to 17 to 100 percent of the recording area (in other words, the combined area of cells containing recording, fire-scarred trees during a given year). Recording area varied among fire years, ranging from 116 to 497 acres. We likely underestimated the extent of low-severity fires because most fires intersected the boundary of the site (fig. O-10).

Table O-1—Distribution of plots at EPH by historical (1860) and modern (2000) forest types (table 2).

Historical forest type (1860)	Modern forest type (2000)					Total plots in 1860
	Spruce-fir	Aspen	Aspen-mixed conifer	Mixed conifer	Pinyon-juniper	
Spruce-fir	2					2
Aspen	1	3	6			10
Aspen-mixed conifer				8		8
Mixed conifer	2			3		5
Oak				3	1	4
Total plots in 2000	**5**	**3**	**6**	**14**	**1**	**29**

Table O-2—Distribution of plots at EPH by historical forest type (1860; table 2) and fire severity (table 3).

Forest type	High	Assumed high	Mixed	Low	Unclassified
Spruce-fir		2			
Aspen	3	5	2		
Aspen-mixed conifer	3	2	2	1	
Mixed conifer	3	1	1		
Oak	1		1		2
Total	**10**	**10**	**6**	**1**	**2**

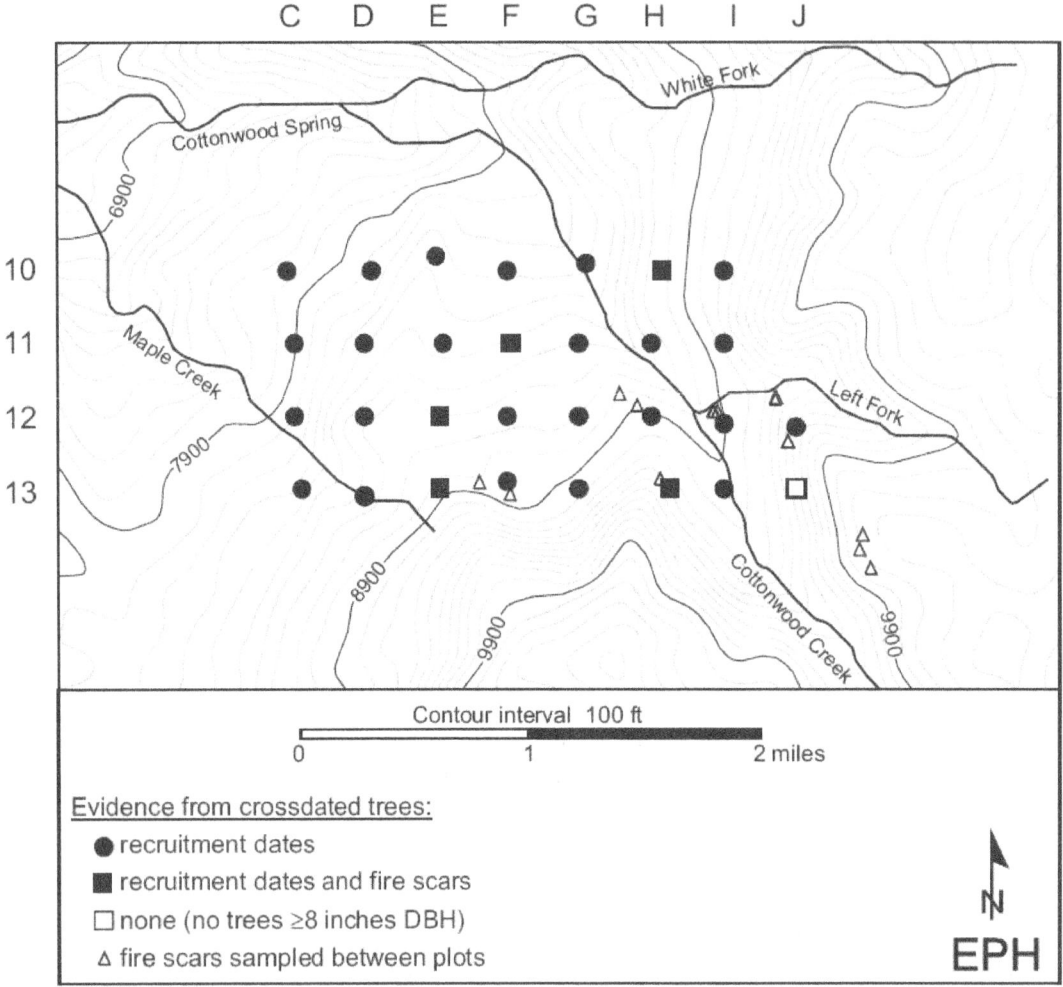

Figure O-1—Locations of plots and crossdated fire-scarred trees that were sampled outside of plots. Nearly half of the fire-scarred trees were sampled within plots and are not mapped individually. Plots are identified by column and row, in other words, the northwestern most plot is 10C, the next plot to the east is 10D, and so forth.

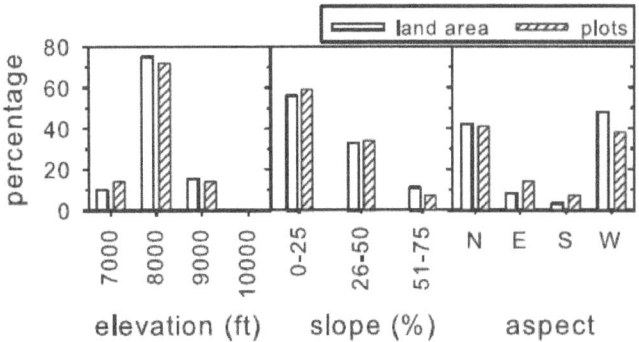

Figure O-2—Distribution of sampled plots and land area at EPH by topography. Aspect classes are 90° wide, beginning with 46° for east (E). Land area was derived from a digital elevation model (Utah AGRC 2004).

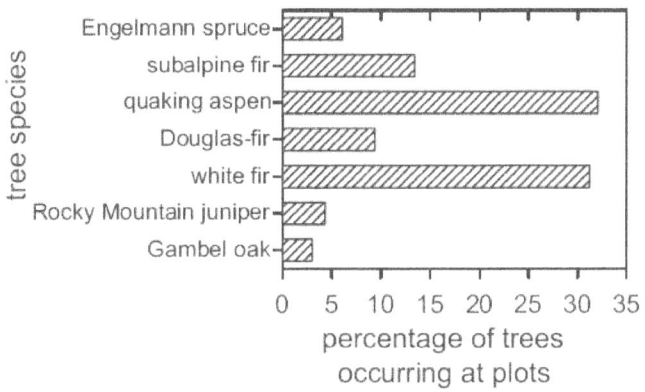

Figure O-3—Distribution by species of the 856 live and dead trees ≥8 inches DBH that occurred in plots at EPH, regardless of whether or not we removed wood samples and crossdated them. Not shown are two bigtooth maple, one ponderosa pine, and five limber pine trees.

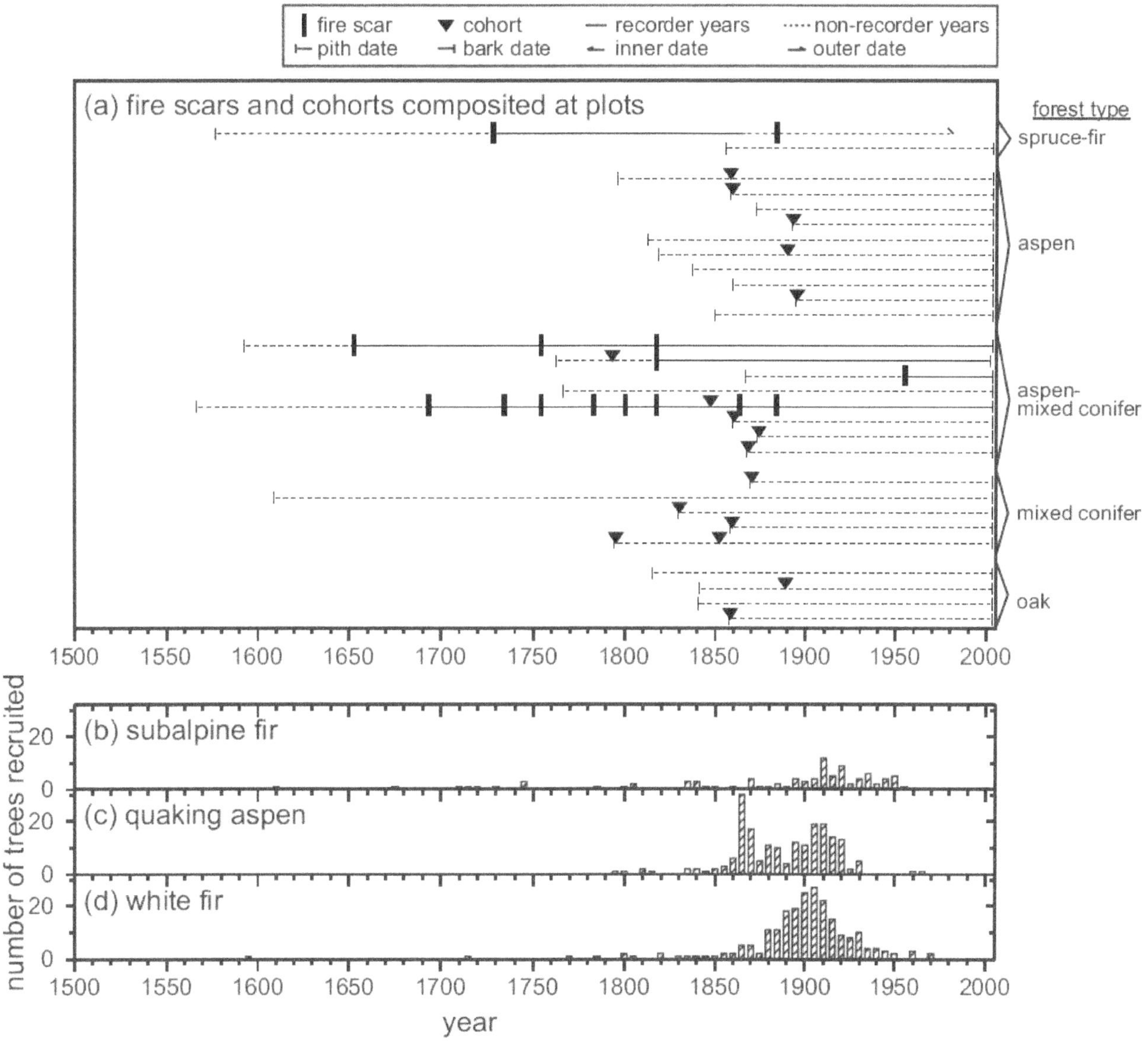

Figure O-4—Chronologies of fire and tree recruitment at EPH. In (a), horizontal lines are plot-composite fire-scar and cohort dates by forest type. Non-recorder years precede the first scar, whereas recorder years generally follow it, but non-recorder years can also occur when the catface margin is consumed by subsequent fires or rot. In (b) through (d), recruitment dates are given for species comprising ≥10 percent of trees with such dates. The latter part of the distribution is incomplete because we only cored trees that were ≥8 inches DBH.

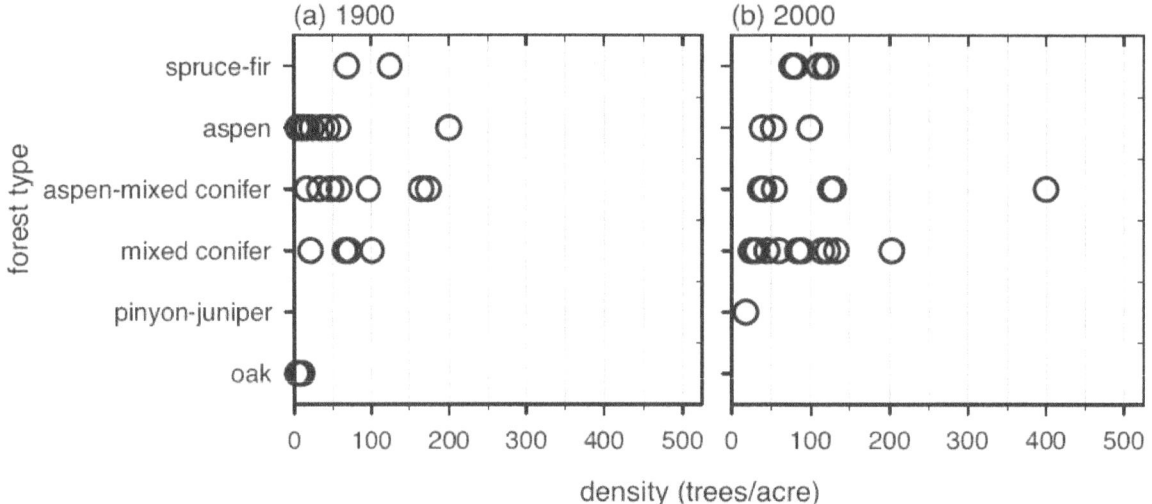

Figure O-5—Density of trees ≥8 inches DBH that were alive at each plot at EPH (a) in 1900 and (b) in 2000, by forest type (table 2).

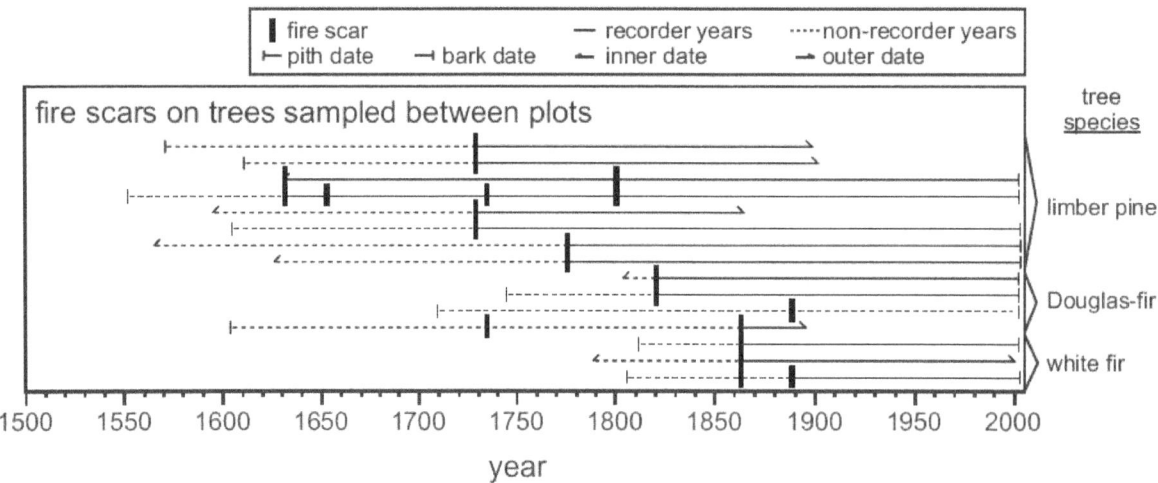

Figure O-6—Chronology of low-severity fires recorded on the 15 trees sampled between plots over approximately, 453 acres at the southeastern end of EPH.

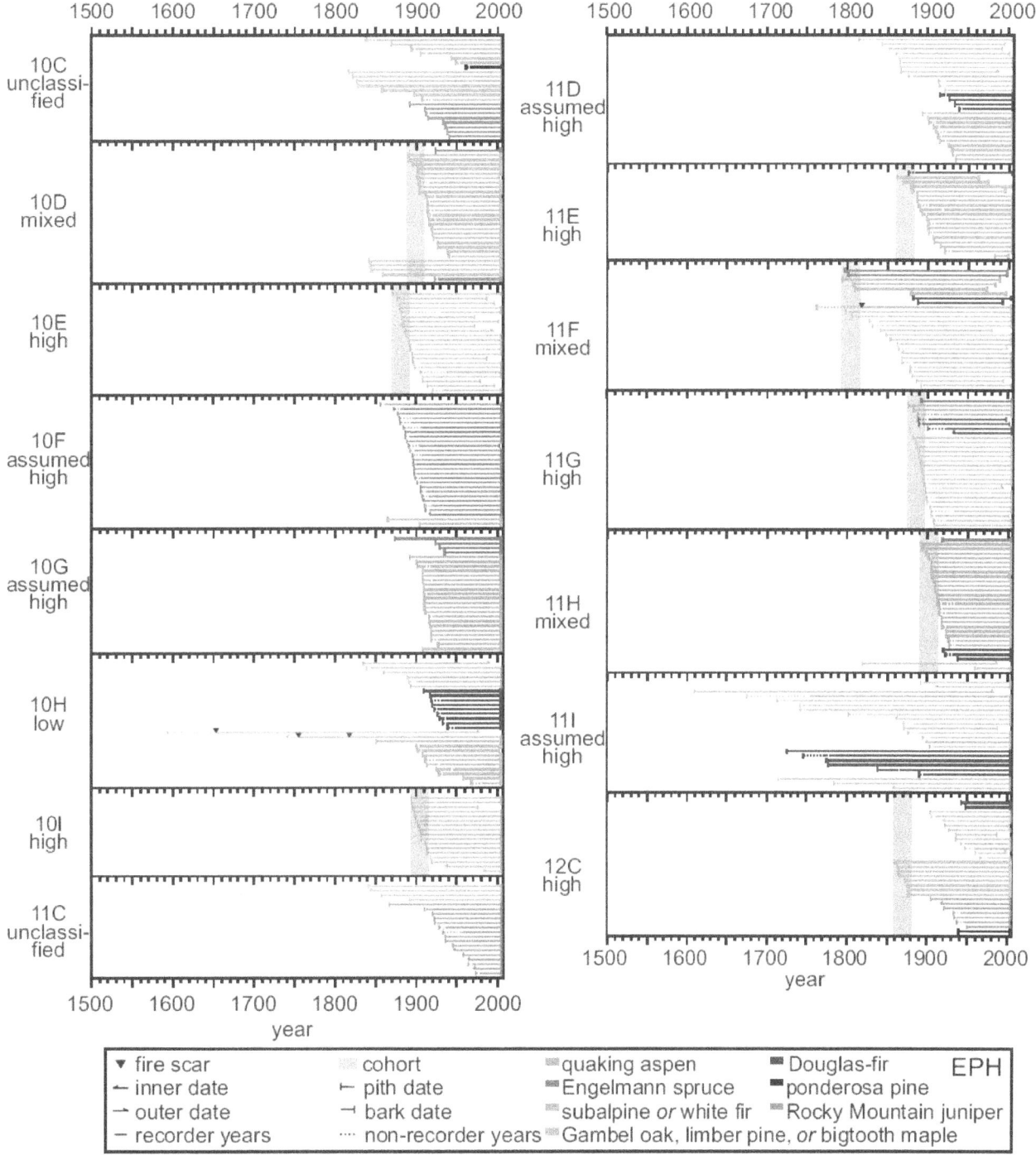

Figure O-7—Fire-demography diagrams (FDDs, Brown and others 2008b) showing chronologies of tree demography (recruitment and death), fire scars, and cohorts at each plot. Bark dates on four stumps are shown as outer dates. Not shown are 15 fire-scarred trees sampled between plots. Inferred fire severity (table 3) is indicated to the left of each panel. Most of the trees (62 percent) in the combined subalpine/white fir category are white fir. Most of the trees (85 percent) in the combined Gambel oak, limber pine, and bigtooth maple category are Gambel oak.

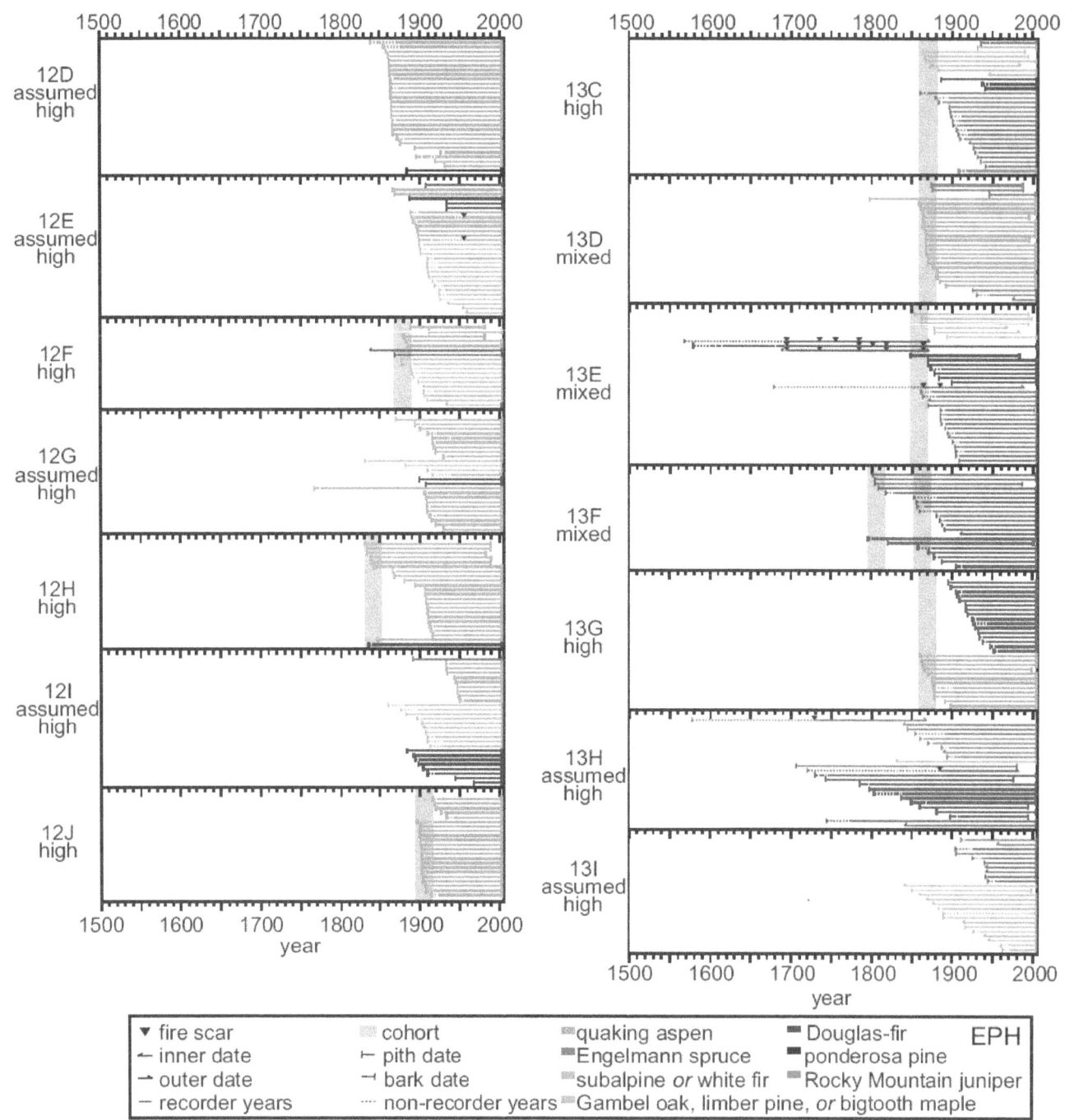

Figure O-7—*Continued.*

USDA Forest Service RMRS-GTR-261WWW. 2011.

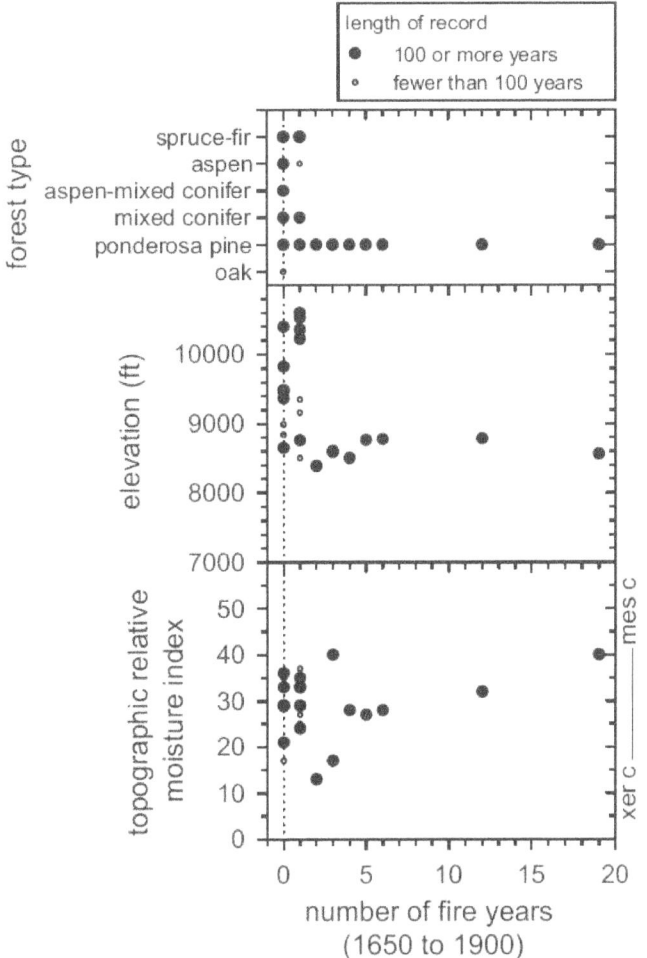

Figure O-8—Variation in fire among plots at EPH with topography, forest type, and relative soil moisture availability (Parker 1982). Number of fire years includes both fire-scar and cohort dates. Plots with no reconstructed fires during this period fall on the dotted line.

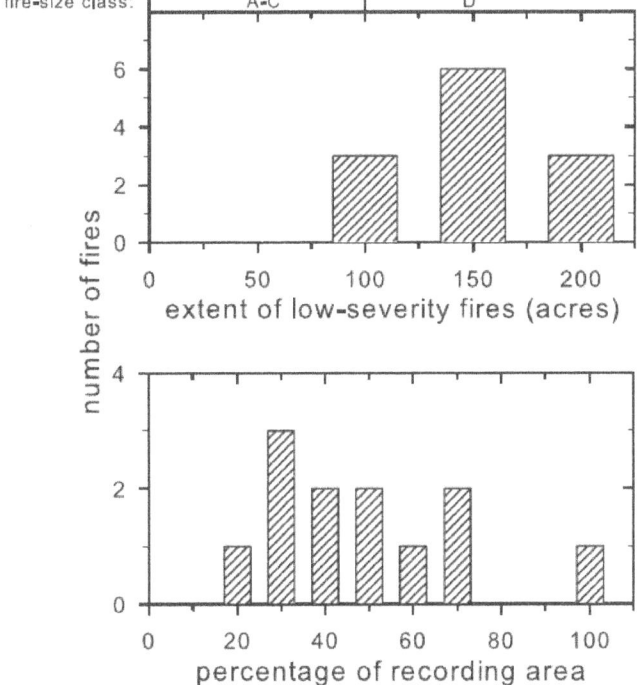

Figure O-9—Relative extent of low-severity fires within the 1876-acre EPH site, from 1650 to 1900, as area (top) and as a percentage of the recording area (in other words, the combined area of cells containing recording, fire-scarred trees during each year; bottom). Commonly used fire-size classes are indicated at the top (NWCG 2007).

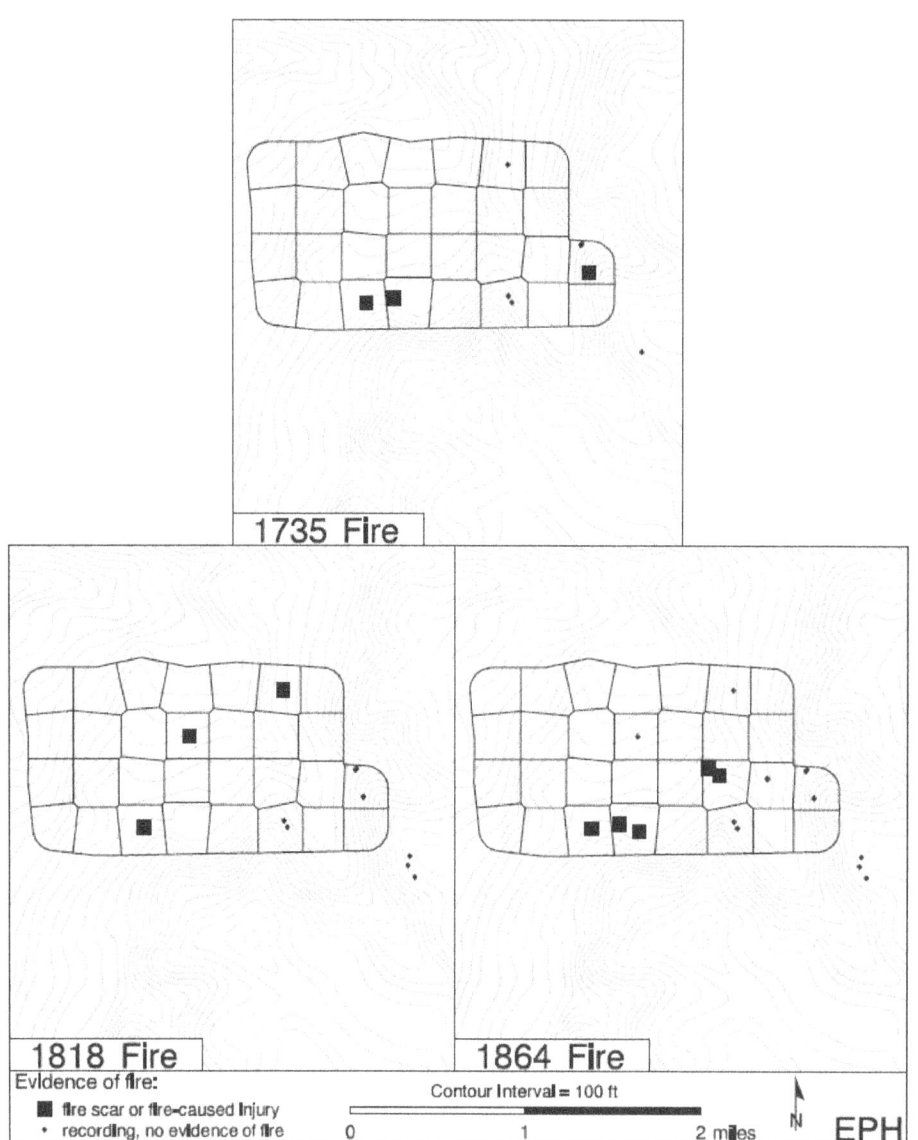

Figure O-10—Maps of years with evidence of low-severity fires in three or more cells at EPH. "Recording, no evidence of fire" indicates at least one tree was alive at that location during that year but did not have a fire scar or fire-caused injury. Empty cells indicate that no fire-scarred trees were recording in that cell during that year. Cohort dates are not mapped.

Appendix P. Western Uinta Mountains, Ashley National Forest (WUN)

Topography

We sampled 25 plots over 2255 acres in Miners Gulch, just south of the High Uintas Wilderness on the Duchesne Ranger District of the Ashley National Forest in Duchesne County, Utah (figs. 1 and P-1). The plots were separated by 0.30 miles on average (range 0.27 to 0.32 miles and averaged 0.48 acres in area (range 0.14 to 1.35 acres). Plots were sampled within cells that averaged 62 acres and ranged from 56 to 69 acres. Plots ranged in elevation from 7352 to 10,437 ft (fig. P-2) and ranged in slope from 5 to 65 percent, but most had slopes between 26 and 50 percent (68 percent of plots). They were sampled on a range of aspects, but most were on south and east aspects (88 percent). The distribution of plots differed from that of land area by more than 10 percent for several categories of topography. Plots were oversampled from elevations of 9000 to 10,000 ft, on moderate slopes, and on east aspects, and plots were undersampled for elevations from 8000 to 9000 ft, on steep slopes and on west aspects (fig. P-2). We took four photographs at each of the plots.

Tree Demography

Of the 745 trees that occurred in the plots, most (99 percent) were ponderosa pine, Douglas-fir, quaking aspen, lodgepole pine, subalpine fir, or Engelmann spruce, but 1 Colorado pinyon and 7 Rocky Mountain juniper also occurred plus 3 trees we could not identify (fig. P-3). Most of these trees were living (84 percent) and the rest were snags (6 percent), logs (10 percent), or stumps (1 percent). We were able to remove and crossdate wood samples from most of these trees (524 trees or 70 percent), and we obtained actual or estimated pith dates for 504 of them. These pith dates ranged from 1514 to 1961 and 103 of them post-dated 1900 (fig. P-4). The death dates we obtained for 49 logs and snags ranged from 1840 to 2003.

Historical and Current Forest Structure and Composition

The plots included a range of historical and modern forest types (ponderosa pine, mixed conifer, lodgepole, and spruce-fir; table P-1). One lodgepole plot converted to mixed conifer between 1860 and 2000. In 1900, tree density averaged 49 trees per acre and ranged from 1 to 153 trees per acre (fig. P-5). In 2000, tree density averaged 69 trees per acre and ranged from 17 to 167 trees per acre. However, we likely underestimated historical tree density because we could not obtain recruitment or earliest-ring dates for 221 of the 745 trees that occurred in the plots and only an earliest-ring date for another 20 trees. One tree had an earliest-ring date between 1901 and 1920 and therefore may have been living before 1900.

Fire Scars

We were able to remove and crossdate fire-scarred samples from 65 trees. Most of these (54 trees) were sampled in 16 of the 25 plots at this site (1 to 10 trees per plot, average 3 trees). We sampled the 11 other fire-scarred trees as we encountered them between plots, over 287 acres at the southwestern end of the site (fig. P-6). Most of the 65 fire-scarred trees were lodgepole pine (45 percent) and ponderosa pine (37 percent) and the rest were Douglas-fir and Rocky Mountain juniper. About half were live trees (52 percent), and the rest were logs and snags. These 65 trees yielded 94 fire scars and 19 eroded fire scars or abrupt changes in ring width (figs. P-4 and P-7). We were able to assign an intra-ring position to 56 percent of the 87 fire scars that occurred during the analysis period (1650 to 1900). Of the scars that occurred on lodgepole pine trees, half (50 percent) occurred on the boundary between two rings (fig. P-8). In contrast, of the scars that occurred on ponderosa pine trees, half (44 percent) occurred in the early- and middle-earlywood.

Post-Fire Cohorts

We identified 13 cohorts of trees from estimated recruitment dates at 10 of the plots. Twelve of these cohorts were recruited before 1900 (1840 to 1863) and were identified from 109 trees (5 to 21 trees per cohort), most of which were lodgepole (39 percent), ponderosa pine (29 percent), or Douglas-fir (26 percent), but a few quaking aspen, Rocky Mountain juniper, and subalpine fir also occurred (figs. P-4 and P-7). The cohorts that were recruited before 1900 occurred in plots with a range of forest types: ponderosa pine (40 percent of cohorts), lodgepole (30 percent), and mixed conifer (30 percent).

Spatial Variation in Fire Regimes

We reconstructed too few fire intervals in plots during the analysis period (1650 to 1900) to compute plot-composite fire intervals by forest type at this site. The tree-ring record before 1900 was less than 100 years long for 3 of the 25 plots at this site (fig. P-9).

We could not infer historical fire severity at one plot because it did not meet our requirements for any of the severity categories (table P-2). We assigned the remaining plots to the mixed or high fire severity categories.

From 1650 to 1900, the 14 low-severity fires we reconstructed within our 2255-acre sampling area averaged 145 acres and ranged from 56 to 813 acres (fig. P-10), equivalent to 8 to 100 percent of the recording area (in other words, the combined area of cells containing recording, fire-scarred trees during a given year). Recording area varied among fire years, ranging from 131 to 815 acres. We likely underestimated the extent of low-severity fires because most fires intersected the boundary of the site (fig. P-11).

Table P-1—Distribution of plots at WUN by historical (1860) and modern (2000) forest types (table 2).

Historical forest type (1860)	Modern forest type (2000)				Total plots in 1860
	Spruce-fir	Lodgepole	Mixed conifer	Ponderosa pine	
Spruce-fir	3				3
Lodgepole		7	1		8
Mixed conifer			10		10
Ponderosa pine				4	4
Total plots in 2000	**3**	**7**	**11**	**4**	**25**

Table P-2—Distribution of plots at WUN by historical forest type (1860; table 2) and fire severity (table 3).

Forest type	Assumed high	Mixed	Assumed mixed	Unclassified
Spruce-fir	3			
Lodgepole	4	3		1
Mixed conifer	2	3	5	
Ponderosa pine		4		
Total	**9**	**10**	**5**	**1**

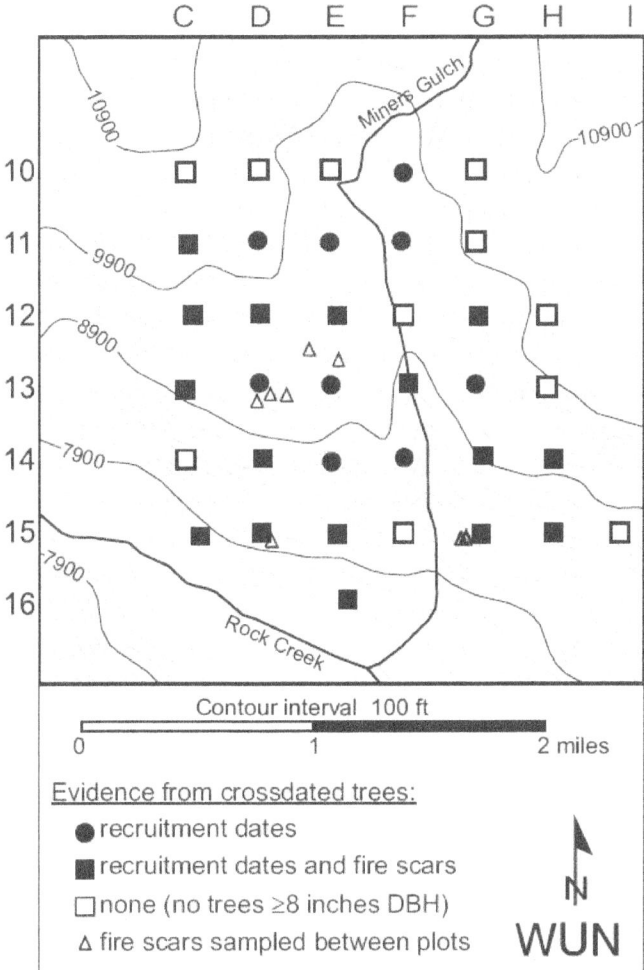

Figure P-1—Locations of plots and crossdated fire-scarred trees that were sampled outside of plots. Most of the fire-scarred trees were sampled within plots and are not mapped individually. Plots are identified by column and row, in other words, the northwestern most plot is 10C, the next plot to the east is 10D, and so forth.

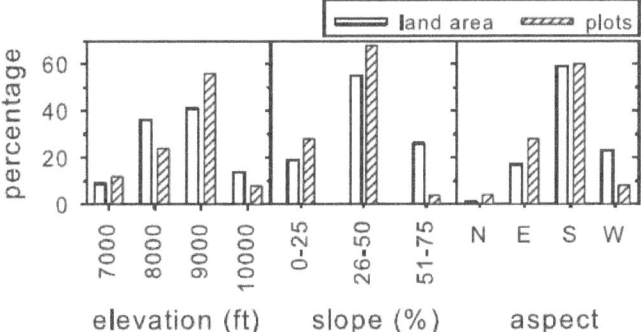

Figure P-2—Distribution of sampled plots and land area at WUN by topography. Aspect classes are 90° wide, beginning with 46° for east (E). Land area was derived from a digital elevation model (Utah AGRC 2004).

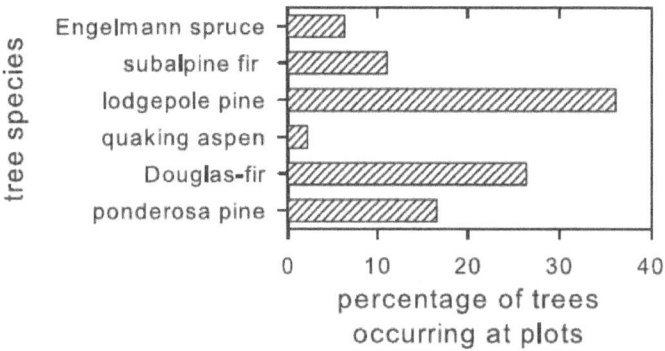

Figure P-3—Distribution by species of the 745 live and dead trees ≥8 inches DBH that occurred in plots at WUN, regardless of whether or not we removed wood samples and crossdated them. Not shown are one Colorado pinyon and seven Rocky Mountain juniper plus three trees of unknown species.

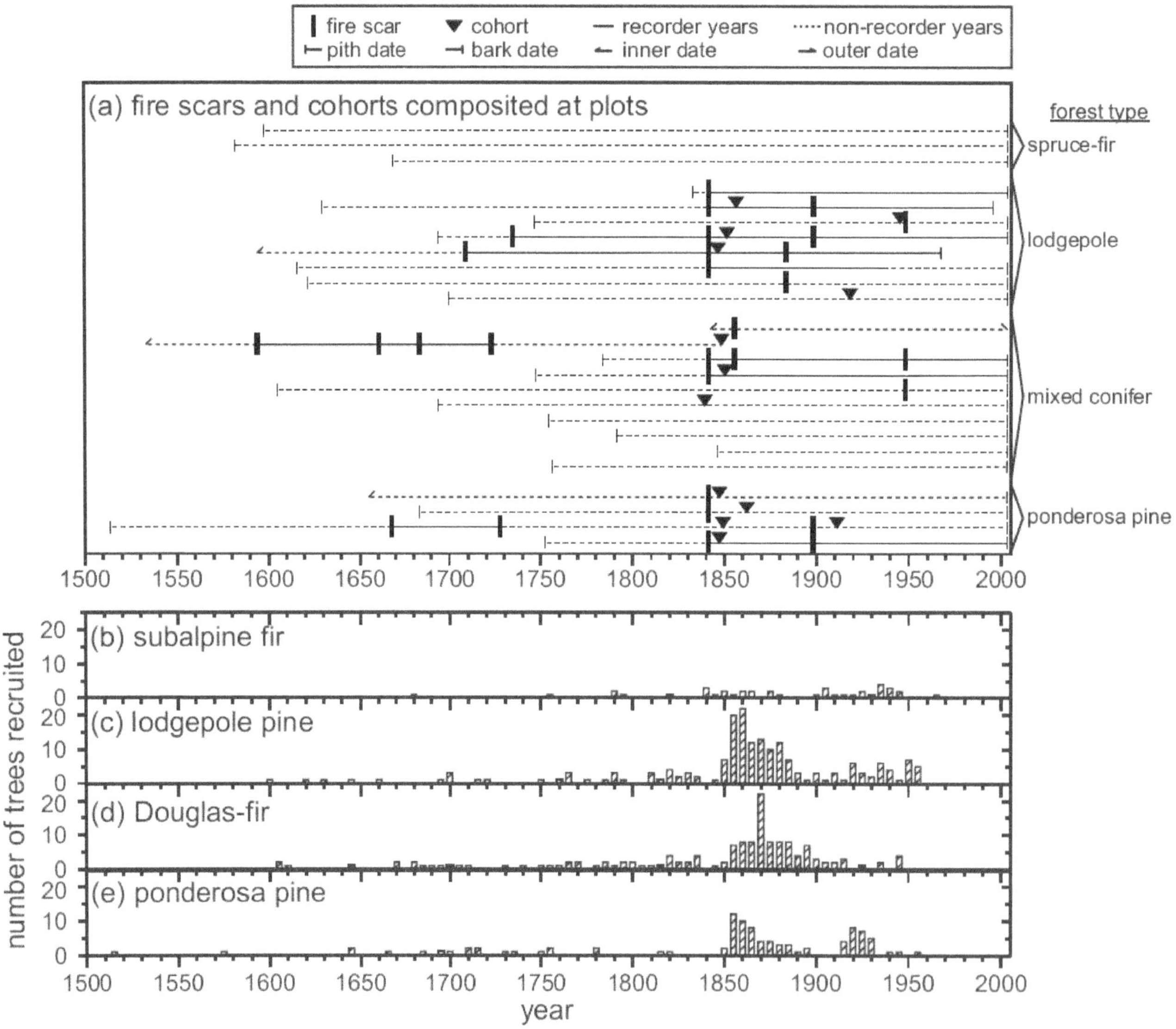

| fire scar | ▼ cohort | — recorder years | ······non-recorder years |
| ⊢ pith date | ⊣ bark date | ⊷ inner date | ⊶ outer date |

(a) fire scars and cohorts composited at plots

forest type

spruce-fir

lodgepole

mixed conifer

ponderosa pine

1500 1550 1600 1650 1700 1750 1800 1850 1900 1950 2000

(b) subalpine fir

(c) lodgepole pine

(d) Douglas-fir

(e) ponderosa pine

number of trees recruited

1500 1550 1600 1650 1700 1750 1800 1850 1900 1950 2000
year

Figure P-4—Chronologies of fire and tree recruitment at WUN. In (a), horizontal lines are plot-composite fire-scar and cohort dates by forest type. Non-recorder years precede the first scar, whereas recorder years generally follow it, but non-recorder years can also occur when the catface margin is consumed by subsequent fires or rot. In (b) through (e), recruitment dates are given for species comprising ≥10 percent of trees with such dates. The latter part of the distribution is incomplete because we only cored trees that were ≥8 inches DBH.

USDA Forest Service RMRS-GTR-261WWW. 2011.

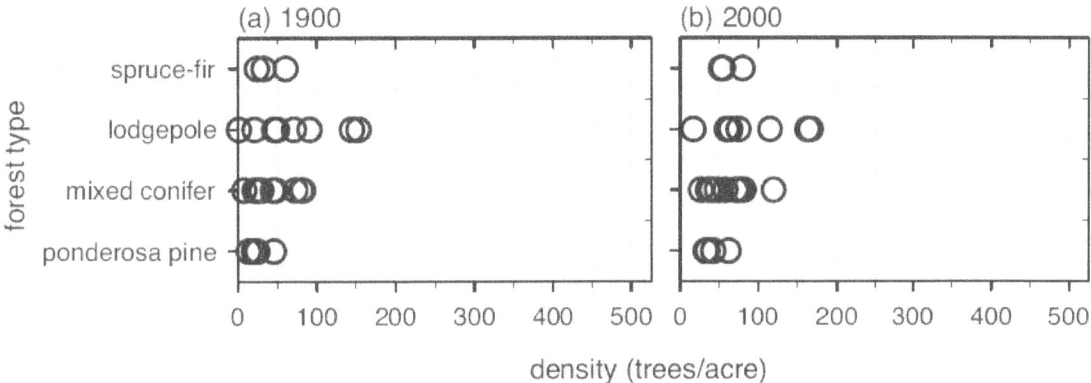

Figure P-5—Density of trees ≥8 inches DBH that were alive at each plot at WUN (a) in 1900 and (b) in 2000, by forest type (table 2).

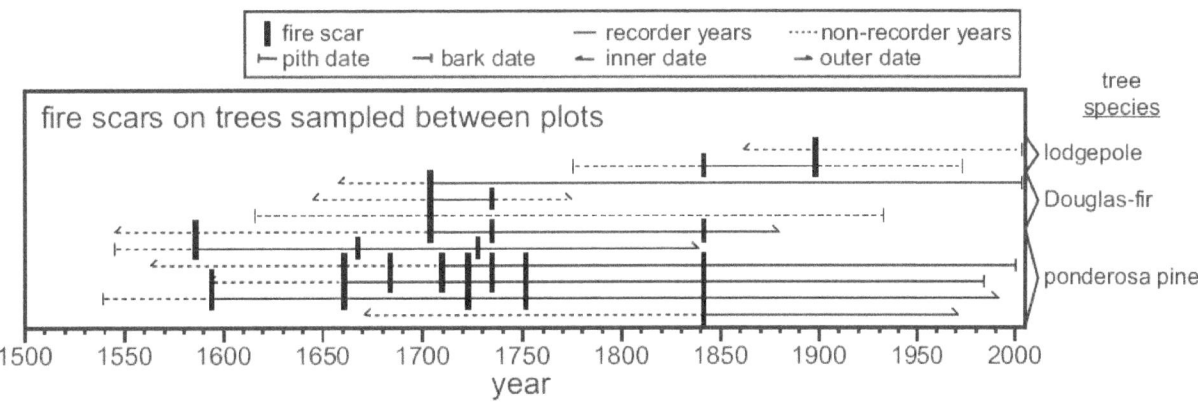

Figure P-6—Chronology of low-severity fires recorded on the 11 trees sampled between plots over approximately, 287 acres at the southern end of WUN.

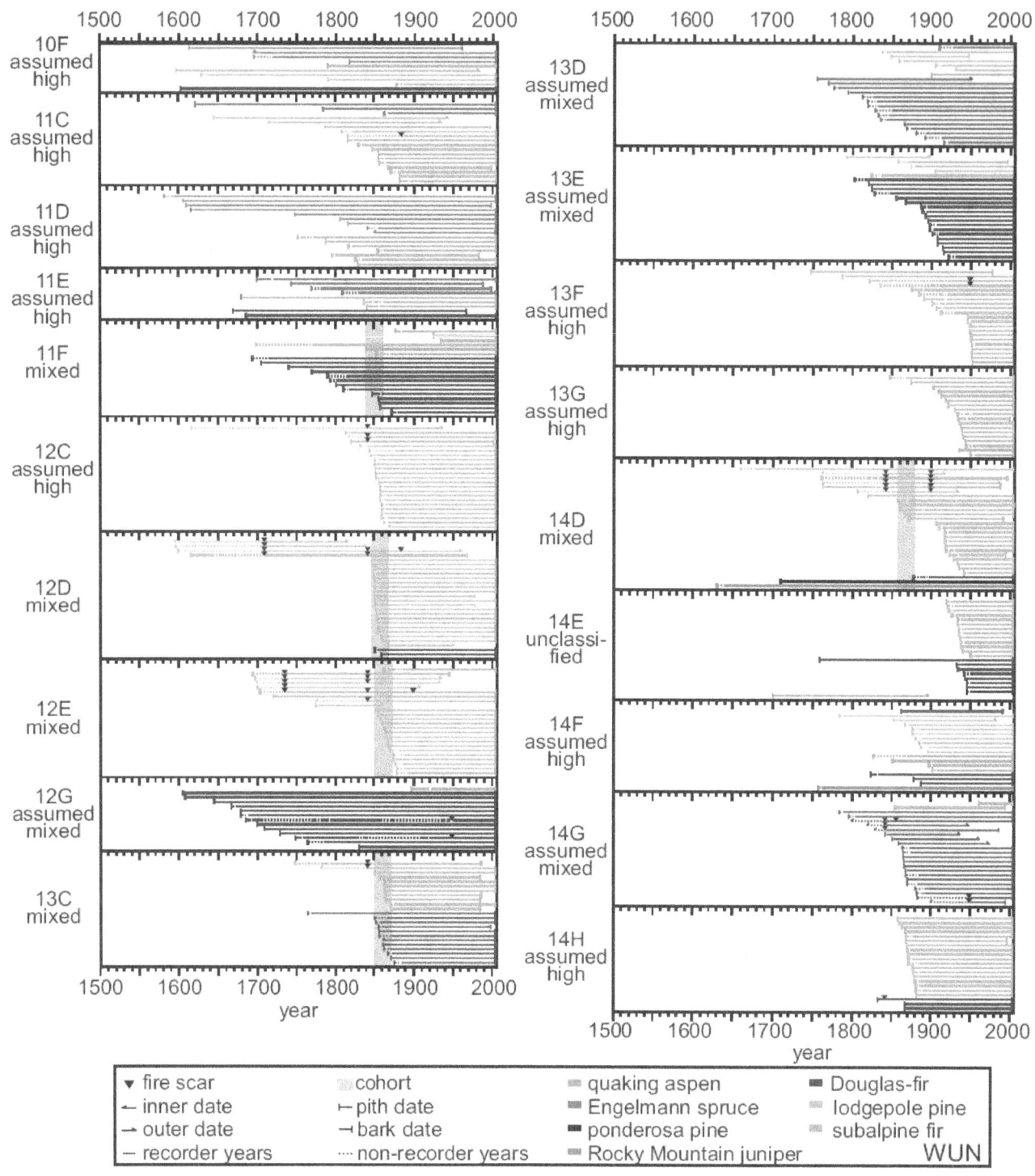

Figure P-7—Fire-demography diagrams (FDDs, Brown and others 2008b) showing chronologies of tree demography (recruitment and death), fire scars, and cohorts at each plot. Bark dates on three stumps are shown as outer dates. Not shown are 11 fire-scarred trees sampled between plots. Inferred fire severity (table 3) is indicated to the left of each panel.

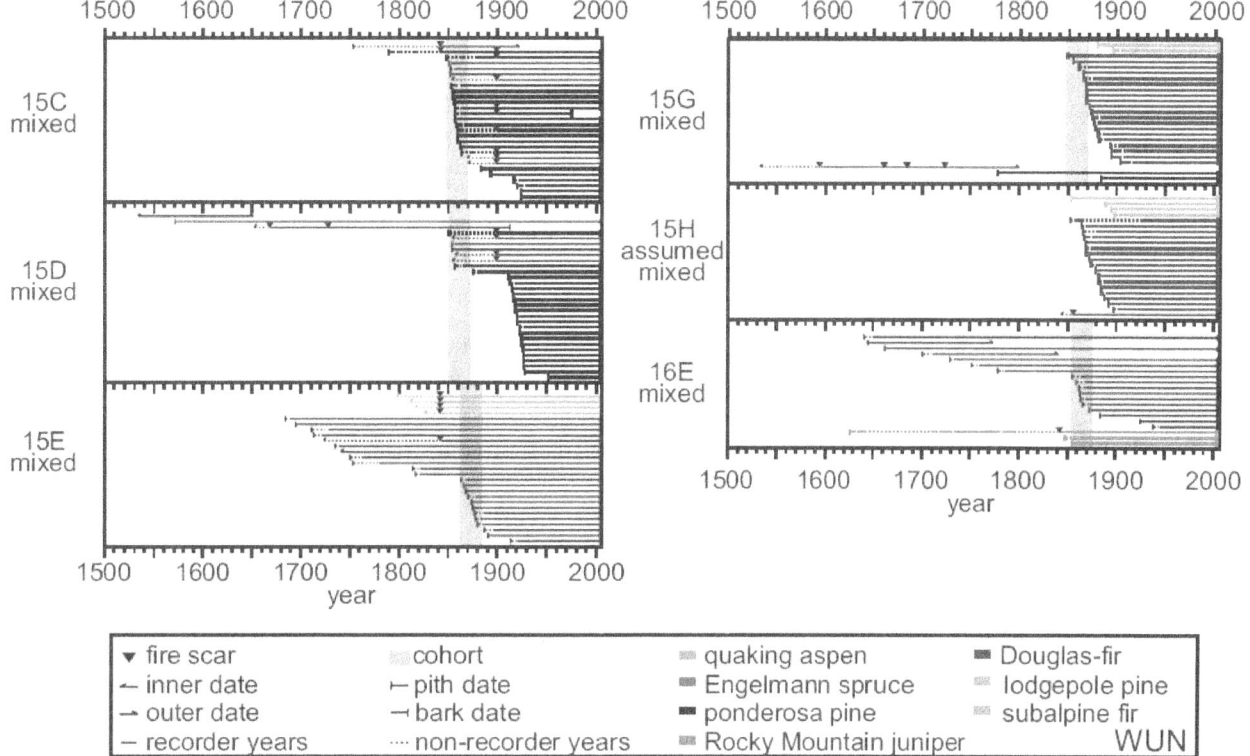

Figure P-7—Continued.

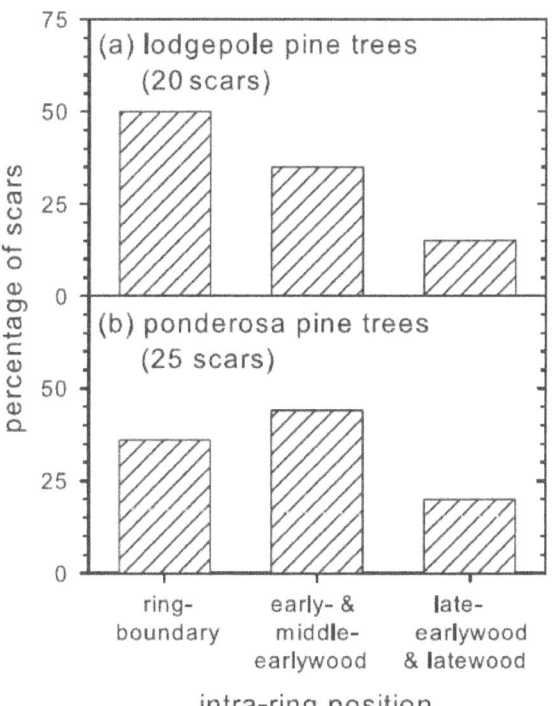

Figure P-8—Intra-ring position of fire scars sampled in and between plots at WUN from 1650 to 1900, as a percentage of the number of scars for which the position could be determined (given in parentheses). Not shown are intra-ring positions for four fire scars on Douglas-fir trees.

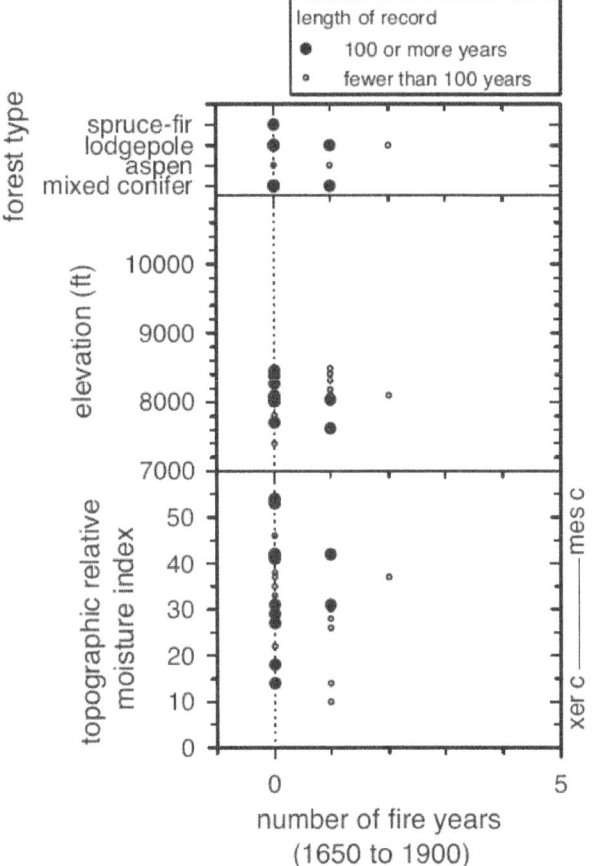

Figure P-9—Variation in fire among plots at WUN with topography, forest type, and relative soil moisture availability (Parker 1982). Number of fire years includes both fire-scar and cohort dates. Plots with no reconstructed fires during this period fall on the dotted line.

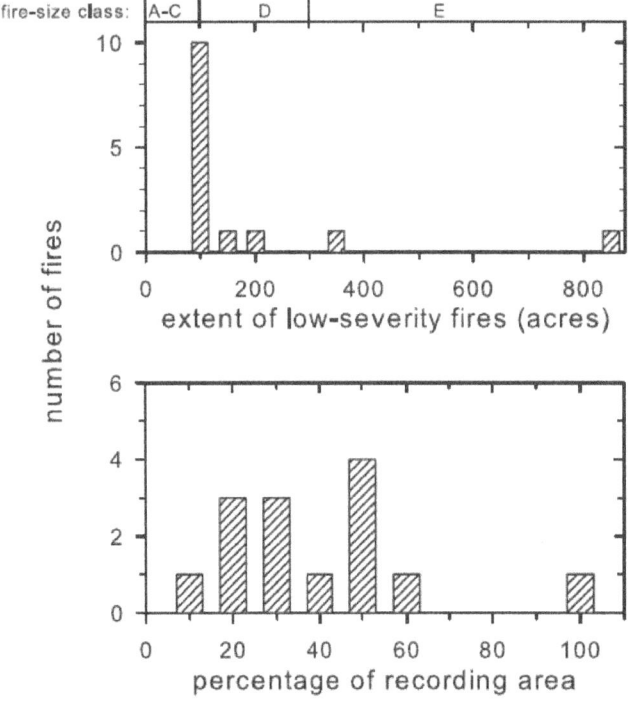

Figure P-10—Relative extent of low-severity fires within the 2255-acre WUN site, from 1650 to 1900, as area (top) and as a percentage of the recording area (in other words, the combined area of cells containing recording, fire-scarred trees during each year; bottom). Commonly used fire-size classes are indicated at the top (NWCG 2007).

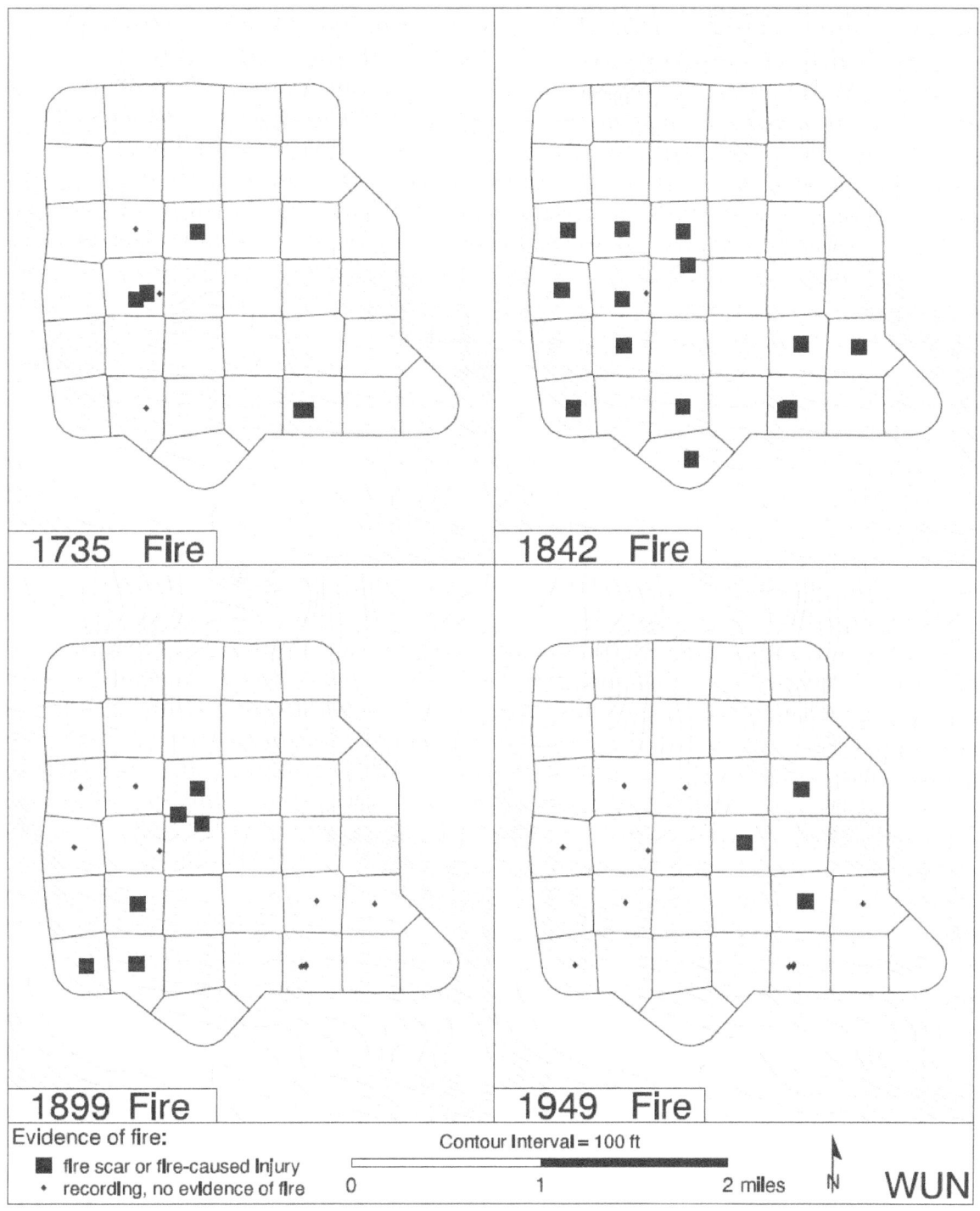

1735 Fire

1842 Fire

1899 Fire

1949 Fire

Evidence of fire:
■ fire scar or fire-caused injury
· recording, no evidence of fire

Contour Interval = 100 ft

0   1   2 miles

N

WUN

Figure P-11—Maps of years with evidence of low-severity fires in three or more cells at WUN. "Recording, no evidence of fire" indicates at least one tree was alive at that location during that year but did not have a fire scar or fire-caused injury. Empty cells indicate that no fire-scarred trees were recording in that cell during that year. Cohort dates are not mapped.

Appendix Q. Central Uinta Mountains, Ashley National Forest (MUR)

Topography

We sampled 30 plots over 2218 acres near Pole and Big Elk Creeks, just south of the High Uintas Wilderness on the Roosevelt Ranger District of the Ashley National Forest in Duchesne County, Utah (figs. 1 and Q-1). The plots were separated by 0.31 miles on average (range 0.30 to 0.32 miles) and averaged 0.33 acres in area (range 0.03 to 1.22 acres). Plots were sampled within cells that averaged 67 acres and ranged from 59 to 81 acres. Plots ranged in elevation from 7567 to 10,656 ft (fig. Q-2) and in slope from 0 to 68 percent, but most were less than 25 percent (63 percent). They were sampled on a range of aspects, but most were on south and east aspects (77 percent). The distribution of the plots by elevation, aspect, or slope did not differ from the distribution of the landscape by more than 10 percent in any category (fig. Q-2). We took four photographs each at 24 of the plots.

Tree Demography

Of the 810 trees that occurred in the plots, most (99 percent) were ponderosa pine, subalpine fir, Douglas-fir, quaking aspen, lodgepole pine, or Engelmann spruce, but 8 Utah juniper also occurred (fig. Q-3). Most of these trees were living (73 percent) and the rest were snags (8 percent), logs (9 percent), or stumps (10 percent). We were able to remove and crossdate wood samples from most of these trees (610 trees or 75 percent), and we obtained actual or estimated pith dates for 484 of them. These pith dates ranged from 1410 to 1974 and 146 of them post-dated 1900 (fig. Q-4). The death dates we obtained for 46 logs and snags ranged from 1806 to 2004.

Historical and Current Forest Structure and Composition

The plots included a range of historical and modern forest types (ponderosa pine, aspen-mixed conifer, aspen, lodgepole, and spruce-fir; table Q-1). Some plots changed forest type between 1860 and 2000: one aspen plot converted to mixed conifer; and one ponderosa pine, one lodgepole, and three aspen plots converted to aspen-mixed conifer. In 1900, tree density averaged 85 trees per acre and ranged from 0 to 716 trees per acre (fig. Q-5). In 2000, tree density averaged 127 trees per acre and ranged from 16 to 1038 trees per acre. However, we likely underestimated historical tree density because we could not obtain recruitment or earliest-ring dates for 200 of the 810 trees that occurred in the plots and only an earliest-ring date for another 126 trees. Sixteen of these trees had earliest-ring dates between 1901 and 1920 and therefore may have been living before 1900.

Fire Scars

We were able to remove and crossdate fire-scarred samples from 84 trees, 1 of which had only scars that were recorded on a single tree and so was excluded from further analyses. Of the remaining 83 trees, about half (47 trees) were sampled in 16 of the 30 plots at this site (1 to 8 trees per plot, average 3 trees). We sampled the 36 other fire-scarred trees as we encountered them between plots, over 2460 acres throughout the site (fig. Q-6). Most of the 83 fire-scarred trees were lodgepole pine (47 percent) and ponderosa pine (41 percent) and the rest were Engelmann spruce and Douglas-fir. Most were logs, snags, or stumps (64 percent) and the rest were live trees. These 83 trees yielded 167 fire scars and 9 eroded fire scars or abrupt changes in ring width (figs. Q-4 and Q-7). However, one of these scar dates was eliminated from further analyses because it was recorded on only a single tree at the site. We were able to assign an intra-ring position to

67 percent of the 148 fire scars that occurred during the analysis period (1650 to 1900). Of the scars that occurred on ponderosa pine trees, half (48 percent) occurred in the late-earlywood or the latewood (fig. Q-8). In contrast, of the scars that occurred on lodgepole pine trees, most (94 percent) occurred either on the boundary between two rings or in the late-earlywood or latewood.

Post-Fire Cohorts

We identified 16 cohorts of trees from estimated recruitment dates at 15 of the plots. Thirteen of these cohorts were recruited before 1900 (1410 to 1898) and were identified from 98 trees (5 to 13 trees per cohort), most of which were quaking aspen (33 percent), lodgepole pine (30 percent), Engelmann spruce (22 percent), or ponderosa pine (12 percent), but a few Douglas-fir and Utah juniper trees also occurred (figs. Q-4 and Q-7). The cohorts that were recruited before 1900 occurred in plots with a range of forest types: lodgepole (31 percent of cohorts), spruce-fir (31 percent), aspen (23 percent), and ponderosa pine (15 percent).

Spatial Variation in Fire Regimes

During the analysis period (1650 to 1900), plot-composite, low-severity fire intervals that were pooled among ponderosa pine plots averaged 42 years (range 5 to 178 years; fig. Q-9). There were more fire years in low-elevation than in high-elevation plots (fig. Q-10). The tree-ring record before 1900 was less than 100 years long for 11 of the 30 plots at this site.

We inferred that one lodgepole plot was not historically forested (table Q-2). We assigned the remaining plots to the low, mixed, or high fire severity categories.

From 1650 to 1900, the 15 low-severity fires we reconstructed within our 2218-acre sampling area averaged 240 acres and ranged from 58 to 976 acres (fig. Q-11), equivalent to 6 to 94 percent of the recording area (in other words, the combined area of cells containing recording, fire-scarred trees during a given year). Recording area varied among fire years, ranging from 312 to 1042 acres. We likely underestimated the extent of low-severity fires because most fires intersected the boundary of the site (fig. Q-12).

Table Q-1—Distribution of plots at MUR by historical (1860) and modern (2000) forest types (table 2).

Historical forest type (1860)	Modern forest type (2000)						Total plots in 1860
	Spruce-fir	Lodgepole	Aspen	Aspen-mixed conifer	Mixed conifer	Ponderosa pine	
Spruce-fir	8						8
Lodgepole		6		1			7
Aspen			4	3	1		8
Aspen-mixed conifer				1			1
Ponderosa pine				1		5	6
Total plots in 2000	**8**	**6**	**4**	**6**	**1**	**5**	**30**

Table Q-2—Distribution of plots at MUR by historical forest type (1860; table 2) and fire severity (table 3).

Forest type	High	Assumed high	Mixed	Assumed mixed	Low	Not historically forested
Spruce-fir	2	4	2			
Lodgepole		2	3		1	1
Aspen	2	5	1			
Aspen-mixed conifer		1				
Ponderosa pine			2	2	2	
Total	**4**	**12**	**8**	**2**	**3**	**1**

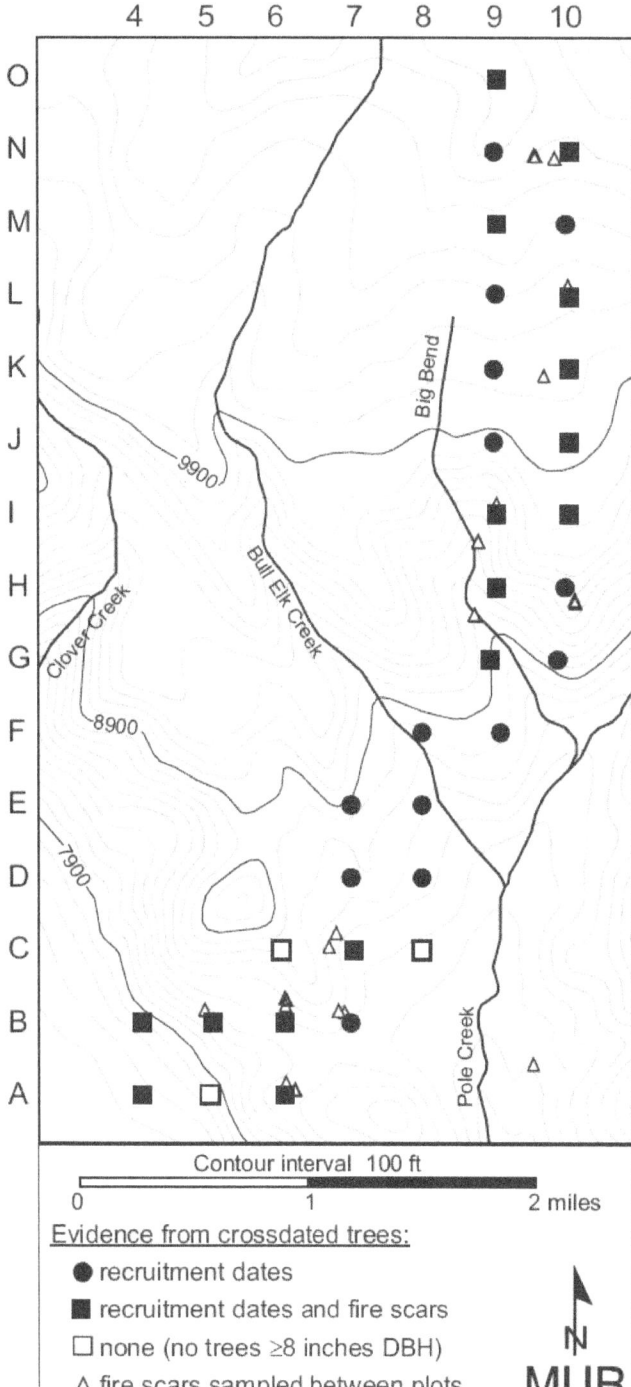

Figure Q-1—Locations of plots and crossdated fire-scarred trees that were sampled outside of plots. More than half of the fire-scarred trees were sampled within plots and are not mapped individually. Plots are identified by column and row, in other words, the southwestern most plot is 4A, the next plot to the east is 5A, and so forth. Note that at most other sites, the rows are identified by number and the columns by letter.

Figure Q-2—Distribution of sampled plots and land area at MUR by topography. Aspect classes are 90° wide, beginning with 46° for east (E). Land area was derived from a digital elevation model (Utah AGRC 2004).

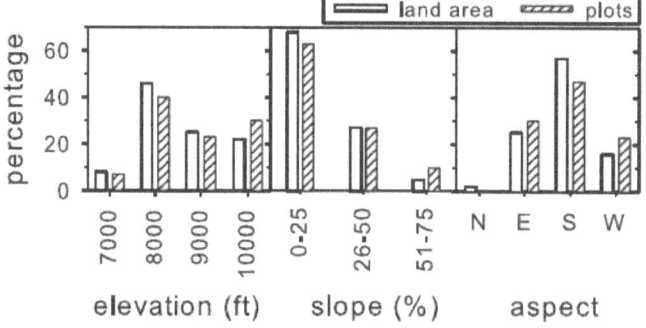

tree species
Engelmann spruce
subalpine fir
lodgepole pine
quaking aspen
Douglas-fir
ponderosa pine
0 5 10 15 20 25 30 35
percentage of trees occurring at plots

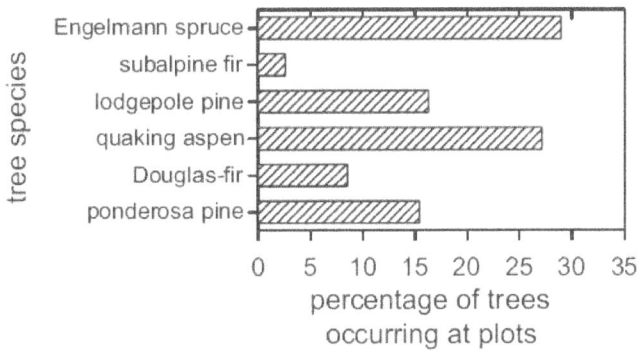

Figure Q-3—Distribution by species of the 810 live and dead trees ≥8 inches DBH that occurred in plots at MUR, regardless of whether or not we removed wood samples and crossdated them. Not shown are eight Utah juniper trees.

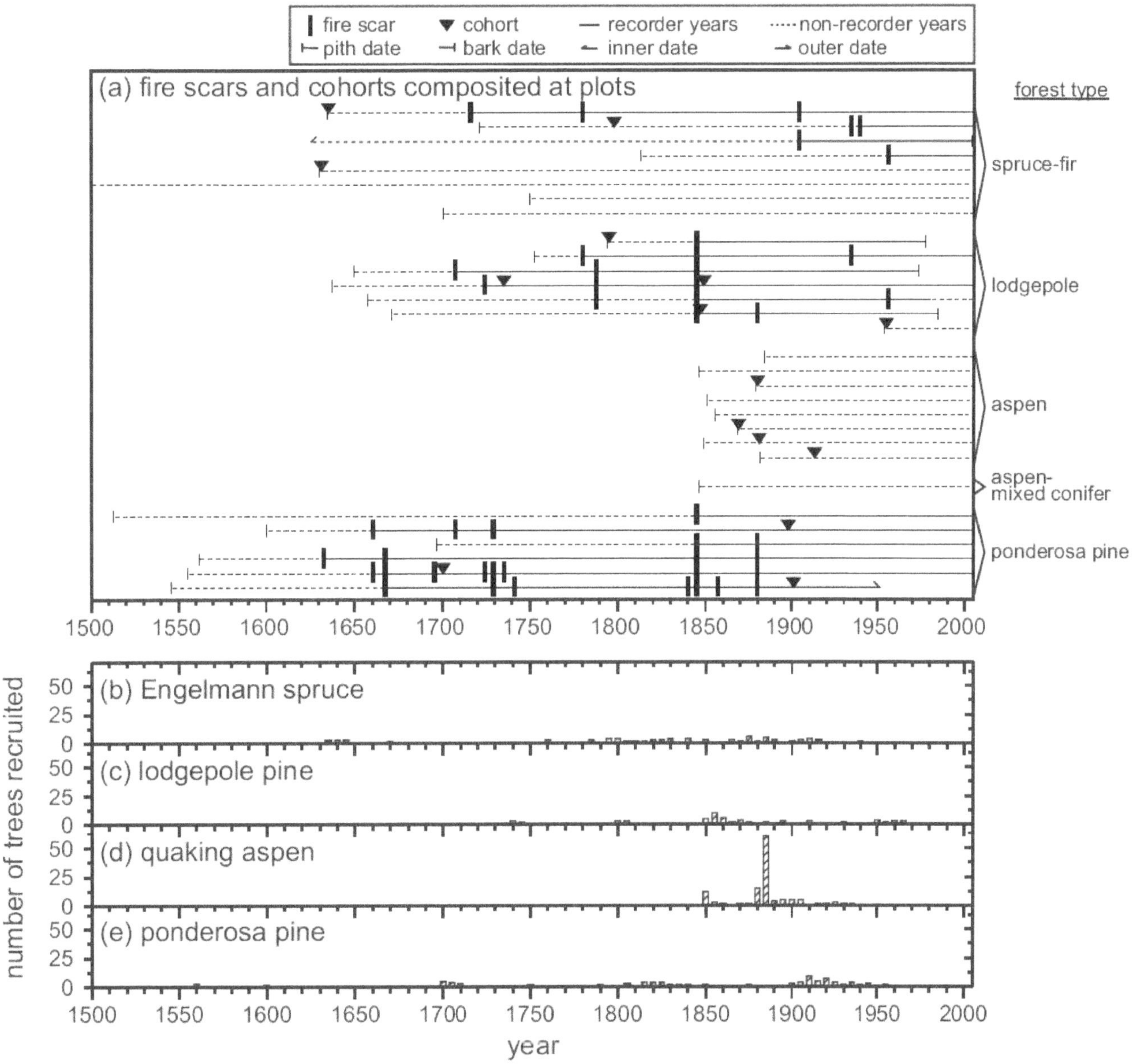

fire scar
cohort
recorder years
non-recorder years
pith date
bark date
inner date
outer date
(a) fire scars and cohorts composited at plots
forest type
spruce-fir
lodgepole
aspen
aspen-mixed conifer
ponderosa pine
1500 1550 1600 1650 1700 1750 1800 1850 1900 1950 2000
number of trees recruited
(b) Engelmann spruce
(c) lodgepole pine
(d) quaking aspen
(e) ponderosa pine
50 25 0
year

Figure Q-4—Chronologies of fire and tree recruitment at MUR. In (a), horizontal lines are plot-composite fire-scar and cohort dates by forest type. Non-recorder years precede the first scar, whereas recorder years generally follow it, but non-recorder years can also occur when the catface margin is consumed by subsequent fires or rot. In (b) through (e), recruitment dates are given for species comprising ≥10 percent of trees with such dates. The latter part of the distribution is incomplete because we only cored trees that were ≥8 inches DBH.

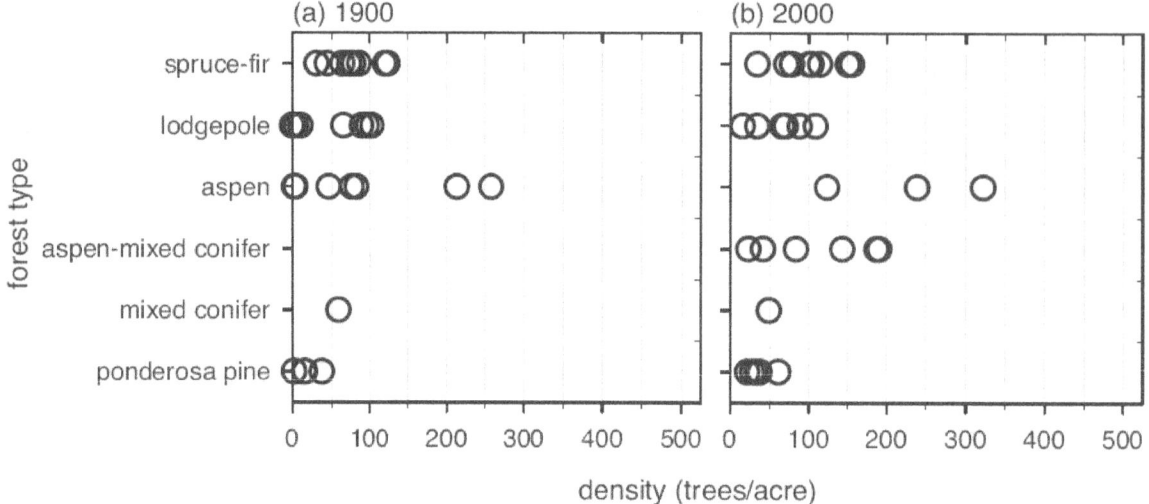

Figure Q-5—Density of trees ≥8 inches DBH that were alive at each plot at MUR (a) in 1900 and (b) in 2000, by forest type (table 2). Not shown is one lodgepole plot (MUR10K), which had a density of 716 trees/acre in 1900 and 1038 trees in 2000.

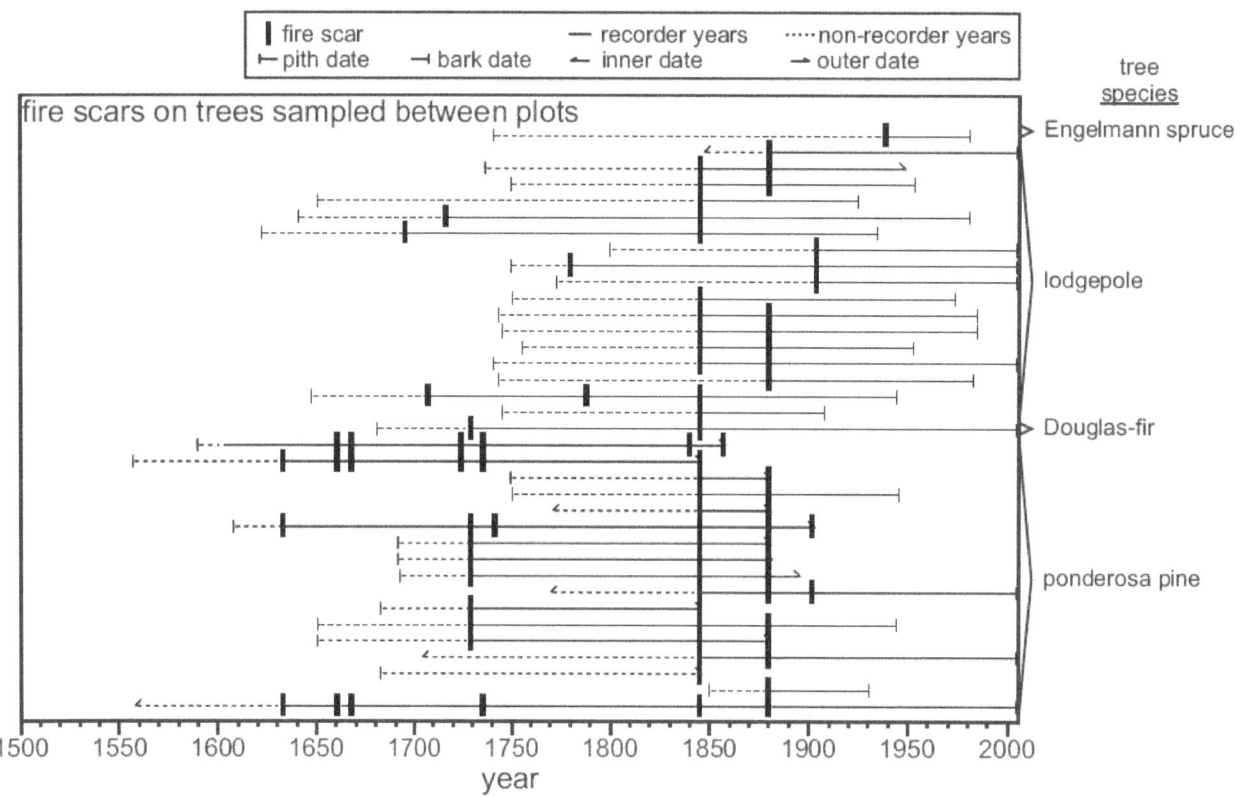

Figure Q-6—Chronology of low-severity fires recorded on the 36 trees sampled between plots over approximately, 2460 acres throughout the MUR site.

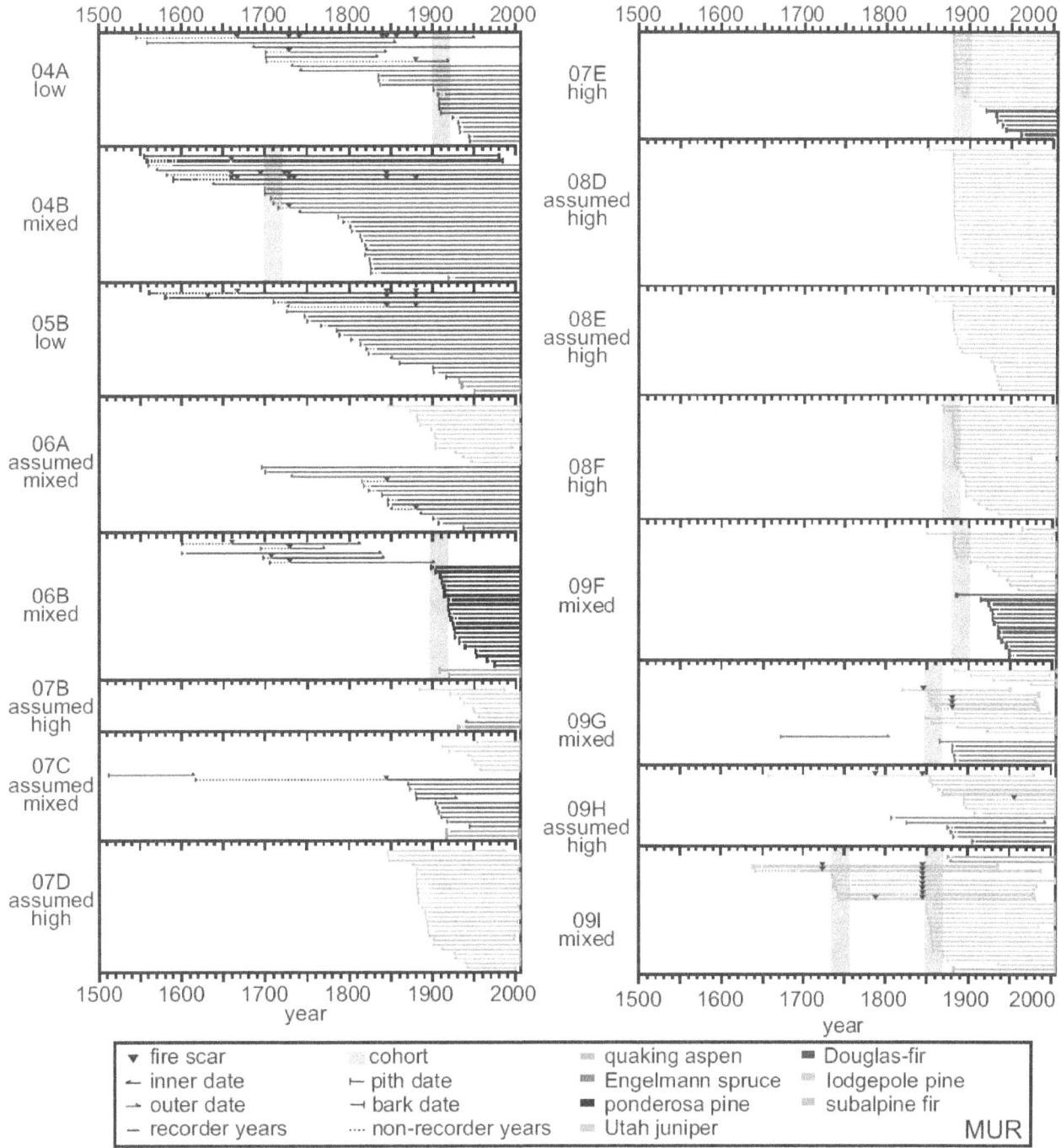

Figure Q-7—Fire-demography diagrams (FDDs, Brown and others 2008b) showing chronologies of tree demography (recruitment and death), fire scars, and cohorts at each plot. Bark dates on 31 stumps are shown as outer dates. Not shown are 36 fire-scarred trees sampled between plots. Inferred fire severity (table 3) is indicated to the left of each panel.

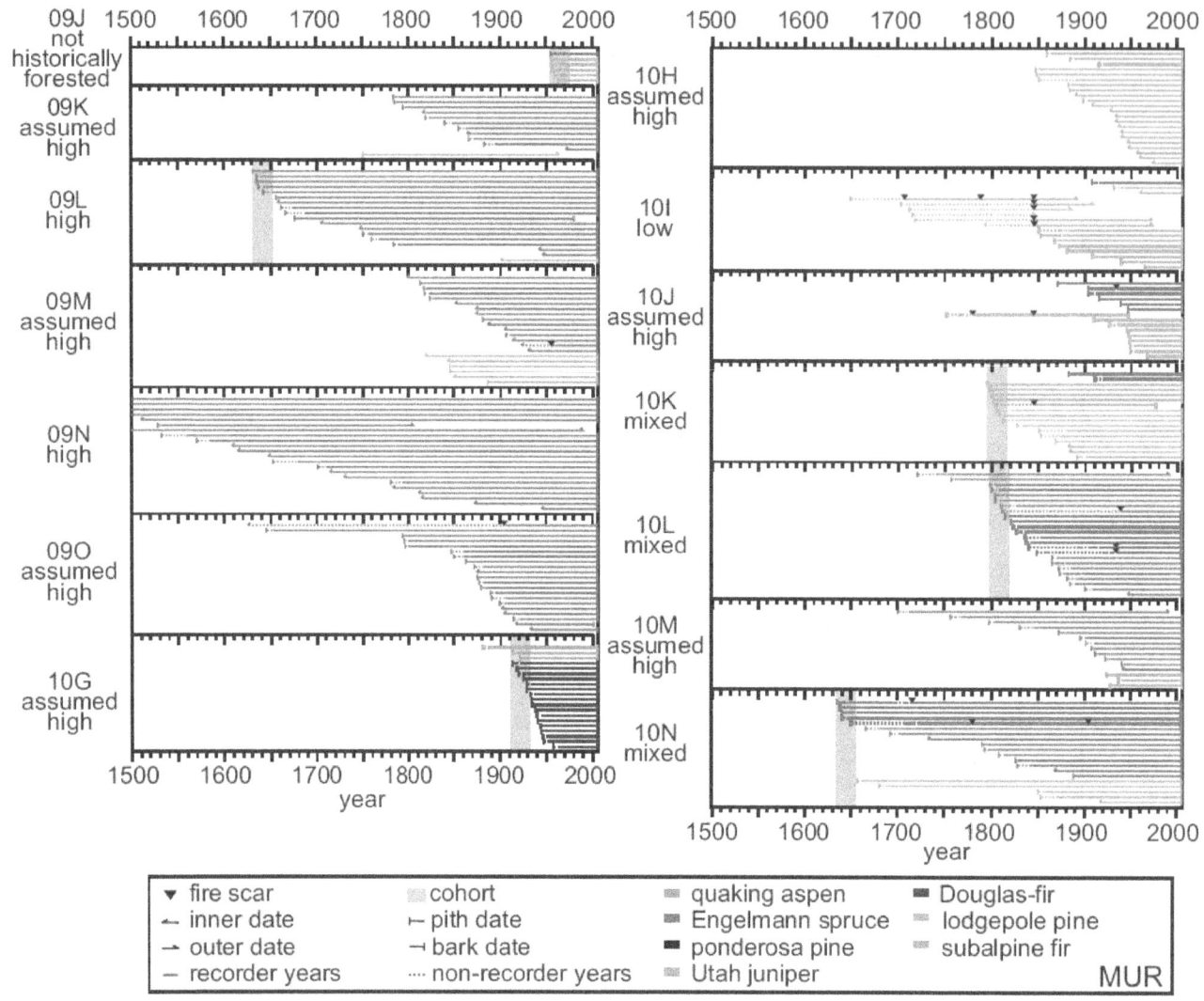

Figure Q-7—*Continued.*

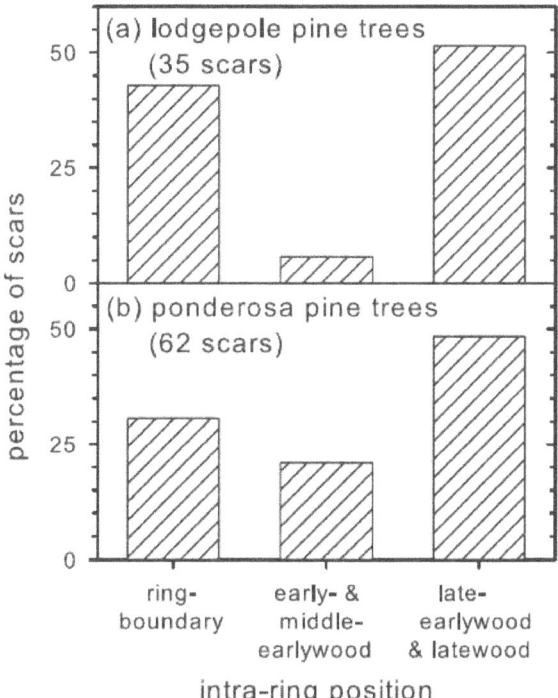

Figure Q-8—Intra-ring position of fire scars on trees sampled in and between plots at MUR from 1650 to 1900, as a percentage of the number of scars for which the position could be determined (given in parentheses). Not shown are intra-ring positions for two fire scars on Douglas-fir trees.

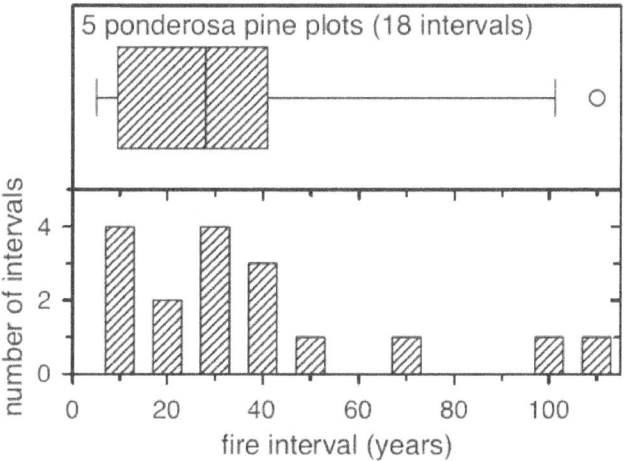

Figure Q-9—Plot-composite intervals between low-severity fires in ponderosa pine plots at MUR from 1650 to 1900. Plots averaged 0.33 acres. The box (top) encloses the 25th to 75th percentiles and the whiskers enclose the 10th to 90th percentiles of the distribution of intervals. The vertical line indicates the median fire interval, and all values falling outside the 10th to 90th percentiles are shown as circles. In the histogram (bottom), the same intervals are plotted in 10-year bins (1 to 10 years, 11 to 20 years, and so forth).

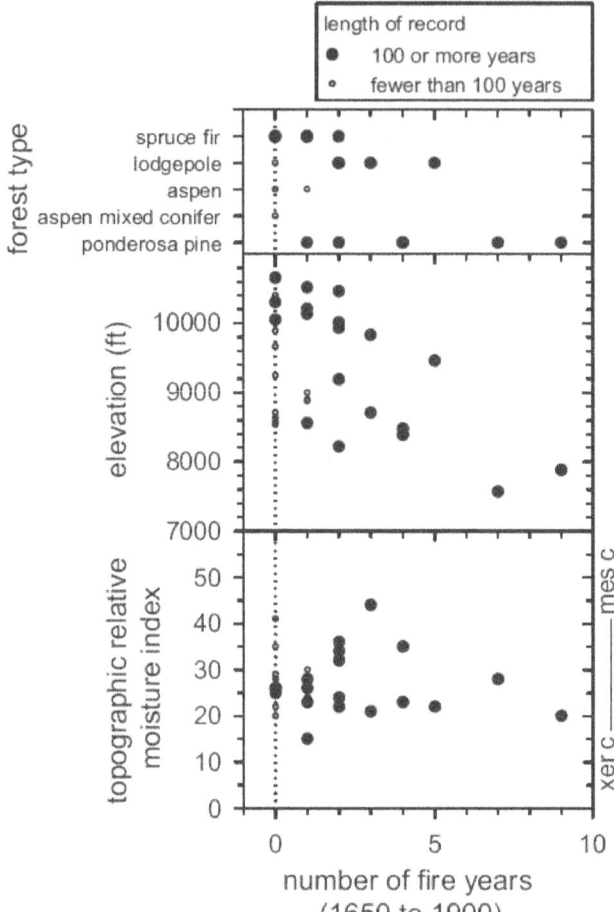

Figure Q-10—Variation in fire among plots at MUR with topography, forest type, and relative soil moisture availability (Parker 1982). Number of fire years includes both fire-scar and cohort dates. Plots with no reconstructed fires during this period fall on the dotted line.

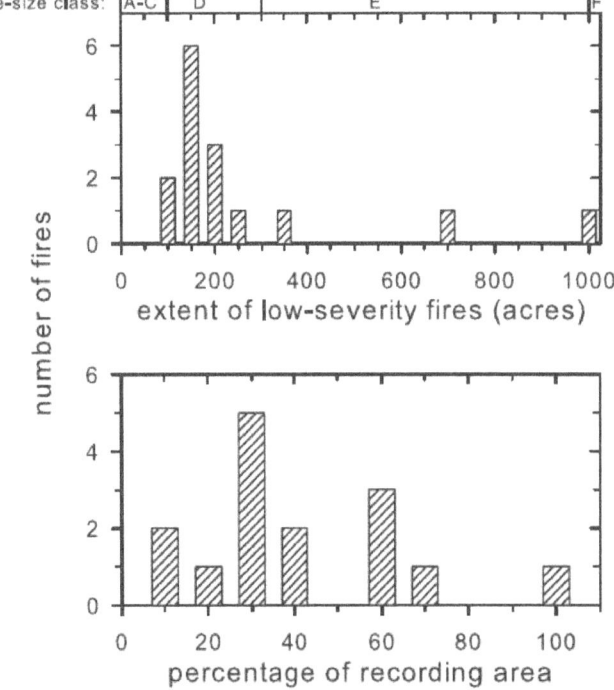

Figure Q-11—Relative extent of low-severity fires within the 2218-acre MUR site, from 1650 to 1900, as area (top) and as a percentage of the recording area (in other words, the combined area of cells containing recording, fire-scarred trees during each year; bottom). Commonly used fire-size classes are indicated at the top (NWCG 2007).

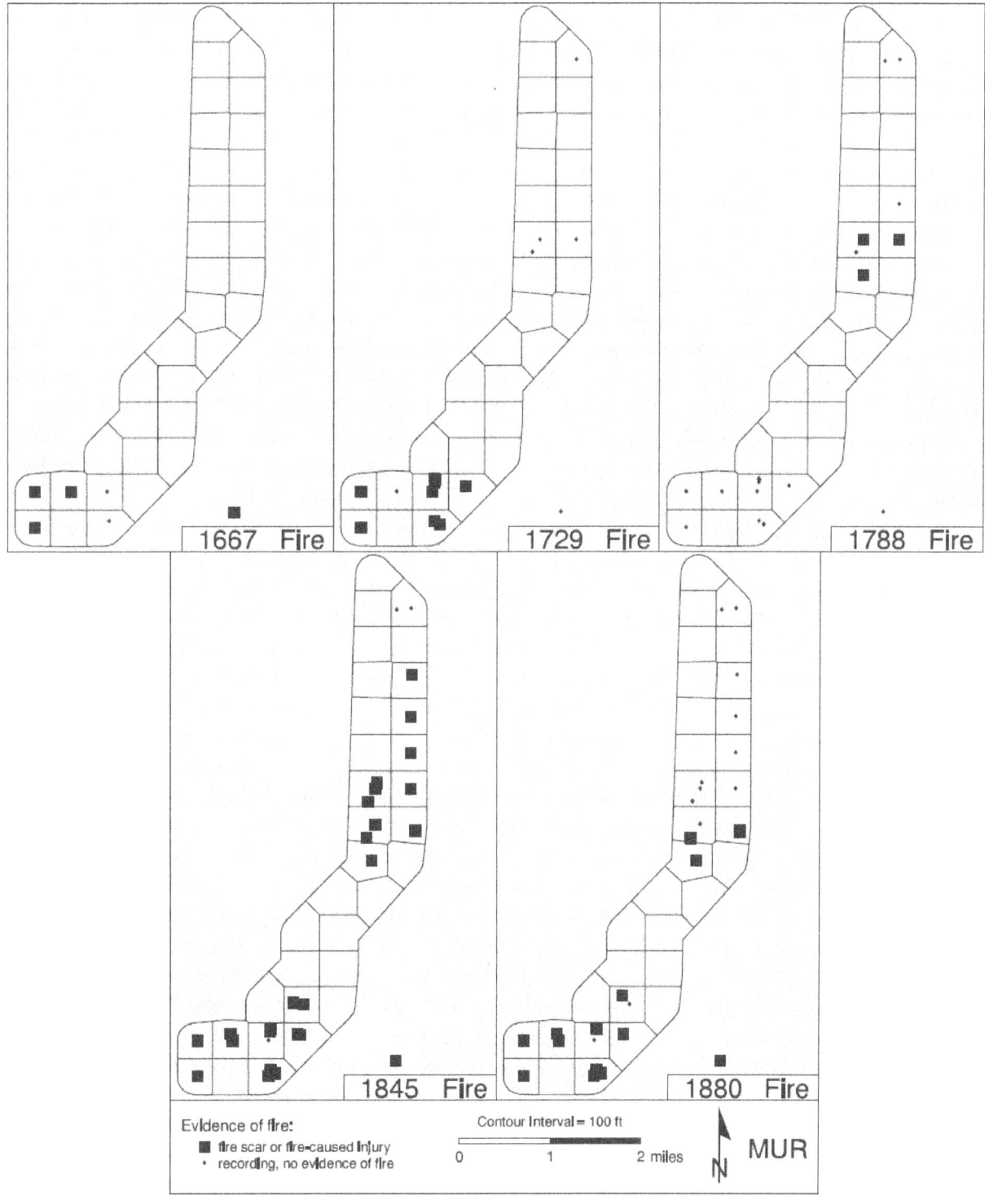

Figure Q-12—Maps of years with evidence of low-severity fires in three or more cells at MUR. "Recording, no evidence of fire" indicates at least one tree was alive at that location during that year but did not have a fire scar or fire-caused injury. Empty cells indicate that no fire-scarred trees were recording in that cell during that year. Cohort dates are not mapped.

Appendix R. Eastern Uinta Mountains, Ashley National Forest (BRO)

Topography

We sampled 30 plots over 1842 acres along Brownie Creek, on the Vernal Ranger District of the Ashley National Forest in Uintah County, Utah (figs. 1 and R-1). The plots were separated by 0.30 miles on average (range 0.25 to 0.31 miles) and averaged 0.38 acres in area (range 0.15 to 1.22 acres). Plots were sampled within cells that averaged 61 acres and ranged from 55 to 70 acres. Plots ranged in elevation from 7778 to 9667 ft (fig. R-2) and in slope from 2 to 72 percent. They were sampled on a range of aspects, but most were on south and west aspects (70 percent). The distribution of the plots by elevation, aspect, or slope did not differ from the distribution of the landscape by more than 10 percent in any category except south and west aspects, which were under and over sampled, respectively (fig. R-2). We took between two and four photographs at each of the plots.

Tree Demography

Of the 841 trees that occurred in the plots, most (98 percent) were Rocky Mountain juniper, ponderosa pine, Douglas-fir, quaking aspen, lodgepole pine, subalpine fir, or Engelmann spruce, but 15 limber pine trees also occurred (fig. R-3). Most of these trees were living (80 percent) and the rest were snags (11 percent), logs (8 percent), or stumps (1 percent). We were able to remove and crossdate wood samples from most of the trees (731 trees or 87 percent), and we obtained actual or estimated pith dates for 669 of them. These pith dates ranged from 1400 to 1973 and many of these post-dated 1900 (196 trees; fig. R-4). The death dates we obtained for 116 logs and snags ranged from 1802 to 2004.

Historical and Current Forest Structure and Composition

The plots included a range of historical and modern forest types (sagebrush, shrubland, pinyon-juniper, ponderosa pine, mixed conifer, aspen-mixed conifer, aspen, lodgepole, and spruce-fir; table R-1). Some plots changed forest type between 1860 and 2000: one sagebrush plot converted to pinyon-juniper; two sagebrush, one shrubland, two pinyon-juniper, and one ponderosa pine plot converted to mixed conifer; and one aspen plot converted to aspen-mixed conifer. In 1900, tree density averaged 65 trees per acre and ranged from 0 to 194 trees per acre (fig. R-5). In 2000, tree density averaged 83 trees per acre and ranged from 11 to 194 trees per acre. However, we likely underestimated historical tree density because we could not obtain recruitment or earliest-ring dates for 110 of the 841 trees that occurred in the plots and only an earliest-ring date for another 62 trees. Ten of these trees had earliest-ring dates between 1901 and 1920 and therefore may have been living before 1900.

Fire Scars

We were able to remove and crossdate fire-scarred samples from 73 trees, 4 of which had only scars that were recorded on a single tree and so were excluded from further analyses. Of the remaining 69 trees, about half (38 trees) were sampled in 17 of the 30 plots at this site (1 to 4 trees per plot). We sampled the 31 other fire-scarred trees as we encountered them between plots, over 688 acres throughout the site (fig. R-6). Most of the 69 fire-scarred trees were ponderosa pine (54 percent) and Douglas-fir (23 percent) and the rest were lodgepole pine, Engelmann spruce, subalpine fir, and Rocky Mountain juniper. About 90 percent were live trees (46 percent) or snags (45 percent) and the rest were logs. These 69 trees yielded 114 fire scars and 20 eroded fire scars or abrupt changes in ring width (figs. R-4 and R-7). However, five of these scar dates were eliminated from further analyses because they were recorded on only a single tree at the site. We were able to assign an intra-ring position to 80 percent of the 94 fire scars that occurred during the analysis period (1650 to 1900). Of the scars that occurred on ponderosa pine trees, half (55 percent) occurred on the boundary between two rings (fig. R-8).

Post-Fire Cohorts

We identified 19 cohorts of trees from estimated recruitment dates at 18 of the plots. Seventeen of these cohorts were recruited before 1900 (1806 to 1895) and were identified from 243 trees (5 to 26 trees per cohort), most of which were lodgepole pine (51 percent), Douglas-fir (20 percent), quaking aspen (14 percent), or Engelmann spruce (9 percent), but a few ponderosa pine and subalpine fir also occurred (figs. R-4 and R-7). The cohorts recruited before 1900 occurred in plots with a range of forest types: lodgepole (41 percent of cohorts), aspen (18 percent), mixed conifer (18 percent), spruce-fir (12 percent), aspen-mixed conifer (6 percent), and pinyon-juniper (6 percent).

Spatial Variation in Fire Regimes

We reconstructed too few fire intervals in plots during the analysis period (1650 to 1900) to compute plot-composite fire intervals by forest type at this site. The tree-ring record before 1900 was less than 100 years long for 13 of the 30 plots at this site (fig. R-9). We inferred that two plots were not historically forested, and we could not infer historical fire severity at two others because they did not meet our requirements for any of the severity categories (table R-2). We assigned the remaining plots to the low, mixed, or high fire severity categories.

From 1650 to 1900, the 10 low-severity fires we reconstructed within our 1842-acre sampling area averaged 284 acres and ranged from 61 to 910 acres (fig. R-10), equivalent to 11 to 94 percent of the recording area (in other words, the combined area of cells containing recording, fire-scarred trees during a given year). Recording area varied among fire years, ranging from 548 to 968 acres. We likely underestimated the extent of low-severity fires because most fires intersected the boundary of the site (fig. R-11).

Table R-1—Distribution of plots at BRO by historical (1860) and modern (2000) forest types (table 2).

Historical forest type (1860)	Modern forest type (2000)						
	Spruce-fir	Lodgepole	Aspen	Aspen-mixed conifer	Mixed conifer	Pinyon-juniper	Total plots in 1860
Spruce-fir	4						4
Lodgepole		7					7
Aspen			1	3			4
Aspen-mixed conifer				1			1
Mixed conifer					7		7
Ponderosa pine					1		1
Pinyon-juniper					2		2
Shrubland					1		1
Sagebrush					2	1	3
Total plots in 2000	**4**	**7**	**1**	**4**	**13**	**1**	**30**

Table R-2—Distribution of plots at BRO by historical forest type (1860; table 2) and fire severity (table 3).

Forest type	High	Assumed high	Mixed	Assumed mixed	Low	Not historically forested	Unclassified
Spruce-fir	1	2	1				
Lodgepole	2		5				
Aspen	3	1					
Aspen-mixed conifer			1				
Mixed conifer			3	3	1		
Ponderosa pine					1		
Pinyon-juniper			1				1
Shrubland				1			
Sagebrush						2	1
Total	**6**	**3**	**11**	**4**	**2**	**2**	**2**

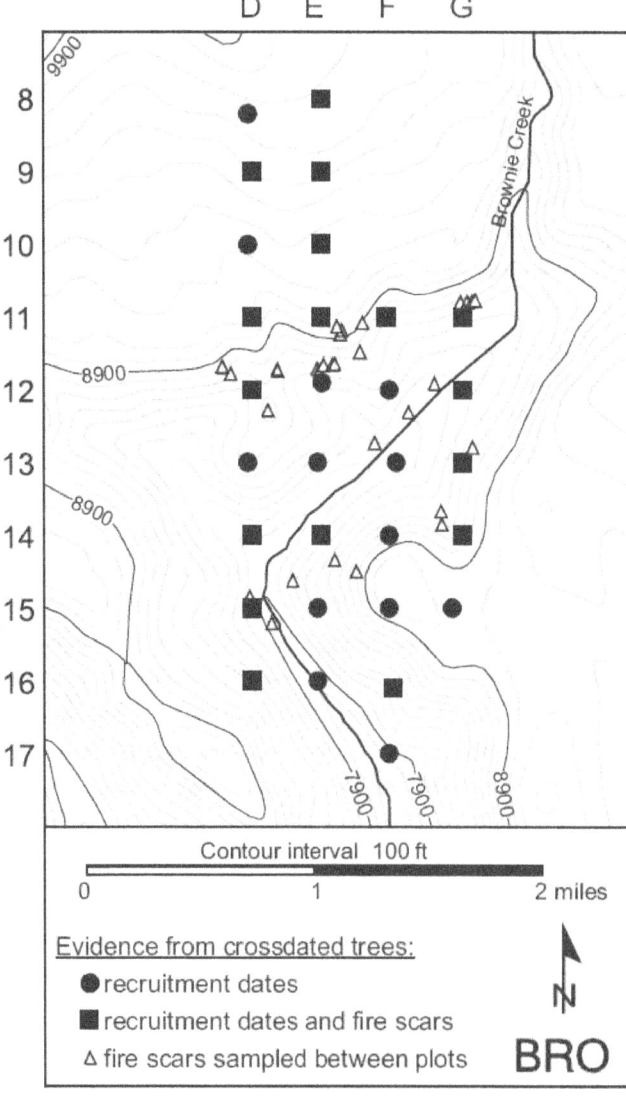

Figure R-1—Locations of plots and crossdated fire-scarred trees that were sampled outside of plots. About half of the fire-scarred trees were sampled within plots and are not mapped individually. Plots are identified by column and row, in other words, the northwestern most plot is 8D, the next plot to the east is 8E, and so forth.

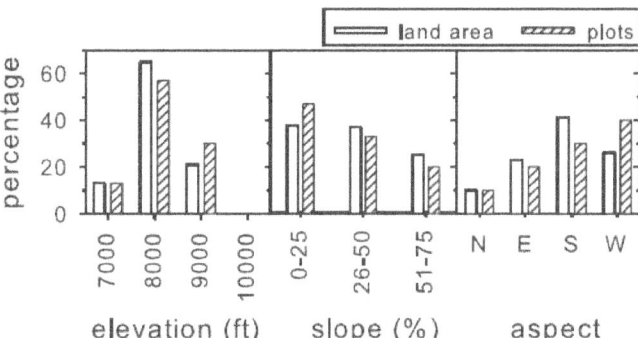

Figure R-2—Distribution of sampled plots and land area at BRO by topography. Aspect classes are 90° wide, beginning with 46° for east (E). Land area was derived from a digital elevation model (Utah AGRC 2004).

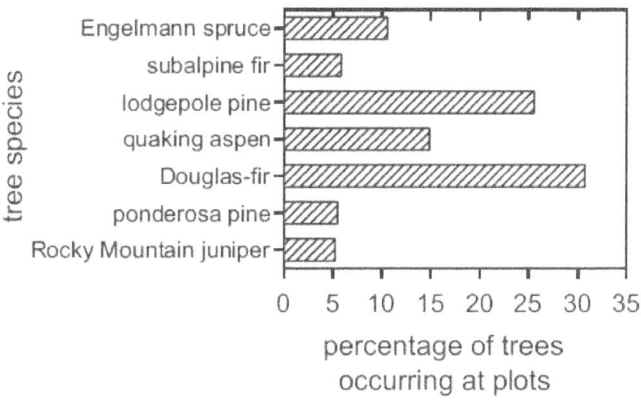

Figure R-3—Distribution by species of the 841 live and dead trees ≥8 inches DBH that occurred in plots at BRO, regardless of whether or not we removed wood samples and crossdated them. Not shown are 15 limber pine trees.

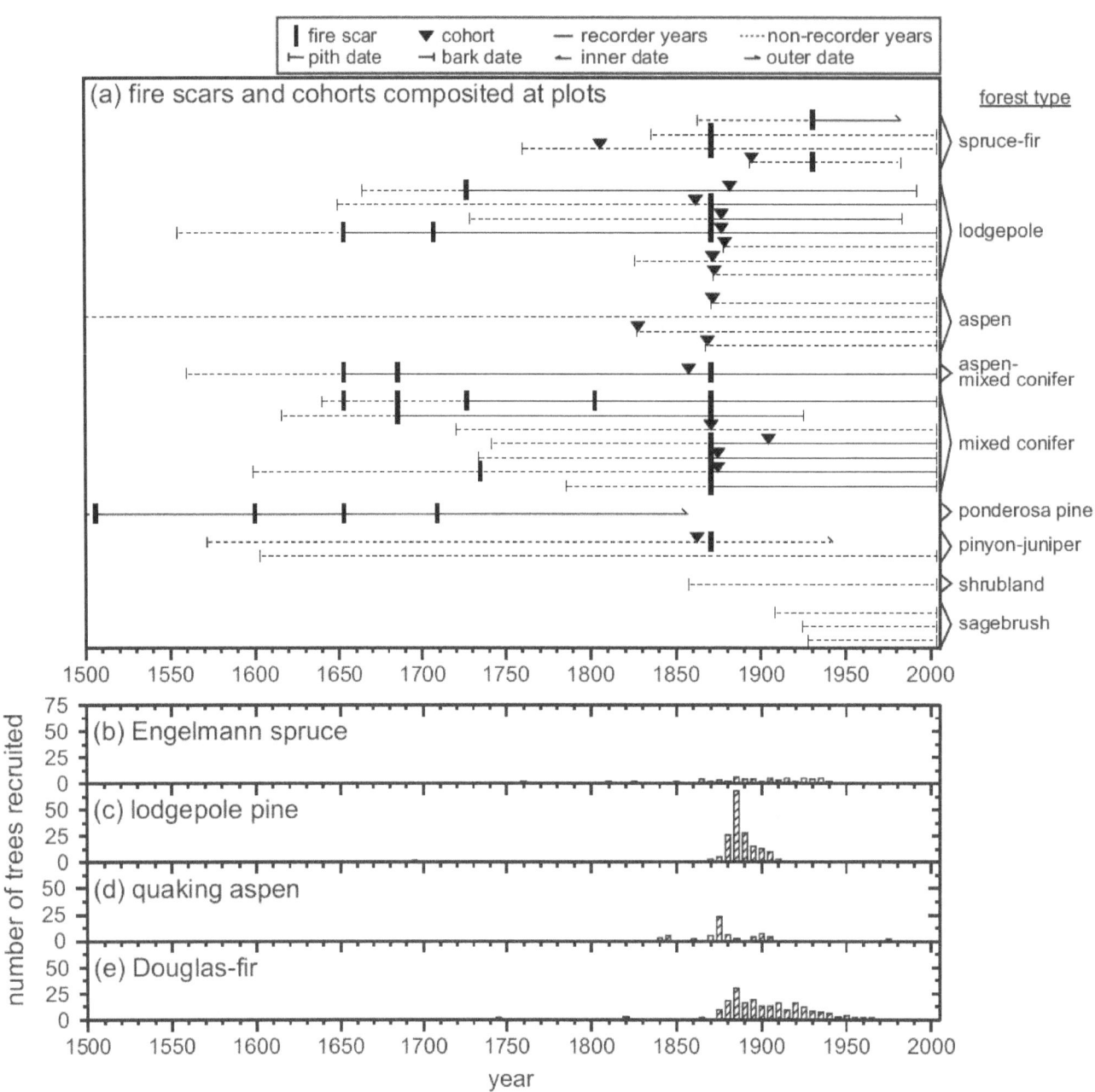

Figure R-4—Chronologies of fire and tree recruitment at BRO. In (a), horizontal lines are plot-composite fire-scar and cohort dates by forest type. Non-recorder years precede the first scar, whereas recorder years generally follow it, but non-recorder years can also occur when the catface margin is consumed by subsequent fires or rot. In (b) through (e), recruitment dates are given for species comprising ≥10 percent of trees with such dates. The latter part of the distribution is incomplete because we only cored trees that were ≥8 inches DBH.

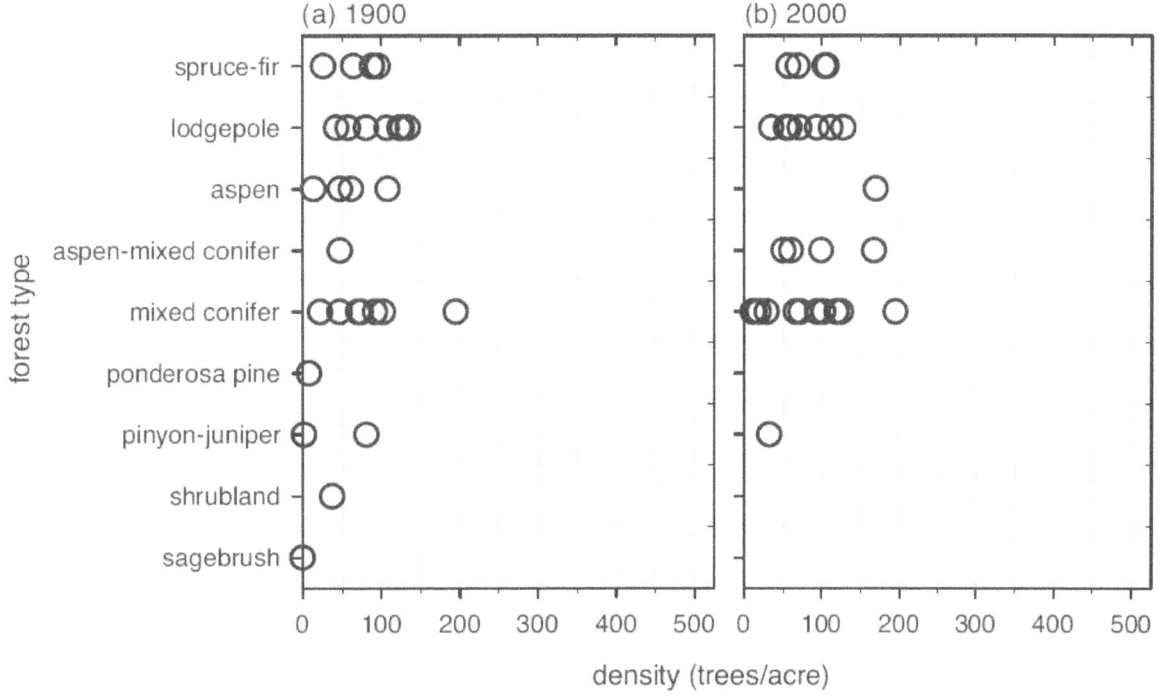

Figure R-5—Density of trees ≥8 inches DBH that were alive at each plot at BRO (a) in 1900 and (b) in 2000, by forest type (table 2).

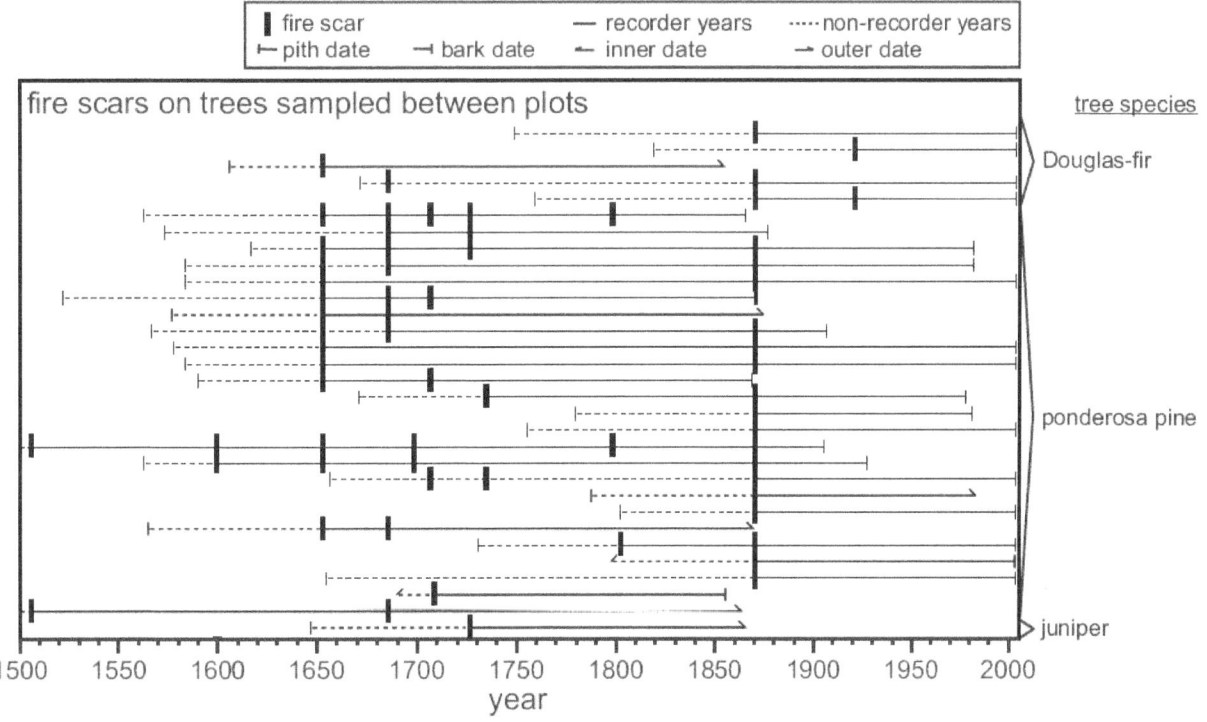

Figure R-6—Chronology of low-severity fires recorded on the 31 trees sampled between plots over approximately, 688 acres at the southern end of BRO.

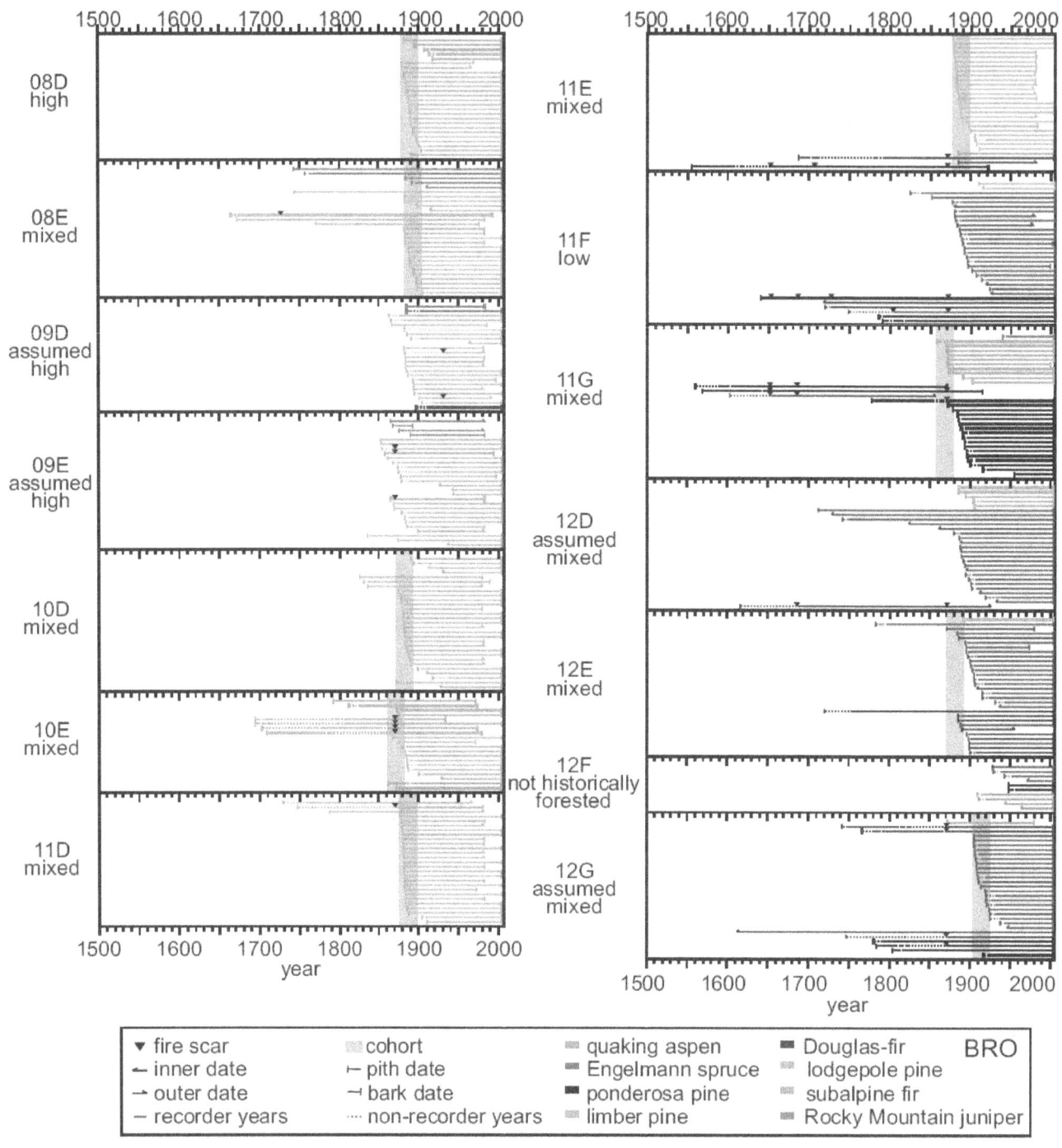

Figure R-7—Fire-demography diagrams (FDDs, Brown and others 2008b) showing chronologies of tree demography (recruitment and death), fire scars, and cohorts at each plot. Bark dates on two stumps are shown as outer dates. Not shown are 31 fire-scarred trees sampled between plots. Inferred fire severity (table 3) is indicated to the left of each panel.

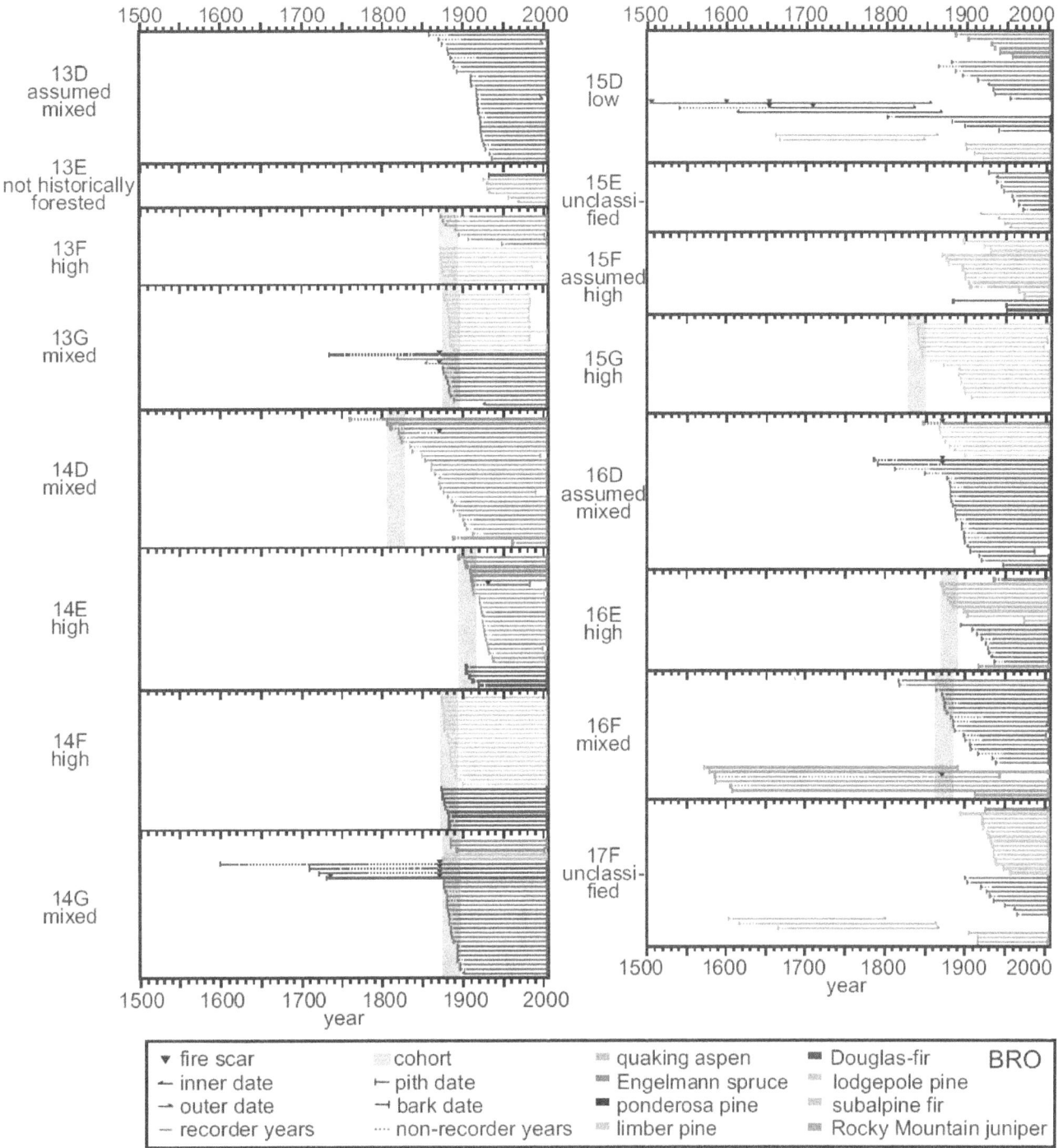

Figure R-7—*Continued.*

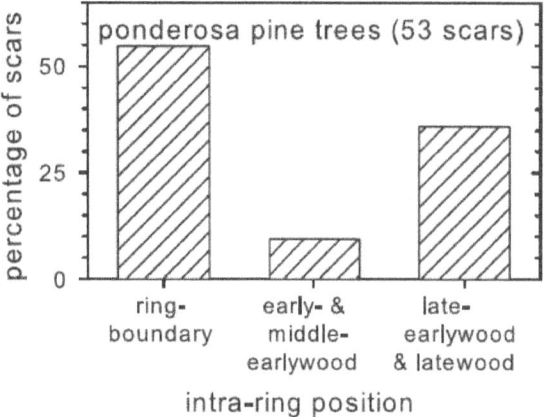

Figure R-8—Intra-ring position of fire scars on trees sampled in and between plots at BRO from 1650 to 1900, as a percentage of the number of scars for which the position could be determined (given in parentheses). Not shown are intra-ring positions for 22 fire scars on Rocky Mountain juniper, Douglas-fir, and lodgepole pine trees.

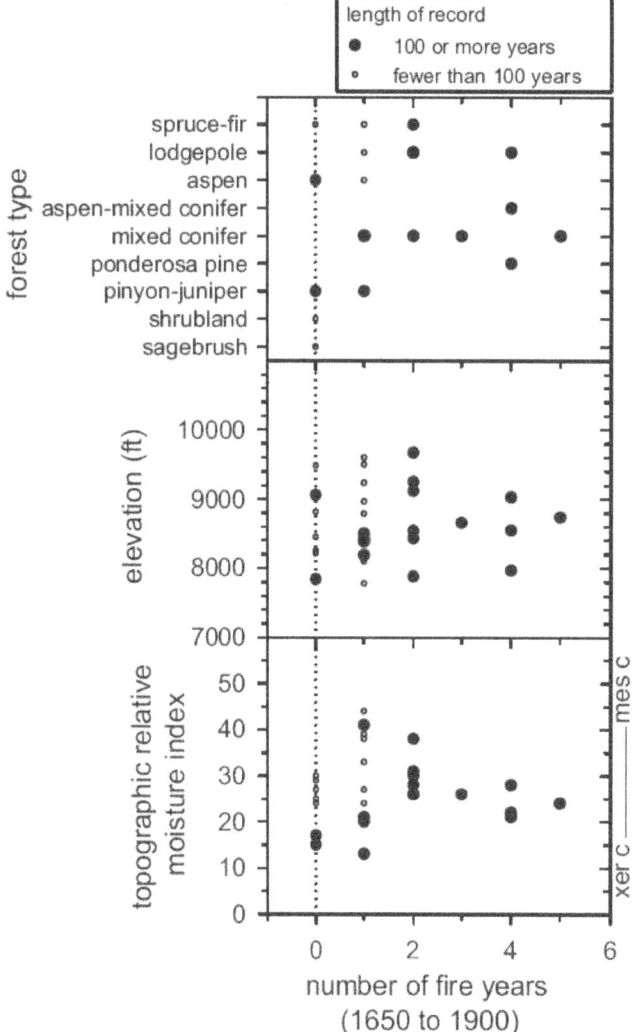

Figure R-9—Variation in fire among plots at BRO with topography, forest type, and relative soil moisture availability (Parker 1982). Number of fire years includes both fire-scar and cohort dates. Plots with no reconstructed fires during this period fall on the dotted line.

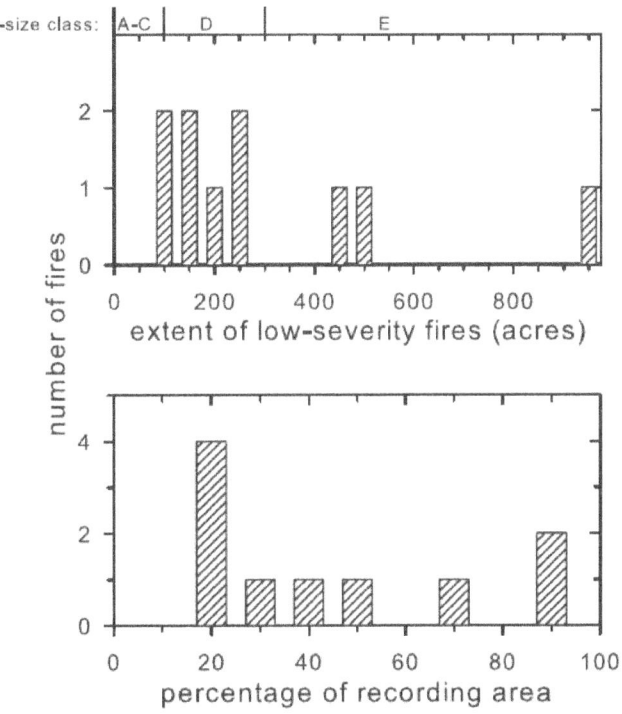

Figure R-10—Relative extent of low-severity fires within the 1842-acre BRO site, from 1650 to 1900, as area (top) and as a percentage of the recording area (in other words, the combined area of cells containing recording, fire-scarred trees during each year; bottom). Commonly used fire-size classes are indicated at the top (NWCG 2007).

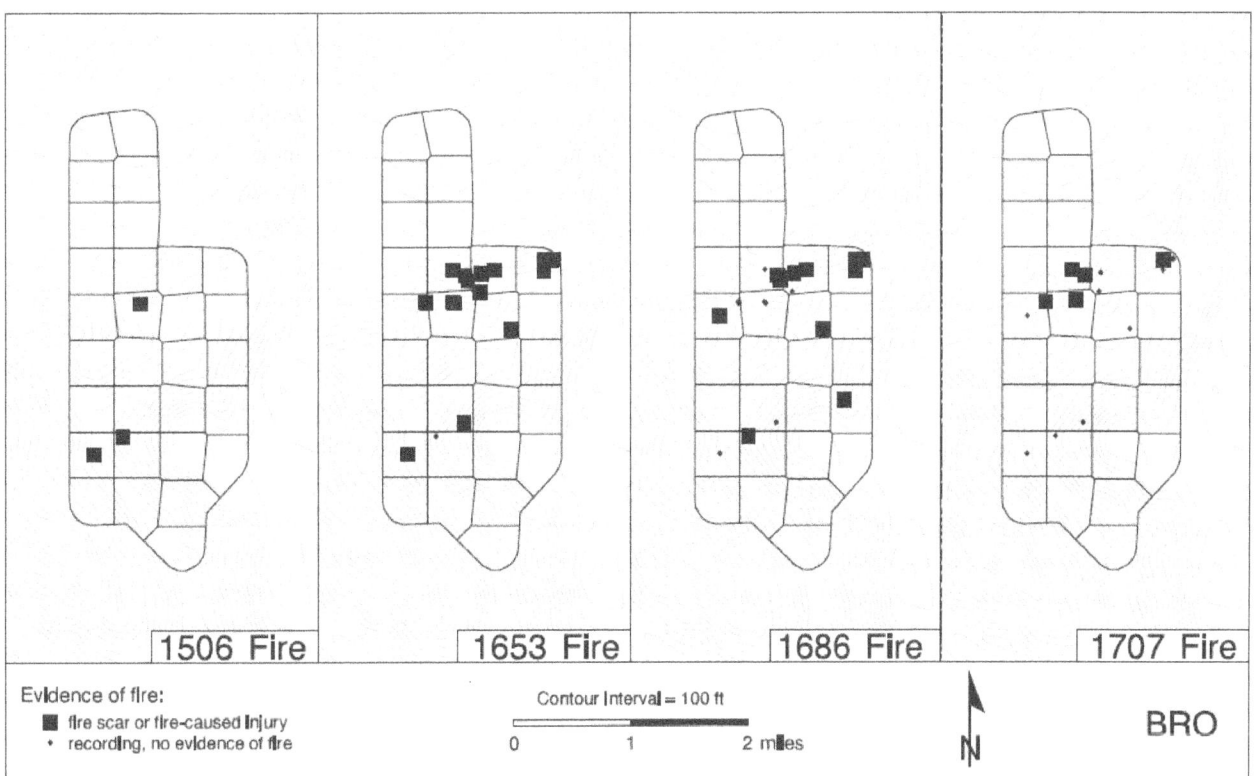

Figure R-11—Maps of years with evidence of low-severity fires in three or more cells at BRO. "Recording, no evidence of fire" indicates at least one tree was alive at that location during that year but did not have a fire scar or fire-caused injury. Empty cells indicate that no fire-scarred trees were recording in that cell during that year. Cohort dates are not mapped.

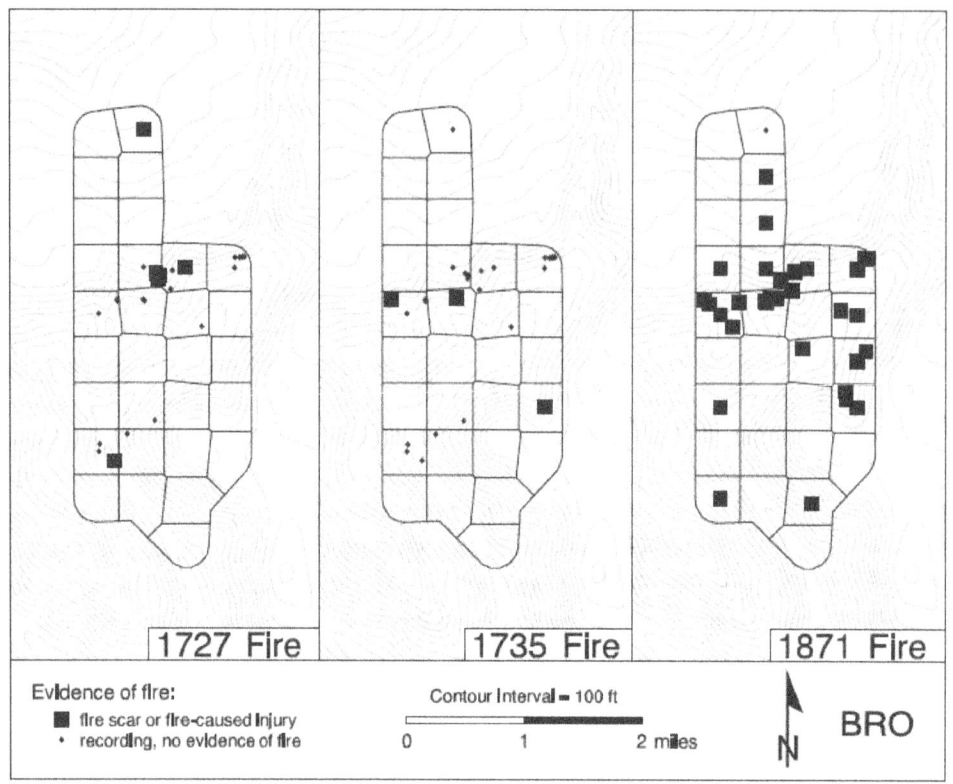

Figure R-11—*Continued.*

USDA Forest Service RMRS-GTR-261WWW. 2011.

Appendix S. Wasatch Range, Uinta-Wasatch-Cache National Forest (WCH)

Topography

We sampled 30 plots over 2166 acres near Little Bear Creek in Logan Canyon on the Logan Ranger District of the Uinta-Wasatch-Cache National Forest in Cache County, Utah (figs. 1 and S-1). The plots were separated by 0.30 miles on average (range 0.28 to 0.40 miles) and averaged 0.33 acres in area (range 0.09 to 1.39 acres). Plots were sampled within cells that averaged 62 acres and ranged from 56 to 68 acres. Plots ranged in elevation from 7393 to 8484 ft (fig. S-2) and in slope from 5 to 55 percent, but most were less than 25 percent (73 percent of plots). They were sampled on a range of aspects. The distribution of the plots by elevation, aspect, or slope did not differ from the distribution of the landscape by more than 10 percent in any category (fig. S-2). We took three or four photographs at each of the plots.

Tree Demography

All of the 909 trees that occurred in the plots were Douglas-fir, quaking aspen, lodgepole pine, subalpine fir, limber pine, or Engelmann spruce (fig. S-3). Most of these trees were living (79 percent) and the rest were snags (15 percent), logs (4 percent), or stumps (2 percent). We were able to remove and crossdate wood samples from fewer trees at this site than at others (564 trees or 62 percent) largely because this site had a higher proportion of trees with rot (29 percent) than any of the other sites. We obtained actual or estimated pith dates for 544 of the crossdated trees. These pith dates ranged from 1679 to 1959 and many post-dated 1900 (179 trees; fig. S-4). The death dates we obtained for 22 logs and snags ranged from 1904 to 2005.

Historical and Current Forest Structure and Composition

The plots included a range of historical and modern forest types (mixed conifer, aspen, lodgepole, and spruce-fir; table S-1). Some plots changed forest type between 1860 and 2000: 3 aspen and 1 spruce-fir plot converted to mixed conifer; three aspen and one spruce-fir plot converted to aspen-mixed conifer; and two aspen plots converted to spruce-fir. In 1900, tree density averaged 58 trees per acre and ranged from 2 to 202 trees per acre (fig. S-5). In 2000, tree density averaged 108 trees per acre and ranged from 14 to 245 trees per acre. However, we likely underestimated historical tree density because we could not obtain recruitment or earliest-ring dates for 345 of the 909 trees that occurred in the plots and only an earliest-ring date for another 20 trees. Nine of these trees had earliest-ring dates between 1901 and 1920 and therefore may have been living before 1900.

Fire Scars

We were able to remove and crossdate fire-scarred samples from 16 trees, all of which were sampled in 5 of the 30 plots at this site (1 to 9 trees per plot, average 3 trees). We did not sample any fire-scarred trees between plots at this site. Most of the fire-scarred trees were lodgepole pine (88 percent) and the rest were Douglas-fir. Most were live trees (88 percent) and the rest were logs. These 16 trees yielded 18 fire scars (figs. S-4 and S-6). We were able to assign an intra-ring position to each of the four fire scars that occurred during the analysis period (1650 to 1900).

Post-Fire Cohorts

We identified 10 cohorts of trees from estimated recruitment dates at 10 of the plots. Eight of these cohorts were recruited before 1900 (1748 to 1885) and were identified from 64 trees (5 to 16 trees per cohort) composed of subalpine fir (38 percent), Douglas-fir (38 percent), lodgepole pine (9 percent), quaking aspen (8 percent), or limber pine (8 percent) (figs. S-4 and S-6). The cohorts that were recruited before 1900 occurred in plots with a range of forest types: aspen (63 percent of cohorts), mixed conifer (25 percent), and lodgepole pine (13 percent).

Spatial Variation in Fire Regimes

We reconstructed too few fire intervals in plots during the analysis period (1650 to 1900) to compute plot-composite fire intervals by forest type at this site. The tree-ring record before 1900 was less than 100 years long for 18 of the 30 plots at this site (fig. S-7).

We could not infer historical fire severity at one plot because it did not meet our requirements for any of the severity categories (table S-2). We assigned the remaining plots to the mixed or high fire severity categories.

From 1650 to 1900, we reconstructed only two low-severity fires within our 2166-acre sampling area. One was 120 acres and the other was 126 acres, equivalent to 66 and 100 percent of the recording area, respectively (in other words, the combined area of cells containing recording, fire-scarred trees during a given year). Recording area during these fire years was 181 and 126 acres, respectively. We likely underestimated the extent of these low-severity fires because both intersected the boundary of the site (fig. S-8).

Table S-1—Distribution of plots at WCH by historical (1860) and modern (2000) forest types (table 2).

Historical forest type (1860)	Modern forest type (2000)					
	Spruce-fir	Lodgepole	Aspen	Aspen-mixed conifer	Mixed conifer	Total plots in 1860
Spruce-fir	4			1	1	6
Lodgepole		6				6
Aspen	2		1	3	3	9
Mixed conifer					9	9
Total plots in 2000	**6**	**6**	**1**	**4**	**13**	**30**

Table S-2—Distribution of plots at WCH by historical forest type (1860; table 2) and fire severity (table 3).

Forest type	High	Assumed high	Mixed	Assumed mixed	Unclassified
Spruce-fir		6			
Lodgepole		5	1		
Aspen	4	3	1		1
Mixed conifer	2	1		6	
Total	**6**	**15**	**2**	**6**	**1**

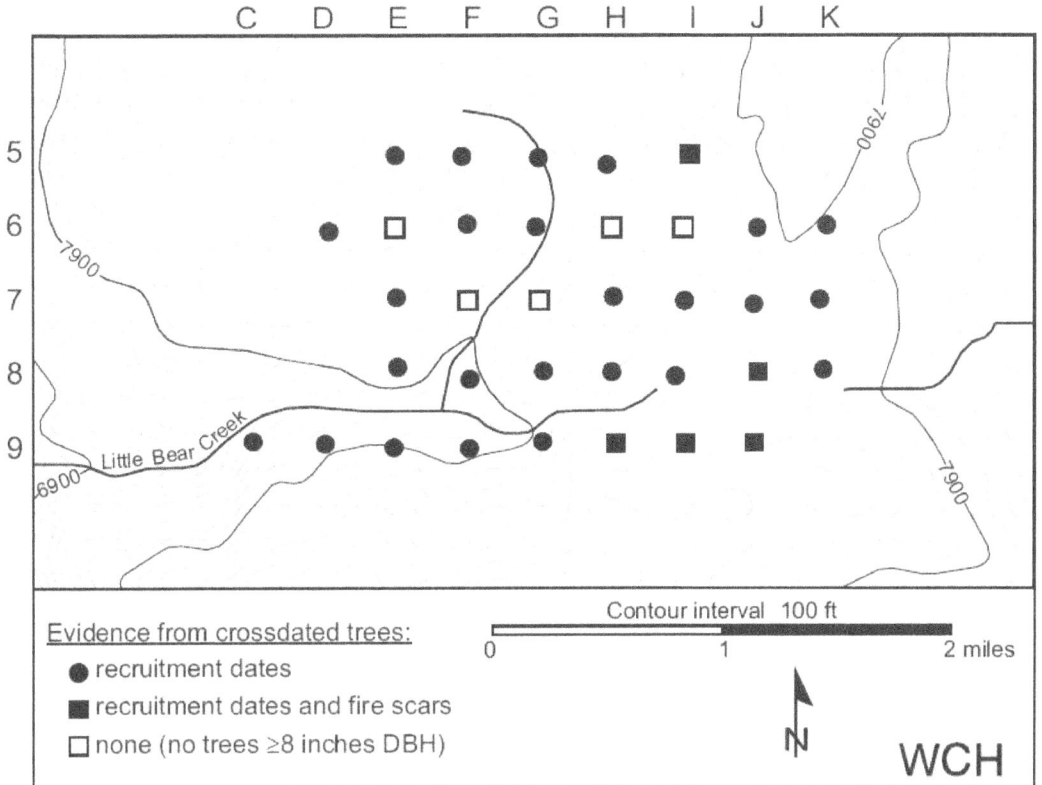

Figure S-1—Locations of plots and crossdated fire-scarred trees that were sampled outside plots. All of the fire-scarred trees were sampled within plots and are not mapped individually. Plots are identified by column and row, in other words, the southwestern most plot is 9C, the next plot to the east is 9D, and so forth.

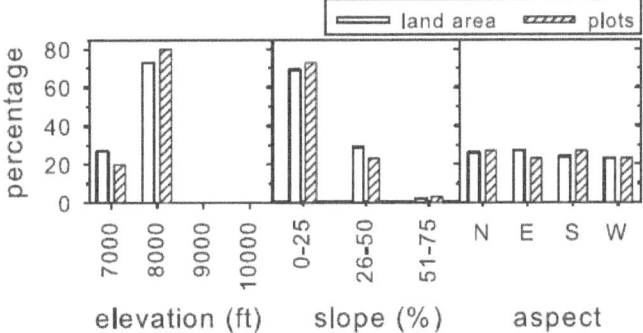

Figure S-2—Distribution of sampled plots and land area at WCH by topography. Aspect classes are 90° wide, beginning with 46° for east (E). Land area was derived from a digital elevation model (Utah AGRC 2004).

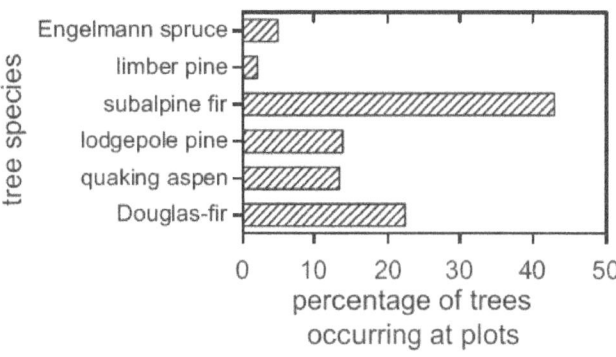

Figure S-3—Distribution by species of the 909 live and dead trees ≥8 inches DBH that occurred in plots at WCH, regardless of whether or not we removed wood samples and crossdated them.

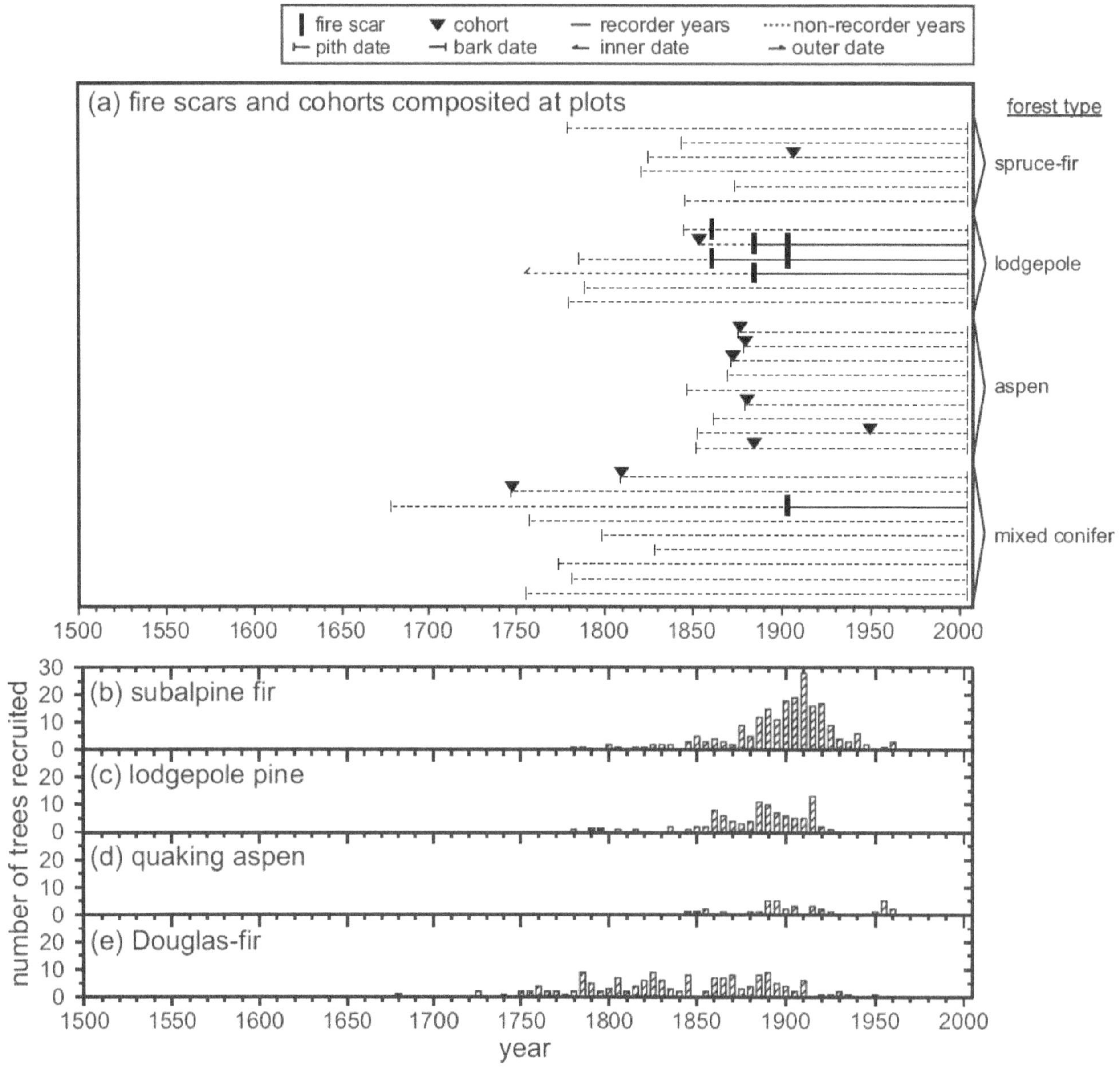

Figure S-4—Chronologies of fire and tree recruitment at WCH. In (a), horizontal lines are plot-composite fire-scar and cohort dates by forest type. Non-recorder years precede the first scar, whereas recorder years generally follow it, but non-recorder years can also occur when the catface margin is consumed by subsequent fires or rot. In (b) through (e), recruitment dates are given for species comprising ≥10 percent of trees with such dates. The latter part of the distribution is incomplete because we only cored trees that were ≥8 inches DBH.

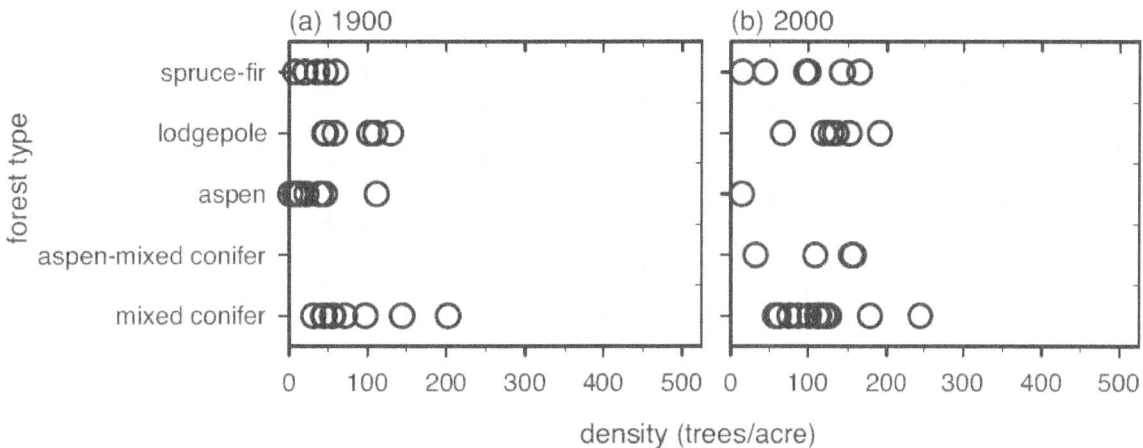

Figure S-5—Density of trees ≥8 inches DBH that were alive at each plot at WCH (a) in 1900 and (b) in 2000, by forest type (table 2).

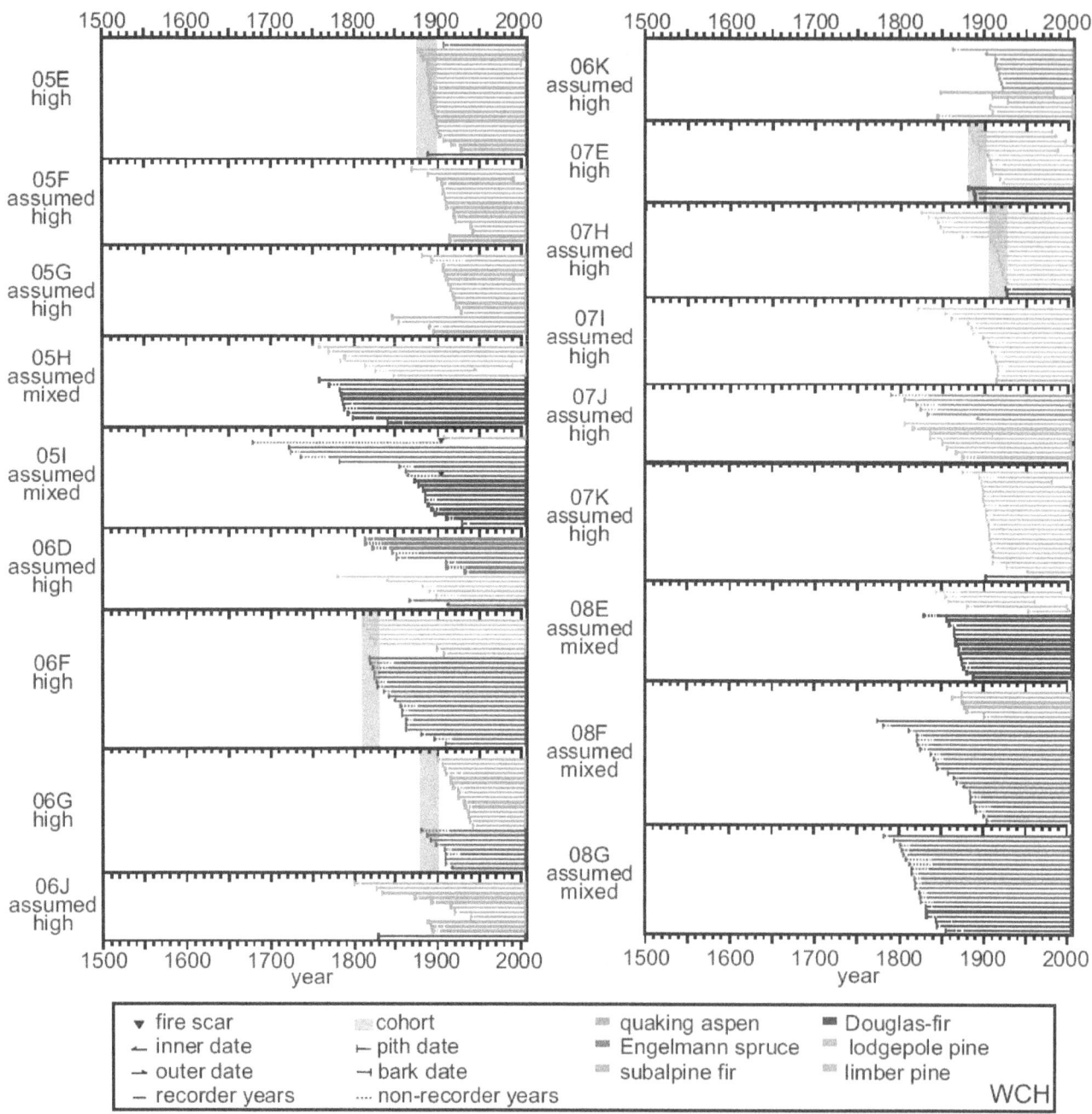

Figure S-6—Fire-demography diagrams (FDDs, Brown and others 2008b) showing chronologies of tree demography (recruitment and death), fire scars, and cohorts at each plot. The bark date on one stump is shown here as an outer date. Inferred fire severity (table 3) is indicated to the left of each panel.

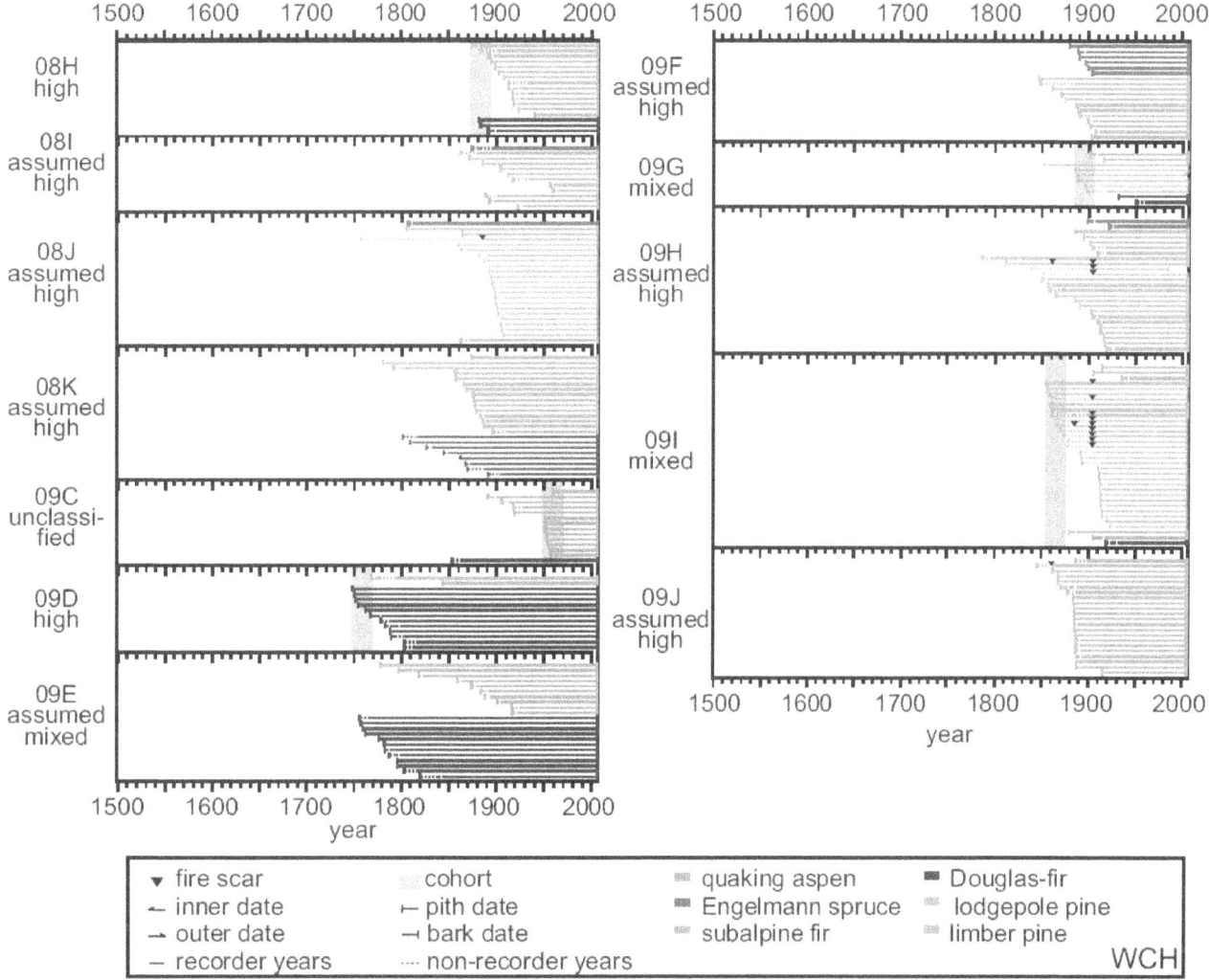

Figure S-6—*Continued.*

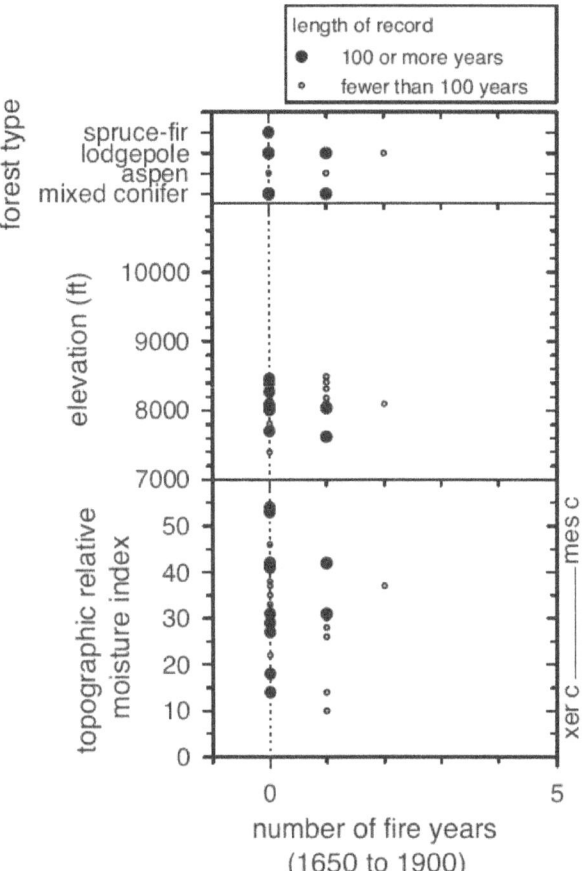

Figure S-7—Variation in fire among plots at WCH with topography, forest type, and relative soil moisture availability (Parker 1982). Number of fire years includes both fire-scar and cohort dates. Plots with no reconstructed fires during this period fall on the dotted line.

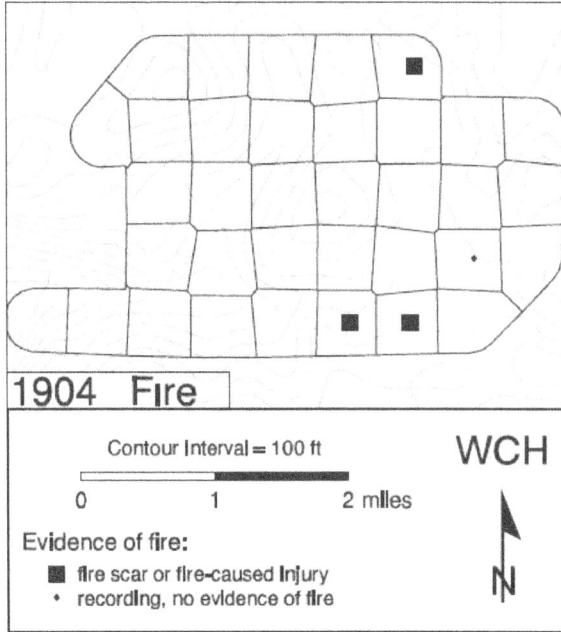

Figure S-8—Map of the one year with evidence of low-severity fires in three or more cells at WCH. "Recording, no evidence of fire" indicates at least one tree was alive at that location during that year but did not have a fire scar or fire-caused injury. Empty cells indicate that no fire-scarred trees were recording in that cell during that year. Cohort dates are not mapped.